Mimesis as Make-Believe

Mimesis as Make-Believe

On the Foundations of the Representational Arts

Kendall L. Walton

Harvard University Press
Cambridge, Massachusetts
London, England
1990

This book has been supported by a grant from the National
Endowment for the Humanities, an independent federal agency.

The excerpt from "Self-Portrait in a Convex Mirror," in *Selected
Poems* by John Ashbery, copyright © John Ashbery, 1985, all rights
reserved, is reprinted by permission of Viking Penguin, a division of
Penguin Books USA, Inc.

"Frame-Tale," from John Barth, *Lost in the Funhouse* (New York:
Doubleday, 1968), is reprinted by permission of Doubleday, a
division of Bantam, Doubleday, Dell Publishing Group, Inc.

"Slithergadee," from Shel Silverstein, *Uncle Shelby's Zoo: Don't
Bump the Glump,* copyright © 1964 by Shel Silverstein, is reprinted
by permission of Simon & Schuster, Inc.

This book is printed on acid-free paper, and its binding materials
have been chosen for strength and durability.

Library of Congress Cataloging-in-Publication Data
Walton, Kendall L., 1939–
    Mimesis as make-believe: on the foundations of the
representational arts / Kendall L. Walton.
        p. cm.
    Includes bibliographical references.
    ISBN 0-674-57619-5 (alk. paper)
    1. Aesthetics.   2. Representation (Philosophy)
3. Mimesis in literature.   I. Title.
BH301.R47W35 1990   89-39455
111'.85—dc20   CIP

For Harold and Vendla Walton

Contents

Illustrations

Acknowledgments

It has been my great good fortune to have had extraordinarily able and generous colleagues and friends during the years in which I have been thinking and writing about the representational arts. I have profited immensely from extended conversations, over periods of months and years, with John G. Bennett, David Hills, Patrick Maynard, Holly Smith, William Taschek, and Stephen White. All of them read large parts of the manuscript in progress, at one time or another, and inspired significant improvements in it. I have consulted David Hills especially often, on everything from the thorniest philosophical issues and the subtlest aesthetic ones to the selection of examples and illustrations, and I have never failed to receive remarkably insightful advice. I am indebted to Kit Fine and Timothy McCarthy for discussions about the metaphysical status of fictional entities, and to Susan Pratt Walton for her expertise on southeast Asian forms of make-believe. The observations and frowns of many perceptive and often skeptical students did much to shape my thoughts. Two of them, Ted Hinchman and Eileen John, also assisted in the preparation of the manuscript.

In taking issue, at times, with the writings of Nelson Goodman, Richard Wollheim, and Nicholas Wolterstorff, I express my admiration for their work. I have probably followed their leads more often than I have departed from them, and if I have emphasized disagreements more than agreements that is only because the former seemed to me more instructive. I recall with pleasure illuminating conversations on a number of occasions with Wollheim and Wolterstorff, about their work and mine.

To facilitate the exposition of my theory of make-believe, I have employed a large cast of characters, some of whom are actual as well as fictional, and I am grateful for their contributions. Special thanks to Gregory and Eric, real characters both.

The issues I address in this book are inherently interdisciplinary ones, and they have engaged the talents of many distinguished scholars in many fields of study. Critics, art historians, literary theorists, psychologists, and philosophers have contributed in many ways to my understanding of the representational arts and to the theory I develop here. The references in the text only hint at my indebtedness to this rich and richly diverse literature.

My fascination with philosophical problems concerning the representational arts began in my early graduate student days and found expression in a series of papers, the first of which appeared in 1973. I have changed my mind about some things over the years, and have found what I believe to be more perspicuous ways of presenting and developing lines of thought I continue to find fruitful. But the present study owes much to these earlier ventures. None of my previous papers escaped dismemberment—and I hope improvement—in being incorporated into this book. But I have helped myself freely to ideas and sentences from them when doing so served my present purposes. The papers I have drawn on are: "Pictures and Make-Believe," *Philosophical Review* 82 (1973); "Are Representations Symbols?" *The Monist* 58 (1974); "Points of View in Narrative and Depictive Representation," *Nous* 10 (1976); "Fearing Fictions," *Journal of Philosophy* 75 (1978); "How Remote Are Fictional Worlds from the Real World?" *Journal of Aesthetics and Art Criticism* 37 (1978); review of Nicholas Wolterstorff, *Works and Worlds of Art,* in *Journal of Philosophy* 80 (1983); "Fiction, Fiction-Making, and Styles of Fictionality," *Philosophy and Literature* 7 (1983); "Do We Need Fictional Entities? Notes toward a Theory," in *Aesthetics: Proceedings of the Eighth International Wittgenstein Symposium,* part I, ed. Rudolf Haller (Vienna: Hölder-Pichler-Tempsky, 1984); and "Looking at Pictures and Looking at Things," in *Philosophy and the Visual Arts,* ed. Andrew Harrison (Dordrecht: Kluwer, 1987). I thank the editors and publishers involved for permission to use material from these publications.

I am grateful to the American Council of Learned Societies, the National Endowment for the Humanities, the Rockefeller Foundation, and the Stanford Humanities Center for fellowships which, on several occasions during the last two decades, freed me from other obligations to concentrate on the writing of this book or the papers that preceded it. I express my appreciation also to the Horace H. Rackham School of Graduate Studies for summer support and support for preparation of the manuscript, and to the University of Michigan College of Literature, Science, and the Arts for assistance with the expenses of acquiring the illustrations. I thank the National Endowment for the Humanities for its generous publication support.

Ben Rogers hove in sight presently; the very boy of all boys whose ridicule he had been dreading. Ben's gait was the hop, skip, and jump—proof enough that his heart was light and his anticipations high. He was eating an apple, and giving a long melodious whoop at intervals, followed by a deep-toned ding dong dong, ding dong dong, for he was personating a steamboat! As he drew near he slackened speed, took the middle of the street, leaned far over to starboard, and rounded-to ponderously, and with laborious pomp and circumstance, for he was personating the *Big Missouri*, and considered himself to be drawing nine feet of water. He was boat, and captain, and engine-bells combined, so he had to imagine himself standing on his own hurricane-deck giving the orders and executing them.

"Stop her, sir! Ling-a-ling-ling." The headway ran almost out, and he drew up slowly towards the side-walk. "Ship up to back! Ling-a-ling-ling!" His arms straightened and stiffened down his sides. "Set her back on the stabboard! Ling-a-ling! Chow! ch-chowwow-chow!" his right hand meantime describing stately circles, for it was representing a forty-foot-wheel. "Let her go back on the labboard! Ling-a-ling-ling! Chow-ch-chow-chow!" The left hand began to describe circles.

"Stop the stabboard! Ling-a-ling-ling! Stop the labboard! Come ahead on the stabboard! Stop her! Let your outside turn over slow! Ling-a-ling-ling! Chow-ow-ow! Get out that head-line! Lively, now! Come—out with your spring-line— what're you about there? Take a turn round that stump with the bight of it! Stand by that stage now—let her go! Done with the engines, sir! Ling-a-ling-ling!"

"Sht! s'sht! sht!" (Trying the gauge-cocks.)

Tom went on whitewashing—paid no attention to the steamer.

—Mark Twain, *The Adventures of Tom Sawyer*

They are playing a game. They are playing at not playing a game. If I show them I see they are, I shall break the rules and they will punish me. I must play their game, of not seeing I see the game.

—R. D. Laing, Knots

Introduction

My starting point is simply the observation of paintings, novels, stories, plays, films, and the like—Seurat's *Sunday on the Island of La Grande Jatte,* Dickens' *Tale of Two Cities,* Hitchcock's *North by Northwest,* Ibsen's *Hedda Gabler,* Mozart's *Magic Flute,* Michelangelo's *David,* Edgar Allan Poe's *Telltale Heart,* for example—together with an awareness of the importance these works have in our lives and in our culture. One cannot help reflecting on and wondering about what they are made of and how they work, the purposes they serve and the means by which they do so, the various ways in which people understand and appreciate them, the shapes of the spaces they occupy in our individual and collective histories. When approached from a more technical perspective, they have other fascinations as well: they pose intriguing problems, often disruptive ones, for metaphysical theories and theories of language.

The scope of our investigation is less easily decided than its starting point. What category of things shall we inquire into? My subtitle promises an investigation of the "representational arts"—a promise I will keep, in a way—and I take our examples to be paradigms of representational art, however uncertain it may be how far and in what directions that category extends. The examples also qualify as central instances of works of "fiction," and this notion too will play a part in determining the field of our exploration. Both phrases point in the right direction, but vaguely and only approximately.

A quick survey of its frontiers shows the notion of representational art to be especially problematic. Does the Sydney Opera House qualify? Would it if it were titled *Sailing through the Heavens?* Is Brancusi's *Bird in Space* representational? Mondrian's *Broadway Boogie Woogie?* Do Jackson Pollock's paintings represent the actions by which they were made? Should we allow that "expressive" music *represents* emotions or the experiencing of emotions? Is expression a species of representation? Program music is representational, no doubt, but what about background music in film? How shall we classify Stravinsky's *Pulcinella Suite,* Jasper Johns's targets and flags, Duchamp's readymades, happenings? The existence of borderline or undecidable cases, even vast numbers of them, is not the problem. What is of concern is the fact that we cannot easily say why something does or does not count as representational or why it is borderline, or what one would have to learn about it to decide. Some problematic works are probably not borderline at all. If only we understood better what representationality is, one may feel, we would see that a given item *definitely* qualifies or that it *definitely* does not. We are not just uncertain about what is representational, we are confused. We need a theory.

If our category is representational *art,* we face the interminable and excruciatingly unedifying task of separating art from nonart. We can save ourselves some grief by fixing our sights on the class of the *representational,* whose members may but need not be art. But this lets in many more puzzles. Does this class include clouds or constellations of stars when they are seen as animals? Do passport photographs qualify? X-ray photographs, live television images, reflections? Are chemistry textbooks, historical novels, Truman Capote's *In Cold Blood,* a love poem, and a love letter written in verse all representational in a single sense, and in the same sense that *The Telltale Heart* is? What about scarecrows, plastic flowers, dollar bills, counterfeit dollar bills, Monopoly money, the bread and wine used in communion, a child's boots bronzed and mounted and displayed, a taste of soup, Madame Tussaud's wax figures, footprints, droodles, coronations, cremations, cockfights, graphs, diagrams, playing cards, chess pieces—and, let us add, hobbyhorses and toy trucks? How might we go about deciding? Every one of these items qualifies as "representational" in *some* reasonable sense of the term, no doubt. The trouble is that there seem to be too many senses criss-crossing the field and interfering with one another.

I will carve out a new category, one we might think of as a principled modification—not just a clarification or refinement—of an ordinary notion of representational art. I will call its members simply "representations," preempting this expression for my own purposes and assigning it an extension both broader and narrower than it is usually understood to possess. I will not take the concept of art very seriously, for the most part, but it is suggestive in one important respect of what I will call representations. The works of "representational *art*" most likely to spring to mind are, like our initial examples, works of *fiction*—novels, stories, and tales, for instance, among literary works, rather than biographies, histories, and textbooks. I will concentrate on fiction, and only fiction will qualify as "representational" in my special sense.

What shall we mean by "fiction"? This expression may not exude quite as much sheer mystery as "representation" originally does, but confusion abounds. We will exorcise some of it in Chapter 2, disentangling one sense of the term from others and refining it. We will find it best not to limit "fiction" to *works*, to human artifacts, and to use it more broadly in other respects than is commonly done. "Fiction" in this sense will be interchangeable with "representation" as we will understand it, although I will favor "representation" except when contrasts with what is commonly called "nonfiction" need emphasis.

The term "representation" is less than ideal for the role I will assign it, but I know of no better one. "Fictional representation" would point more clearly to the exclusion of nonfiction. But I resist the implication that our category is a species of a larger class of "representations," understood to include "nonfictional" as well as "fictional" ones. And "fictional" will have another job to do anyway. "Mimesis," with its distinguished history, can be understood to correspond roughly to "representation" in my sense, and it is associated with important earlier discussions of many of the issues I will address. Hence its use in my title. But I disavow any implied commitment either to a picture theory of language (or "symbols") or correspondence theory of truth, or to an imitation or resemblance theory of depiction. "Representation," too, may suggest to some a commitment of the former sort. But in one respect at least it is unexcelled: It is used so multifariously, in such a confused profusion of senses and nonsenses, and in the service of such a variety of theoretical designs, that no current use can claim exclusive rights to it. It is so obviously in need of a fresh start that there can be no objection to my giving it one.

My decisions about how to shape the category of representations and the reasons for them will emerge gradually as our theory develops. Indeed, to construct a theory, to achieve an understanding of things, is in large part to decide how best to classify them, what similarities and differences to recognize and emphasize. Determination of the scope of our investigation will thus be largely a result of it. We won't know just what, beyond my initial examples, the theory is a theory of until we have it in hand.

But we do have the initial examples, a loose collection of cultural objects commonly described both as "representational art" and as "works of fiction." Even when this classification, or these, gives way to the more perspicuous and more illuminating category of representations in our special sense, paintings, novels, stories, plays, and films such as *La Grande Jatte, A Tale of Two Cities, The Telltale Heart, Hedda Gabler,* and *North by Northwest* will remain central in our attention. My primary purpose in devising this category and developing the theory to which it belongs is to deepen our understanding of works like these and their surroundings. It is in this way that I will keep the promise to investigate the foundations of the "representational arts."

There is enormous diversity among even the initial examples. I note now that they include both literary works and works of the visual arts, as well as hybrids such as theater, film, and opera. We will examine this and other differences among them in due course, but it is essential first to see what representations of all varieties have in common. Concentrating just on literature, or just on the visual arts, has sometimes led to serious misconceptions that are best corrected by placing representations of one sort alongside ones of the other. Not until Part Three will I systematically distinguish literary and depictive representations and consider more than in passing other differences among them. Until then we will focus on what can be said about representations generally.

What all representations have in common is a role in *make-believe.* Make-believe, explained in terms of imagination, will constitute the core of my theory. I take seriously the association with children's games—with playing house and school, cops and robbers, cowboys and Indians, with fantasies built around dolls, teddy bears, and toy trucks. We can learn a lot about novels, paintings, theater, and film by pursuing analogies with make-believe activities like these.

This suggestion is hardly a daring innovation; nor was it when Ernst Gombrich, in a famous essay, compared pictures to hobbyhorses.[1] That make-believe (or imagination, or pretense) of *some* sort is cen-

1. "Meditations on a Hobby Horse." (Complete bibliographical information on works cited in short form in the notes appears in Works Cited.) Gombrich's suggestion that a picture of a man is a "substitute" for a man as a hobbyhorse is a "substitute" for a horse points around several mistakes. But it is also misleading. A hobbyhorse does not substitute for a horse in the way a horseless carriage substitutes for a horse-drawn one. One rides in the horseless carriage as one rides in the horse-drawn one, but the child does not actually ride his stick. Moreover, it is crucial that the child *think of* his stick as a horse, whereas the user of an automobile may long have forgotten the horse-drawn carriage that it replaces.

tral, somehow, to "works of fiction" is surely beyond question. Establishing this much is like pulling a rabbit out of a hutch. But there have been few concerted attempts to explain what make-believe is or to trace the roots of fiction (or representation in anything like our sense) in that direction. And the consequences of taking make-believe to be central have not been appreciated. Some of them are surprising. As obvious and as innocuous as the basic insight may seem, we will find ourselves endorsing some quite unexpected and unorthodox conclusions in the course of developing it. In the end one might think the hutch must actually have been a hat. But by then the rabbit will be in our hands.

Many recent theorists, especially, look to language—to the workings of natural languages in standard, ordinary, nonfictional contexts— for models on which to understand novels, paintings, theater, and film. My emphasis on make-believe is designed in part to counteract the excesses of this approach. I don't deny that linguistic models have much to offer. Theorists have clarified significant features of the works we are interested in by considering them together with "serious" uses of language and by bringing theories of language to bear on them. But every model has its dangers, and linguistic ones have so dominated recent thinking about fiction and the representational arts that many of their limitations have gone unnoticed. It is time to look at things from a fresh perspective. A make-believe theory needn't be in conflict with linguistically based ones, of course. The genuine insights of one theory can be accepted along with those of others. Some will argue that games of make-believe can themselves be illuminated by thinking of them in linguistic terms (as "semiotic"). No doubt there is some truth in this. It is equally true, however, that the notion of make-believe can clarify significant aspects of language, as we shall see. In any case it is essential to break the hold that the preoccupation with language has exerted on our thinking about representation and to see through the distortions it has engendered. We can always come back to linguistic models later to appreciate what is right about them.

I alluded earlier to a distinction between two kinds of questions to be investigated. On the one hand, there are questions about the role representations have in our lives, the purposes they serve, the nature of appreciators' responses. The very fact that people make up stories and tell them to one another, the fact that they are interested at all in what they know to be mere fiction, is astonishing and needs to be explained. On the other hand, there are more technical issues concerning the ontological standing of characters and other fictitious entities and the semantic role of names and descriptions purportedly designating them. There has been a remarkable and unfortunate separation between discussions of these two groups of issues, between, broadly speaking, *aesthetically* and *metaphysically* oriented theorizing about fiction. Seldom do investigations of the two kinds intersect or interact. Aestheticians rarely worry about whether there *really* is a Tom Sawyer or a Moby Dick. Metaphysicians and philosophers of language typically betray little interest in what the point or value of the institution of fiction might be. It goes without saying that an integrated theory in which both aesthetic and metaphysical matters are treated in a unified fashion is much to be desired, a theory in which the answers to questions of each sort point toward and reinforce the answers to questions of the other.

There are good reasons to think that such an integrated theory is to be found. It is reasonable to assume that the institution of fiction is well adapted to the purposes it serves, and we ought to be able to see how it is so adapted. Any account of its logical, semantic, and ontological structure that leaves mysterious why there should be an institution with that structure ought to be highly suspect. If the institution involves recognition of fictitious entities, we should expect an explanation of why it does, what purposes this recognition serves, and how it serves them. We have a right to demand that a convincing metaphysical treatment of the nature of the institution, including its ontological presuppositions, make significant contact with aesthetic questions about what the point of the institution is.

There is also a more specific reason for expecting links between aesthetic and metaphysical matters. The experience of being "caught up in a story," emotionally involved in the world of a novel or play or painting, is central to the appreciation of much fiction, and explaining the nature of this experience is an important task for the aesthetician. It is extraordinarily tempting to suppose that when one is caught up in a story, one loses touch with reality, temporarily, and actually believes in the fiction. The reader of *Anna Karenina* abandons himself to the novel and is convinced, momentarily and partially at least, of Anna's existence and of the truth of what the novel says about her. Otherwise why would he be moved by her predicament? Why would one even be interested enough to bother reading the novel? Yet it also seems that the normal appreciator does not (of course!) *really* believe in the fiction. The central metaphysical problem concerning fiction is thus mirrored in the very experience of appreciation. It is hard to believe that the two are not intimately intertwined, that the question of whether appreciators really do believe in fictions does not bear significantly on the question of whether we theorists are to accept them.

The connections will be apparent in my treatment of the two kinds of issues. Make-believe will be central in both cases. In Parts One, Two, and Three I concentrate on developing the theory of make-believe and applying it to aesthetic problems (broadly construed). Metaphysical and semantic concerns will not be far from the surface, however, and I will treat them directly in Part Four, using resources acquired earlier.

The metaphysical and semantic problems as well as the aesthetic ones arise in part from the role make-believe plays in the arts. But make-believe is a pervasive element of human experience, important not just in the arts but in many other areas of our lives as well. Nor is make-believe centrally or paradigmatically or primarily a feature of the arts or an ingredient of "aesthetic" experience—one that sometimes spills over to other things. There is nothing distinctively "aesthetic" about make-believe itself at all. And works of art are neither the sole nor the primary instances of representation in our sense. They are merely the ones I have chosen to focus on in this study. I will discuss make-believe in children's games, however, in the course of clarifying it and examining its role in the arts. And I will propose a way of understanding assertions of existence and nonexistence and also certain nonliteral uses of language in terms of make-believe, including ones unconnected with works of fiction or representational works of art. I suspect that make-believe may be crucially involved as well in certain religious practices,[2] in the role of sports in our culture, in the institution of morality, in the postulation of "theoretical entities" in science, and in other areas in which issues of metaphysical "realism" are prominent, although I will offer only the barest hints or less of how my theory might be applied in these directions.

The plausibility of applications in other domains is significant. It helps to confirm the theory and to reinforce the ambitious claims I will be making for its explanatory power within the arts. We will be able to see representationality in the arts as continuous with other familiar human institutions and activities rather than something unique requiring its own special explanations. Yet the theory will provide a framework rich enough and flexible enough to account for discontinuities between the representational arts and other areas in which

2. See Pavel, *Fictional Worlds*, pp. 57–61.

make-believe is involved, as well as within the representational arts themselves.

My ambitious claims about the role of make-believe in the arts involve many familiar issues (and some unfamiliar ones as well): how (and whether) fiction is to be distinguished from nonfiction (Chapter 2); what principles guide (or describe) our readings or interpretations (Chapter 4); problems of narrative theory, ones concerning reliable and unreliable narration, the mediating roles of narrators, and how prevalent narrators are in literary works (Chapter 9); the relation between appreciation and criticism; the character of appreciators' emotional responses to fiction (Part Two); paradoxes of tragedy (why appreciators willingly and even eagerly let themselves in for the unpleasant experiences tragedies seem to induce in them, for instance); the nature of pictorial representation, how depiction differs from description and whether depiction is "natural" or "conventional" (Chapter 8). We will examine notions of *realism* and *points of view* in both literary and pictorial representations. We will explore the (apparent or actual) outskirts of the representational, with particular attention to nonfigurative painting (§ 1.8), to literary nonfiction (§ 2.7), to the decorative arts (§ 7.6), and to music (§§ 8.6, 8.7). We will have occasion to contribute to discussions of photography and film, of legends and myths, of the "time" arts and the "static" ones—not to mention the traditional philosophical perplexities about the metaphysical status of fictional entities. The territory is vast, even if it is limited to the workings of make-believe within the arts, and different readers will be drawn to different parts of it. To a considerable extent one can concentrate on the topics one is most interested in, locating them with the help of the contents and the index. But all readers should look first at the discussions of make-believe in the early chapters and the development of the basic elements of the make-believe theory of representation. I advise reading at least Chapter 1 (especially the odd-numbered sections), sections 1–6 of Chapter 3, Chapter 5, and the first several sections of Chapters 6 and 7 before skipping ahead. Cross-references will guide one to sections on which a given discussion is especially dependent, and browsing beyond the more abstract presentations of the theory will help to give a concrete sense of how it works. This study is not a compendium of separate responses to particular problems but an attempt to construct a single comprehensive and unified theory, one with many applications.

Let's begin.

PART ONE

Representations

1

Representation and Make-Believe

The lunatic, the lover, and the poet
Are of imagination all compact.
One sees more devils than vast hell can hold;
That is the madman. The lover, all as frantic,
Sees Helen's beauty in a brow of Egypt.
The poet's eye, in a fine frenzy rolling,
Doth glance from heaven to earth, from earth to heaven.
And as imagination bodies forth
The forms of things unknown, the poet's pen
Turns them to shapes, and gives to airy nothing
A local habitation, and a name.
Such tricks hath strong imagination,
That if it would but apprehend some joy,
It comprehends some bringer of that joy.
Or in the night, imagining some fear,
How easy is a bush supposed a bear!
—Shakespeare,
A Midsummer Night's Dream

In order to understand paintings, plays, films, and novels, we must look first at dolls, hobbyhorses, toy trucks, and teddy bears. The activities in which representational works of art are embedded and which give them their point are best seen as continuous with children's games of make-believe. Indeed, I advocate regarding these activities as games of make-believe themselves, and I shall argue that representational works function as props in such games, as dolls and teddy bears serve as props in children's games.

Children devote enormous quantities of time and effort to make-believe activities. And this preoccupation seems to be nearly universal, not peculiar to any particular cultures or social groups.[1] The urge to engage in make-believe and the needs such activities address would seem to be very fundamental ones. If they are, one would not expect

---

1. Opie and Opie, *Children's Games*. Some have suggested that all or nearly all children's play consists in pretense or make-believe—that tag is pretended chase and capture, for instance. See Aldis, *Play Fighting*, pp. 14, 128.

children simply to outgrow them when they grow up; it would be surprising if make-believe disappeared without a trace at the onset of adulthood.

It doesn't. It continues, I claim, in our interaction with representational works of art (which of course itself begins in childhood). The forms make-believe activities take do change significantly as we mature. They become more subtle, more sophisticated, less overt. The games children play with dolls and toy trucks are in some ways more transparent and easier to understand than their more sophisticated successors. This is one reason why children's games will help illuminate the games adults play with representational works of art.

It goes without saying that in speaking of "games" of make-believe we must disavow any implication that they are mere frivolity. Children's games serve purposes far more significant than that of keeping them happy and out of mischief. It is generally recognized, I believe, that such games—and imaginative activities generally—do indeed, as their prevalence suggests, have a profound role in our efforts to cope with our environment.[2] Children in the Auschwitz concentration camp played a game called "going to the gas chamber."[3] Some may be horrified at the thought of treating such a tragic matter so lightly. But this "game" is probably best regarded as an earnest attempt by the participants to comprehend and come to grips with their terrible situation. In "playing" it they were, I suspect, facing the reality of genocide with the utmost seriousness.

Much needs to be learned about the benefits of make-believe, about just what needs it serves and how it serves them. But suggestions come easily to mind: that engaging in make-believe provides practice in roles one might someday assume in real life, that it helps one to understand and sympathize with others, that it enables one to come to grips with one's own feelings, that it broadens one's perspectives. An advantage of regarding paintings, plays, and the like as props in games of make-believe is that whatever we may learn about the functions of children's games of make-believe, and whatever we may feel we know already, are likely to help explain how and why such representational works are valuable and important.

Games of make-believe are one species of imaginative activity; specifically, they are exercises of the imagination involving *props*. Before explaining what "props" are and how they operate, I must make several observations about imagining.

2. See references in §7.5, note 22.
3. Opie and Opie, *Children's Games*, p. 331.

1.1. IMAGINING

When we think about the imagination, examples like the following naturally come to mind: Fred finds himself, in an idle moment, alone with his thoughts. Feeling unsuccessful and unappreciated, he embarks on a daydream in which he is rich and famous. He calls up images of applauding constituents, visiting dignitaries, a huge mansion, doting women, and fancy cars. But alas, reality eventually reasserts itself and Fred gets back to selling shoes.

This is indeed a paradigm instance of an exercise of the imagination. But it is not in all respects typical. We must be wary of mistaking peculiarities of Fred's experience for features to be found in imaginings generally. An enormous variety of experiences come under the heading of exercises of the imagination.

One peculiarity of Fred's imaginings is that they do not make use of props. Another is that they consist partly in having mental images; imagining can occur without imagery. But I will focus now on three other characteristics of Fred's daydream that are not common to imaginings generally: It is *deliberate;* it consists of *occurrent* mental events (or actions); and it is *solitary,* something he does by himself. Imaginings can be spontaneous. They need not be occurrent. And they are sometimes social rather than solitary activities or experiences.

Before proceeding we should note the independence of imagining from truth and belief. Much of what Fred imagines is false and is known by him to be false. But he imagines, also, that his name is Fred, that he prefers warm climates, that France is in Europe, and much else that he knows to be true. To say that someone imagines such and such is sometimes to *imply* or *suggest* that it is not true or that the imaginer disbelieves it. Nevertheless, imagining something is entirely compatible with knowing it to be true.

I postpone consideration of the differences between imagining a *proposition,* imagining a *thing,* and imagining *doing* something—between, for instance, imagining that there is a bear, imagining a bear, and imagining seeing a bear—and the relations among them. But they will be important later.

Spontaneous and Deliberate Imaginings

We sometimes decide on what to imagine, as Fred did; we form intentions to imagine this or that and carry them out. Imagining is sometimes deliberate. But not always. Often we just find ourselves imagining certain things. Our fantasizing minds stray, seemingly at random, without conscious direction. Thoughts pop into our head unbidden. Imagining seems, in some cases, more something that happens to us than something that we do. Like breathing, imagining can be either deliberate or spontaneous.

The line between deliberate and spontaneous imaginings is not sharp. Varying degrees and kinds of control may be exerted over what (and whether) we imagine. And both deliberate and spontaneous imaginings are often combined in a single imaginative experience. A chain of imaginings begun deliberately almost always develops further on its own. One who decides to imagine a bear will find himself imagining a bear of a certain sort—a large, ferocious grizzly pacing back and forth, for instance. Elaborations of what we imagine deliberately occur spontaneously.

Nevertheless, imaginative experiences involving relatively many relatively spontaneous imaginings differ significantly from more deliberate ones. Insofar as our imaginings are deliberate, we are well aware of their dependence on us. It is obvious to the imaginer that the "world of his imagination" is an artificial contrivance, something dreamed up, something he constructed, bit by bit, by his choices of what to imagine. Spontaneous imaginings have a life of their own. The imaginer is more a "spectator" than the perpetrator of them. Rather than constructing her imaginary world, she "watches" as it unfolds. It seems less her own contrivance than something created and existing independently of her. She may be surprised at how it turns out. She may be amazed to find herself imagining a bear with candy cane stripes, and then "watch" with astonishment as (so to speak) this extraordinary beast jumps over the moon. Spontaneously created imaginary worlds are like the real world in their capacity to surprise us. Imagining spontaneously can be more fun, more exciting than doing so deliberately. It is likely to be a more "vivid" or "realistic" experience, one which, in its independence of the will, is more like actually perceiving or otherwise interacting with the real world.[4]

4. Berkeley implies that ideas that arise spontaneously are not ideas of imagination at all but real things. "The ideas formed by the imagination . . . have . . . an entire dependence on the will. But the ideas perceived by sense, that is, real things, . . . being imprinted on the mind by a spirit distinct from us, have not the like dependence on our will" (*Three Dialogues,* p. 197). See also Locke, *Essay,* bk. 4, chap. 11, sec. 5. Richard Wollheim suggests that "it is the involuntariness of what [one] imagines, [one's] passivity in imagination, that conduces to the accompaniment of imagination by feeling," by terror, for example, when, while watching *King Lear,* one imagines Gloucester being blinded ("Imagination and Identification," pp. 68–69).

A deeper explanation of why spontaneous imaginings tend to be more vivid than deliberate ones might go like this: The relevant general principle is that evidence of the falsity of a proposition imposed forcefully on one's consciousness makes it difficult to imagine vividly that the proposition is true. If I want to imagine myself in a trackless wilderness, I may enhance the vivacity of my experience by closing my eyes or blotting out the automobile traffic and skyscrapers from my field of vision with my hand so that I see only trees and sky. Staring intently at skyscrapers and automobiles does not make it difficult to imagine oneself in the wilds. What is not so easy is imagining this *vividly* while glaring evidences of civilization dominate one's consciousness. Closing my eyes does not make me forget that I am surrounded by cars and skyscrapers, nor does it create an illusion. I know just as surely as I ever did that I am not in the wilds. The point is not that my beliefs affect the vividness of my imagining. What is important is, rather, how *conspicuous* certain facts which I believe are to me, how persistently they intrude into my thoughts, how difficult it is to avoid thinking (occurrently) about them.

If Jennifer imagines herself coming across a bear in the forest, she has bearish thoughts; she entertains, considers, turns over in her mind the proposition that there is a bear in front of her, and probably more specific propositions as well, such as that there is a ferocious grizzly pacing back and forth in front of her. She may also visualize a bear. If her imagining is deliberate, the fact that she rather than a (real) bear is the source of these bearish thoughts and images, the fact that she dreamed up the bear, is sure to be prominent in her awareness and difficult to ignore. It is not so difficult to ignore this if her imagining is spontaneous. She *knows* perfectly well that no real bear is responsible for her thoughts and images; she may have no doubt that they flow from somewhere in the dark recesses of her own unconscious. But when her imagining is spontaneous, nothing forces her to dwell on this fact; it does not intrude into her occurrent thoughts, even though if asked she would not hesitate to acknowledge it. This is why the imagining is likely to be more vivid, more gripping, more "frightening" if it is spontaneous than if it is deliberate.

Spontaneous imaginings may be *subject* to the imaginer's control. The imaginer may have the option of intervening deliberately in her imaginative experience even if she chooses not to exercise this option. If I find myself musing, spontaneously, about a candy-striped polar bear jumping over the moon, I may nevertheless realize that I could, if I wanted to, imagine instead a polka-dotted grizzly jumping over a star, or that I could stop imagining altogether. This realization limits my sense of the independence of my imaginative experiences from me. The imaginary world does unfold under its own power, but only with my (implicit) permission, only because I allow it to do so.[5]

Sometimes, however, we seem not to have even potential, unexercised control over what we imagine. This is so when we are asleep or in a trance. Dreams are spontaneous, undeliberate imaginings which the imaginer not only does not but cannot direct (consciously).[6] This helps to explain why dreaming is often such a powerful experience, why dreams tend to be more compelling, more "realistic" than daydreams in which the imaginer either directs the course of his imaginings or deliberately refrains from interfering.

Occurrent and Nonocurrent Imaginings

Each of us holds a great many beliefs and has an enormous number of intentions and desires, only a tiny fraction of which occupy our attention at any given moment. Thus arises the traditional distinction between occurrent and nonoccurrent (dispositional?) beliefs, intentions, and desires. Marilyn occurrently believes that the Democrats will win the next election when the thought that they will occurs to her, when she thinks or says to herself, with conviction, that the Democrats will win. She holds many other beliefs at the same time. She believes that Thomas Edison invented the telephone, that the Vikings were the first Europeans to visit America, that she is not a professional wrestler, and much more. But few of these other beliefs occur to her at this time. Some never do.

So it is with imaginings. Suppose that Fred launches his daydream by (occurrently) imagining himself winning a huge lottery prize and using it to finance a successful political campaign, and that he then goes on to imagine winning the affection and admiration of millions while in office, eventually retiring to a villa in southern France. All of these thoughts course through Fred's consciousness as he fantasizes. But it may well be true also that he imagines winning the election without resorting to stuffing ballot boxes or bribing powerful oppo-

5. See Casey, *Imagining*, pp. 63–64.

6. Occasionally one does have the impression of making decisions about what to dream. But it seems to me that what one decides is, at most, the topic of one's dream, its details being beyond one's (conscious) control. One deliberately starts the dream in a certain direction and then lets it go as it will. The experience might best be understood as a cross between a dream and a (deliberate) daydream. One might *dream* that one chooses to imagine certain things; there may be a daydream in (the world of) one's dream. But dreaming about choosing is not actually choosing.

nents, that he imagines his place of retirement to be in a warm climate on the Mediterranean, that he imagines being in good health when he retires—even if *these* thoughts do not explicitly occur to him. The question of whether his election is fair and square may never arise in his mind; he just takes for granted that it is. Once he occurrently imagines retiring to southern France, he has in the back of his mind the thought that his retirement is in a warm climate on the Mediterranean, even if he never gets around to saying this to himself. He thinks of himself, implicitly, as being in good health when he retires; he imagines that he is, but not occurrently. These thoughts are, we might say, part of his "mental furniture" during the daydream.

After Fred has occurrently imagined himself becoming a millionaire by winning a lottery and has gone on to think about his political career and retirement, he doesn't cease imagining that he won a lottery. His imagining this is a persisting state that begins when the thought occurs to him and continues, probably, for the duration of the daydream. After the initial thought it is a nonoccurrent imagining which forms a backdrop for later occurrent imaginings about his political career and retirement. (An effect of this background imagining might be a vague gnawing feeling, as the fantasy progresses, that his successes are unearned and undeserved insofar as his wealth is responsible for them.)

It is a mistake to think of a daydream as simply a disconnected series of individual mental events, acts of imagining, as one imagines first one thing, then another, then a third, and so on. The various imaginings are woven together into a continuous cloth, although only some of the strands are visible on the surface at any particular spot.

We need not decide what constitutes nonoccurrent imaginings and how they differ from their occurrent cousins. Perhaps they are dispositions to imagine occurrently. But we must be careful here. A person who has recurrent dreams or daydreams of fame and fortune is disposed, between the occurrences, to imagine himself rich and famous. But he need not actually be imagining this nonoccurrently then; he might even imagine the opposite during the intervals. Fred might have been disposed, during his daydream, to imagine occurrently his marrying Greta Garbo: he is infatuated with her, and if the question of who or whether he marries had occurred to him, he would have imagined himself marrying her. But it does not follow that Fred did nonoccurrently imagine marrying Garbo. Some nonoccurrent imaginings seem to consist in an (occurrent?) *experience* of some kind—the experience of having a thought in the back of one's mind, or at least in a coloring of one's other experiences. This may be true of Fred's continued imagining of his having struck it rich in a lottery, as he thinks about his plush retirement with the feeling that it is unearned or undeserved.

It should be clear that nonoccurrent, nonepisodic imaginings are not necessarily unconscious ones. We may well be at least nonoccurrently aware of them. (Perhaps noticing them *occurrently* would constitute imagining occurrently.) I suspect also that occurrent imaginings need not be conscious.

Many questions remain about the nature of nonoccurrent imaginings, how they differ from occurrent ones, and how to classify various particular instances. It is enough for our purposes simply to remember that imaginings do not have to be occurrent.

Solitary and Social Imaginings

We have understood imagining so far to be a solitary affair, something a person does or experiences by himself. But people do not always engage in imaginings alone. Fantasizing is sometimes a social event. There are collaborative daydreams as well as private reveries.

We sometimes make agreements with one another about what to imagine: "Let's imagine traveling on a spaceship headed for Pluto." "OK, and let's say that while passing Saturn we are attacked by a band of space pirates." Joint fantasizing allows people to pool their imaginative resources. Together they may be able to think of more exciting things to imagine than they could come up with separately, or more interesting or satisfying ones. And participants in a joint fantasy can share their experiences with one another. They can discuss what they imagine and compare their reactions to it.

The social activity I call collective imagining involves more than mere correspondence in what is imagined. Not only do the various participants imagine many of the same things; each of them realizes that the others are imagining what he is, and each realizes that the others realize this. Moreover, steps are taken to see that the correspondence obtains. And each participant has reasonable expectations and can make justified predictions about what others will imagine, given certain turns of events.

Making explicit agreements about what to imagine, as was done in the space travel daydream, is one method of coordinating imaginings. But it has a serious drawback. Insofar as the participants decide, collectively, on what to imagine, their imaginings are bound to be deliberate; each must decide, individually, to imagine whatever it is that is agreed upon. The price of coordination by agreement is the "vivacity" of imagining spontaneously. But, as we shall see shortly, coordination can be effected by other means without paying this price—by enlisting the aid of such things as dolls, hobbyhorses, snow forts, toy trucks, mud pies, and representational works of art.

Imagining and Entertaining

What is it to imagine? We have examined a number of dimensions along which imaginings can vary; shouldn't we now spell out what they have in common?

Yes, if we can. But I can't. Fortunately, an intuitive understanding of what it is to imagine, sharpened somewhat by the observations of this chapter, is sufficient for us to proceed with our investigation. But it will be revealing to look briefly at one promising but inadequate way of understanding imagining. In order to simplify things, let us restrict our attention to propositional imagining—imagining that something is the case. To imagine that *p,* it might be said, is to entertain the proposition that *p,* to attend to it, to consider it.[7]

Entertaining, attending to, considering seem most naturally construed as occurrent mental events. If they are occurrent, can sense be found for "nonoccurrently imagining that *p*"? That might be taken to mean "having the proposition that *p* in the back of one's mind." But this notion is no clearer than imagining itself. If it is to be any help to us, it must be possible to have a proposition in the back of one's mind without believing it (even implicitly), since one can imagine what one does not believe. Shall we say that one "nonoccurrently entertains," has in the back of one's mind, whatever propositions one is nonoccurrently aware of or knows about? This would allow much too much. I suppose that for most of my life I have been nonoccurrently aware of the proposition that Saint Anselm was born in August; I have realized implicitly that there is such a proposition, although I have never believed it or disbelieved it or desired it or had any other particular psychological attitude toward it except possibly that of being unaware of its truth value. Did I *imagine* nonoccurrently, all these years, that Anselm was born in August? Surely not. This proposition

7. According to Alvin Plantinga, the author of a work of fiction "exhibits" propositions and "calls them to our attention, invites us to consider and explore them" (*Nature of Necessity,* p. 62). See also Scruton, *Art and Imagination,* chap. 7; and Wolterstorff, *Works and Worlds,* pp. 233–234.

has not had anything like the role in my imaginative life that the proposition that Fred retires in good health has in his daydream— when he thinks implicitly of himself as retiring in good health while saying to himself only that he retires. If to imagine a proposition is to entertain it, to have it in mind, we need a more restricted notion of entertaining or having in mind, yet one that allows for doing so nonoccurrently. What sense is there in which I have rarely or never— prior to the writing of these pages—entertained or had in mind, even implicitly, the proposition that Anselm was born in August, yet in which Fred during his daydream did entertain or have in mind, implicitly, the proposition that he retired in good health? Well, the sense in which to entertain or have in mind a proposition is to imagine it. We are back where we started: What is imagining?

It is doubtful that the notion of entertaining propositions can be made to work even as an account of occurrent imagining. When Helen believes occurrently, thinks to herself, that there will be an earthquake in San Francisco before the year 2000, surely part of what she is doing is entertaining this proposition. Perhaps we can accept without too much strain that she is also imagining it, and that in general people imagine what they occurrently believe, disbelieve, fear, intend, desire. But suppose Dick thinks to himself that it is *not* the case that San Francisco will have an earthquake by 2000. He would seem to be entertaining the proposition that San Francisco *will* have an earthquake by 2000, as well as its negation. Must we allow that he is imagining both of them, both that the earthquake will occur and that it won't? Occurrent imagining, as we ordinarily understand it and as we need to understand it in order to explain representation, involves more than just entertaining or considering or having in mind the propositions imagined. Imagining (propositional imagining), like (propositional) believing or desiring, is *doing* something *with* a proposition one has in mind.[8]

Other strategies for explaining what it is to imagine face unusual difficulties. It is not easy to see what behavioral criteria might throw light on imagining, or what the relevant functions of a functional account might be. Imagining seems less tractable than more frequently discussed attitudes such as believing, intending, and desiring,

8. "The entertaining of propositions is the most familiar of all intellectual phenomena. It enters into every form of thinking and into many of our conative and emotional attitudes as well. Indeed, one might be inclined to say that it is the basic intellectual phenomenon; so fundamental that it admits of no explanation or analysis, but on the contrary all other forms of thinking have to be explained in terms of it" (Price, *Belief,* p. 192).

as well as emotional states such as being happy or sad or feeling guilty or jealous.

These negative conclusions illustrate and underscore some of the difficulties facing any attempt to construct a full-fledged account of what it is to imagine. I hope they have at least won the reader's sympathy for my decision not to make the attempt. It remains to be shown that we can get along without such an account. In any case, the difficulties do not provide an excuse to settle for some notion weaker than imagining—that of considering, for example—which, however clear, cannot do the job that needs to be done. "Imagining" can, if nothing else, serve as a placeholder for a notion yet to be fully clarified.

We noted that dolls, toy trucks, and representational works of art contribute to social imaginative activities by assisting in the coordination of imaginings. This is only one of many important ways in which real things enrich our imaginative lives. A conception of imaginative experiences as, in general, free-floating fantasies disconnected from the real world would be narrow and distorted. Sometimes, to be sure, imagining is a means of escape from reality, and we do frequently imagine what is not really the case. But even when we do, our experience is likely to involve the closest attention to features of our actual environment, not a general oblivion to it. Most imaginings are in one way or another dependent on or aimed at or anchored in the real world. I will examine three major roles that real things often have in our imaginative experiences: They *prompt* imaginings; they are *objects* of imaginings; and they *generate fictional truths*. The third is the defining characteristic of "props," as I shall use the term.

1.2.   PROMPTERS

While walking in the woods, Heather comes across a stump shaped strikingly like a bear, or so it seems to her anyway, and she imagines a bear blocking her path. Her imagining is prompted by the stump; but for it she would not have done so. The twittering of sparrows induces a person to imagine the sounds of a cocktail party; a child imagines a big red dump truck upon unwrapping a new toy one; a dreamer imagines that a school bell is ringing, as a result of hearing the ringing of his alarm clock. These are cases in which things in our environment prompt our imagination. Hallucinogenic drugs and brain operations can also affect what we imagine. But the prompters I am interested in are ones that prompt by being perceived or otherwise experienced or cognized. The stump, for example, provokes Heather to imagine a bear only because she sees it.

Prompters contribute to our imaginative lives in several ways. Most obviously, they broaden our imaginative horizons. They induce us to imagine what otherwise we might not be imaginative enough to think of. It might not occur to me to imagine a monster sitting atop a mountain were it not for the influence of certain suggestive rock formations. Imagining is a way of toying with, exploring, trying out new and sometimes farfetched ideas. Hence the value of luring our imaginations into unfamiliar territory.

Not every new idea is equally worth toying with. Natural objects like stumps and rock formations may or may not prod our imaginations in fruitful directions. What they prompt us to imagine is partly a matter of chance, depending on what shapes or other characteristics they happen to have. So people sometimes make artificial prompters or alter natural ones in order to direct the imaginings of others in predetermined ways. Snowmen, dolls, and toy trucks are designed by their makers to induce those who see or use them to imagine men, babies, and trucks of certain sorts. One might carve a stump into an unmistakable bear "likeness" in order to make sure that it will prompt people to imagine a bear. By constructing artificial prompters, we share our imaginative thoughts with others; and all of us can profit from those who are unusually imaginative, creative, perceptive, those who possess special talents for thinking up provocative or illuminating or comforting lines of imagination.

Why not just give verbal instructions in order to direct other people's imaginings? Why not just say, "Imagine a ferocious grizzly bear blocking your path," rather than going to the trouble of carving a stump? In the first place, it may be difficult to put into words exactly what one wants someone else to imagine. ("Imagine a bear poised to attack, but with a look on its face of, well, more of fear than of hatred, if you know what I mean.") And even if one does manage to say what one wants to say, the instructions may not be readily understood. It may be easier to communicate precisely what one wants others to imagine by constructing a "likeness" of some sort than by issuing explicit verbal instructions. (Some literary works might be construed simply as explicit instructions to readers about what to imagine. But most have a more complicated role than this, as we shall see in Chapter 9, one more like that of sculpted stumps and other "likenesses.")

A second advantage that carved stumps and the like have over verbal instructions is this: Following instructions is more likely to require reflection and deliberation on the part of the imaginer, especially if the instructions are complicated. One may well respond more automatically to a reasonably realistic "likeness." Heather doesn't need to *decide* whether to imagine a bear when she confronts the stump, or whether to imagine that it is large or small, facing her or facing away from her, and so on. The stump makes many of these decisions for her. Imaginings induced by prompters like stumps and toy trucks, even elaborately detailed imaginings, are often less contrived and deliberate, more spontaneous, than are imaginings in response to instructions.

Prompters are obviously a boon to collective imaginative activities. A toy truck or a well-executed snowman induces all who see it to imagine approximately the same things—a truck or a man of a certain sort. It coordinates their imaginings. And since the coordination does not involve agreements, stipulations, collective deliberation, the imaginings can be spontaneous. Moreover, it is probably obvious to each participant that the others will imagine what he does. Each can reasonably assume that the snowman will induce others, as it does him, to imagine a man of a certain sort. The prompter coordinates the imaginings of the participants and also gives them grounds to expect such coordination—both without disruptive discussion.

A natural prompter can serve as well as an artificial one in this regard. A sufficiently bearlike stump will prompt all observers to imagine a bear and give each reason to think the others are similarly prompted. A stump that is not naturally sufficiently bearlike may require judicious carving. But an easier alternative might be to make do with the stump as it is by making an initial stipulation or agreement ("Let's call that stump a bear," or just "Look at that bear"), and then allowing the stump to guide our more specific imaginings. Once the basic stipulation is made, further deliberation may be unnecessary; the characteristics of the stump may prompt all participants to imagine, nondeliberately, a large and ferocious bear rearing up on its hind legs, and each may confidently expect the others to imagine likewise. (Compare paintings and sculptures that depend heavily on their titles: the late Monets in the Musée Marmottan, Jacques Lipchitz's *Reclining Nude with Guitar*.)

There is another sort of agreement or stipulation which participants in joint imaginative activities may make, one that looks forward to crucial features of the representational arts. Rather than agreeing to imagine a bear in some particular instance, the participants may agree to imagine a bear whenever they come across a stump, *any* stump ("Let's say that all stumps are bears"). With practice they may "internalize" this convention sufficiently so that when they see a stump, even a not very bearlike one, it provokes them automatically and unreflectively to imagine a bear. It may even make them "jump with fright."

The prompting function of such things as stumps, snowmen, and toy trucks, important as it is, should not be overemphasized. Suppose that Kate and Steve build a snow fort—an imposing structure with turrets and a central tower, protected by a moat. The finished structure did not give them the idea of imagining a fort, or a fort with turrets, a central tower, and a moat. It is because they already had that idea that they built the snow edifice and built it as they did. In fact, they probably imagined this before building it, or anyway before finishing it. Perhaps they intended their work to prompt the imaginings of others, but they may not have. They may have built it only for their own use and enjoyment. It is unlikely that the snow fort does no prompting at all. A cavity in the wall which was not especially intended might later be interpreted as a seat; it may induce Kate and Steve to imagine a seat. The creators of a snowman may adjust the features of its face with only a vague idea of what expression they are giving it. The result then prompts them to imagine a man with a very particular expression, one they did not foresee. Nevertheless it is obvious that the prompting function of the snow fort is only a small part of its contribution to Kate's and Steve's imaginative activity.

Even toy trucks, which are made for the benefit of people other than their makers and are obviously designed to prompt their imaginings, are important in other ways also. A child playing with a toy truck does not merely look at it and imagine what it prompts him to imagine. He "makes it go"—fast or slow, into one room and another, and so on. When he does he imagines a (real) truck behaving in these ways. The toy is hardly to be credited with prompting *these* imaginings, nor is its movements. He made the toy move in certain ways because of how he wanted to imagine a truck moving, rather than vice versa.

Such things as snow forts and toy trucks do not always do very much in the way of expanding our imaginative horizons, provoking us to imagine what we would not have thought to imagine otherwise. Among the other roles they may play in our imaginative activities is that of being *objects* of imaginings.

1.3. OBJECTS OF IMAGININGS

When Kate and Steve finish their snow fort, they do not merely imagine a (real) fort with turrets, a tower, and a moat; they imagine of the actual sculpted heap of snow that *it itself* is such a fort. A child playing with a rag doll not only imagines a baby; he imagines the doll to be a baby. (This is not to imagine that there is something which is both a rag doll and a baby. The child imagines, of something which is in fact a rag doll, that it is not a doll but a baby.) A child imagines a stump to be a bear or a hollow log a house. While dreaming, one may imagine of the sound of an alarm clock that it is the sound of a school bell. Many imaginings are thus about real things. And many of the things that prompt imaginings prompt imaginings about themselves. Things that a person imagines about are objects of his imagining.[9]

Not all prompters are objects of the imaginings they prompt. While fantasizing about a trip to Italy, Nathan might be prompted by the sight of a water faucet to imagine that it is raining in Italy. But he probably does not imagine anything about the faucet itself; it is only a stimulus. It is also possible for something—the snow fort, for instance—to be an object of imaginings without prompting them. My present interest is in objects of imaginings whether or not they prompt the imaginings.

There are notable differences among imaginings about objects. Suppose Sarah imagines George Bush to be a bookie. Bush is the object of her imagining, but his role in her experience differs significantly from the roles objects such as dolls, stumps, and snow forts usually have in imaginings. For one thing, the latter are props as well as objects, whereas Bush is not (at least he does not function very extensively as a prop). We are not yet in a position to appreciate this difference. But we can appreciate another one which is not unrelated to it.

Sarah chose Bush as an object of her imagining because he is of special interest to her. She might relish the absurdity of the idea of his being a bookie if she considers him actually to be a righteous, upstanding, Boy Scoutish sort of person. Alternatively, she may wish to explore the perhaps surprising naturalness of this thought, the compatibility of being a bookie with what she takes to be underlying

9. Imaginings *de se* are imaginings about the imaginer himself. But I will suggest in the following section that the imaginer *de se* need not be a *de re* object of his imagining, and that it may not be appropriate to describe him as imagining, "*of himself*, that . . . " By "objects" of imaginings I will mean *de se* as well as *de re* objects.

characteristics of Bush's personality. In either case Bush is the focus of the exercise. Its purpose, or at least an important probable consequence of it, is a deepening of Sarah's understanding of Bush or a clarifying of her attitudes about him.

When Eric imagines a stump to be a bear, he probably does not have any substantial interest in the stump itself. He is interested in the idea of there being a bear blocking his path; perhaps he wonders how he would react, how brave he would be, whether he would freeze in terror if there actually were a bear there. But he is not especially concerned with the thought of that particular stump's being a bear. (He may even believe that the stump *could not* be a bear, that its being a nonbear is one of its essential properties.) Gaining insight into the stump is not among his objectives in imagining as he does. The stump is not the focus of his interest in the way in which Bush is the focus of Sarah's.

What, then, is the point of imagining the stump to be a bear? Why not simply imagine a bear in the path? How does the stump's role as an object of imagination, not just a prompter, contribute to the imaginative experience? An intuitive answer is that the stump "gives substance," as we might describe it, to the imaginary bear. When the stump is imagined to be a bear, there *is* something—something real and solid and kickable—which can be called the imaginary bear. No such substantial object can be identified as the imaginary bear when one merely imagines a bear at a certain spot. I believe that this difference partly accounts for the impression which I have, and which I suspect others share, that an experience of imagining a bear is likely to be more "vivid" if one imagines of some actual object that it is a bear than if one does not. I will cite two pieces of evidence suggesting that my impression is not idiosyncratic.

It has been argued that an important feature of theater, one that is lacking in films, is the actual presence to the audience of actors, real people.[10] The significance of the presence of actors may be explained by the fact that they are objects of the spectators' imaginings. Spectators imagine of Sir Laurence Olivier, when he plays Hamlet, that he is Prince of Denmark; there is a real person before them who they imagine to be faced with the task of avenging his father's murder, to hesitate in carrying it out, and so forth. Viewers of a film are in the presence of nothing but images on a screen. The images prompt them to imagine people robbing stagecoaches, falling in love, and so on, but

10. See Bazin, *What Is Cinema?*, I, 96–98. But Bazin denies that theater and film differ significantly in this respect.

the viewers do not imagine of the images that *they* do these things. The images are prompters but not objects of their imaginings. The point is not that the imaginings of the movie audience do not have real things as objects. The screen images probably prompt the audience to imagine of the movie actors that they rob stagecoaches and fall in love. But the actors are not present in the theater. So the point must be that imaginings are made more vivid by the *presence* of the actors. My suggestion is that their presence is important only because they are objects of imagining. And perhaps even absent objects are better than none. Perhaps a photographic film is in a certain way (though not in others) more "vivid" than an animation in which there are no actors to serve as objects. (This is most likely to be true, I suspect, if we have some independent acquaintance with or knowledge of the film actors.)

My second piece of evidence is a fifteenth-century handbook for young girls which advises them to imagine the Passion story using familiar things as objects:

> The better to impress the story of the Passion on your mind, and to memorize each action of it more easily, it is helpful and necessary to fix the places and people in your mind: a city, for example, which will be the city of Jerusalem—taking for this purpose a city that is well known to you. In this city find the principal places in which all the episodes of the Passion would have taken place—for instance, a place with the supper-room where Christ had the Last Supper with the Disciples, and the house of Anne, and that of Caiaphas, with the place where Jesus was taken in the night, and the room where He was brought before Caiaphas and mocked and beaten. Also the residence of Pilate where he spoke with the Jews, and in it the room where Jesus was bound to the Column. Also the site of Mount Calvary, where he was put on the Cross; and other like places . . .
>
> And then too you must shape in your mind some people, people, well known to you, to represent for you the people involved in the Passion—the person of Jesus Himself, of the Virgin, Saint Peter, Saint John the Evangelist, Saint Mary Magdalen, Anne, Caiaphas, Pilate, Judas and the others, every one of whom you will fashion in your mind.
>
> When you have done all this, putting all your imagination into it, then go into your chamber. Alone and solitary, excluding every external thought from your mind, start thinking of the beginning of the Passion starting with how Jesus entered Jerusalem on the ass.[11]

11. *Zardino de Oration* (Venice, 1494). Quoted in Baxandall, *Painting and Experience*, p. 46.

Notice that the advice is to utilize real things as objects of one's imaginings, but not to do the imaginings in the presence of those objects.

Among the most important objects of imaginings are the imaginers themselves. They call for special treatment.

1.4.   IMAGINING ABOUT ONESELF

Fred imagined himself rich and famous; he was the central character of his daydream. His fantasy is not at all atypical in this respect. It is my impression that virtually all of our imaginings are partly about ourselves. Even when we are not central characters, *heroes* of our dreams, daydreams, and games of make-believe, we usually have some role in them—at least that of an observer of other goings-on. Imagining an elephant in Central Park is likely to involve imagining oneself seeing an elephant in Central Park, especially if one visualizes the elephant. If one doesn't visualize it, one still probably imagines knowing about it. (This need not involve imagining having learned about the elephant in one way or another. It may but need not involve imagining reacting to the news with amazement, excitement, terror, or whatever.)

It is not surprising that so much of our imagining centers on ourselves. People are egocentric. But I am inclined to think that imagining is *essentially* self-referential in a certain way, as intending is. (To intend that something be the case is to intend to do something oneself to bring it about should the occasion arise; otherwise one merely hopes or expects rather than intends.) Christopher Peacocke has argued that imagining does indeed essentially involve imagining about oneself.[12]

There are significantly different ways in which imaginings may have the imaginer as an object. Sometimes a self-imaginer imagines himself *as himself,* we might say; sometimes not. Sometimes one imagines oneself *in a first-person manner,* or *from the inside;* sometimes not. I will not attempt to provide anything like full accounts of these distinctions. But examples will illustrate that there are important distinctions to be made, and will bring out some salient features of the different varieties of self-imaginings.

Peacocke's proposal is that "to imagine something is always at least

12. "Imagination, Experience, and Possibility."

to imagine, *from the inside,* being in some conscious state."[13] My suggestion is weaker: that all imagining involves a kind of self-imagining (imagining *de se*), of which imagining from the inside is the most common variety. Specifically, the minimal self-imagining that seems to accompany all imagining is that of being aware of whatever else it is that one imagines.

An article about Ted appears in a newspaper, but it uses a pseudonym to protect his identity. Ted reads it without realizing that it is about himself. He then imagines of the person referred to—himself—that he is rich and famous. Ted is an object of his own imagining, though he doesn't realize that he is. He imagines of himself that he has certain experiences, that he enjoys his fame and fortune, for instance. But he does not imagine this "from the inside." To do that is, in part, to imagine about oneself in such a way that one cannot be unaware that it is oneself about whom one imagines.

Imagining from the inside is one variety of what I will call "imagining *de se*," a form of self-imagining characteristically described as imagining *doing* or *experiencing* something (or *being* a certain way), as opposed to imagining merely *that* one does or experiences something or possesses a certain property. Fred imagines winning the lottery, moving to France, and feeling the sun on his back. Ted, however, imagines only that he acquires and enjoys fame and fortune; he does not imagine *acquiring* them or *enjoying* them. Imagining *de se* is also characteristically described using "he himself" locutions. It would be a little out of place to describe Ted as having imagined that *he himself* acquired and enjoyed fame and fortune.

De se imaginings in general are such that the imaginer cannot be unaware that his imagining is about himself. But these are not the only imaginings with objects whose identity enjoys a certain immunity from doubt. Wittgenstein observed that when a person imagines King's College on fire, there may be no room for questioning his claim that it is King's College which he imagines—even if another college or a Hollywood movie set perfectly matches his visual image (if he has one).[14] Doubt about the identity of the imagined college is not entirely out of the question, however. If the imaginer has previously mistaken another college for King's, and if his intention is to imagine *that* college, he may think the college he is imagining is King's when it

---

13. Ibid., p. 21 (my emphasis). Peacocke's account of what "from the inside" means is in *Sense and Content,* chap. 5.

14. *Blue and Brown Books,* p. 39.

is actually the other one. If he saw King's College without realizing it was King's, he might then imagine King's College on fire without realizing that King's is the college he is imagining.

No mistakes of this sort seem possible when Fred imagines (*de se*) feeling the sun on his back. There is a story to be told about how an imagining about King's College gets to be about King's College, or what makes Ted's imagining an imagining about himself—a story in part of causal links between the object and one's previous experiences (one's seeing the college, Ted's reading of the paper) and between these and one's imagining. To identify something as an object of one's imagining in these cases is to forward a hypothesis about what sort of story is to be told, a hypothesis that can be mistaken. There seems to be no similar story about what makes *de se* imaginings imaginings about oneself.

If it is King's College that I imagine on fire, it might be said that I imagine it "under a certain description" or "mode of presentation," that, for example, I imagine it "as the college I saw on such and such an occasion." Ted imagines Ted "as the subject of the newspaper article." It isn't clear that such can be said about Fred's imagining (*de se*) about himself when he imagines feeling the sun on his back.

Imagining *de se* is not always imagining *from the inside*.[15] I understand Fred to imagine from the inside the warmth of the sun on his back. When Gregory imagines playing in a major league baseball game and hitting a home run, he may imagine this from the inside, imagine feeling in his hands the shock of the bat connecting with the ball, and so on. But suppose he imagines hitting the home run from the perspective of a spectator in the stands. He visualizes the scene from that point of view, and his image of the field includes Gregory as he slams the ball over the center field fence and rounds the bases. This imagining is, I believe, best classified as *de se*. It is perfectly natural to describe Gregory as imagining *hitting* a home run, and as imagining that *he himself* hits one. There is no room for doubt that he is himself the player who hits the home run in his imagination. No conceivable evidence about the causal antecedents of his imaginative experiences could make him question that he is. There seems to be no story of the relevant sort to be told about how it got to be Gregory whom he imagines. And he seems not to imagine himself under a description analogous to "the subject of the newspaper article" or "the person I saw on such and such an occasion." Yet his imagining is not from the

---

15. David Hills convinced me of this. The reasons I give are approximately his.

inside. It is as though he is watching someone else hit the ball and round the bases, despite his unshakable realization that he is himself that person. (He may imagine himself from the inside watching the game from the stands.[16] And of course his imagining, from the stands, hitting the home run may alternate with imagining this from the inside.)

The question of whether an imagining is from the inside arises only when what is imagined is an experience (broadly construed). But one can imagine possessing properties that are not experiences. One may imagine (de se) being a descendant of a thirteenth-century sailor or having a rare blood type, but not from the inside.

Is imagining from the inside necessarily imagining about oneself? Yes, I take it, and so is imagining experiencing or doing something or being a certain way in general, whether from the inside or not. (If these are not self-imaginings, we should not call them imaginings de se.) To imagine seeing a rhinoceros is to imagine oneself seeing a rhinoceros, not just to imagine an instance of rhinoceros seeing. One who imagines Napoleon's seeing a rhinoceros, or imagines a seeing of a rhinoceros without imagining whose seeing it is, does not thereby "imagine seeing a rhinoceros" as this phrase is ordinarily understood. And unless one also imagines (oneself) seeing a rhinoceros, one's imagining cannot be from the inside.[17] "Imagine" fits a common pattern in this regard. To remember giving a speech is to remember oneself giving one, not merely to remember an instance of a speech being given. To start swimming is to start one's own swimming. To try climbing a mountain is to try to climb it oneself. To think about or consider applying for a job is to think about or consider applying for it oneself.

The notion of the self that figures in imaginings de se need not be a very rich or full one, however, and this may help to mollify skeptics. When I imagine (myself) seeing a rhinoceros, there may be a sense in which I do not imagine that Kendall Walton sees a rhinoceros, or imagine Walton's seeing one, or imagine of Walton that he sees one. No verbal representation of myself (neither my name nor a description of myself nor a first-person pronoun) need figure in my thoughts as I imagine; I may think something like "That is a rhinoceros," rather than "I see a rhinoceros," although the former imaginatively

16. How is it that he is both spectator and player in the imaginary game? Perhaps he imagines being the spectator and imagines being the player, without imagining being both at once.

17. One might imagine, from the inside, watching Napoleon looking at a rhinoceros.

locates the rhinoceros in relation to me. I don't *pick out* a person—myself—and then proceed to imagine about him. Nor do I in any ordinary manner *identify* someone (myself) as the object of my imagining. We might express this point by saying that the self whom I imagine to be seeing a rhinoceros may be a "bare Cartesian I." And we might reasonably decline to characterize my imagining as an instance of *de re* imagining about myself. I propose thinking of imagining *de se* not as a species of imagining *de re* but rather as a *different* way in which imaginings can be "about" oneself.[18]

One can imagine *being Napoleon,* as we say, and seeing a rhinoceros through *his* eyes. Suppose Joyce does. There is more than one way of understanding her experience, but the most plausible ones seem to me to involve Joyce's imagining *herself* seeing a rhino.

The most straightforward construal would have it that she imagines herself seeing a rhinoceros while imagining herself to be identical with Napoleon.[19] But it is metaphysically impossible that she should be Napoleon. Can one imagine what is metaphysically impossible? Perhaps. That would seem to be what one does when one sees a cartoon depiction of a pig whose face is recognizably that of a familiar politician: one imagines of the politician that he is a pig. Some will allow that metaphysically impossible identities like that between Joyce and Napoleon can be believed. Seeing Brian Mulroney from a distance, I mistake him for William Rehnquist. Don't I then believe of Mulroney that he is identical with Rehnquist? Of course I don't realize that it is Mulroney whom I believe to be Rehnquist and hence that what I believe is impossible. Joyce does realize that she is Joyce and that her being Napoleon is impossible. This makes it difficult for her to *believe* that she is Napoleon, but it is not clear that it should hinder her imagining this. One might speak of different "modes of presentation" here: I believe of Mulroney, under a demonstrative mode of presentation ("*that* man"), that he is Rehnquist. Joyce imagines of herself qua *herself,* that she is Napoleon, where Napoleon is identified descriptively or in some other way. The mode of presentation under which Joyce imagines herself is construed by some to be a demonstrative one ("*this* person," said while pointing inwardly to oneself); others may deny that any mode of presentation is involved.

18. I take this suggestion from David Hills. Lewis understands belief *de se* to be an instance of belief *de re* about oneself, and Chisholm does as well, although in the broader of two senses of "belief *de re.*" Both would presumably say the same about imagining. (Lewis, "De Dicto and De Se," p. 156; Chisholm, *First Person,* pp. 108–109.)

19. This is consistent with there being a sense in which she does not imagine that *Joyce* and Napoleon are identical.

Richard Wollheim denies that to say "I imagine myself being Sultan Mahomet II" is to say that one imagines an identity between oneself and the sultan. Although identity is symmetrical, he observes, "imagining myself being Sultan Mahomet II" is not the same as "imagining Sultan Mahomet II being me"; these are "two different imaginative projects."[20] The reason is insufficient. There may merely be *more* to imagining myself being the sultan than imagining an identity between me and the sultan. (What more is involved may be *implied* by the use of this phrase rather than said.) When I imagine myself being the sultan, what I go on to imagine, besides the identity, will be different from what I go on to imagine when I imagine the sultan being me. In the first case I imagine myself (= the sultan) living in the fifteenth century and directing a siege of Constantinople; in the second I imagine myself (= the sultan) living in the twentieth century and writing about the representational arts. Also, "imagining myself being the sultan" is likely to suggest that I imagine myself (= the sultan) from the inside, or at least in a *de se* manner, whereas "imagining the sultan being me" does not.

There may still be resistance to the idea that Joyce imagines an impossibility. Could it be that she merely imagines herself in Napoleon's shoes, where this means that she imagines being in a situation like one she takes Napoleon to have been in, not that she imagines an identity between herself and Napoleon? This is not what is meant by "imagining being Napoleon," for Napoleon doesn't figure in the content of the imagining. Wollheim once suggested that one's imagining in such cases involves the "master thought" that Napoleon doesn't otherwise exist;[21] but this doesn't do the job. When Joyce imagines being crowned at Notre-Dame and suffering defeat at Waterloo, she could be imagining simply that she existed *in place of* Napoleon, and that it was she rather than he who was crowned at Notre-Dame and defeated at Waterloo. This is not imagining herself "being Napoleon."

To imagine being Napoleon it is not even *necessary* that one imagine having experiences of kinds one believes Napoleon to have had. I might imagine being Napoleon and landing on the moon, without thinking that Napoleon did land on the moon, and without imagining being crowned or doing or experiencing anything else I think Napoleon actually did or experienced. There is, to be sure, the question of what makes it Napoleon whom I imagine being. But the

20. *Thread of Life*, p. 75. See also Wollheim, "Imagination and Identification," p. 80.
21. "Imagination and Identification," pp. 82–83.

answer does not lie in the descriptive content of the imagining, in what I imagine doing or experiencing.

The best way to avoid supposing that Joyce imagines a metaphysical impossibility, if one feels obliged to avoid it, is something like this:[22] She imagines (herself) seeing a rhinoceros. And *by means of* this first-person self-imagining she imagines Napoleon to be seeing a rhinoceros. Let us say that she illustrates for herself what she imagines Napoleon to experience, by imagining experiencing it herself. (Compare Kurosawa's film *Rashomon*. The portrayal of the bandit killing the man illustrates what fictionally the bandit testifies to have happened. See §8.7.) Joyce does not imagine an identity between herself and Napoleon. But she does imagine both herself and Napoleon, and these two imaginings, though distinct, are significantly linked.

I will make little use in what follows of the notion of imagining being someone (other than oneself). But imagining (*de se*) doing things or having experiences and, more specifically, imagining from the inside will be central. Such self-imaginings are crucial components of our imaginative experiences. It is chiefly by imagining ourselves facing certain situations, engaging in certain activities, observing certain events, experiencing or expressing certain feelings or attitudes that we come to terms with our feelings—that we discover them, learn to accept them, purge ourselves of them, or whatever exactly it is that imagining helps us do. These self-imaginings are important even when our main objective is to gain insight into others. In order to understand how minorities feel about being discriminated against, one should imagine not just instances of discrimination but instances of discrimination against *oneself;* one should imagine *experiencing* discrimination. It is when I imagine *myself* in another's shoes (whether or not I imagine *being* him) that my imagination helps me to understand *him*. (Such imaginative understanding may be what has been called *Verstehen*.) And when I imagine this I also learn about myself.

Earlier I contrasted Sarah's fantasy about George Bush with Eric's imaginings about stumps. Most imaginings *de se* seem to belong more with the former than the latter. The objects of both Sarah's and the self-imaginer's imaginings are especially important to them. Sarah's imagining is motivated and guided by a special interest in Bush, and she may hope to achieve insight about him through her experience. Likewise, it is typically because people are especially important to themselves that they imagine about themselves as much as they do,

---

22. William Taschek suggested this alternative.

even if a certain minimal self-imagining is automatic. Even when imaginers' primary purpose is to understand others, the insight they also gain into themselves is a significant if partly incidental consequence of their imaginings. Imaginers as objects of their imaginings rarely serve as mere means, as frames on which to hang imaginings about other things, in the way that stumps are likely to.

But imaginers, when they are objects of *de se* imaginings, function in *some* ways more as the stumps do than as I am supposing Bush does in Sarah's experience. The imaginers, like the stumps, are *props* as well as objects.

1.5. PROPS AND FICTIONAL TRUTHS

Let us turn now to the settings in which imaginings occur rather than the acts of imagining themselves—to dreams, daydreams, games of make-believe, and the experiencing of representational works of art.

When it is "true in a game of make-believe," as we say, that Jules goes on a buffalo hunt, the proposition that he goes on a buffalo hunt is *fictional,* and the fact that it is fictional is a *fictional truth.* In general, whatever is the case "in a fictional world"—in the world of a game of make-believe or dream or daydream or representational work of art—is fictional. When Fred dreams of fame and riches, it is fictional that he is rich and famous. In Seurat's *Sunday on the Island of La Grande Jatte* a couple is strolling in a park; fictionally this is so. It is fictional that there is a society of six-inch-tall people called Lilliputians, and also that a certain Gregor Samsa was transformed into an insect.[23]

To call a proposition fictional amounts to saying only that it is "true in some fictional world or other." Sometimes we will want to specify which "world" something is "true in." So let's say that the proposition that there is a society of six-inch-tall people is not only fictional but, more specifically, fictional in *Gulliver's Travels,* or *Gulliver's Travels*–fictional. It is *Gulliver's Travels*–fictional also that a war was fought over whether eggs should be broken on the large or the small end. But the proposition that a couple is strolling in a park belongs to a different world; it is *La Grande Jatte*–fictional. "It is fictional that *p*" can be thought of as analogous to "It is believed (or

23. The notion of fictionality obviates the need for Danto's "is's" of artistic and other special sorts of identification (*Transfiguration,* pp. 126–27). It is fictional that a doll is a person or an actor Hamlet, in the usual sense of "is." (The identities in some of Danto's examples are fictional only in what I will call "unofficial" games of make-believe.)

desired, or claimed, or denied) *by someone or other* that *p,*" and "It is *Gulliver's Travels*–fictional that *p*" as analogous to "It is believed (desired, claimed, denied) *by Jones* that *p.*" So much for terminology.

In taking fictionality to be a property of propositions, I am brashly begging controversial questions of metaphysics and philosophical logic. We needn't be very fussy about how propositions are understood, except that I will, for present purposes, take some of them to have individual objects as constituents: Fred is a constituent of the proposition that Fred is rich and famous. *De re* fictional truths consist in the fictionality of propositions having particulars as constituents.[24] "Modes of presentation" or something of the sort are needed also— to distinguish the first- and third-person manners in which Fred and Ted imagine themselves rich and famous, for instance. I do not think of modes of presentation as constituents of propositions, but they have a lot to do with the character of Fred's and Ted's daydreams and imaginative experiences generally.

There are other ways of setting things up. I choose this familiar one less from conviction than for convenience, and in the belief that in the long run this choice will not substantively affect matters at hand. Readers who reject propositions or prefer to understand them differently are invited to reformulate my claims about fictionality however their philosophical conscience dictates—in accordance with their preferred way of treating (so-called) propositional attitudes generally.[25] It is my belief that any reasonable reformulation will be recognizably the same, that the substance of the problems it treats and its ways of treating them will remain.

What is fictionality? We understand intuitively what it is for something to be "true in a fictional world"; if we didn't, criticism as we know it would be impossible. But how is fictionality to be analyzed? The first step toward an analysis is to investigate the relation between

24. Purely fictional entities are not constituents of propositions, for there aren't any. And since there is no Gregor Samsa, there is no such thing as the proposition that he became an insect. But it will be convenient for now to pretend that the universe does contain fictitious entities and propositions about them. I will speak, for now, as though the proposition that Gregor became an insect is fictional. But this is just pretense. (In this respect much of this book is itself a work of fiction.) In Part Four we will see how to understand what people actually say when they appear to be, or pretend to be, talking about fictitious entities.

25. I find especially attractive the suggestion by Lewis ("De Dicto and De Se") and Chisholm (*First Person*) that propositional attitudes be understood in terms of the ascription of properties to oneself. So far as I can see, my theory could be stated in these terms without altering it substantively. In place of the imagining of propositions, we will have imaginative self-ascription of properties. This fits nicely with the idea that imagining is, necessarily, in part self-directed.

fictionality and the imagination. In doing so we shall see, finally, what props are and how they are important.

Being fictional and being imagined are characteristics that many propositions share. Readers of *Gulliver's Travels* imagine that there is a society of six-inch-tall people. Fred imagines that he is rich and famous. But it would be a serious mistake simply to identify the fictional with what is imagined. What is fictional need not be imagined, and perhaps what is imagined need not be fictional.[26]

"Let's say that stumps are bears," Eric proposes. Gregory agrees, and a game of make-believe is begun, one in which stumps—all stumps, not just one or a specified few—"count as" bears. Coming upon a stump in the forest, Eric and Gregory imagine a bear. Part of what they imagine is that there is a bear at a certain spot—the spot actually occupied by the stump. "Hey, there's a bear over there!" Gregory yells to Eric. Susan, who is not in on the game but overhears, is alarmed. So Eric reassures her that it is only "in the game" that there is a bear at the place indicated. The proposition that there is a bear there is fictional in the game.

Or so Eric and Gregory think. They approach the bear cautiously, but only to discover that the stump is not a stump at all but a moss-covered boulder. "False alarm. There isn't a bear there after all," Gregory observes with surprise and relief. And for the benefit of outsiders, "We were mistaken in thinking that, in the world of the game, there was a bear there." Eric and Gregory did imagine that a bear was there, but this did not make it fictional in their game. They do not say that fictionally there was a bear which evaporated when they approached, nor that it is *no longer* fictional that a bear was there at the earlier time. Gregory takes back his previous claim that fictionally a bear was in the place indicated, and he is right to do so.

Meanwhile, however, unbeknownst to anyone, there is an actual stump buried in a thicket not twenty feet behind Eric. Fictionally a bear is lurking in the thicket, although neither Eric nor Gregory realizes the danger. No one imagines a bear in the thicket; it is not fictional that a bear is there because somebody imagines that there is. But it is fictional. What makes it fictional? The stump. Thus does the stump generate a fictional truth. It is a prop. Props are generators of fictional truths, things which, by virtue of their nature or existence, make propositions fictional. A snow fort is a prop. It is responsible for

26. For any imagining, we might recognize a fantasy in which what is imagined is fictional. But it need not be fictional in the "world" the imaginer is mainly concerned with—e.g., that of a game of make-believe.

the fictionality of the proposition that there is a (real) fort with turrets and a moat. A doll makes it fictional in a child's game that there is a blonde baby girl.

Representational works of art are props also. What makes it fictional in *La Grande Jatte* that a couple is strolling in a park is the painting itself, the pattern of paint splotches on the surface of the canvas. It is because of the words constituting *Gulliver's Travels* that fictionally there is a society of six-inch-tall people who go to war over how eggs are to be broken.

Props generate fictional truths independently of what anyone does or does not imagine. But they do not do so entirely on their own, apart from any (actual or potential) imaginers. Props function only in a social, or at least human, setting. The stump in the thicket makes it fictional that a bear is there only because there is a certain convention, understanding, agreement in the game of make-believe, one to the effect that wherever there is a stump, fictionally there is a bear. I will call this a *principle of generation*. This principle was established by explicit stipulation: "Let's say that stumps are bears." But not all principles are established thus. Some, including most involving works of art, are never explicitly agreed on or even formulated, and imaginers may be unaware of them, at least in the sense of being unable to spell them out. I do not assume that principles of generation are, in general or even normally, "conventional" or "arbitrary," nor that they must be learned. Nevertheless, what principles of generation there are depends on which ones people accept in various contexts. The principles that are in force are those that are understood, at least implicitly, to be in force.

Props are often prompters or objects of imagining also; even all three. Any stumps Eric and Gregory discover during their game have all three roles; they prompt Eric and Gregory to imagine certain things, and among the imaginings they prompt are imaginings about themselves (imaginings, of the stumps, that they are bears). But the three functions are distinct. It is clear already that props need not be prompters or objects of any imaginings. An undiscovered stump prompts no imaginings and is not imagined about, although it is a prop. Nor must prompters or objects be props. Suppose Eric associates raspberries with poison ivy; it was after picking raspberries that he suffered his worst outbreak of poison ivy, and he hasn't forgotten. He sees raspberry bushes in the forest and imagines poison ivy. Let's say that he also imagines of the raspberry bushes that they are poison ivy plants. This does not make it fictional in his game that poison ivy is growing in the forest, for there is as yet no principle of generation in effect, no even implicit understanding, whereby the raspberry bushes "count as" poison ivy. No such principle need be in force even if it happens that Gregory too associates raspberry bushes with poison ivy for some reason and is prompted to imagine as Eric does. Without the relevant understanding, Eric's and Gregory's imaginations simply wander—in similar directions, as it happens. They interrupt the game to engage in their own personal fantasies.

We are still lacking a positive account of fictionality. We know that being fictional is not the same as being imagined, and we have seen how some fictional truths are established—by props working in conjunction with principles of generation. But what is thus established? The answer will emerge when we consider what connections do obtain between fictionality and imagination.

Imagining is easily thought of as a free, unregulated activity, subject to no constraints save whim, happenstance, and the obscure demands of the unconscious.[27] The imagination is meant to explore, to wander at will through our conceptual universes. In this respect imagination appears to contrast sharply with belief. Beliefs, unlike imaginings, are correct or incorrect. Belief aims at truth. What is true and only what is true is to be believed. We are not free to believe as we please. We are free to imagine as we please.

So it may seem, but it isn't quite so. Imaginings are constrained also; some are proper, appropriate in certain contexts, and others not. Herein lies the key to the notion of fictional truth. Briefly, a fictional truth consists in there being a prescription or mandate in some context to imagine something. Fictional propositions are propositions that are *to be* imagined—whether or not they are in fact imagined.

The agreements which participants in a collective daydream make about what to imagine can be thought of as rules prescribing certain imaginings. It is a rule of a certain joint fantasy that participants are to imagine traveling to Saturn in a rocket, or that they are to imagine of a particular stump that it is a bear. True, the agreements are made, the rules established voluntarily, and their prescriptions are relative to one's role as a participant in the imaginative activity in question. But they do prescribe. Anyone who refuses to imagine what was agreed on refuses to "play the game" or plays it improperly. He breaks a rule.

These rules are categorical. But I shall be interested mostly in condi-

---

27. "Nothing is more free than the imagination of man" (Hume, *Enquiry*, sec. 5, pt. 2).

tional rules, ones to the effect that *if* certain circumstances obtain, certain things are to be imagined. The principle of generation in Eric's and Gregory's game is a conditional rule—the rule that if there is a stump at a certain place, one is to imagine that there is a bear there. Given that a stump does occupy a certain spot, imagining that a bear occupies that spot is mandated. Of course if participants in the game are unaware of a particular stump—because it is buried in a thicket, for example—their failure to imagine as prescribed is understandable; one can only do one's best to follow the rule. But to refuse to imagine that there is a bear where there is a stump in full view would be to flout the rule, to refuse to play the game.

The fictionality of the proposition that there is a bear at a certain place consists in the fact that imagining it is prescribed by a rule of the game. The rule is conditional, its prescription dependent on the presence of a stump. Thus does the stump generate the fictional truth.

Is there, for *every* fictional proposition, a requirement that it be imagined? If a stump is exactly 4 feet $5\frac{1}{2}$ inches tall, presumably it is fictional ("true in the game") that there is a bear of precisely that height. Must Eric and Gregory imagine *that*, on pain of playing the game improperly? Must they imagine (even nonoccurrently) that, like all bears, this one has a heart that pumps blood through its body, and that it likes blueberries? Is the appreciator of a picture of a flock of birds required to notice that fictionally there are exactly forty-seven birds in the flock and to imagine accordingly? To do *that* might well be to view the picture inappropriately, to let trivial details distract one from what is important about it. A proposition is fictional, let's say, if it is to be imagined (in the relevant context) *should the question arise,* it being understood that often the question *shouldn't* arise. In normal cases the qualification can be understood thus: If *p* is fictional, then should one be forced to choose between imagining *p* and imagining not-*p,* one is to do the former.[28] When I speak of prescriptions to imagine in what follows, I will take them to be so qualified.

Principles of generation can in general be construed as rules about what is to be imagined in what circumstances, but only if we are careful to disavow certain likely implications of this term. Calling them rules may suggest that they are established by explicit fiat or agreement and consciously borne in mind in the contexts in which they are operative, as is the rule of Eric's and Gregory's game. I repeat: I make no such assumptions. A principle is in force in a

28. This construal will not do for the special cases in which *p* and not-*p* are both fictional. I will not attempt to say how the qualification is to be understood generally.

particular context if it is understood in that context that, given such-and-such circumstances, so and so is to be imagined. The understanding need not be explicit or conscious. I do not assume that it must be "arbitrary" or "conventional." It may be so ingrained that we scarcely notice it, so natural that it is hard to envision not having it. We may have been born with it, or with a nearly irresistible disposition to acquire it. Nevertheless, principles of generation, whether or not we call them rules, constitute conditional prescriptions about what is to be imagined in what circumstances. And the propositions that are to be imagined are fictional.

Fictionality has turned out to be analogous to truth in some ways; the relation between fictionality and imagining parallels that between truth and belief. Imagining aims at the fictional as belief aims at the true. What is true is to be believed; what is fictional is to be imagined.

There is a persistent temptation to go one step further and to think of fictionality as a species of truth. (Imagining might then be regarded as a kind of believing, one appropriate to this species of truth.) The temptation is both reflected in and nourished by the fact that what is fictional is colloquially described as *true in a fictional world.* "Fictional worlds" are easily thought of as remote corners of the universe where unicorns really do roam, where a war is actually fought over how eggs should be broken, where it is true that a bear hides in a thicket a few feet from Eric. Moreover, we often feel free to omit phrases such as "It is true in a fictional world that" entirely, just as we omit "It is true that" thereby asserting what is true rather than describing it as true. We say, simply, "A bear was hiding in the thicket" instead of "It is true in the game of make-believe that a bear was hiding in the thicket," and we say it in an assertive tone of voice. "A unicorn has been captured," we declare, in place of, "In (the world of) the Unicorn Tapestries a unicorn has been captured." "We are on our way to Saturn" does the job of "We are on our way to Saturn, in the world of our daydream." Thus we *seem* to assert that a bear was (really) hiding in the thicket, and so forth; we talk as though fictional propositions are true. Could it be that they are? Granted, they do not generally enjoy the kind of truth possessed, for example, by the proposition that there are no unicorns and the proposition that children sometimes play games of make-believe. "Truth in a fictional world" must be distinguished from "truth in the real world." But the temptation to regard both as species of a single genus is manifest.

I resist. What we call truth in a fictional world is not a kind of truth. The phrase "In the world of the Unicorn Tapestries," preceding "a unicorn was captured," does not indicate in what manner or where or in what realm it is true that a unicorn was captured, or anything of the sort. This is *not* true, *period*. "It is believed (desired, claimed, denied) that *p*" is used not to assert that *p* is true but to attribute a different property to it, to assert that this proposition is believed, or that someone desires or claims or denies it to be true. Likewise, "It is fictional that *p*" and its colloquial variants attribute not truth but fictionality to *p*.

My reasons for rejecting the temptation to construe fictionality as a variety of truth will emerge only when we begin to understand why we are tempted. Understanding the temptation is in any case at least as important as combating it. It is no accident that we speak as we do—as though there really are unicorns, as though a war actually was fought over how to break eggs—and an explanation is needed of why we do. The explanation and the source of the temptation lie at the very foundation of the human institution of fiction.

Although fictionality is not truth, the two are perfectly compatible. We noted earlier that people often imagine what is true and what they know to be true. Such imaginings are sometimes prescribed. It is fictional in Fred's daydream that he likes warm climates, as he actually does. It is *Tom Sawyer*–fictional, and true as well, that the Mississippi River runs alongside the state of Missouri. This point would seem to be too obvious to need emphasis. But it does.

The role of props in generating fictional truths is enormously important. They give fictional worlds and their contents a kind of objectivity, an independence from cognizers and their experiences which contributes much to the excitement of our adventures with them. This objectivity constitutes another affinity between fictionality, insofar as it derives from props, and truth. The stump game shows that what is fictional, when props are involved, is detached not only from our imaginings but also from what people think and what they take to be fictional. We can be unaware of fictional truths or mistaken about them as easily as we can about those aspects of the real world on which they depend. Eric and Gregory are genuinely surprised to discover that fictionally a bear is lurking in the thicket. It is not thinking that makes it so; the prop does. Fictional worlds, like reality, are "out there," to be investigated and explored if we choose and to the extent that we are able. To dismiss them as "figments of people's imaginations" would be to insult and underestimate them.

One final note: It is by mandating the imagining of *propositions* that props generate fictional truths. But imagining is not exclusively propositional. *Imagining a bear* goes beyond imagining that there is one. To imagine swimming or climbing or giving a speech is not just to imagine of oneself that one swims or climbs or gives a speech, if it is even partly that. (See §1.4.) Props prescribe nonpropositional imaginings as well as propositional ones. They do not thereby generate fictional truths, but the mandated nonpropositional imaginings are a distinctive and important part of our games of make-believe. Our focus now is on propositional imaginings and the generation of fictional truths, but nonpropositional ones will play crucial roles at several later junctures.

1.6. FICTIONALITY WITHOUT PROPS: DREAMS AND DAYDREAMS

The observations above apply to fictional worlds whose contents are generated by props. But not all fictional truths are generated by props. Those of dreams and daydreams seem not to be. In Jeremy's dream he is being chased by a monster; fictionally this is so. But there appears to be nothing that makes this fictional in the way that stumps generate fictional truths in Gregory's and Eric's game. Nor is the fact that fictionally in Fred's daydream he is rich and famous generated by a prop. Do these fictional truths depend simply on Jeremy's and Fred's actual imaginings? The fictional threatens to collapse back into the imagined in the case of dreams and daydreams.

But we needn't let it. What is fictional in dreams and daydreams, like what is fictional in games of make-believe and representational works of art, can be construed as a matter of what is to be imagined rather than what actually is imagined. What we say about dreams and daydreams is incidental to our larger project. But it will be reassuring to know that a unified account of fictionality along the lines I have suggested is possible.

I begin with an easy case: collaborative daydreams. A decision is made by the collaborators to imagine traveling to Saturn in a rocket, to adopt the categorical rule that participants are to imagine rocketing to Saturn. They do so imagine. But what makes it fictional in the daydream that they rocket to Saturn is not their imagining this; it is rather the rule prescribing their doing so. Suppose the matter was discussed before the decision was made. Some suggested Pluto rather than Saturn as a destination, and some preferred to take a flying saucer rather than a rocket. It is likely that during the deliberations each of the participants imagined each of the proposed alternatives, to try them out. But nothing was fictional in the collective daydream until a collective decision was made, a rule established. It never was fictional in the daydream that the participants embarked for Pluto or that they traveled by flying saucer, since it was a rocket trip to Saturn that was eventually agreed upon. What is fictional in the daydream is what they, qua participants in the daydream, are supposed to imagine; what they actually do imagine is irrelevant. Since the rule adopted is categorical, its prescription does not depend on a prop. But as in games of make-believe, what imaginings are prescribed determines what is fictional.

Individual daydreams can be understood similarly, at least insofar as they are deliberate. Fred decides to imagine retiring to southern France. His decision amounts to adopting a rule for himself, stipulating to himself, that this is to be imagined. And it is by virtue of this stipulation that it is fictional, in his fantasy, that he retires to southern France.

What about nondeliberate imaginative experiences: dreams and spontaneous daydreams? We can preserve a unified theory by construing them as governed by a blanket rule—call it the *acceptance* rule—that whatever is in fact imagined as part of the dream or daydream is to be imagined.[29] The imaginer simply accepts the imaginings he finds himself engaged in as proper and appropriate. (The acceptance rule, like the rules constituting principles of generation, is conditional.) If in a spontaneous fantasy I imagine that I am an Indian chief, the fact that I imagine this constitutes a mandate (relative to my role as the subject of this fantasy) to do so. True, I already did. But this does not make the prescription idle. It is prescribed that I, qua dreamer of this daydream, am to continue thinking of myself as an Indian chief, to continue at least nonoccurrently imagining this. Were I to imagine instead that I am a white sheriff, I would be "playing a different game," starting a new fantasy, or (if you prefer) changing the rules of the old one.

The acceptance rule makes for a very close connection between what is fictional in dreams and spontaneous daydreams and what is imagined. Spontaneously imagining something (as part of such a fantasy) does, in effect, make it fictional (in that fantasy). But it does so

---

29. Not every imagining that occurs while one is engaged in the dream or daydream should count as part of it. One can, in the midst of one fantasy, engage in another one, and without ceasing to engage (nonoccurrently anyway) in the first. Whether something is imagined as part of a given dream or daydream depends, I suppose, on whether the subject thinks of his imagining it as a continuation of that dream or daydream. I will not try to say more than this.

by establishing a prescription to imagine it. Here again the fictional can be understood as what is to be imagined.

This maneuver to preserve the unity of our account of fictionality is not as ad hoc as it might seem. I accept that whatever is imagined as part of a spontaneous fantasy is fictional in that fantasy. But it is not clear that the reverse holds. Unimagined propositions can be fictional in a spontaneous fantasy, I suggest, and it is not implausible that what makes them fictional is a prescription that they be imagined.

One morning Doris reports a dream as follows:

> In my dream I telephoned Jones in New York from Chicago. Later I had another conversation with him, this time in person in his New York office . . . I must have traveled to New York in the meantime.

(If "in real life" Doris habitually travels to New York by air, she might be more specific and say that—in the world of her dream—she must have *flown* to New York.)

The implication is that Doris did not dream that she traveled to New York, she did not imagine doing so, but that nevertheless it is "true in her dream"—that is, fictional in it—that she did. I am inclined to accept this implication at face value. And the dream report itself seems a natural and perfectly coherent one. So fictionality in a dream does not reduce to being dreamed.

Should we suppose that Doris did, somehow, dream that she traveled to New York? Perhaps she did so nonoccurrently, as Fred imagined himself in good health when he retired to southern France, or even unconsciously. I do not think that we must assume this. It is with some surprise that Doris notes, as she recounts the dream, that she "must have traveled" from Chicago to New York. This feels to her like a discovery. But Fred is not surprised to realize that he retired in good health in his fantasy, even though this thought did not explicitly occur to him while he was fantasizing. It was in the back of his mind, it seems, in a sense in which Doris seems not to have had in the back of her mind the thought of traveling from Chicago to New York. Hence her surprise. (The line between nonoccurrently imagining something and its being fictional in one's dream or daydream without having been imagined is an especially fuzzy one.)

The hypothesis that Doris dreamed this unconsciously would explain the sense of discovery or surprise, or so one might suppose. But why must she have done so? Certainly there need be no explanation of the usual sort, in terms of repression, for example, of why her dreaming was not conscious. And her discovery is not much like the usual paradigms of becoming aware of what one has been unconscious of. A person who, in psychotherapy, comes to recognize previously unconscious motives or feelings is not surprised in quite the same way. He has the impression that he was dimly aware of the motives or feelings all along; they feel familiar, not especially surprising. He simply "owns up" to them, finally admits them to himself. Doris does not "own up" to having dreamed of the trip, or finally admit to herself that she did. She comes to realize for the first time, as she recounts her dream, that "in the world of her dream" she made the trip. She doesn't merely "recognize" this, acknowledge it, but infers it from other things, from the fact that fictionally she was first in Chicago and later in New York.

What constitutes the fictionality of the proposition that Doris traveled to New York? Following my earlier characterization of fictionality, we should say that Doris was supposed to imagine the trip to New York even though she did not; that there was a rule enjoining her, qua dreamer of that dream, to imagine this. The relevant rule, I suggest, is one to the effect that the body of propositions fictional in the dream is to be filled out in certain natural or obvious ways, preserving the coherence of the whole.[30] (The details of what fillings-out are called for involve something analogous to the principles of implication I will discuss in Chapter 4.) I will call this a *supplementation* rule. Given what is fictional by virtue of Doris' having dreamed it, in accordance with the acceptance rule, certain other things are to be imagined also and so are fictional also. Since it is fictional in the dream that Doris was in Chicago on one occasion and in New York later, imagining that she traveled from Chicago to New York is called for, and it is fictional in the dream that she did. This rule is also conditional, like those constituting principles of generation. But its injunction is conditional not on the existence or nature of props but on what propositions are fictional by virtue of another rule.

That Doris is enjoined to imagine that she made the trip seems to me consistent with the phenomenological facts. When she recounts the dream, she may well have the feeling that her dreaming was unfinished or incomplete, that imagining the trip (or imagining having made it) was somehow called for. The feeling is, I think, akin to this: I unexpectedly meet an old friend on the street. In my enthusiasm I fail

30. This does not mean that dream worlds cannot be incoherent, but only that they cannot be made incoherent if they aren't already, or made less coherent than they would be otherwise, by this rule.

to notice that he is no longer in jail where he is supposed to be, that he got out somehow. This is an obvious fact which I have not gotten around to believing, not even nonoccurrently. Finally I do, and when I do I feel that I should have noticed it, believed it, earlier. While relating her dream, Doris comes to realize that the proposition that she traveled to New York was fictional, and obviously so; she should have imagined it.

Here is an objection: How can dreams be subject to rules, or dreamings prescribed? Rules govern action; prescriptions apply to things that we do. But dreaming (and spontaneous imagining generally) is not an action. It is something that happens to us, not something we do.

The objection misses the point. The prescription is not to dream something but to imagine it. Dreaming is one kind of imagining. If one dreams the right thing one is, inadvertently perhaps, in compliance with the rule. But there is another way of complying: by imagining deliberately what is prescribed. The prescription makes sense, since one can comply deliberately; the fact that one might find oneself in compliance without doing anything to comply is irrelevant. (Breathing is often involuntary. Nevertheless it makes perfect sense for a choirmaster or a swimming instructor to request or command someone to breathe. This is because breathing *can* be deliberate; one can choose to comply with the request or obey the command.)

The prescription is not *simply* to imagine something, however, but to imagine it as part of the dream. Doesn't that mean it is a prescription to dream something? No. One is enjoined to imagine something as part of a particular fantasy, which happens then to be a dream. But a dream need not remain such. Spontaneous imaginative experiences can become deliberate. What begins as a dream may be continued, after the dreamer awakes, as a deliberate daydream. (Continuing a dream as a daydream is not the same as recalling it or reporting it.) Upon awakening, Doris can follow through with the fantasy which was previously a dream. She can then deliberately imagine as part of this fantasy whatever she, as subject of the fantasy, is enjoined to. And it does seem to me that, insofar as she thinks of herself as continuing what was her dream, she is likely to feel bound to imagine certain things—to continue thinking (nonoccurrently anyway) of herself as having phoned Jones from Chicago, for example, and to imagine having traveled from Chicago to New York.

Let us remember that imaginers cannot be expected to imagine what conditional rules enjoin them to imagine if they are unaware that the condition is satisfied. Eric's and Gregory's failure to imagine a bear in the thicket is excused by their ignorance of the stump. Likewise, if during the deliberate phase of her fantasy Doris does not recall having dreamed both that she phoned Jones from Chicago and that she later talked to him in person in New York—or if she fails to put the two together—we can excuse or anyway understand her not imagining traveling to New York. But if she does recall those two dreamings and does "put them together," yet refuses to imagine the trip, she can fairly be accused of not "playing the game" properly or of converting the fantasy into a different one.

Suppose that Doris does not simply refuse to imagine making (or having made) the trip but imagines *not* doing so. Perhaps she imagines herself undergoing an instantaneous discontinuous change of place (a genetic reconstruction of her body in New York coupled with the simultaneous obliteration of her body in Chicago, for example) rather than making an (ordinary) trip. She is not now guilty of playing the game improperly. For now it is fictional that she did not travel (in an ordinary manner) to New York but was instantaneously transplanted there. (If her new imagining was deliberate, she stipulated to herself that the instantaneous transplant is to be imagined; if it was spontaneous, the acceptance rule applies.) In this case the supplementation rule does not prescribe imagining an ordinary trip; in fact it prescribes imagining that there was no such trip. For the supplementation rule is supposed to preserve the coherence of the body of fictional truths, the fictional world. A fictional world in which someone disappears from Chicago and at the same moment pops into existence in New York may be strange, but it would be stranger still, still less coherent, if the person on some occasion got to New York both in this way and also by some ordinary means.

The fact that Doris imagines the instantaneous transplant removes the obligation to imagine a trip. But it does not prohibit her from imagining one. Suppose she does. Then it is fictional in her fantasy that her arrival in New York resulted from an instantaneous transplant and also from an ordinary trip, that she took both American Airlines and Genetic Reconstruction, Inc., for example. The dream/daydream world is incoherent, but no rules of the fantasy have been violated.

An important moral about the nature of dreams is to be drawn from our observations so far. Dreams are not simply phenomenological experiences people have while asleep, successions of imaginings of a certain kind. They are sleep experiences understood in a particular way—in accordance with rules not given in the experiences themselves but imposed on them.[31] It may be that these rules are culturally conditioned, a matter of traditions that have grown up with the practice of telling dreams. If so, or to the extent that this is so, dreams are cultural objects. But perhaps the rules are determined more by fixed features of our psychological makeup than by culture, experience, and tradition. The acceptance rule especially is an exceptionally natural one, one that is not in any strong sense "conventional" or "arbitrary." Nevertheless it could be different (even if we are not at liberty to change it), and so could the supplementation rule. It could be understood that only what is dreamed is fictional in the dream; then it would not be fictional in Doris' dream that she traveled to New York, even if her phenomenological experiences were exactly as I supposed them to be. (It does not follow, of course, that it would have been fictional that she *didn't* travel to New York.) There could even be an understanding whereby not everything that is dreamed is fictional. It is a contingent fact, a fact about our psychological makeup if not our cultural heritage, that we understand dreams as we do. And the properties of a dream depend on our way of understanding them as well as on the phenomenological character of our sleep experiences.

Dreams are beginning to look more and more like games of make-believe, and dream experiences like representational works of art and other props. Just as what is fictional in a painting depends not only on splotches of paint on canvas but also on relevant traditions about how to interpret them, what is fictional in a dream depends on our understandings about how to interpret the dreamer's phenomenological experiences as well as on those experiences themselves. We might even say that the experiences are props, that dreams (and spontaneous daydreams as well) are games of make-believe of a certain kind. If we do, *deliberate* daydreams (personal and collaborative ones) will stand out as the only contexts in which fictionality exists without props.

There are differences, of course. When we dream, and often when we daydream, we seem to be more exclusively absorbed in our fantasies than we usually are when, in fantasizing, we use external props. Appreciators of paintings and novels and also players of ordinary games of make-believe typically have a kind of dual perspective. They both participate in their games and observe them. They attend to the propositions that are fictional, and also to the fact that they are

---

31. No doubt our ways of understanding dreams affect our dream experiences.

fictional and the means by which their fictionality is generated, noting which features of the props are responsible and, sometimes, what principles of generation are operative. Appreciators of a novel or painting may admire the skill and ingenuity with which the artist assembled the fictional world by manipulating the prop. Gregory and Eric may note the awkwardness of regarding an especially tall and thin stump as a bear; they may even consider changing the rules of the game so that it will count as a giraffe. Or, when they come upon a stump that is remarkably bearlike, they may marvel at the coincidence.

But the dreamer is likely to be immersed solely in the fictional world, and the daydreamer may be also. He concentrates on what is fictional—not on the fact that it is fictional but on the propositions that are in fact fictional, his mode of attention to them being imagining. He is likely not to pay any more attention to the props, to his own dream experiences, than perceivers ordinarily pay to their perceptual experiences; the perceiver looks through his perceptions to what they reveal about the (real) world, and the dreamer looks through his imaginings to the world of his dream. Neither concentrates on the experiences themselves.

There is no *necessary* link between using external or internal props in fantasizing and whether or not one observes as well as participates in the fantasy. Daydreamers can focus and reflect on their acts of imagining, the props, and their manner of generating fictional truths. Dreamers sometimes have the impression of watching themselves dream. External props do not rule out absorption in a fantasy in the manner typical of dreaming. The ringing of the alarm clock which, in a dream, is fictionally the sound of a school bell does not lessen the dreamer's absorption. External props are used in Balinese trance dances: masks, costumes, the kris (dagger), a white cloth to ward off the witch Rangda, and the participants' own bodies. But the participant in trance is lost in the fictional world—oblivious, probably, to the manner in which fictional truths are generated. He is attentive to the props in a certain way, to be sure. But his only thoughts, I suspect, are for the fictional truths they generate; he may not even notice that they are props.

Perhaps he doesn't even realize that the propositions in question are *merely* fictional; perhaps he thinks Rangda really is attacking him. (This would not rule out his also taking it to be fictional that she is.) Perhaps (as Descartes assumes) dreamers believe what is only fictional in their dreams, as well as imagining it. We needn't decide.

So much for dreams and daydreams. We return now to the main course of our investigation, which leads through games of make-believe—those with external props—to the representational arts.

1.7. REPRESENTATIONS

La Grande Jatte, Michelangelo's *David, Gulliver's Travels, Macbeth,* and representational works of art generally are props in games of make-believe.[32] So are dolls, toy trucks, the stumps in Eric's and Gregory's game, and also cloud formations and constellations of stars when we "see" animals or faces in them, if we understand them to prescribe the imaginings they prompt. The differences among these various props need to be seen against the background of their commonality, the fact that all prescribe imaginings, generate fictional truths. But the differences are important. One of them merits early consideration. The stumps and cloud formations especially are likely to seem oddly sorted with representational works of art. I propose to understand "representation" in a way that will exclude them.

The stumps are ad hoc props, pressed into service for a single game of make-believe on a single occasion. Dolls and toy trucks, by contrast, are designed to be props; they were made specifically for that purpose. That is their function, what they are for, as it is the function of chairs to be sat in and of bicycles to be ridden. Moreover, dolls and toy trucks are meant to be not just props but props in games of certain kinds, ones in which they generate certain sorts of fictional truths: dolls are intended to "count as" babies and toy trucks as trucks. I will call games of the kind a given prop has the function of serving in *authorized* ones for it. A given doll is not designed for any *particular* game (token), of course, and it is expected to serve in many different ones; it will play its part in the games of several generations of children if it hangs together long enough. (A snow fort, however, may be built with just one specific game in mind.)

La Grande Jatte and other representational works of art are more like dolls than stumps. They are made specifically for the purpose of being used as props in games of certain kinds, indefinitely many of them played by different appreciators on different occasions.

32. Is it *Gulliver's Travels* and *Macbeth* themselves that are props, or just *copies* of the novel and *performances* of the play? What the reader or spectator is to imagine depends on the nature of the work itself, the novel or play; copies or performances serve to indicate what its nature is. So the work is a prop. In the case of *Macbeth* peculiarities of a particular performance—costumes, gestures, inflections—enjoin imaginings in addition to those prescribed by the work, so the performance is a prop also.

Some might prefer to classify only things *created* to be props, things whose function in *that* sense is to be props, as representations. This would exclude not only stumps but also constellations of stars such as Ursa Major and natural objects generally (unless one wants to count the intentions of a creative deity), as well as artifacts created for other purposes (a table used as a "house" in a game of make-believe, for instance).

I favor limiting "representation" to things whose function is to be props, but in a looser and less restrictive sense of "function," which I will not define rigidly. (I will have more to say in §2.7.) A thing may be said to have the function of serving a certain purpose, regardless of the intentions of its maker, if things of that *kind* are typically or normally meant by their makers to serve that purpose. This may allow one to say that a pattern of cracks in a rock or a doodle drawn unthinkingly but which happens to resemble a drawing of a face has the function of making it fictional in games of make-believe that there is a face. Or something might be said to have a given function (for a certain social group) if there is a tradition or common practice or convention (in that social group) of using it or things like it for that purpose. Thus the function of coal may be to heat houses, of gold to serve as a medium of exchange, of Ursa Major to make it fictional that there is a bear.

(Even if we do understand a thing's function to be linked to the objectives of its creator, this may be so only because there happens to be a tradition or convention or understanding whereby this is so.)

Functions may in some cases be thought of as a matter of rules about how things are to be used. There may be rules that certain things, or things of certain kinds, or things made with certain intentions or in certain social contexts are to be used as props of certain sorts in games of make-believe. Such rules must not be confused with the rules of any particular games. They are rather meta-rules—rules about what sorts of games, games with what rules, are to be played with the things in question. I suggest that meta-rules of this sort (implicit ones) apply to standard instances of representational works.

It can be something's function to serve as a prop even if it never actually does so, even if the relevant game is never actually played. So representations needn't actually be used as props. A painting that is never seen and a forever unread novel will count as representations. (Such works are props in game *types* which, given their functions, they establish, even if the types have no instances or tokens.)

Functions are society relative. Coal and gold and constellations and dolls have functions only with reference to a given social context. An object may have a make-believe function for one social group but not for another, and so may be a representation for the one but not the other. Stumps that are merely ad hoc props relative to our society as a whole might have the function of serving as props in a more local context; a few children might constitute a temporary society relative to which the stumps are full-fledged representations.[33]

It is the function, in any reasonable sense of the term, of ordinary representational works of art to serve as props in games of make-believe. This is a notable fact about them, quite apart from how "representation" is defined. If it is understood that a given object's function is to be a prop in games of certain sorts, the games do not need to be set up anew each time they are played. Stipulations are not required to establish the relevant principles of generation. This is like having an established language available to use for any conversation, rather than having to set up an ad hoc code for each one. The gain is not only in convenience, however. Insofar as it is the object's recognized function to be a prop in certain kinds of games, the principles are likely to seem natural, to be accepted automatically, to be internalized, and the prescribed imaginings are likely to occur spontaneously. Moreover, creators of props can predict how their creations will be used, and so can direct people's imaginings by designing props appropriately.

Appreciating paintings and novels is largely a matter of playing games of make-believe with them of the sort it is their function to be props in. But sometimes we are interested in the props themselves, apart from any particular game. And we are interested, sometimes, in seeing what contributions it is their *function* to make to games of make-believe, what fictional truths it is their function to generate, and what sorts of games would accord with their function, without necessarily actually playing such games. This is often the interest of critics, those who seek to understand and evaluate representations. It is also the interest of those who would draw inferences from a work about the artist, about his personality, style, talent, or originality. We shall see (§7.6) that appreciation as well as criticism often involves interest of this kind. But no such interest is appropriate to ad hoc props like stumps—those lacking the function of being props.

Characterizing representations as things with the function of being

33. But if the make-believe functions of representational works of art, e.g., are essential to their identity, they are representations absolutely, not just relative to one or another society. (See §2.7.)

props in games of make-believe leaves unsettled many questions about what qualifies. Is the listener to imagine that Stravinsky's *Pulcinella Suite* was written in the late baroque period, or does she just note that its style is in some ways like that of baroque works? Do live television broadcasts have the function of prescribing imaginings? The bread and wine used in communion? A child's bronzed boots? Some questionable examples need to be understood more fully, but others will never submit to anything but arbitrary and pointless stipulation. That is no objection to our theory. The illumination claimed for it does not depend on the sharpness of the lines it inscribes. But there should now be less mystery in the uncertainty.

Several further questions about what does and what does not qualify as representations will be considered later. But let us turn to what is called "nonrepresentational" or "nonobjective" or "nonfigurative" art, including the paintings of such artists as Albers, Malevich, Mondrian, Pollock, Rothko, and Stella.

1.8. NONFIGURATIVE ART

"To see something as a representation," Richard Wollheim contends,

> is intrinsically bound up with, and even in its highest reaches is merely an elaboration or extension of, the way in which, when the black paint is applied to white canvas, we can see the black on the white, or behind the white, or level with it. [An objection:] things like diagrams, arabesques, doodles, . . . are cases where we see one thing on another, [but] surely [they] are not representational. We see one line cross *over* another, we see one edge of the cube stick out *in front of* another . . . I agree: but then I do not see why we should not regard these as cases where we see something as a representation. Indeed, the only reason I can think of for not doing so is a prejudice: . . . that is, the crude identification of the representational with the figurative. For, of course, we cannot see the diagram of a cube, or a grid-like doodle, . . . as something figurative.[34]

In Kasimir Malevich's *Suprematist Painting* (1915) (figure 1.1) we "see," in the upper part of the canvas, a diagonally positioned yellow rectangular shape in front of a horizontal green line (or elongated rectangle), and that in turn in front of a large black trapezoid oriented on the opposite diagonal. This is how we see the painting, not how it

34. Wollheim, "On Drawing an Object," pp. 27–28.

1.1 · Kasimir Malevich, *Suprematist Painting,* 101.5
× 62 cm, oil on canvas (1915). Collection Stedelijk
Museum, Amsterdam.

is. Actually the yellow, green, and black are all on (virtually) the same
plane; there are not one but two horizontal green shapes, separated
by a corner of the yellow rectangle; and the black is not a trapezoid
but a complex shape surrounding an assortment of rectangular areas.
To see the painting this way is, in part, to imagine (nondeliberately) a
yellow rectangle in front of an elongated green one, and so on. And
this is how the painting is supposed to be seen; imagining the yellow
in front of the green is prescribed by virtue of actual features of the
canvas. So the painting is a prop; it makes it fictional in games of

make-believe played by viewers that there is a yellow rectangle in front of a green one. Surely, also, it is the painting's function, in any reasonable sense, to serve as such a prop. So *Suprematist Painting* is representational.

I see no way around this argument. It might be thought that what we have here is simply an illusion—it *appears* to the viewer that there is a yellow rectangle, in front of a long green one, in front of a black trapezoid—not a case of imagining. But, in the first place, it is not clear that this is a full-fledged illusion. For there is a sense in which the painting appears to be a flat surface, with no part of it significantly in front of any other. We can easily tell by looking that this is so, even while we "see" the yellow in front of the green. And even if there is an illusion, this does not mean that viewers do not imagine the yellow in front of the green. The illusion, if such it is, does not fool us; we realize full well that the painting's surface is flat. Why not say that it induces an imagining instead? Saying this will be especially reasonable if, rather than ignoring or trying to escape the "illusion," the "appearance" of the yellow's being in front of the green and so on, the viewer cultivates it, dwells on it.

But if *Suprematist Painting* is representational, there will be few if any paintings that are not. Any "nonfigurative" or "nonobjective" painting that is to be seen in some figure-ground configuration will qualify. So, probably, will any design making use of what Gestalt psychologists call *closure:* such a design will mandate our imagining a square, for example, when it contains only hints of one. Jackson Pollock's dripped and splashed paintings may turn out to generate fictional truths about drippings and splashings. Most or even all music will likely have to be considered representational for analogous reasons.

I do not find these conclusions distressing. They underscore easily overlooked but important similarities which supposedly "nonobjective" works do indeed bear to obviously representational ones. But they also leave us with a problem: There is a significant discontinuity between works like *Suprematist Painting* and works like *La Grande Jatte* that needs to be accounted for, even if both qualify as "representations." Wollheim offers some terminology; for him *Suprematist Painting,* though "representational," is not "figurative," whereas *La Grande Jatte* is both. But it is not clear how he would spell this out.

Here is a suggestion: The imaginings *Suprematist Painting* prescribes are imaginings about parts of that work itself. We are to imagine of the actual rectangular patch of yellow on the canvas that it is in front of the green, and so on. This distinguishes *Suprematist Painting* from *La Grande Jatte* and aligns it with dolls and sculptures. We are not to imagine anything of *La Grande Jatte* or its parts, but we are to imagine of a doll that it is a baby and (I presume) of a bronze bust of Napoleon that it is (part of) Napoleon. But in each of the latter two cases the object of our imaginings is imagined to be something very different from what it is, something which (arguably) it *necessarily* is not. A molded piece of plastic, for example, is imagined to be a flesh-and-blood baby. The yellow rectangle in *Suprematist Painting*, however, is imagined to be what it is: a yellow rectangle. It is also imagined to be related to other things in ways in which it isn't actually—to be in front of a horizontal green rectangle, for instance. But it *could* have been related to such other things in these ways. The yellow rectangle in *Suprematist Painting* is more like the actual mirror in Juan Gris's collage *The Marble Console* than the doll. The mirror is imagined to be a mirror, which it is, and to be attached to a marble tabletop, which it is not. (It is attached to a depiction of a marble tabletop.)

We might express this suggestion by saying that figurative paintings "point beyond" themselves in a way that *Suprematist Painting* does not. *La Grande Jatte* portrays people and objects distinct from the painting itself (fictitious ones perhaps), whereas *Suprematist Painting* merely depicts its own elements in a certain manner. *La Grande Jatte* induces and prescribes imaginings about things external to the canvas; *Suprematist Painting* calls merely for imaginative rearrangement of the marks on its surface. This formulation of the difference will not stand if we decide not to recognize fictitious objects. Nevertheless, we think of *La Grande Jatte* as portraying fictitious things beyond itself and *Suprematist Painting* as not doing so.

1.9. FICTIONAL WORLDS

Our pretheoretical notion of fictional worlds is a dangerous one, one that can easily mislead the unwary theorist. I noted that it is linked to the temptation to think of fictionality as a species of truth. Other dangers arise from the inevitable tendency to associate fictional worlds with the possible worlds of recent semantic theory. I suspect that our intuitive idea of fictional worlds helped to inspire the thinking that led to current technical notions of possible worlds. But these notions diverge sharply from fictional worlds as we commonly understand them. I prefer to rely as little as possible on any notion of fictional worlds. But we cannot ignore fictional worlds entirely. For whatever the dangers, ordinary notion(s) of fictional worlds undeniably play a central role in our thinking about representation. And since representation is a cultural phenomenon, our thinking about it is part of what needs to be understood.

I have appealed twice already to the notion of fictional worlds. I characterized fictionality, initially, in terms of it: a proposition was said to be fictional just in case it is "true in a fictional world." But that was just a starting point. This characterization was superseded later by the more considered explanation of fictionality in terms of prescriptions to imagine.

My second use of fictional worlds still stands. I said that some propositions are fictional "in the world of Eric's and Gregory's game of make-believe," that some are fictional "in the world of *La Grande Jatte*" or "in the world of *Gulliver's Travels*," and so on. We would like to be able to explain what it is for something to be fictional "in a given fictional world," and what it is for two propositions to be fictional "in the same fictional world," or "in different ones," without relying any more than necessary on a merely intuitive notion of fictional worlds.

Fictionality in a World

There are fictional worlds of games of make-believe, fictional worlds of representational works, and fictional worlds of dreams and daydreams. Let's adopt the working assumption that there is a one-to-one correspondence between worlds on the one hand and games, works, and dreams or daydreams on the other. Of course the individuation of works, not to mention games and dreams, is not always unambiguous. (Is a serialized cartoon strip one work or many?) And we may sometimes want to say that certain pairs or parts of works (ones that are not works themselves) have their own fictional worlds, or that an ambiguous work has two or more fictional worlds corresponding to different legitimate interpretations. But we need not be concerned with these complexities now.

Among game worlds are the worlds of games in which representational works are props. If Richard is a viewer contemplating *La Grande Jatte,* there is the world of his game. We must be careful not to confuse this world with the world of *La Grande Jatte* itself, and in general not to confuse the worlds of games that appreciators play with representational works with the worlds of the works.

Such confusion is encouraged by the fact that the game worlds and work worlds share many fictional truths. The propositions fictional in the world of a game are those whose fictionality is generated by virtue of the principles and props of the game—the propositions which, because of the principles in force and the nature of the props, are to be imagined by participants in the game. *La Grande Jatte,* the prop in Richard's game, makes it fictional in the world of his game that a couple is strolling in a park, that there are sailboats on a lake, and so on. These propositions are fictional in the world of the painting as well.

But we must insist on distinguishing between the two worlds. If work worlds are not distinct from game worlds in which the works are props, how are we to decide which of the worlds of the various games that different appreciators or appreciators on different occasions play with *La Grande Jatte* is to be identified with the world of *La Grande Jatte?* If this cannot be decided nonarbitrarily, we are forced to regard the world of the painting as a world over and above those of appreciators' games.

Moreover, although there is considerable overlap between the propositions fictional in Richard's game and those fictional in *La Grande Jatte,* some of the former are not among the latter. It is fictional in Richard's game, I will argue, that he sees a couple strolling in a park. But this is not fictional in the painting. Richard is not among the characters in the painting he is looking at. So the two worlds are distinct.

More needs to be said about what fictional truths do belong to the world of a work. It is conceivable that very few or even none of the propositions fictional in an appreciator's game should be fictional in the world of the work he appreciates. People can play any sort of game they wish with a given work. We could arbitrarily decide to adopt a principle of generation whereby, because of the patterns of paint sported by *La Grande Jatte,* we are to imagine a pair of hippopotamuses wallowing in a mud hole rather than a couple strolling in a park. This would make the former proposition fictional in our game and the latter not. But it would not change the world of the painting. It would not then be *La Grande Jatte*–fictional that hippos are wallowing in a mud hole, not even if all viewers of the painting should for some reason choose to play games in which this is fictional. And it would still be *La Grande Jatte*–fictional that a couple is strolling in a park.

Our notion of function comes into play here. It is *La Grande Jatte*'s

function, its purpose, to serve as a prop in certain sorts of games—
games involving a principle of generation which results in the fictionality (in those games) of the proposition that a couple is strolling
in a park. It is not the function of *La Grande Jatte* to be a prop in
games in which fictionally hippos are wallowing in a mud hole, no
matter what games people actually play with it. The hippopotamus
game is inappropriate for the painting, *unauthorized* (in the sense
defined earlier); to play it is to misuse the work. This is why it is not
La Grande Jatte–fictional that hippos are wallowing in a mud hole.

Shall we say that every proposition fictional in authorized games—
games it is the function of the work to serve in—is fictional in the
work? This would make it *La Grande Jatte*–fictional that a couple is
strolling in a park, as it should. But it would also make it *La Grande
Jatte*–fictional that Richard sees a couple strolling in a park, for
Richard's game (let's assume) is in accordance with the painting's
function. Of course there are games authorized for the painting in
which the proposition about Richard is not fictional. Its fictionality in
Richard's game results partly from peculiarities of that game, from
the fact that it is Richard who is playing it; it is not generated by the
painting alone.

This points to the conclusion that what is fictional in *La Grande
Jatte* is what is (or would be) fictional in *any* game in which it is the
function of the painting to serve as a prop, and whose fictionality in
such games is generated by the painting alone. I take this to be basically right.

This way of specifying what propositions are fictional in a work
world brings out the connections between worlds of works and
worlds of games played with them. But it may make fictionality in a
work seem very different from fictionality in a game. In a way this is
as it should be, for works and games are different in important ways.
But these and other contexts in which propositions are fictional also
have a significant commonality which is revealed by indicating in
another way what it is for something to be fictional in a work world.

It is the function of a representation to be used as a prop in certain
sorts of games. Function in this case might be thought of as a matter
of there being rules or conventions about how the work is to be used.
Appreciators are supposed to play certain sorts of games with the
work. And these are games whose players are subject to prescriptions,
deriving from rules of the games and the nature of the work, to
imagine certain propositions—those that are fictional in the work. So
we can say that what is fictional in a work is what appreciators of it

(qua appreciators of it) are to imagine. Likewise, what is fictional in a dream or daydream is what is to be imagined by the dreamer of that dream or daydream, and what is fictional in a game is what players of the game are to imagine. In general, a proposition is fictional if there is a prescription to the effect that it is to be imagined. And which world a proposition is fictional in is a matter of who is subject to the prescription, what role it applies to. Different kinds of contexts and their associated worlds are distinguished by what is responsible for the prescriptions. In some cases (deliberate daydreams) the prescriptions result simply from categorical rules that certain propositions are to be imagined. In others (games of make-believe, dreams, and spontaneous daydreams) there are conditional rules which prescribe by virtue of the satisfaction of the relevant conditions. In the case of representations, the prescriptions are established even less directly; there are meta-rules, constituting the works' functions, which prescribe the playing of certain sorts of games, and these games have their own prescriptions based on conditional rules conjoined with the works serving as props.

Props without Worlds

Not all props have their own fictional worlds, apart from the worlds of games played with them. Ad hoc props do not. This is an important respect in which ad hoc props differ from representations.

The stumps of Eric's and Gregory's game are used as props, but it is not their function to be so used. This means that there is nothing which appreciators of the stumps, qua appreciators of them, are obliged to imagine. The propositions fictional in the world of a work are those that are or would be fictional in worlds of games in which it is the work's function to serve as a prop. The stumps have no such function. So if there is a stump world, it is empty of fictional truths. There is no point in recognizing such a world.

What about dolls and toy trucks? They do have the function of serving as props in games of make-believe. Yet we do not easily speak of worlds of such things (distinct from worlds of games played with them). It makes little difference whether our theory recognizes such worlds or not. But the reasons for our pretheoretical hesitation are interesting. There seem to me to be three rather different ones.

1. It is not clear that dolls have the function of serving as props, in a sense which implies that there is a *prescription* to play certain sorts of games with them. Doll makers expect that they will be used in certain

ways, and it is customary to use them in those ways. But is there any sort of *requirement* that "appreciators" of dolls use them in these ways? Nonconventional uses of dolls (using them in games in which they "count as" pillows rather than babies, for instance), are not *mis*uses in the same way as using *La Grande Jatte* in a game in which it makes it fictional that a pair of hippopotamuses are wallowing in a mud hole. The propriety of certain uses of representational works is connected with the kinds of judgments or evaluations we make of them; using a work improperly is likely to distort one's judgment of it. But it is not obvious that dolls (ordinary dolls from the toy store) are judged or evaluated in a similar way. It is not obvious that the propositions fictional in games in which it is the "function" of dolls to serve are ones that people, qua "appreciators" (users?) of dolls, are mandated to imagine. So it may be reasonable not to count these propositions as fictional in the worlds of the dolls.

2. To speak of a fictional world is, in part, to speak of the class or cluster of fictional truths belonging to it. One reason for having a notion of fictional worlds is to be able to refer conveniently to such clusters. Why should we be particularly interested in the cluster of fictional truths belonging to the world of *La Grande Jatte* (rather than the larger clusters belonging to games played with it)? Because it reflects the contribution the painting makes to games in which it is a prop. Insofar as we are interested in the painting itself, in its character or style or value, or in the talent, imagination, and creativity of the artist, we will pay special attention to the fictional truths of the work world, those the painting alone generates. We are not as often interested in dolls themselves apart from games played with them. The contributions most dolls make to such games are relatively insignificant. What is important is usually the fictional truths generated by what is done with the dolls—that fictionally Heather bathes or dresses or scolds a baby, for instance. The fictional truths generated by a doll alone may include little more than that fictionally there is a baby with two arms, two legs, and one head. Paintings, novels, and other representational works obviously make much more substantial contributions to the games in which they are props.

3. It might be said that paintings (many of them anyway) create their own "fictional spaces," whereas dolls operate in "real space," in Heather's playroom, for instance. What might this mean? Partly, I presume, that a doll's location in real space is significant in a way in which the actual location of a painting is not. The fact that a doll is in Heather's arms or on her bed probably makes it fictional (in her

game) that a baby is in her arms or on her bed. But the fact that the Unicorn Tapestries hang on walls of the Metropolitan Museum does not make it fictional that there are unicorns *there*. It is fictional that there are unicorns someplace else—at a "fictional place" which we might think of as a "fictional world." But the place where, fictionally, there is a baby is just the actual place where the doll happens to be; there is no "fictional place" to be thought of as a "fictional world."[35] Statues and sculptures are sometimes thought of in the way that dolls are, in this respect. The Minute Man statue on Concord Bridge makes it fictional that there is a soldier *on Concord Bridge*. And indeed I find it not especially natural to speak of the "world of the statue" (although I will do so).

The conception of fictional worlds as "fictional spaces" seems unrelated to the notion of fictional worlds that I am using. It is important nonetheless, and so is the difference just described between dolls and the Unicorn Tapestries.

Much later we will come across a rather different kind of case in which there is some plausibility in regarding works as props lacking their own fictional worlds—the case of music.

What Are Fictional Worlds?

> The main character of the book is a customs official. This character is not an official but a high-ranking employee of an old commercial company. This company's business is going badly, rapidly turning shady. This company's business is going extremely well. The chief character—one learns—is dishonest. He is honest, he is trying to re-establish a situation compromised by his predecessor, who died in an automobile accident. But he had no predecessor, for the company was only recently formed; and it was not an accident. Besides, it happens to be a ship (a big white ship) and not a car at all.
>
> Alain Robbe-Grillet, *Jealousy*

To say that for each dream or daydream, game of make-believe, and representational work there is a fictional world, and to say what it is for a proposition to be fictional in the world of a particular dream or game or work, is not to say what kinds of entities fictional worlds are.

35. Some pictures make it fictional that there are things in New York or Paris or other real places, though not by virtue of the location of the pictures. Perhaps we think of the worlds of such pictures as fictional places which correspond to or are versions of the real ones.

It will turn out not to be crucial for our purposes to settle this question. But several observations about what fictional worlds are *not* do need to be made.

Each fictional world is associated with a particular class or cluster of propositions—those propositions that are fictional in that world. Some will be tempted to identify fictional worlds with these clusters of propositions. The world of *La Grande Jatte* may be thought to be the class of propositions that are *La Grande Jatte*–fictional. This would make fictional worlds look very much like possible worlds, for a standard way of construing possible worlds is as sets of propositions. But fictional worlds are not possible worlds. Two differences, especially, have been discussed elsewhere: Fictional worlds are sometimes impossible and usually incomplete, whereas possible worlds (as normally construed) are necessarily both possible and complete. These differences have significant ramifications that have not been fully explored, and there are other differences as well.

The world of William Hogarth's engraving *False Perspective* (figure 1.2) is impossible; the propositions fictional in it, those that on the present suggestion constitute its world, could not all be true. It is *False Perspective*–fictional that a tree which is nearer the foreground than several others is nevertheless behind a sign which they are in front of, and that a woman in a second-story window is within reach of a man on a distant hill (close enough to light his pipe with a candle). M. C. Escher's impossible pictures are well known, and so is the "Triple-Pronged Bifurcation" and other trick drawings. The worlds of time-travel stories are impossible if time travel is impossible. (That of H. G. Wells's *Time Machine* is impossible in any case.) So, probably, are the worlds of Kafka's *Metamorphosis* and fairy tales in which people turn into pumpkins or frogs or deer, though the impossibility in these cases (and some time-travel stories) may be metaphysical rather than logical. There is nothing to stop anyone from telling a story about an elf who squares the circle.

Can one imagine impossibilities? Not, presumably, if imaginability is a good test of possibility. But then can contradictory or metaphysically impossible propositions be fictional, on our account? I am inclined to think that even contradictions can be imagined in the relevant sense. But our understanding of fictionality is safe even if they cannot be. There can be prescriptions to imagine a contradiction even if doing so is not possible. (A badly drafted law might require one to do something and also to refrain from doing it.) There may also be separate prescriptions to imagine p and to imagine not-p,

without a prescription to imagine their conjunction. The set of propositions fictional in a given world might be inconsistent even if no contradiction is fictional.

Sometimes the impossibility of a fictional world is noteworthy. The very point of *False Perspective* centers on the fact that it makes contradictions fictional. But readers of fairy stories may be expected to accept without batting an eye the fact that fictionally people are transformed into frogs or deer, and may scarcely notice the impossibility of what is fictional.

It is not fictional in *Metamorphosis* that Gregor's great-grandfather was a locksmith, nor is it *Metamorphosis*-fictional that this is not the case. The story neither says nor implies anything about his great-grandfather's occupation. Its world is *indeterminate* or *incomplete* in this respect. It is *La Grand Jatte*–fictional neither that the couple in the foreground is married nor that they are not married. Obviously most fictional worlds are indeterminate in many respects. But possible worlds as usually construed are complete; the class of propositions constituting any given possible world includes either p or not-p for every proposition p (or every proposition not about particulars absent from that world).

We have seen no reason so far not to identify fictional worlds with classes of propositions, provided only that we allow that the classes constituting fictional worlds, unlike those constituting possible worlds, need not be either consistent or complete. But other considerations should make us wary. It is natural to think of fictional worlds as existing contingently. The world of *La Grande Jatte* exists only because the painting does; it was created by Seurat when he produced the painting. But propositions and classes of propositions exist necessarily (or at least their existence depends only on any particulars they are about). The class of propositions that are *La Grande Jatte*–fictional would have existed even if *La Grande Jatte* did not, and that class did exist before the painting was made.

Moreover—and more important—two different works might generate exactly the same fictional truths. Two authors working in ignorance of each other might write novels that happen to make exactly the same propositions fictional. (The two novels might be word-for-word identical, but they might conceivably generate the same fictional truths even if they were not.) In such a case we should still, I believe, regard each work as having its own distinct world even though the same propositions are fictional in each.

These two objections could be circumvented by identifying fictional worlds not with sets of propositions but with sets of *propositions-as-indicated-by-a-given-work* (or game of make-believe or dream or daydream).[36] But this (and the simple set-of-propositions theory as well) would prevent us from saying that a given world *could* have had different propositions fictional in it from those that actually are. If different propositions had been fictional in it, "it" would not have been the fictional world that it is. So it would not be true to say that had Kafka added such and such to his story, it would have been fictional in (what is in fact) the world of *Metamorphosis* that Gregor's great-grandfather was a locksmith.

I will say no more about the nature of fictional worlds. A number of options are open. Probably a theory in which they are thought of as classes of propositions, or one in which they are thought of as *indicated* classes of propositions, could be made to work, regardless of departures from ordinary conceptions of fictional worlds. Alternatively, we might look for a metaphysically respectable kind of entity more in accord with the ordinary conception. But we need not decide what fictional worlds are; indeed, we need not even recognize such things. What is important is various properties that propositions sometimes possess: the property of being fictional and that of being fictional in a particular representational work or game of make-believe or dream or daydream. It is natural to express these properties with the help of phrases appearing to refer to fictional worlds ("the property of being fictional *in the world of* . . . "), and for convenience I will often do so. But my explanations of these properties do not presuppose any such reference.

I.IO. THE MAGIC OF MAKE-BELIEVE

Make-believe—the use of (external) props in imaginative activities—is a truly remarkable invention. We have seen how props insulate fictional worlds from what people do and think, conferring on them a kind of objective integrity worthy of the real world and making their exploration an adventure of discovery and surprise (see §1.5). Yet worlds of make-believe are much more malleable than reality is. We can arrange their contents as we like by manipulating props or even, if necessary, altering principles of generation. We can make people turn into pumpkins, or make sure the good guys win, or see what it is like for the bad guys to win. The excitement of exploring the unknown

36. Levinson, "What a Musical Work Is"; Fine, "Problem of Non-Existence."

will be lost to the extent that we construct the worlds ourselves. But if we let others (artists) construct them for us, we can enjoy not only the excitement but also the benefits of any special talent and insight they may bring to the task.

There is a price to pay in real life when the bad guys win, even if we learn from the experience. Make-believe provides the experience—something like it anyway—for free. Catastrophes don't really occur (usually) when it is fictional that they do. The divergence between fictionality and truth spares us pain and suffering we would have to expect in the real world. We realize some of the benefits of hard experience without having to undergo it.

This last advantage is common to imaginative activities generally. But only make-believe offers the remarkable combination of other features I am claiming for it. Worlds of deliberate daydreams (like Fred's) are amenable to human control, but they do not enjoy the independence that make-believe worlds do. Dreams and spontaneous daydreams can boast a certain independence; the dreamer waits to see what will happen, and is sometimes surprised.[37] But neither he nor anyone else can effectively manipulate them. (Drugs or mushrooms or spicy food may have some, mostly unpredictable, effects.) One must accept dream worlds as they come.

Dreaming is, moreover, inevitably a solitary activity. One may have lots of company *within* a dream; one may dream about others as well as oneself. And the dreamer can share his experiences at breakfast. But what he shares then is merely his reflections on the dream from outside of it. We do not do the dreaming together; we do not join with others in experiencing a dream. Deliberate daydreams, by contrast, can be social. But they sacrifice not only the objectivity of their fictional worlds but also the vivacity of spontaneous imaginings. Games of make-believe, however, are easily shared; we play them together. And doing so neither compromises the objectivity of the fictional worlds nor lessens the spontaneity of participants' imaginings.

Objectivity, control, the possibility of joint participation, spontaneity, all on top of a certain freedom from the cares of the real world: it looks as though make-believe has everything. There are reasons for engaging in other modes of imagining, no doubt, purposes they serve that make-believe does not. But the magic of make-believe is an extraordinarily promising basis on which to explain the repre-

---

37. But waiting is the only manner of exploration available. In a game of make-believe one can actively direct the inquiry.

sentational arts—their power, their complexity and diversity, their capacity to enrich our lives.

Representations, I have said, are things possessing the social function of serving as props in games of make-believe, although they also *prompt* imaginings and are sometimes *objects* of them as well. A prop is something which, by virtue of conditional *principles of generation,* mandates imaginings. Propositions whose imaginings are mandated are *fictional,* and the fact that a given proposition is fictional is a *fictional truth. Fictional worlds* are associated with collections of fictional truths; what is fictional is fictional in a given world—the world of a game of make-believe, for example, or that of a representational work of art. This, in brief outline, is the skeleton of my theory. Let's flesh it out and see what it can do for us.

2

Fiction and Nonfiction

Where are we to place Darwin's *Origin of Species,* Prescott's *History of the Conquest of Peru,* and Sandburg's biography of Abraham Lincoln, not to mention philosophical treatises, mathematics textbooks, instruction manuals, recipes, legal documents, and requests to pass the salt? How do such "works of nonfiction" compare with novels and other works of fiction?

Postponing for the moment certain qualifications and refinements, we can say this: It is not the function of biographies, textbooks, and newspaper articles, as such, to serve as props in games of make-believe. They are used to claim truth for certain propositions rather than to make propositions fictional. Instead of establishing fictional worlds, they purport to describe the real world. We read the *New York Times* to find out what actually happened in Washington or Walla Walla, not what happened "in the world of the *Times.*" Works of nonfiction do not, in general, qualify as representations in our special sense.

Here is an objection: Darwin's *Origin of Species,* for example, is designed to elicit beliefs. It is arguable that believing something involves imagining it (or at least that occurrent believing involves imagining, and perhaps Darwin's work is designed to induce occurrent beliefs). So doesn't *The Origin of Species* prescribe imaginings, and thus generate fictional truths?

No. In writing his book Darwin no doubt intended to get readers to believe certain things. But there is no understanding to the effect that readers are to believe whatever the book says just because it says it. If we are to believe the theory of evolution, it is because that theory is true, or because there is good evidence for it, not because it is expressed in *The Origin of Species*—although of course *The Origin of Species* might convince us of the theory's truth or inform us of evidence for it. Darwin's book itself does not prescribe believings. So we cannot conclude that it prescribes imaginings, even if believing involves imagining.

Perhaps the reader of *The Origin of Species*, qua reader of that work, is obliged at least to consider, understand, attend to, entertain the propositions expressed in it, regardless of their truth or falsity. If he does not do so, perhaps he is not "playing the game" of reading the book properly. But as we saw earlier (§1.2) considering or entertaining propositions falls short of imagining them.

An important symptom of the difference between *The Origin of Species* and works like *Gulliver's Travels* which I count as representational is that what is said in *The Origin of Species* does not of itself warrant assertions like "Species evolved by means of natural selection." It justifies such assertions only insofar as it provides good reason to think they are true. But the sentences in *Gulliver's Travels* warrant the assertive utterance "A war was fought over how to break eggs," quite apart from whether they give us reason to think such a war actually was fought.

Of course it is possible to *read* histories or biographies or treatises or committee reports as novels. One can resolve to imagine whatever propositions Sandburg's biography of Lincoln expresses; one can adopt a principle that one is to do so. (This may but need not involve ignoring whether the propositions are true or false.) One thus plays a game of make-believe in which the biography is a prop of the kind novels usually are. If one does, we might allow that the biography is a representation *for that reader*. But we might deny that it is a representation *simpliciter* (in our sense), on the ground that its *function*, in the relevant sense, is not to be a prop in games of make-believe, no matter how anyone chooses to use it.

Some works straddle the fence. Many historical novels, for instance, are best understood as prescribing the imagining of the propositions they express and *also* seeking to elicit the reader's belief in many of them. (It is usually understood, however, that the reader is not to believe propositions about details of conversations between historical figures which the novelist could not possibly be in a position to know, for example.) Some histories are written in such a vivid, novelistic style that they almost inevitably induce the reader to imagine what is said, regardless of whether or not he believes it. (Indeed this may be true of Prescott's *History of the Conquest of Peru*.) If we think of the work as prescribing such a reaction, it serves as a prop in a game of make-believe. We might even allow that its function is partly to serve as a prop, although this function may be subordinate to that of attempting to inform the reader. There are differences of degree along several dimensions here.

We thus find ourselves with a way of distinguishing *fiction* from *nonfiction*. Works of fiction are simply representations in our special sense, works whose function is to serve as props in games of make-believe. Except for the fact that representations need not be *works*, human artifacts—an important fact, as we shall see—we could use "representation" and "work of fiction" interchangeably.

This notion of fiction is a natural descendant of the one used by booksellers and librarians in separating fairy tales, short stories, novels, and Superman comic books from newspaper articles, instruction manuals, geography textbooks, biographies, and histories. This is not to say that we should expect to draw the line just where they do, however; the rough everyday classification needs refining in order to serve our theoretical purposes. Berkeley's *Dialogues between Hylas and Philonous,* for example, containing those two fictional characters as they do, will fall in our category of fiction.

Berkeley's *Dialogues* constitute a serious attempt to illuminate the reader about the real world, and the manner in which he pursues this objective is similar in many respects to the way Hume, for example, pursues it in *The Treatise of Human Nature,* notwithstanding Berkeley's use of fictional characters. We can understand why the *Dialogues* are commonly classified as "nonfiction." But this classification, together with an understanding of "fiction" in the spirit of ours, raises the disconcerting specter of an overlap between "fiction" and "nonfiction." We might find ourselves counting the *Dialogues,* and also certain histories and historical novels, as *both.* Better to find a more perspicuous way of characterizing the complexities of these works. For the sake of clarity I will mean by "nonfiction" simply "not fiction." Any work with the function of serving as a prop in games of make-believe, however minor or peripheral or instrumental this function might be, qualifies as "fiction"; only what lacks this function entirely will be called nonfiction.

I have not drawn a precise line around the category of fiction. Nor is it desirable to do so; that would obscure some of the most interesting features of the many complex and subtle works in the border area. But one of the aims of my theory is to develop tools for understanding works that resist classification, works that are in one way or another mixed or marginal or indeterminate or ambiguous. This will be the burden of §2.7.

It is important to consider this way of understanding "fiction" against the background of alternatives. In the following several sections we will examine a selection of more standard accounts. Their shortcomings will point all the more strongly to my own rather unorthodox one, and will reinforce the make-believe approach as a whole. In particular, we will note important advantages that the make-believe theory enjoys over certain linguistically based ones.

2.2.   FICTION VERSUS REALITY

Our present concern is not with "fiction" as opposed to "reality," nor with contrasts between "fiction" and "fact" or "truth." These oppositions have little to do with the intuitions on which my recent suggestions are based, and little to do, I think, with the intuitions dominant in the shelving practices of booksellers and librarians. The difference we are interested in is between *works of fiction* and *works of nonfiction*. The potential for confusion here is considerable and has been amply realized.[1]

Let us put aside for the moment my proposal to understand "work of fiction" in terms of make-believe and start from scratch, reverting to a preanalytic conception of a fundamental, if rough, differentiation between novels, stories, fables, and fairy tales on the one hand and biographies, histories, textbooks, instruction manuals, and newspaper articles on the other. This conception is by no means univocal, and it is murky in various ways, but one can plausibly claim it to be a conception of a distinction essentially independent of the family of differentiations between fiction and reality or truth.

The distinction we are after is certainly not that between things that are real and things that are merely "fictional." Novels and comic books are no less real than newspaper articles and textbooks. Obviously. But the presumption persists that the two senses of "fictional" are somehow crucially connected, and that the notion of works of fiction is to be understood in terms of fictitious entities. A not infrequent suggestion is that novels and stories, though real themselves, are works that are largely *about* mere fictions, whereas biographies and textbooks are about real things. (Let's allow for the sake of

1. Even the phrases "work of fiction" and "work of nonfiction" fail to point unambiguously in the right direction. Their use, in theorizing as well as in practice, is a muddle capable of driving the conscientious commentator up a skyscraper. Suffice it to say that the distinction I will draw is one of considerable importance, and is a prominent ingredient, at least, in the confused mix of ordinary uses of "fiction" and its compounds.

argument that there are things that are merely fictional.) "When we call a piece of literature a work of *fiction* we mean no more than that the characters could not be identified with any persons who have lived in the flesh, nor the incidents with any particular events that have actually taken place."[2]

This will not do. William Hazlitt's *Characters of Shakespeare's Plays* (1817) is largely about mere fictions, yet nothing is more unambiguously a work of nonfiction. Tomasso Landolfi's incredible fantasy "Gogol's Wife" is about something real—Nikolay Vasilyevich Gogol. Joyce Carol Oates's story "How I Contemplated the World from the Detroit House of Corrections" is about the Detroit House of Corrections, Detroit itself, and many of its streets, stores, suburbs—actual existents all. Both are works of fiction nonetheless. No doubt some or all of the characters in these stories are fictitious. But there is no reason why a work of fiction could not be exclusively about people and things (particulars) that actually exist. Reality can be the subject of fantasy.

But when works of fiction are about real things, what they say about them is frequently untrue. Does the difference consist in the fact that works of nonfiction express truths whereas works of fiction express falsehoods or untruths? No. A fantasy remains fiction even if it happens to correspond to the actual course of events. A novel set in the future or on an alien planet might turn out, by coincidence or otherwise, to be prophetically "accurate" down to the last detail without endangering its status as fiction. We did not have to compare George Orwell's *1984* with the events of that year to decide whether it is fiction or nonfiction, nor must we wait until 2002 to classify *2002*. Conversely, an inaccurate history is still a history—a false one. Even a totally fabricated biography or textbook would not for that reason qualify as a novel, a work of fiction. Fact can be fiction and fiction fact.[3]

(Does the difference depend on whether the author *claims* truth for what he writes, whether or not his claims are correct? No, as we shall see in §2.4.)

2. A. J. Toynbee, quoted in *Webster's Third New International Dictionary*, p. 844. See also MacDonald, "Language of Fiction," p. 342; Beardsley, "Fiction as Representation," p. 300; and Wilshire, *Role Playing*, p. 28.

3. "Literal falsity distinguishes fiction from true report," Goodman claims, although he thinks that fiction must be literary, as well as literally false. "The novel containing a high percentage of literally true statements approaches nonfiction; the [literary] history with a high percentage of false statements approaches fiction" ("Fiction for Five Fingers," pp. 124, 126).

The moral of this section is scarcely profound, but it is absolutely essential. Notions of works of fiction akin to ours, in the library and bookstore spirit, are in many discussions intertwined irresponsibly with fiction-reality contrasts, with chaotic results. Understanding fiction in terms of make-believe keeps these distinctions appropriately distinct.

But we need to consider other more thoughtful alternatives to our way of understanding fiction than those just mentioned. Some depend less directly on contrasts between fiction and reality; some not at all.

2.3.   LINGUISTIC STRATEGIES

Most attempts to separate works of fiction from works of nonfiction focus on fictional uses of language. The home of the distinction lies in literature. Partly because of this, no doubt, theories of language have played prominent roles in attempts to explain it. But herein lies a danger. Not all fiction is linguistic. Any adequate theory of fiction must accommodate pictorial fictions, for instance, as well as literary ones. A theory that does not will not be adequate to explain even literary fiction. If our aim is to understand novels, stories, tales, and yarns, we need to know what it is about them that makes them works of *fiction,* and that requires knowing what fictionality in general is— what literary works of fiction have in common with works of fiction of other kinds. Distortions arise from concentration on literary fictions and too exclusive reliance on theories of language, as we shall see.

Theories of language invariably focus on standard, literal, nonfictional discourse.[4] The usual procedure, in developing an account of fiction, is first to devise or adopt a theory of language and then to utilize its central concepts in explaining how fictional discourse deviates from "normal," nonfictional uses of language. Eventually perhaps, and as an afterthought, one attempts to stretch the account of literary fiction to cover fiction in other media. A central assumption underlying this procedure—that fiction is to be understood in terms of and as derivative from nonfiction—is fundamentally mistaken.

4. "Typically issues of much literary interest such as metaphor, simile, transference of sense, irony, satire, allegory, fictionalisation, and so on, are set aside at the beginning of logical and semantical studies, where the emphasis has always been on literal meaning and reportative discourse, to the cost of most of the remainder of discourse. The literary phenomena set aside are at best given perfunctory treatment after the important work of dealing with literal reportative discourse has been accomplished" (Routley, *Exploring Meinong's Jungle,* p. 537).

This is dramatically evident when nonliterary fiction is considered at an earlier stage than is usually done, and more seriously.

Theories of language of some kinds have been more prominent than others in discussions of fiction. Emphasis on semantic properties such as *denotation* and *truth* lead quickly to questions about "fiction" as opposed to fact or reality—not the questions we are now concerned with—forcing one to consider what if anything names like "Gulliver" denote and whether sentences like "Gulliver visited Lilliput" are true. Goodman speaks of *fictive* representations, works like unicorn-pictures which are representational but do not represent anything.[5] But there is little connection between fictive representation as he understands it and the notion of fiction we are interested in now. I think it is fair to say that Goodman's theory simply does not countenance a distinction corresponding even vaguely to ours. This neglect may be deliberate on Goodman's part. It is ill advised nonetheless.

Fiction and nonfiction differ more on pragmatic than on semantic grounds. So it is not surprising that speech-act theories of language have been used more often in attempts to understand the distinction than have theories like Goodman's. John Austin's notion of "illocutionary actions"—actions such as asserting, questioning, and requesting—has seen wide service in this area. In the following three sections we will examine several popular ways of accounting for the distinction within the framework of speech-act theories. My conclusions will be largely negative: speech-act theories will prove to be remarkably unhelpful in explaining fiction. We have here an unfortunate instance of the "Have theory will travel" syndrome—the tendency of theorists, when faced with a new problem, to dust off an old theory they know and love, one devised with other questions in mind, shove it into the breach, and pray that it will fit. In this case it does not fit, and the result is confusion rather than illumination.

Lest I step on toes other than the ones I am aiming at, let me emphasize that my present concern is not with the viability of speech-act theories as theories of language. Nor do I deny that they can be used fruitfully to illuminate important features of literary and other fictions. I am now addressing only the basic question of what fiction is, how works of fiction are to be differentiated from other things. Whatever the other merits of speech-act theories, their applications to this question have been distinctly infelicitous.

Speech-act theories have been applied to the question of the nature

5. *Languages of Art*, pp. 21–26.

of fiction in various ways, but most applications share an emphasis on the action of fiction-making. Fiction, it is thought, is to be understood in terms of the actions whereby works of fiction are produced. This is not surprising, since speech-act theories propose to understand language in terms of actions performed by language users. But it is exactly backwards. The basic notion is that of works of fiction, or rather that of things, whether human artifacts or not, which function as works of fiction do, not the notion of acts of fiction-making.

2.4.   FICTION AND ASSERTION

Whether a literary work is fiction or nonfiction does not necessarily show in its words. The very same sequence of words, the same sentences, might constitute either a biography or a novel.[6] Nor does the essential difference lie in the relation of the words to the world. We have already seen that it is not a matter of being about real or fictitious entities, and that it does not consist in the truth values of a work's sentences, in whether or not they correspond to the facts.

Perhaps what is crucial is not whether what the author writes is true but whether he *claims* truth for it, whether he *asserts* the sentences (the declarative ones anyway) he inscribes.[7] Are literary works of fiction to be understood as texts that are unasserted, and that are not vehicles of other (ordinary) illocutionary actions? This proposal has the advantage of putting some distance between the notion of works of fiction and that of "fiction" as contrasted to reality, fact, and truth. It is obviously much too crude as stated. But its difficulties run deeper than might first appear.

It is true that in writing fiction an author typically does not perform the illocutionary acts that a person using the same words in a nonfictional setting is likely to be performing. In writing (the original German version of) "I have completed the construction of my burrow

6. Sometimes there are hints in the words, e.g., the phrase "Once upon a time." Certain grammatical constructions occur frequently in fiction but rarely or never in nonfiction. See Banfield, "Narrative Style" and *Unspeakable Sentences*.

7. This, with some qualifications, is Beardsley's proposal (*Aesthetics*, pp. 419–423). See also Ohmann, "Speech Acts," pp. 13–14.

It will not be necessary for us to decide on an account of *assertion*. One might understand it along the lines of Grice's notion of a person's meaning something by an utterance, i.e., in terms of an intention to produce in hearers a certain effect by means of their recognition of that intention (Grice, "Meaning"). Or one might adopt an analysis such as Searle's in *Speech Acts*, in which the idea of the speaker's taking responsibility for the satisfaction of certain conditions plays an important role. The choice between these and other reasonable ways of understanding it will not affect what I say here and in what follows.

and it seems to be successful,"[8] Kafka was not asserting, claiming that he had actually finished making a burrow. But this simple observation leaves us far from the heart of the notion of fiction.

It is immediately obvious that to inscribe a series of declarative sentences without asserting them (or performing any other standard illocutionary action) is not necessarily to produce a work of fiction.[9] One might compile a list of sentences for purposes of a grammar lesson or to test a microphone. Fiction is not just language stripped of some of its normal functions; it is something positive, something special.

Is the absence of normal illocutionary force at least a necessary condition of a work's being fiction? Writing fiction has often been said to be somehow incompatible with writing assertively. But it certainly is not. Assertions can be made in any number of ways: by producing a declarative sentence while delivering a lecture, by raising a flag, by honking a horn, by wearing a rose, by extending one's arm through a car window. There is no reason why, in appropriate circumstances, one should not be able to make an assertion by writing fiction. Indeed there is a long tradition of doing just that. There is what we call *didactic* fiction—fiction used for instruction, advertising, propaganda, and so on. There is the not uncommon practice, even in ordinary conversation, of making a point by telling a story, of speaking in parables. (Perhaps writing fiction is more often a means of performing other illocutionary actions—suggesting, asking, raising an issue, reminding, encouraging to act—than a means of making assertions.)

This point would hardly require mention were it not so often denied. Sir Phillip Sidney's observation "Now, for the poet, he nothing affirms, and therefore never lieth,"[10] which (when seen out of context anyway) can be construed as such a denial, is echoed and endorsed with great regularity in contemporary discussions of fiction.[11]

But what fiction writers assert when they make assertions is usually not what their sentences explicitly express, not what they would be

8. "The Burrow," p. 325.

9. As Mary Louise Pratt points out (*Toward a Speech Act Theory,* pp. 91–92).

10. *An Apology for Poetry,* p. 123.

11. "I assert nothing when I make up a story as fiction" (Urmson, "Fiction"). See also Beardsley, *Aesthetics,* pp. 421–423; Gale, "Fictive Use of Language," pp. 324–339; Ohmann, "Speech Acts," pp. 11–14, 16–18; Plantinga, *Nature of Necessity,* pp. 161–162; Van Inwagen, "Creatures of Fiction," p. 301. "Practically all writers on the topic . . . agree that in such cases authors of fiction do not *assert* or *report* or *describe* what they write" (Parsons, "Review of Woods," p. 158). Some of these writers may mean to be making weaker claims than those they seem committed to.

asserting if they used those sentences nonfictionally. One does not tell a story about a boy who cried wolf too often as a way of stating that just such an event actually transpired, but rather as a way of pointing out the possibility of analogous occurrences—the possibility, for example, that public officials who warn too often of recessions or communist takeovers will lose their credibility. Shall we say, then, that what is necessary for a work to count as fiction is that in writing it the author did not assert what his sentences explicitly say, even if he was, indirectly, making other claims?

I think not. Historical novels are, or at least can be, exceptions. It is expected that the author of a historical novel will make up many details, of course—especially ones no historian could hope to discover, such as the precise words of private, unbugged conversations. But the author may well be held responsible for the accuracy of his portrayal of the general outline of events. Part of his purpose may be to inform readers about historical events, to get across facts that are explicitly expressed by some of the sentences he writes. If he does have this purpose, and even, perhaps, if he does not, it is highly likely that, on any reasonable account of assertion, he inscribes the relevant sentences assertively. (There is no sharp division between those sentences of a historical novel that are asserted and those that are not; the limits of the novelist's license to reconstruct history are not well defined.)

It will not do to regard asserted sentences in a historical novel as, in general, interruptions in the fiction, interpolations of nonfiction woven into an otherwise fictional fabric. Tolstoy does not stop work on his fiction when he writes that Napoleon invaded Russia, even if in writing this he was claiming that Napoleon actually did invade Russia. He constructed a "fictional world" in which Napoleon not only had various conversations, the details of which Tolstoy invented, but in which Napoleon also invaded Russia. It was *by means of* making it fictional (in my terms) that Napoleon invaded Russia that Tolstoy asserted that this event actually did occur.

Could an author be claiming truth for every sentence he writes and still be writing fiction? I see no reason why not, why there couldn't be a genre of historical novel in which authors are allowed no liberties with the facts and in which they are understood to be asserting as fact whatever they write.[12] We might attribute the words of a novel in such a genre to a fictional narrator, a dramatic speaker, and at the

12. Fish points out something like this possibility ("How to Do Things," p. 235). See also §2.7.

same time regard the narrator as "speaking for the author" in something like the way Philonous in Berkeley's *Dialogues* speaks for
Berkeley or Sartre's characters sometimes speak for him. (Readers
can, if they choose, ignore the fact that the author is making claims
about the real world and concern themselves only with the narrator
and what happens "in the fictional world.")

It is arguable that what has been called the New Journalism, which
combines conscientious efforts to get the facts right with the deliberate utilization of novelistic techniques, approaches such a genre.[13]
Insofar as accuracy is expected, the New Journalist, like journalists of
old, can probably be construed as asserting what he writes. But a
glance at a few samples of his work leaves no doubt that it, no less
than most novels, has the function of prescribing imaginings. It is
fiction in our sense. Here is a passage from Norman Mailer's *Executioner's Song*, a detailed account of the events leading up to the execution of Gary Gilmore:

> By the second day of November, after all the phone calls came in,
> Bessie began to hear echoes again. The past rang in Bessie's ear, the
> past reverberated in her head. Steel bars slammed into stone.
> "The fool," Mikal screamed at her. "Doesn't he know he's in
> Utah? They will kill him, if he pushes it." She tried to calm her
> youngest son, and all the while she was thinking that from the time
> Gary was 3 years old, she knew he was going to be executed. He had
> been a dear little guy, but she had lived with that fear since he was 3.
> That was when he began to show a side she could not go near . . .
> Everything was shades of brown. One poverty after another. Even
> the icebox was brown. It was that shade of gloom which would not
> lift. The color of clay. Nothing could grow.
> Outside were fifty trailers in this lot off the highway they called a
> Park. It parked old people. At little expense. Had her trailer cost
> $3,500? She could no longer remember. When people asked if it had
> one bedroom or two, she would say, "It's got one and a half bed-
> rooms, if you can believe it." It also had a half porch with a half
> awning.[14]

(New Journalism obviously has a lot in common with older, more
literary styles of scholarly historical writing, and also with novels—
not just overtly historical ones—in which the author takes great pains

13. Norman Mailer describes *The Executioner's Song* as a "true life story" written "as if
it were a novel" ("An Afterword," in *Executioner's Song*, p. 1053).
14. Mailer, *Executioner's Song*, pp. 494–495.

to get things right, researching the geographic, historical, and cultural setting for his story and whatever actual personages and incidents figure in it. It is more a revival than something new.)

Although writing fiction is not incompatible with making assertions or performing other illocutionary acts, there is a simple but important truth which probably underlies the words of those who seem to say that it is: Works of fiction are not *necessarily* vehicles of assertion or of any other illocutionary acts; to produce a work of fiction is not in itself to perform an illocutionary act. On this point I disagree markedly with many who claim to derive an account of fiction from speech-act theory in other ways.

2.5. PRETENDED AND REPRESENTED ILLOCUTIONARY ACTIONS

Some theorists construe storytelling as an act of *pretending* to assert or pretending to perform other illocutionary acts, and works of fiction as vehicles or products of such acts of pretense. John Searle is among those who have taken this line.[15] Iris Murdoch, he says, uses sentences in her novel *The Red and the Green* which would ordinarily be used to make assertions about the thoughts and actions of a certain Second Lieutenant Andrew Chase-White. But this is not what Murdoch does with them. Instead she pretends to make such assertions. In general, Searle claims, "An author of fiction pretends to perform illocutionary acts which he is not in fact performing" (p. 325).

Searle is quick to point out that Murdoch's pretense is not a form of deception. She is not trying to fool anyone. The sense in which she is pretending is one in which "to pretend to . . . do something is to engage in a performance which is *as if* one were doing . . . the thing and is without any intent to deceive" (p. 324).

This won't do as an account of pretending, not even with the qualification Searle adds later that "one cannot truly be said to have pretended to do something unless one intended to pretend to do it" (p. 325). A harpsichordist who plays his instrument as though he were playing a piano, using pianistic techniques, is not necessarily pretending to play the piano, not even if his pianistic style of playing is intentional. We can improve the account by adding that to pretend

15. Searle, "Logical Status of Fictional Discourse," pp. 319–332. A similar theory was advanced by Gale, "Fictive Use of Language." See also Lewis, "Truth in Fiction," p. 266 ("Storytelling is pretense. The storyteller purports to be telling the truth about matters whereof he had knowledge").

to do something one must imagine oneself to be doing it. (Eventually I will explain pretense in terms of make-believe, but this can wait.)

I will ignore Searle's contention that the author of fiction is not actually performing the illocutionary acts in question. As we have seen, he might be doing so. But one might devise an appropriate sense of "pretense" in which one can pretend to do something which one is also actually doing. In any case, there are more serious objections to Searle's way of understanding fiction.

I suppose that creators of literary fictions do sometimes pretend to assert what they say or write. A storyteller, an old man spinning yarns about his youthful exploits, may be pretending to claim that he made a fortune in the Yukon gold rush and lost it in a poker game. It is possible that when Murdoch wrote *The Red and the Green* she was pretending to make assertions about a certain Andrew Chase-White. But she may not have been so pretending. Whether or not she was is of no particular significance, and has nothing to do with what makes her work a work of fiction.

The quickest way to see what is wrong with this pretense account of fiction is to remind ourselves that *literary* fictions are not the only ones, and that a crucial test of the adequacy of any account of what makes fictional literature fictional is whether it can plausibly be extended to other media. The pretense theory fails this test resoundingly.

Pierre-Auguste Renoir's painting *Bathers* and Jacques Lipchitz's sculpture *Guitar Player* surely belong in the fiction category. But I very much doubt that in creating them Renoir and Lipchitz were pretending to make assertions (or to perform other illocutionary acts). Painting and sculpting are less standard or obvious ways of asserting than uttering declarative sentences. So it is not clear that painting *Bathers* or sculpting *Guitar Player* should count as behaving as if one were making an assertion. And it is unlikely that either artist imagined himself to be asserting anything.

It is undeniable that in painting or sculpting one *can* be pretending to assert. There are traditions in which to produce pictures or sculptures is actually to make assertions. Courtroom sketches in newspapers constitute claims about courtroom events. Perhaps traditional portraits, on canvas or in stone, are vehicles of assertions about the appearance of the sitters. An artist might pretend to assert by mimicking such traditions. But it is unlikely that the creators of *Bathers* and *Guitar Player* thought of themselves as mimicking the making of assertions, or that they are to be so regarded by appreciators of their works. In any case, they need not have been pretending to assert, and the reader need not understand them to have been doing so in order to understand and appreciate their works as works of fiction. Constructing a painted or sculpted work of fiction is not thereby pretending to make truth claims. It is not pretending at all. Compare the manufacturing of dolls. That, surely, is not an act of pretense, and I see no reason to regard painting or sculpting differently. To paint or sculpt or manufacture dolls is rather to produce props for others to use in their imaginative activities.

If doubts remain, consider the possibility of a society which has no tradition at all of using pictures or sculptures as vehicles of assertion (or as vehicles of any other illocutionary acts). Artists in this society create pictures and sculptures of animals and people, of bathers and guitar players, but never as a means of informing anyone else of the existence or nature of actual animals or people, nor as a means of communicating any other information to them. They regard the act of drawing a bison, for example, always as "making" a new, fictional bison, never as explaining to anyone something about an actual animal. Such a drawing surely qualifies as a work of fiction. But the artist, just as surely, was not pretending to assert anything in creating it. He was not mimicking a tradition of making truth claims with paint, for there is no such tradition to mimic.

The possibility of a society like this one seals the fate of the pretended assertion theory of fiction. Nothing is a work of fiction by virtue of being a pretended vehicle of assertion, not even works that happen to have this additional role. This goes for literary works as well as paintings and sculptures. The fiction writer need not be pretending to perform illocutionary acts any more than any fiction maker need be.

The pretense theory has a cousin who might at first sight appear in better health: the view that works of fiction are *representations* of speech acts. Several theorists have advanced such an account of "literature" or "poetic language" or "fictive discourse."

> The composition of a fictional text is the representation (i.e., depiction) of an illocutionary action, or series of them, in basically the same sense in which a painter depicts a cow, or an actor on the stage depicts an act of punching.[16]

16. Beardsley, *Aesthetics*, p. xliv.

> A literary work *purportedly* imitates (or reports) a series of speech acts which, in fact, have no other existence.[17]

If this is taken as a theory of fiction in general, not just literary fiction, it collapses immediately. Fictional pictures obviously need not represent speech acts. A picture of a unicorn does not represent anyone's asserting that there is a unicorn or anyone's performing any other illocutionary act. It just represents a unicorn. This means that the theory will not help us understand the fictionality of literary fictions, even if it fits the class of literary fictions.

Do literary works of fiction represent speech acts? Those with narrators do. Conrad's *Lord Jim* makes it fictional that Marlow utters certain words—the words of the text—thereby making various assertions, asking questions, and so on. I favor recognizing narrators in nearly all literary works, however much some of them fade into the background. (See §9.5.) But the option of regarding some works as lacking narrators is certainly viable, and it may be close to mandatory for works of a literary tradition in which obvious, forefronted narrators are unknown. So we must allow that there can be works of literary fiction that do not represent speech acts.

Even if we disallowed this possibility, the theory would not tell us what makes fictional works of literature *fictional*, since it fails as an account of fiction (in general). What we need to know is what it is to represent anything at all, in the appropriate sense. That what a literary fiction represents is discourse, or illocutionary acts, is (at best) merely what makes it *literature*.

It is essential to see that the ills of the theories of fiction as pretended and as represented illocutionary actions are not superficial ones that might respond to topical treatment. Tinkering with the notion of pretense or that of a narrator will not help. The theories are wrong to the core. The core of both of them is the idea that fiction is parasitic on "serious" discourse, that fictional uses of language, pictures, or anything else are to be understood in terms of their use in making assertions, asking questions, issuing orders, or engaging in other activities characteristic of nonfictional language. These "serious" uses are primary, it is thought, and fictional uses are based on or derived from them in one way or another. What is crucial, according to the

17. Ohmann, "Speech Acts," p. 14. See also Beardsley, *Possibility of Criticism*, pp. 58–61; Eaton, "Liars, Ranters, and Dramatic Speakers," pp. 356–371; and Smith, *Margins of Discourse*, pp. 24–40.

core of the theories, is that fiction necessarily involves the use of tools designed primarily for "serious" discourse, and that it is their primary "serious" function that makes possible their use in fiction.

We have seen that works of fiction—pictorial and sculptural ones at least—are not things of sorts which need have any "serious" uses. Indeed, I see no reason to suppose that there must be any such thing as "serious" discourse, involving language or pictures or anything else, or that anyone must have any conception of such, in order for pictures and sculptures to be fictional. The notion of fiction is not parasitic on that of "serious" discourse.

Why has anyone thought otherwise? Mainly, it seems to me, because of a narrow concentration on literature coupled with the naive assumption that whatever works for literature will work for the other arts as well. Fictional *literature* may be parasitic on "serious" discourse. Literature, fictional or otherwise, necessarily involves the use of language, and perhaps nothing counts as language unless it is sometimes used for "serious" discourse. If so, fictional literature is to be explained partly in terms of "serious" discourse—but because it is literature, not because it is fiction.

Even this is open to challenge. Consider a society in which there is no "serious" discourse, but in which people construct works of fiction out of what look like English sentences. Their works are not vehicles of pretended illocutionary actions. Nor do they represent illocutionary actions; like pictures and sculptures, they have no narrators. Shall we say that they are composed of *language,* and that they are works of *literature?* If so, we will have to grant that even the notion of literary fiction is independent of that of "serious" discourse.

2.6.   FICTION MAKING AS AN
       ILLOCUTIONARY ACTION?

Let us consider one final way in which speech-act theory has been thought to illuminate the nature of fiction. Fiction making is sometimes said to be not one of the standard varieties of illocutionary actions that constitute "serious" discourse, nor an action of pretending to perform such illocutionary actions or one of representing them, but rather a special, sui generis sort of illocutionary action itself. Works of fiction are thought of as essentially vehicles of the illocutionary action of fiction making.[18] It is incumbent on propounders of

18. Wolterstorff, *Works and Worlds*, pp. 219–234. See also Gale, "Fictive Use of Language"; Eaton, "Liars, Ranters, and Dramatic Speakers"; and Currie, "What Is Fiction?"

this view to spell out what kind of illocutionary act fiction making is, of course. But they face a difficulty more serious than this, one infecting the very idea that fiction making is an illocutionary action and that works of fiction are essentially vehicles of such an action.

Speech-act theories attempt to understand language fundamentally in terms of actions that speakers perform rather than properties of words or sentences. Linguistic expressions are regarded as essentially vehicles of speakers' actions; their salient properties, such as their having certain meanings, are explained in terms of their roles in such actions. If the action of fiction making is to be regarded fruitfully as an illocutionary action, as analogous to asserting, questioning, and promising, it must be similarly fundamental. Works of fiction must be understood primarily as vehicles of acts of fiction making, just as sentences are vehicles of acts of asserting, questioning, and promising.

Although we can describe sentences as "assertions," the notion of assertion applies primarily to human actions. No doubt this is because it is the actions, not the sentences, that are fundamental. Assertive sentences are important as means whereby people assert. Sentences are assertions in a merely derivative or parasitic sense. A sentence is an "assertion" if it is a sentence of a kind people ordinarily or typically or normally use to make assertions. Likewise, it is argued, fictionally representing is fundamentally a human action, something people do.[19] They do it by producing texts or pictures or other artifacts; hence we can, if we like, speak in a derivative sense of texts or pictures as fictional representations. But it is the action that is primary—an action that can be classified along with asserting, promising, and requesting as an illocutionary action in its own right.

This analogy fails dramatically. The action of fiction making does not have a place in the institution of fiction similar to that which illocutionary actions have in ordinary conversation.

Consider a naturally occurring inscription of an assertive sentence: cracks in a rock, for example, which by pure coincidence spell out "Mount Merapi is erupting." And suppose we know for sure, somehow, that the cracks were formed naturally, that nobody inscribed (or used) them to assert anything. This inscription will not serve anything like the purposes vehicles of people's assertions typically serve. It will not convince us that Mount Merapi is erupting, or that there is reason to believe it is, or that someone thinks it is or wants us to think so. Ordinarily we are interested in vehicles of a person's assertions pre-

19. Wolterstorff, *Works and Worlds*, pp. 198–200.

cisely because they are just that; an assertive inscription or utterance gets its importance from the fact that someone asserted something in producing it. Our ultimate interest may be in the truth of what is said; but if the words convince us of this truth, they do so, typically, because we take the speaker to have uttered them assertively. Likewise for other illocutionary actions. The *action* of promising, requesting, apologizing, or threatening is crucial. Sentences are important as vehicles of such actions. A naturally occurring inscription of a sentence of a kind normally used to promise or request or apologize or threaten would be no more than a curiosity.

Contrast a naturally occurring story: cracks in a rock spelling out "Once upon a time there were three bears . . ." The realization that the inscription was not made or used by anyone need not prevent us from reading and enjoying the story in much the way we would if it had been. It may be entrancing, suspenseful, spellbinding, comforting; we may laugh and cry. Some dimensions of our experiences of authored stories will be absent, but the differences are not ones that would justify denying that it functions and is understood as a full-fledged *story*. We will not achieve insight into the author or her society if there is no author, nor will we admire her skill as a storyteller or marvel at the perceptiveness of her vision of the human condition. Neither will we acknowledge her affirmations or protestations or receive her promises or apologies. But these opportunities, when we have them, are *consequences* of the author's having told a story, having produced an object whose function is to serve as a prop of a certain sort in games of make-believe. It is because she did this that we achieve insights about her or marvel at her perceptiveness or whatever. This make-believe function needs to be recognized apart from the interests in fiction makers which things possessing it often serve. To restrict "fiction" in its primary sense to actions of fiction making would be to obscure what is special about stories that does not depend on their being authored, on their being vehicles of persons' storytellings. The basic concept of a *story* and the basic concept of *fiction* attach most perspicuously to objects rather than actions.

Stories do not often occur in nature, but fictional pictures do. We see faces, figures, animals in rock patterns and clouds. The patterns or clouds are not vehicles of anyone's acts of picturing, of fiction making. But to rule that this automatically disqualifies them as pictures or that it makes them such only in a secondary sense would be to slight their role as props. This is a role they share with painted pictures, but it need not involve thinking of them as things of a kind normally produced in acts of picture making (or things of a kind normally presented or displayed as pictures). Naturally occurring designs are best regarded as pictures, full-fledged ones, when it is understood to be their function to serve as props in games of a specifically visual sort.

The fundamental disanalogy between illocutionary actions and acts of fiction making comes out in differences in the roles of agents' intentions. A crucial question for a person on the receiving end of an illocutionary action is almost always, Did he mean it? Did he intend to assert this, to promise that, to issue such and such an order or apology? But one may well read a story or contemplate a (fictional) picture without wondering which fictional truths the author or artist meant to generate. Photographers, especially, can easily be unaware of fictional truths generated by their works. Authors and other artists may be surprised at where extrapolation from the fictional truths they intentionally generated leads. This need not make any particular difference to the appreciator—unless he is concerned with what the artist might be asserting in producing the fiction, what illocutionary actions she might be performing in the process of, and in addition to, producing it. And it does not justify a judgment that the action of fiction making was defective or did not come off at all. The notion of accidental fiction making is not problematic in the way that that of accidental assertion is.

Fiction making is not reasonably classified as an illocutionary action, and works of fiction are not essentially vehicles of acts of fiction making. It may be that *language* is centered on the actions of speakers. The institution of fiction centers not on the activity of fiction makers but on objects—works of fiction or natural objects—and their role in appreciators' activities, objects whose function is to serve as props in games of make-believe. Fiction making is merely the activity of constructing such props.

The fiction maker does come into play insofar as function is understood to depend on her intentions. But it need not be understood to depend on them. Our theory of fiction applies across the board independently of any particular means of fixing functions. In our society the function of a text or picture, how it is to be used, may be determined partly by its maker's intentions. But another society might give less weight to this consideration or none at all, and even we determine the functions of natural objects differently.

Functions are cultural constructs in any case, however, and nothing is fiction independent of a social (or at least human) context or setting. The naturally occurring story of the Three Bears is fiction only by virtue of people's understandings about how to treat certain kinds of texts. Such understandings need not involve anything like someone's making—or presenting or displaying—an inscription for a certain purpose, or meaning something by it, or doing something with it. It may be understood that *any* textual inscription beginning "Once upon a time" is to serve as a prop, including any that no one even knows about.

Along with the act of fiction making (and that of presenting or displaying a fiction) we must exclude *communication* in any sense involving human communicators from the essence of fiction. Language may be essentially a means whereby people communicate with one another; hence the plausibility of basing a theory of language on actions of communicators, language users. To suppose that fiction is essentially a means of communication is no more plausible than to suppose it incapable of serving this purpose.

People do communicate by means of fictions, and we are often interested in what their makers or users do with them or mean by them. Nothing I have said should detract from the role fictions often play as vehicles of action. What I insist on is separate recognition of the primary function of being a prop in games of make-believe, whether or not someone's producing or displaying something with this function is also of interest, and whether or not that function is conferred on it by the maker or displayer.

In addition to being independent of language—of its "serious" uses in particular—the basic notion of fiction has turned out to be strikingly disanalogous to it.

2.7. MIXTURES, INTERMEDIATES, AMBIGUITY, INDETERMINACY

The actual literary works that populate our libraries do not come neatly differentiated into two discrete piles, fiction and nonfiction, nor do works of other media. It is not at all obvious, in practice, where to draw the line. Much of the territory is gray, speckled, even chameleonlike. Perhaps there are at least *some* clear instances of each category, but even this must not be taken for granted.

We can put aside uncertainties that rest on the endemic confusion exorcised in §2.2. But even if we stick to the notion of fiction I have recommended, separating it clearly from those that oppose reality or truth or claims of truth, we will have plenty of puzzles on our hands.

This fuzziness, and its persistence through serious attempts to clarify and refine commonsense notions of fiction, has encouraged skepticism about the viability and significance of the distinction.[20] It does not support such skepticism. Our objective is illumination; the purpose of an account of fiction is not to make classification easy but to promote insight into the sometimes complex and subtle character of particular works. And insight does not consist in assigning each definitively to its own box. We do need to appreciate why works that resist classification do so, why and in what ways they are marginal or intermediate or mixed or ambiguous or indeterminate or whatever. But an account of fiction may serve this purpose without inscribing a precise line—even, indeed, if it does not enable us to identify any unambiguous cases at all. What we face is not a threat to the viability of the distinction or our account of it, but a challenge to understand the ways in which works fail to fit comfortably on one side or the other. To throw up our hands in frustration would be to abandon the quest for illumination.

Some works are mixtures of fiction and nonfiction. These are hardly problematic from a theoretical point of view. In a philosophical treatise passages presenting hypothetical examples (examples of evil geniuses, primitive "language games," waiters who behave too much like waiters, brains in vats, unexpected executions) may qualify as fiction while the rest of the work does not. Metaphors or irony embedded in otherwise nonfictional contexts can sometimes be understood to have the job of serving as props in momentary games of make-believe. (See §6.3.) Novels and other predominantly fictional works may contain passages of nonfiction, no doubt, but entirely unambiguous instances are not easy to come by. It is reasonably obvious, often enough, that a passage in a novel is to be construed as a more or less straightforward observation or pronouncement about the actual world, addressed by the author directly to the readers. The opening sentence of *Anna Karenina* ("Happy families are all alike; every unhappy family is unhappy in its own way") is frequently cited; there are discussions of love and other matters of real-world interest in Henry Fielding's novels;[21] in footnotes to *Kiss of the Spider Woman* Manuel Puig presents a series of apparently straightforward essays recounting the views of Freud, Norman O. Brown, Herbert Marcuse, Wilhelm Reich, and others on sexuality. But it is rarely wholly clear that such passages do not *also* have the function of

20. See, for example, Fish, "How to Do Things," pp. 235–237.
21. See, for instance, *Tom Jones,* bk. 6, chap. 1 ("Of Love").

eliciting imaginings, of making it fictional, for instance, that someone—a character through whom the author speaks or even the author himself—is making those pronouncements. If, in setting down the opening lines of *Anna Karenina,* Tolstoy was claiming (with allowance for some exaggeration) that all happy families really are alike but that there are many different kinds of unhappy ones, his words may also make it fictional that someone—the narrator—utters them assertively. If this is their function, the passage is fiction in our sense.[22]

I was deliberately vague about the notion of *function,* introduced in §1.7. Fiction, understood in terms of function, inherits this vagueness. What is it for a work to have as one of its functions the job of serving as a prop in games of make-believe? What counts as fiction will depend on whether we understand a work's function to depend on how its maker intended or expected it to be used; or on how, typically or traditionally, it actually is used; or on what uses people regard as proper or appropriate (whether or not they do so use it); or on how, according to accepted principles, it is in fact to be used (whether or not people realize this); or on one or another combination of these. There is no point in trying to be precise here. But we should be able to say in what sense or senses a particular work has the function of serving as a prop in games of make-believe and in what sense or senses it does not.

Since functions are society relative, so is fiction. The ancient Greek myths may have been nonfiction for the Greeks but fiction for us. (But see §2.8.) Perhaps nonfiction for adults is sometimes fiction for children. The fuzziness of the distinction derives partly from uncertainties about what to take as the relevant social group.

But something is fiction for one society and not for another less often than one might suppose. It is not uncommon for a work (or a text) to be used differently in different social contexts; but its function in a given society need not be assumed to coincide with the way it is used (normally or even universally) in that society. We have a tradition of respect for the genesis of works from other cultures and other times. We often consider it proper or obligatory to do our best to find out how works were used or understood in the society in which they

22. Another possibility is that the words make it fictional that they are true—that all happy families are alike, and so on—but *without* making it fictional that anyone asserts this. Still another is that they merely announce to the reader that this is fictional, its being understood to be left to later parts of the novel, or to an assumption that the novel world is like the real world in this respect, to make it so. The passage does not qualify as fiction by virtue of its having the function of making this announcement.

were produced, or how their makers intended or expected them to be used, and to use them similarly. Our rules for determining functions can be understood to require deferring, sometimes, to the society of origin; they may decree that a work's function *for us* is whatever it was for them, even if we are under severe misapprehensions about what its function was for them and even if we actually use it very differently.[23] If the Greek myths were nonfiction for the Greeks, perhaps they are nonfiction for us also, despite the fact that we use and understand them as fiction.

Alternatively, one might take functions to be essential to the identity of works. Perhaps a given painting or story necessarily has the function of serving as a prop in games of make-believe; without that function it would not be the thing that it is. This would mean that works are fiction or nonfiction absolutely, not just relative to one or another society. We might think of the myths as told by us as distinct from their Greek precursors (even if they share the same *texts*), the former being fiction absolutely and the latter nonfiction absolutely.

Function is a matter of degree even when it is relativized to societies, and so is fictionality. It may be *more or less* the function of a given work, for a given society, to serve as a prop in games of make-believe. But there are differences of degree along several other relevant dimensions. A particular function which a work possesses to a greater or lesser extent may be more or less one of prescribing imaginings, as opposed to merely prompting them, more or less one of serving as a prop in games of make-believe. What a work has the function of prescribing may be, to a larger or lesser extent, imaginings rather than mere contemplatings of propositions. Borderline cases come in several varieties.

We have seen that service as a prop in games of make-believe can coexist happily with service in other capacities: props may also be vehicles of assertion, or vehicles of attempts to convey knowledge or induce understanding or cultivate wisdom or spur action. A single work may have the function of performing all or any several of these roles. No doubt such combinations have encouraged hesitations about where to draw the line between fiction and nonfiction, especially since a work's make-believe role may be a distinctly minor one. Our notion of fiction suffers no indefiniteness on this account. A work (or a passage of a work) with the job of prescribing imaginings is definitely fiction in our sense, no matter what other purposes it may

---

23. See Savile's defense of the "historicist" conception of art against the "autonomous" one (*Test of Time,* chap. 4).

have and no matter how insignificant this one may be. But we need to be sensitive to the variety of tasks that may be assigned to a given work, their relative importance, and interactions among them. Although Berkeley's *Dialogues between Hylas and Philonous* presumably have the job of prescribing imaginings (about a conversation between a certain Hylas and Philonous),[24] this is obviously not their main purpose, and it is rather incidental to the accomplishment of their main purpose—that of presenting Berkeley's views on the nature of reality and his arguments for them. Berkeley might have forgone using Philonous as a mouthpiece with no great loss, and Hylas might have been replaced by more staid references to what an objector does or might say. The result would have been less colorful but probably no less convincing and no less illuminating. The fictional element in the *Dialogues* is scarcely more than a rhetorical flourish.

In more interesting instances it may not be clear which of a work's several purposes is the main one, and its various functions may interact with and reinforce one another in complex and subtle ways. In §2.4 I mentioned the "nonfiction novels" or "factual fictions" of the New Journalism. There can be no doubt that a central purpose of Mailer's *Executioner's Song* is to serve as a prop in games of make-believe. Its role in make-believe is in part, however, a means to the end of conveying information and insight about actual historical events.[25] This role is especially crucial, no doubt, in achieving and communicating *understanding* (*Verstehen*), in a sense that goes beyond the acquiring of factual information,[26] although the imaginative activities the work inspires in readers also help to make the factual details of the historical events memorable.

But the cognitive dimensions of this and similar works contribute in turn to their role in make-believe. The vivacity of the reader's imaginings may be enhanced by the knowledge that what he imagines is true,

24. This might be questioned. Perhaps one isn't to imagine the conversation very vividly anyway. Or perhaps one is merely to imagine imagining it.

25. Advocacy is frequently a significant objective of the New Journalism as well. "Participation and advocacy remain the touchstones of the new insurgent journalism . . . We are in special need of writers, who like Agee, Orwell and Camus, are committed in their bones, to not just describing the world, but changing it for the better" (Newfield, "Journalism," p. 65).

26. "The closer a serious writer gets to his material, the more understanding he gets, the more he is there to record those decisive moments of spontaneity and authenticity. He gets inside the context and sees scenes and details that distance and neutrality deny to the more conventional reporters. He does not have to write about impersonal public rituals like ghost-written speeches, well-rehearsed concerts, and staged and managed press conferences. He is there to see and react to the human reflexes exposed late at night that illuminate a man's character" (ibid., p. 65).

by his realization of the reality of the setting of a story and its characters and events. Even if *The Executioner's Song*—or Tolstoy's *War and Peace,* for that matter—is read mainly as a tragic fable or an adventure story and not with an eye to improving (in any direct way) one's knowledge or understanding of the actual historical events, it is likely to be more exciting, more gripping, if one takes it to be largely accurate than it would otherwise be.[27] (This point is related, no doubt, to the contribution actual objects of imagination make to the vivacity of one's imaginings. See §1.3.) To the extent that "artistic" purposes are distinct from cognitive ones, they may be served by getting the facts right. The enormous efforts novelists sometimes expend in researching the settings of their fictions and the historical figures they use as characters are not to be explained solely, sometimes probably not at all, by an interest in informing the reader about them. The purpose may be—to use an exceptionally obscure word—to enhance "realism."

Should we go by the *primary* or *dominant* function of a work in classifying it as fiction or nonfiction, insofar as that can be ascertained, rather than tying its status to the mere presence or absence of a given function? This seems to me an awkward alternative, especially if our goal is a recognizable refinement of the practice of librarians. No one will be tempted by the idea that nonfiction is distinguished from fiction by having as its primary purpose the achieving of cognitive aims (broadly speaking), any make-believe elements being subservient to this. Cognitive ends are by no means the proprietary property of nonfiction. Promoting understanding is arguably the primary objective of many paradigmatic works of fiction, including ones in which no unusual efforts are made to get the particulars right. Nor will it do to think of fiction as aimed primarily at achieving or conveying *understanding* (*Verstehen*), as opposed to merely imparting information (assuming, as I do, that this distinction can be made out). *Great* fiction may go for *Verstehen,* but lesser though still paradigmatically fictional works may settle for imparting information. Moreover, *Verstehen* is probably the ultimate objective of much nonfiction—of much psychological and anthropological writing, for instance, as well as many histories and biographies (including ones that do not to any noticeable extent prescribe imaginings). The mere citation of well-

---

27. This is not to deny that imaginings in response to fairy tales can be as vivid as imaginings ever are. A lot of different things affect the vivacity with which we imagine. And no doubt several kinds of "vivacity" need to be distinguished.

chosen factual details can contribute to a deep understanding of historical persons or events, and this may be the purpose of citing them.

2.8. LEGENDS AND MYTHS

One welcome hypothesis encouraged by these observations is that our own understanding of legends and myths originating in ancient or alien cultures—the ancient Greek myths and the Hindu *Ramayana* and *Mahabarata* epics, for instance—may have a lot more in common with the ways they were understood in their original settings than is usually supposed.

It is clear that many such legends are told and understood by us as fiction. Originally, according to a familiar story, they purported to be accurate reports of actual historical events. We cannot take them seriously in this spirit, in our enlightened age, so we reinterpret them as fiction.[28] The tale of Orpheus' tragic attempt to rescue Eurydice from the Underworld was regarded in ancient Greece—so the meta-myth goes—much as we regard Sandburg's biography of Lincoln and *The Rise and Fall of the Third Reich*. For us the Orpheus story is more like *The Hobbit* or *The Wizard of Oz*. This radical transformation may have occurred gradually, of course, and at intermediate stages the status of the myth may have been indeterminate.

This crude scenario is doubly dubious: many myths may never have been straightforward truth claims,[29] and even if they were, they may have been fiction all along.

Ancient and Hindu myths in their original settings may have functioned, like the New Journalism, both to convey information about matters of fact and also to serve as props in games of make-believe. They may have been fiction originally, as they are for us, even if they were presented and accepted as faithful chronicles of past events.

But the presumption that they were thought of as faithful chronicles of past events at all should not be accepted lightly. Not all cul-

28. One might say either that the *original* myth, which is not fiction even by our lights, was replaced by a homologous story which is, or that there is but one enduring myth which was nonfiction for its originators and is fiction for us. In any case the original *tellings* of the story were supposedly straightforward truth claims, but contemporary tellings are fiction instead, i.e., they have the function of serving as props in games of make-believe.

29. That is, in telling the myths, speakers may not have been claiming literal truth for them. I am not advancing skepticism about whether telling them was a means of propounding morals or making general observations about the structure of the universe or the human condition or how best to live our lives.

tures are as constantly preoccupied with truth and falsity as ours is.[30] Hindu tellers of the *Ramayana* story and their audiences may not be much interested in whether Rama, Sita, and Rawana *actually* existed, or in whether a messenger of Rawana really did take the form of a deer in order to deceive Sita. Perhaps these questions simply do not arise. Tellings of the *Ramayana* story need not be understood as claims that such events did take place. If they are not, their *main* if not exclusive role must be in make-believe. The *Ramayana* story—and the ancient Greek myths as well—may serve primarily as fiction in their home cultures. That is precisely their role in ours.[31]

How could anyone fail to care whether stories told to him by his elders and which he in turn passes on to his progeny are *true*? If this attitude surprises us, a little reflection will suggest that it is no less surprising, sometimes, that we do care as much as we do.

Why are we interested in history, in the truth about past occurrences? Events of the remote past, especially, rarely impinge on our lives very directly. The massing of armies for an attack on a fiefdom four centuries ago is of much less immediate concern to us now than the East-West arms race, or preparations for war among contemporary African tribes or Mafia families. To be sure, ancient sieges and other remote events may have had consequences that affect us enormously; the Norman conquest of England did. The point is that our need to *know* about those events is usually not nearly as pressing as our need to know about more current ones.

This is not to deny that history has lessons for us, of course, or that knowledge of even the most remote events does and should influence our lives. Sometimes one can generalize from the past and extrapolate to the future. Data about the causes of previous wars might help us to take steps to prevent the next one. But one or a few isolated incidents provide only anecdotal grounds on which to base predictions. The truth or falsity of a given story passed down to me by my ancestors is unlikely to affect significantly the inductive basis on which I live my life.

Many of the most important lessons of history are not of this sort. Past events can be richly illuminating in innumerable ways without themselves constituting grounds for the adoption of new beliefs. They

---

30. I am indebted to Elizabeth Eisenstein for urgings in this direction.

31. Differences remain, of course. Whereas we actively disbelieve the myths (construed literally), the ancients or the Hindus may not have. A more important difference, probably, is that the stories occupied a more central position in their original cultures than they do in ours.

can suggest possibilities, reveal promising lines of thought and experiment, inspire visions of the future, clarify and crystallize thoughts, facilitate the articulation of vague intuitions. They can force us to accept facts we would prefer not to know. Facts of history operate not in a vacuum, of course, but in conjunction with nonhistorical information and other resources. Our *evidence,* insofar as the insights achieved are based on evidence, may be entirely contemporary. Knowledge gained from historical researches acts as a catalyst, prompting the reorganization of information already in our possession as we notice analogies and contrasts between past situations and current ones, encouraging us to see things in a new light, revealing patterns and connections.[32]

Sometimes imagination is crucial. Imagining myself in a historical figure's shoes may afford insight into my own or another's psyche or into the spirit of a people or a culture. Historical accounts of his situation or behavior or state of mind may induce the appropriate imaginings, whether or not they provide significant evidence concerning matters of contemporary interest.

Let us not assume that the benefits of historical knowledge are solely or even mainly "cognitive"—nor, for that matter, that there is a distinguishable category of cognitive effects or values. Knowledge of the past influences feelings and attitudes and behavior. It encourages people to accept or resist their fate, promotes satisfaction, foments revolution, soothes and stimulates. Past events are, again, catalysts in many cases rather than reasons for feeling or thinking or acting differently.

There is no news in these observations, although the details of the manner in which historical knowledge induces insight and affects us in other ways deserve more study than they have received. What is important for us now is that for many such purposes legend or myth may be as good as history. An avowedly unveridical tale may be as suggestive and stimulating as a trustworthy account of actual events, and may inspire similar insight. Fantasies, parables, hypothetical examples can often do the job of factual reports when the job does not involve using the actual occurrence of the reported events as evidence or reasons. Sophocles' portrayal of the Oedipus story may improve my understanding of matters of contemporary interest as much if I consider it apocryphal as it would if I thought it true.

So why *should* we care whether the stories we hear of primeval

32. See Lewis, "Truth in Fiction," pp. 278–279.

happenings are true or false? Why not just accept the insight and stimulation they offer without bothering to evaluate their veridicality? When imagining is important, we may want to understand a story as fiction, as prescribing imaginings. We still need not decide whether it is true, or even ask. This, I am suggesting, may be essentially the attitude some cultures have toward their myths.

While we are in the business of speculating about empirical matters, we might as well also consider the attitudes of children toward fairy tales. I am suspicious of the idea that very young children swallow fairy tales whole, taking them to be reports of received fact, and only later come to regard them as fiction. The question of their truth or falsity may simply not arise at first, and the naive younger child as well as the enlightened older one may use tales as props in games of make-believe, imagining appropriately in response to them.[33]

These speculations are just that. It is not my purpose to decide historical and psychological questions about how the Greeks or the Hindus regarded their myths or about children's attitudes toward fairy tales. But the picture I have sketched needs to be kept in mind. I take it to be a point in its favor that it avoids postulating that the "enlightenment" of a person or a culture effects a radical transformation in the nature of his or its interest in legends or tales. If that were the case, it would be hard to explain why the stories often have such strong appeal both before and after. The possibility of continuity across the enlightenment is likely to remain unnoticed if we fail to distinguish clearly between fiction understood in terms of make-believe and what is not true or not believed or not asserted. Otherwise, one may be so impressed with the change of cognitive attitude toward the stories in question—even if it is only from agnosticism to disbelief—that one overlooks the continuation of their role in make-believe.

2.9.   A NOTE ON TRUTH AND REALITY

> If men really could not distinguish between frogs and men, fairy-stories about frog-kings would not have arisen.
>
> J. R. R. Tolkien, "On Fairy-Stories"

I have spoken freely of *truth, reality,* and *facts* in this chapter and earlier without mentioning the notorious philosophical perplexities

---

33. I recall Frank Sibley suggesting something along these lines.

attending these notions. I brazenly assume that it makes sense to speak thus, that there is a difference between what is and what is not, and that telling it like it is differs from telling it otherwise.

This stance is less daring than it may seem (to those who find it daring).[34] For I have not endorsed any specific conception of the nature of reality or truth or facts. In particular, I do not assume that reality is a realm of things-in-themselves independent of sentient observers, nor that to be true is somehow to picture or mirror this objective reality, to correspond to the way things "really" are. There may be a significant sense in which facts are not found but made, in which reality is the product rather than (simply and straightforwardly) the target of thought and word. What is true and what is false may be dependent on or relative to or conditioned by a culture or a language or a conceptual scheme or a theoretical framework or the constitution of the human mind. It may make sense to ask how things are only from within a particular "language game" or "root metaphor" or "paradigm" or "theoretical framework," or only with reference to certain "forms of intuition and categories of understanding." We can remain neutral as to how truth and reality are to be understood. If our objective were to investigate "fiction" as opposed to reality or truth, probably we would have to take sides. But it isn't and we don't.[35] This is fortunate, for the rivalry between correspondence theories and their competitors (coherence and pragmatic theories, conceptions of truth as warranted assertability or in terms of utterance conditions, reductions of reality to appearance) will not be resolved in a day or a chapter or a book, and we must get on to fiction.

There is a way of making worries about the objectivity of truth and reality look dangerous to our enterprise, however, at least to the casual eye—a way that does not rest entirely on confusions involving "fiction" as opposed to reality or truth. If reality is less than "objective," our own invention rather than something "out there" for us to discover, how does it differ from realms of fiction, which we invent also? Could it be that "the real world" is no more than a fancy name for just another fictional one? If so, what becomes of the difference between discourse about it and discourse concerning the worlds of Oz and *Anna Karenina*? Stanley Fish raises the specter thus:

34. Readers who see no risk at all may skip this section.
35. I have argued elsewhere ("Linguistic Relativity") for the plausibility of the old idea that there is no such thing as the way the world is in itself, that things as they are conceived by one or another sentient being may be all there is.

"Shared pretense" is what enables us to talk about anything at all. When we communicate, it is because we are parties to a set of discourse agreements which are in effect decisions as to what can be stipulated as a fact. It is these decisions and the agreement to abide by them, rather than the availability of substance, that make it possible for us to refer, whether we are novelists or reporters for the *New York Times*. One might object that this has the consequence of making all discourse fictional; but it would be just as accurate to say that it makes all discourse serious, and it would be better still to say that it puts all discourse on a par.

The distinction between serious and fictional discourse . . . cannot be maintained if the implications of speech-act theory are clearly and steadily seen.[36]

Fish and others have suggested that it is discourse itself which creates our "reality."[37] Novels and other works of fiction establish fictional worlds. What then is the difference?

An answer to these worries sufficient for our purposes is simply that reality is reality and facts are facts, however they are to be understood, and that what is the case obviously *does* differ from what is not the case, even if the difference is somehow conventional, culturally specific, dependent on this or relative to that, or whatever. The insight that facts are not "brute," if indeed they are not, is a far cry from collapsing the distinction. Many of the philosophers who have gone farthest in questioning the "objectivity" of the real world and arguing its dependence on us have made a point of retaining that notion and contrasting it to falsehood or unreality.

Of course, we must distinguish falsehood and fiction from truth and fact; but we cannot, I am sure, do it on the ground that fiction is fabricated and fact found . . .

Recognition of multiple alternative world-versions betokens no policy of laissez-faire. Standards distinguishing right from wrong versions become, if anything, more rather than less important.[38]

36. Fish, "How to Do Things," pp. 197, 242–243.

37. "The France you are talking about will always be the product of the talk about it, and will *never* be independently available" (ibid., p. 199). "All writing, all composition, is construction. We do not imitate the world, we construct versions of it" (Scholes, *Structural Fabulation,* p. 7). "As the argument went, nonfiction could no more chronicle reality than fiction since all forms of writing offer models or versions of reality rather than actual descriptions of it; consequently, nonfiction was as inherently 'irrealistic' as fiction" (Weber, *Literature of Fact,* p. 14).

38. Goodman, *Ways of World-Making,* pp. 91, 107. Kant did not doubt that we can be right or wrong about the objects of possible experience, conditioned though they are by our

Fish himself concurs: "I am not claiming that there are no facts; I am merely raising a question as to their status."[39]

So what's the fuss? Is it that, although there are such things as truth and reality, they are not nearly as significant as we naively suppose? Some of Fish's remarks suggest as much (though Goodman just expressed dissent). Of the various "stories" we tell one another, Fish says, the "true" ones are merely more "popular," more "prestigious" than others. What counts as "reality" is given by the story or stories which happen to be "standard"; nonstandard ones are merely "nonauthorized."[40]

But truth and reality, whatever they are, obviously *do* matter. However unconcerned the ancients may have been about the truth value of the Eurydice story, they surely did care whether reports of an impending attack or the death of a leader were true or merely fictional. It is fictional in *Dr. Strangelove* that the world is destroyed by nuclear war. We fervently hope that this will not turn out to be true. The difference is enormous and nothing could matter more.

Are the notions of truth and reality important theoretically, as well as in everyday life? Berkeley, Kant, and Goodman certainly thought so, and we must agree. They are so central to our thinking (indeed it is hard to imagine what it would be like to think without them) that they are surely inseparable from the subject matter of any investigation of human institutions. An investigator cannot dispense with the very thing he is investigating. The subject of this study is the institution of representation, and an integral part of it is the difference between truth and fictionality, the possibility of propositions' being true but not fictional, or fictional but not true (or both, or neither), and the role of these combinations in our personal and social experience.

One fundamental difference between the real world and fictional ones, if both are somehow man-made, lies in the manner in which we make them. A particular work of fiction, in its context, establishes its

---

forms of intuition and categories of understanding. Berkeley, while contending that nothing has "*absolute* existence, distinct from being perceived by God, and exterior to *all* minds," was careful to preserve the ordinary distinction between "real things, and chimeras formed by the imagination, or the visions of a dream" (*Three Dialogues*, p. 197). Rorty argues for a pragmatic theory of truth as against correspondence theories, but allows that "in one sense of 'world' . . . there is no argument about the point that it is the world that determines truth" and calls this an "uncontroversial triviality" ("World Well Lost," pp. 662, 664). We need not ask for more.

39. "How to Do Things," p. 237.
40. Ibid., p. 239.

fictional world and generates the fictional truths belonging to it. A particular biography or history does not itself establish the truth of what it says or produce the facts it is concerned with. What generates facts, if they are our own creations, is not individual pieces of writing but something more like the whole body of a culture's discourse, or the language itself as opposed to what is said in the language, or the conceptual scheme embodied in either of these. Every piece of discourse or thought which aspires to truth has a reality independent of *itself* to answer to, whatever role sentient beings might have in the construction of this reality. The fictional world corresponding to a given work of fiction is not thus independent of it.

Fish himself ends up observing that in denying the "absolute opposition" between "language that is true to some extra-institutional reality and language that is not" he is not denying "that a standard of truth exists and that by invoking it we can distinguish between different kinds of discourse: it is just that the standard is not brute, but institutional, not natural, but made. What is remarkable is how little this changes."[41]

Indeed, *nothing* relevant to our conception of fiction seems to have changed. We do not have to solve all of reality's problems in order to treat our own.

2.10.   TWO KINDS OF SYMBOLS?

We have seen that fictionality has nothing essentially to do with what is or is not real or true or factual; that it is perfectly compatible with assertion and communication, including straightforward reporting of the most ordinary matters of fact, yet entirely independent of them; that it is not essentially the product of human action nor paradigmatically linguistic; and that fiction is not parasitic on "serious" discourse or nonfictional uses of symbols. These results, unexpected though some of them are, flowed easily from the simple intuition that to be fictional is, at bottom, to possess the function of serving as a prop in games of make-believe.

The boundaries of the fictional have not become much more distinct than they were when we began, although they have been relocated somewhat. But it is hoped that asking whether a given work is fiction or nonfiction, as we now understand this question, will lead to

41. Ibid., p. 243. It is unclear how this remark is to be reconciled with his claim that "the distinction between serious and fictional discourse . . . cannot be maintained" (p. 197).

a better appreciation of what it is and how it works and in what ways it is like and unlike various other things, even when no straightforward answer is forthcoming.

Works of fiction are simply *representations* in the sense defined in Chapter 1, except that they are works, human artifacts, whereas representations need not be. The class of representations needed to be differentiated, on one side, from "nonrepresentational" or "nonobjective" works of art, as Rothko and Mondrian paintings and Bach inventions might seem to be (although I have suggested they are not), and from ordinary trees and chairs. On the other side, representations must be distinguished from works of nonfiction: committee reports, economics textbooks, and so on. By construing works of fiction and other representations in terms of make-believe, we draw both distinctions at once. Neither trees and chairs and whatever "nonobjective" works of art we might want to exclude, nor economics textbooks and committee reports, have the function of serving as props in games of make-believe.

This procedure is itself unorthodox. It is natural to think of the two distinctions as arising in sequence. First one recognizes a large class of "symbols" or "signs" (or "symbol systems" or "symbolic behavior")—what might be called "representations" in a sense broader than mine—excluding ordinary trees and chairs and any "nonrepresentational" works of art but including both fiction and nonfiction. After that one turns to the task of separating the two species of this genus.

This picture obscures the breadth of the gap between fiction and "serious" discourse or "nonfictional" uses of symbols (and it does not sufficiently discourage thinking of fiction as a deviation from "serious" discourse). The only genus big enough to hold both—"serious" discourse and "symbols" used nonfictionally, as well as what I call representations, works of fiction—will, I fear, be too big to be illuminating.

Shall we understand the genus to be the class of things that "pick out" or "specify" propositions? Perhaps its species can then be distinguished by what is done with the propositions—whether they are asserted or questioned or made fictional, for instance. (This makes the genus a semantic category and its division into species a matter of pragmatics.) We should not assume that picking out propositions is always (logically) *prior* to using them for some purpose or other. Perhaps it is in the case of linguistic symbols. Perhaps a text (in its context) specifies propositions by virtue of the semantics of the language, independently of whether it asserts them or makes them fictional or what.[42] But often, I suspect, it is only by virtue of making a proposition fictional or by being used to assert it that something can be said to pick it out at all.[43]

This does not invalidate the genus; the class of things that "pick out" propositions may constitute a recognizable kind even if the devices by which they do so are different in different cases. But the kind threatens to expand out of control. What about things that make propositions *true?* The act of throwing a ball through a hoop in the course of a basketball game "picks out" the proposition that a goal is scored; what it does with this proposition is to make it true. (Perhaps it does the former by accomplishing the latter.) The arrival of Amundsen at the South Pole, given the circumstances, made true the proposition that Scott came in second. A perfectly spherical stone makes it true that there is a perfectly spherical stone; doesn't it then "pick out" this proposition? Will our genus have to include absolutely everything? It is not obvious that making a proposition fictional is any less like making it true than like, for instance, serving as a vehicle for asserting it.

Some uses consist of being employed by a *person* for some purpose and others do not. The assertive use of a textbook consists in someone's using it to assert. Making it true that there is a spherical stone is something the spherical stone itself does. But in this respect fiction belongs with the stone rather than the textbook. (See §2.6.)

Some may look for relief to the idea that "conventional" means of specifying propositions are to be distinguished from "natural" ones. Shall we count pictures and texts, whether fiction or nonfiction, and also presumably the throwing of a basketball through a hoop "symbols" on the ground that it is by virtue of conventions that they pick out propositions, and justify excluding the round stone because it is not? Possibly; but after reading Quine and Wittgenstein we should be less than sanguine about the prospects of making this distinction stick.

Is it only within a cultural context that a picture or a story or a textbook picks out the propositions it makes fictional or serves to assert? No doubt. But the operation of the round stone in picking out

42. Even this is doubtful. The propositions a novel makes fictional are often not those that its words, given the semantics of the language, express, and not those that would be asserted by someone who spoke or wrote those words assertively. One must know that it is a novel, that its job is to generate fictional truths, in order to decide what propositions it picks out and makes fictional.

43. In §8.8 I suggest that it is by virtue of their role in make-believe that pictures pick out the propositions they do.

and making true the proposition that there is a round stone may also be culturally relative. Perhaps the cultural context comes in differently, but this will have to be shown.

Chiseling out a usefully limited natural kind comprising both fictional and nonfictional "symbols" is a formidable task at best. I do not know whether it is possible. But we can take the category of representations, of works and nonworks of fiction, understood as things with the function of serving as props in games of make-believe, and run with it.

3

Objects of Representation

War and Peace is a novel about Napoleon. *A Tale of Two Cities* is about London, Paris, and the French Revolution. Cézanne's *Montagne Sainte-Victoire* is a picture of Mount Sainte-Victoire. Let us say that Napoleon is an *object* of *War and Peace,* that London, Paris, and the French Revolution are among the objects of *A Tale of Two Cities,* and that *La Montagne Sainte-Victoire* has as its most prominent object Mount Sainte-Victoire. A thing is an object of a given representation if there are propositions about it which the representation makes fictional. We have seen that many of our imaginings are about actual things. Such imaginings are sometimes prescribed by props. When it is the function of a work to prescribe imaginings about a thing, the work generates (*de re*) fictional truths about it; it is an object of the representation. Paris is an object of *A Tale of Two Cities* because *A Tale of Two Cities* makes it fictional of Paris that it exists, that it was the site of knittings by a certain Madame Defarge, and so on.

To say what a work is "of" or "about" or what it "represents" or "portrays" or "depicts" is often to specify its objects. But these expressions have other jobs also; they are too promiscuous to provide a reliable guide to the objects of representation. I will usually limit them to this role, however. Unless it is clear to the contrary, when I say that a work is of or about a given thing, or represents or portrays or depicts it, I will mean that the thing is an object of the work in the sense indicated, that the work generates fictional truths about it.

Representation-as is a matter of which propositions about its objects a work makes fictional. To represent a person as being tall or clever is to make it fictional of him that he is tall or clever. Ordinarily works represent their objects as existing. But not always. One could write a story in which someone wakes up one morning to discover that George Bush's election to the presidency in 1988 was only a dream, and in which Mao Tse-tung was a myth perpetrated by publicity agents working for an anonymous Chinese bureaucracy.[1] The story makes it fictional of Bush's election that it did *not* occur and of Mao Tse-tung that he did *not* exist. Nevertheless, it is Bush's actual election and the real Mao Tse-tung which, fictionally, have no existence. The real Mao is an object of the story, even though *in the story* he is not real. He is represented—misrepresented—as being nonexistent. So objects of representations are not to be thought of simply as things that reside in their fictional worlds.

Many have remarked that all representation is representation-as. This follows easily from my definitions. To represent a thing is not just to pick it out somehow but to make some proposition about it fictional, and to do *that* is to represent it *as* something, as being such that that proposition is true. It is by representing its object as such and such that a work represents the object at all.

It is not clear that all representations have objects, even though all can appropriately be described as being "of" or "about" something or as "representing" something. (Such is the promiscuity of "of," "about," and "represent.") In any case, not all representations have *actual* things as objects.[2] The Unicorn Tapestries are "pictures of unicorns," but there are no actual unicorns that they picture. Edgar Allan Poe's story "The Tell-Tale Heart" is "about a man who commits murder," but no real-world man or murder is among its objects. We can say that the Unicorn Tapestries are *unicorn-representations* (specifically, unicorn-pictures) and that "The Tell-Tale Heart" is a *man-representation* and a *murder-representation* (a man-story and a murder-story),[3] but we are not yet in a position to explain what this means. These works generate at least *de dicto* fictional truths, ones not about any particular things. It is Unicorn Tapestries-fictional that *there are* unicorns, and it is "The Tell-Tale Heart"-fictional that *there is* a man (at least one) who commits a murder. It is tempting to think that these representations also generate (*de re*) fictional truths about certain *nonactual* unicorns and about a certain nonactual man and a nonactual murder, ones to be found not in the real world but "in the pictures" and "in the story." We shall confront this temptation

1. Jorge Luis Borges has not, to my knowledge, written a story of this kind.
2. Unless we wish to say, rather vacuously, that the world or the universe is an object of every representation, that every representation makes it fictional of the universe that it contains unicorns, or a man and a murder, or whatever.
3. Following Goodman, *Languages of Art,* pp. 21–26.

shortly (see §3.8). But until then we will be concerned only with objects of representation that are actual.

3.2.   REPRESENTATION AND MATCHING

It is of the utmost importance that we distinguish representing from another relation that may obtain between representations and things in the world, one I will call *matching*.

A fat-man-representation can be said to correspond in one respect to all fat men. Informally, "the man in the picture" and any given fat man are alike in that both are fat. A fat-man-representing picture that is a portrait of a man who actually is fat, one representing a fat man as being fat, corresponds thus to its object. The picture and its object may of course fail to correspond in other ways. The man may be short or poor and the picture a tall-man-representation or a rich-man-representation. What I call "matching" is *complete* correspondence between a representation and something in the world. Informally again, a man-picture matches a man if the man is in *every* detail exactly like "the man in the picture." A story matches a person if that person is and does everything that a character in the story is and does.[4]

This explanation of "matching" assumes that there are such things as (purely fictional) people in pictures and characters in stories. There are no such things, I believe, but we do not now have the resources to define "matching" without making this assumption. (One way to define it would be to say what I just did, taking this not literally but in the primary way statements appearing to make reference to fictitious entities and which involve unofficial games of make-believe are to be taken. See §10.4.)

A work may represent something it does not match, or match something it does not represent. Representing without matching is simply misrepresentation. Longfellow's ballad "The Midnight Ride of Paul Revere" portrays Paul Revere as riding to Concord on April 18, 1775, to warn the Americans of the approaching British army. Revere didn't actually do this; he was captured by the British before he got to Concord. The ballad misrepresents him, fails to match him. The Paul

---

4. The character need not possess all the properties that the person does for the story to match him, although the reverse must be true. The person may have blond hair, for instance, while the story is indeterminate with respect to the color of the character's hair.

Revere "in the poem" made it to Concord, whereas the real one did not. But misrepresenting is representing nonetheless; the poem does represent Revere. Some of the propositions it makes fictional are about him, even if they are false.

What about matching without representing? If a portrait of John is perfectly accurate, if it matches him, it just might match his identical twin brother as well. Or it might happen to match the brother even if it does not quite match John. Neither circumstance makes it a picture of the brother. The fictional truths it generates are about John, not about his twin. Suppose that Tom Sawyer, the character in *The Adventures of Tom Sawyer*, has a double in the real world. There happens actually to have been a boy of that name who was and did everything Mark Twain's novel has the fictional Tom Sawyer being and doing—a boy, in other words, whom the novel matches. Mark Twain knew nothing of the real "Tom Sawyer"; the correspondence between him and the character is purely coincidental. (Let's assume also that the boy lived out his life in obscurity and that few if any readers of the novel notice the correspondence or could be expected to.) *The Adventures of Tom Sawyer* is not about this actual boy. He is not one of its objects.

Must we say this? Could we regard Twain as having, accidentally, written a novel about a real person? We must resist the inclination to think that the issue here is a merely verbal one. Mark Twain's novel does not prescribe any imaginings about the real-world counterpart of his character. Readers are in no way obliged or expected to imagine of the actual "Tom Sawyer" that he got his friends to whitewash a fence, that he attended his own funeral, and so on. The fact that he happens actually to have done all these things has no bearing on what the novel asks us to imagine. This, at bottom, is why the real boy is not an object of the novel. To have something for an object is to generate fictional truths about it, to prescribe imaginings about it. Objects thus have a special role in the games of make-believe that are to be played with representations. What a representation matches has no such role, unless it happens to be an object also. To call both of them objects of representation would be to run roughshod over this important difference.

We will shortly come to appreciate the distinction more fully. But if there is any lingering doubt that it is an intuitively natural one, consider the possibility of the fictional Tom Sawyer having more than one counterpart in the real world. Unless we are willing to say that *The*

Adventures of Tom Sawyer is a novel about *all* of them, we will have to agree that matching does not suffice for representing.

3.3.   DETERMINANTS

What determines what a work represents or whether it represents anything? This is a matter of what principles of generation are in effect. The principles in question—those whereby certain works prescribe imaginings about certain (actual) things—are loose, variable, and complex. I will undertake a more general examination of these and other principles in Chapter 4. But it will be useful to keep in mind several circumstances which, in some traditions and for some genres with which we are familiar, appear have a part in determining the objects of representations. Readers acquainted with recent philosophical discussions of reference will find most of the suggestions that follow familiar. I regard representing (in our sense), along with the relation between names and what they name, for example, as a species of reference.

Some representations utilize ordinary linguistic reference to effect contact with their objects. Using the name of a well-known personage ("Napoleon," "Julius Caesar") for a character in a literary work commonly serves to establish the "identity" of the character with that person, to render the work a novel or play or poem about him. It is arguable that the person must be reasonably well known to the intended audience, that an author's using the name of an utterly obscure acquaintance does not suffice to make the acquaintance an object of his work. A work does not prescribe imaginings about someone, perhaps, unless it is reasonable to expect the audience to recognize that it does. It is arguable, also, that an accidental use of even a well-known name does not do the trick, that the author must have knowingly and deliberately used the name of the person in question. Otherwise we have mere homonymy: the occurrences of the name in the text do not denote the person, and the work does not represent him.

Pictures often pick out their objects by means of titles. John Sloan's *McSorley's Bar* is, by virtue mainly of its title, a painting of McSorley's Bar in New York. Again, the mere fortuitous coincidence of a painting's title with the name of a real thing is probably insufficient. But it is my impression that the familiarity of the object to appreciators is usually understood to be less important in the case of painting than in that of literature. It may not matter if no one has heard of McSorley's Bar. Sometimes nonverbal signs play a role.

Halos help to specify objects of Renaissance paintings by limiting the possibilities to saints.

Some may contend that only the intentions of the artist are operative, that works represent whatever their makers mean them to represent, and that names, titles, and nonverbal clues serve merely to indicate artists' intentions. No doubt there *could* be principles of generation to this effect; it could be understood that appreciators are to engage in imaginings about whatever artists intend them to engage in imaginings about. But I find it more reasonable to regard the artist's intention, in most cases, as but one of a loose collection of circumstances bearing on determination of what a work represents.

When an artist paints from life, the slice of life from which he paints—the mountain or city or person he scrutinizes over his easel—is probably what his painting is a painting of. Intentions are involved, but not just the intention that a particular scene or thing be the object of the painting. The object guides the artist's hand as he paints, and he intends it to do so. The objects of a photograph may sometimes be understood to be whatever reflected light into the lens of the camera and onto the film thus producing the image, regardless of the photographer's intentions.

My examples so far suggest that for something to be an object of a representation it must have a causal role in the production of the work; it must in one way or another figure in the process whereby the representation came about, either by entering into the intentions with which the work was produced or in some more "mechanical" manner. This seems to me to be right. And it separates representing sharply from matching, since no such causal link is required for matching. But even if representations must in fact be causally related to their objects, it is only a contingent fact that there is such a requirement. There could be a convention to the effect that works represent whatever they bear a high degree of correspondence to, or even one to the effect that they represent only what they match. (The latter convention would be impractical since matching is so difficult both to achieve and to ascertain.)

Even in actual cases we probably want to allow that how close a representation comes to matching something has some bearing on whether it represents it. René Magritte's painting *L'Annonciation* portrays a weight lifter holding a bone in one hand and a barbell in the other, one of whose weights is his head. It hardly depicts the Annunciation, despite the title, even if Magritte intended it to (which is unlikely). It may be in some way "symbolic" of that event but is not a picture of it. This suggests that there must be *some* correspondence between representations and their objects. Perhaps to represent the Annunciation something must be at least an announcing-representation. If so, having an appropriate causal relation to a representation is not sufficient for being its object, even if it is necessary.

We must not overemphasize the causal relation that obtains between paintings and photographs done from life and the life they are done from. Fra Filippo Lippi used a local nun, Lucrezia Buti, as a model for his *Madonna della Cintola*. She posed for the picture just as many a nobleman has posed for his portrait. Yet *Madonna della Cintola* is not in the same sense a portrait of Lucrezia.[5] She is not its object; rather the biblical Mary is. The imaginings prescribed are about Mary, not about Lucrezia. Authors sometimes model characters on people with whom they are familiar, or fictional events on actual ones. But this does not make the models objects of the authors' works; no fictional truths *about them* need be generated. They simply assist the author in deciding what sorts of characters and fictional events to include in his work, what fictional truths to have it generate, however invaluable this assistance may be. *David Copperfield* is in one sense "autobiographical." But it need not be regarded as generating fictional truths about Charles Dickens.

I have attempted only the roughest of sketches of what considerations bear on the determination of a representation's objects. It will suffice for now to note that, typically, some combination of titles and like signs, artists' intentions, and other causal relations, together perhaps with a certain degree of correspondence, serves to establish the relation of representing. Part of the purpose of this observation is to clarify further the distinction between representing and matching. It also helps us to see how representing is related to referring.

3.4.   REPRESENTING AND REFERRING

Lippi's *Madonna della Cintola* does not *represent* Lucrezia Buti because it does not *refer* to her. If *David Copperfield* does not refer to Charles Dickens, it does not represent him. Representing is a kind of referring.

But not all referring is representing, not even all referring by representations. Reference is sometimes effected by means of a purely fic-

---

5. Cf. Monroe Beardsley's distinction between "nominal" and "physical" portrayal (*Aesthetics*, p. 277).

tional character who signifies, stands for, calls to mind an actual person. Dr. Pangloss in Voltaire's *Candide* stands for Leibniz, to whom the work refers. Spenser's *Faerie Queen* refers to Queen Elizabeth by means of a stand-in in the fictional world, the character Gloriana. But I prefer not to regard these works as *representing* Leibniz and Queen Elizabeth in our sense. It is not fictional *of Leibniz* that his name is "Pangloss" and that he became a "beggar covered with sores, dull-eyed, with the end of his nose fallen away, his mouth awry, his teeth black, who talked huskily, was tormented with a violent cough and spat out a tooth at every cough," and in this sorry state met his old philosophy student, Candide, to whom he continued to prove that all is for the best.[6] We are not asked to imagine this of Leibniz, although we are expected to *think* about him when we read about Pangloss, to notice and reflect on certain "resemblances" between the two. Pangloss is Voltaire's device for referring to Leibniz, but he refers to Leibniz in order to comment on him, not in order to establish fictional truths about him. Reference thus built on the generation of fictional truths, ones not about the things referred to, is one common kind of allegory.

Confusion can arise from the fact that we commonly speak of allegorical references in the same language that we use for representing. *Candide* is said to be *about* Leibniz, or to *represent* him. *Madonna della Cintola* is described as a picture *of* Lucrezia Buti, although it neither represents nor refers to her. Again, we must be wary of the promiscuity of these expressions.

In a series of three anonymous French broadsheets, "Effet de la Ligue," Philip II of Spain and the Guises are "portrayed" as a three-headed monster trampling the people while a town burns in the background (see figure 3.1). The monster is later conquered by a courageous lion, Henry IV. We do not have to hold that fictionally Philip and the Guises *are* a three-headed monster and Henry a lion. My preference is to say that in the fictional world a (purely fictional) three-headed monster is destroyed by a (purely fictional) lion, and that by arranging for this to be the case, the anonymous artist allegorically refers to and comments on Philip, the Guises, and Henry. (If the pictured animals had faces resembling those of the real people, it would be more natural to hold that fictionally the people are animals.)

Allegorical reference is sledgehammer obvious in *Candide* and the

6. *Candide,* chaps. 3 and 4.

French broadsheets. Less definite allegorical references can be found almost wherever one wants to find them: think of Kafka's *Metamorphosis* and Beckett's *Waiting for Godot*. But they are hard to prove. This is one of the great virtues of allegory; it is a trick to outwit the censor, including sometimes the appreciator's own internal censor. The Javanese puppeteer who chooses an episode from the *Mahabarata* epic in which an ancient evil king is deposed may get his message about current events across without running afoul of the authorities.[7]

3.1 · Anonymous French, "Effet de la Ligue," $6\frac{1}{4} \times 4\frac{7}{8}$ inches, etching and burin (1594). Bibliothèque Nationale, Paris. Photo Biblio. Nat. Paris.

3.5. USES OF OBJECTS

What is the point of having works represent actual things? There is a strangely persistent tendency to consider connections with the real world gratuitous, at least from an "aesthetic" point of view. What matters, it is supposed, is what *sorts* of people and places and events are to be found in a fictional world, not whether any of them are actual. Even with this attitude one must allow objects of representation a certain practical value. If a storyteller wants the setting for his

---

7. I am indebted to A. L. Becker for this example. Here it is the performance of the episode, not the work performed, that carries the allegorical reference.

tale to be a large modern industrial city in a nation with both imperialist and democratic traditions and with economic and class structures of certain kinds, he can provide such a background in a stroke by locating the action in London, by making it fictional of (the actual) London that the action takes place there. (This can usually be accomplished just by calling the city in which the action occurs London.) This spares storyteller and reader alike tedious time- and page-consuming specification of details about the setting. It also avoids placing undue emphasis on the setting at the expense of the action. The reader simply assumes that, except where there are specific indications to the contrary, the fictional London is like the real one. Fictionally, the city in which the action takes place is large and modern and industrial and whatever else London actually is, unless the story indicates otherwise. (But see Chapter 4.) With the setting thus in place, the author is free to focus the reader's attention on the characters and their doings.

The representing of objects is more than a device of convenience, however. Some representations contain statements or assertions about real things, and that requires reference to them. The referring need not be representing, as we have seen. But it can be, and representing is sometimes the method of choice. The indirectness of allegory is useful in effecting veiled references, and even obvious allegorical references carry a certain air of pretense, transparent though it may be. When simple, straightforward references are desired, as in historical novels, portraiture, and religious icons, representing may be preferable. Moreover, a statement that includes a representation of a thing can be especially powerful and compelling. For to represent something is to prescribe imaginings about it; and engaging in imaginings about something—George Bush, the French Revolution, oneself—is a good way to deepen one's understanding of it. Indeed the statement may be unnecessary; representations of objects prescribe imaginings about them even if they are not to be understood also as vehicles of statement or assertion.

This, incidentally, brings out one failing of the fashionable practice of regarding representations in a quasilinguistic light. Linguistic utterances are informative, typically, because they are vehicles of assertion. It is because in uttering certain words a speaker is *asserting* or *stating* that a building is on fire or that a train is about to depart that one learns from his words that this is so. But a representation, by inducing appropriate imaginings, provides its illumination quite apart from any such communicative role. (See §2.8.)

We inherit from Aristotle (or his commentators) the notion that the job of poetry is to reveal *general* truths, not truths about particular things. Even so, representing particulars can be helpful. One way to demonstrate the evils of war in general is to cite, for example to represent, a specific instance such as the Spanish civil war. The work can thus engage and utilize what appreciators know independently about that particular case and the insight achieved by their imaginings about it to guide them toward general conclusions. Again, this may be accomplished even if the work is not construed as a comment on the particular case or as a statement of the general truths.

Not all objects of representations interest us particularly, even as instances of general truths, and the work does not always direct our interest toward them. They can be rather remote from the point of the work. This is sometimes true of settings, backgrounds, and locations. The purpose of locating the action of *King Kong* in New York, thus making New York an object of the work, is not to deepen our understanding of New York or especially to direct our attention to that city.

What is the purpose then? We noticed in §1.3 that our imaginings are sometimes about things that are not themselves focuses of interest, such things as stumps, a pile of snow, a plastic doll. I am convinced that these objects contribute significantly to the imaginative experience. If they do not, it is hard to understand why imaginings so often have such incidental things as objects. (I have suggested rather vaguely that they provide "substance" to one's imaginings, thereby enhancing their "vivacity.") Works whose objects are not central to our interests (at least while we are appreciating the work), ones that prescribe imaginings about such objects, utilize the contribution they make to the imaginings.

The fact that it is in New York, an actual city and a familiar one, that King Kong escapes and has his various adventures, the fact that he looks down from the skyscraper on the well-known landmarks of Manhattan, gives the movie a distinctive flavor strikingly different from that of fantasies like *Gulliver's Travels* and *The Hobbit* which unfold in purely fictional lands or on purely imaginary planets, or even the Faulkner stories set in the fictitious but typical Yoknapatawpha County. Some may propose that the familiar real-world setting lends an air of "believability" to the unbelievable. I think it is more a matter of engaging our personal interest in the unbelievable events, of our being able to say such things as "I once stood at the very corner where (fictionally) Kong captured the little girl." I am reminded of the difference it makes in reading about historical events to have visited the places where they transpired: the Tower of London, the Parthenon, Gettysburg, Rome, Jerusalem.

3.6.   REFLEXIVE REPRESENTATION

Some representations are their own objects. We saw in Chapter 1 that props in children's games can be objects of the imaginings they prescribe. A doll directs players of the game not just to imagine a baby but to imagine the doll itself to be a baby. So it generates fictional truths about itself; it represents itself. Let's call it a *reflexive* representation.

The reader of *Gulliver's Travels* is to imagine that a certain ship's physician named "Gulliver" traveled to various exotic lands and kept a journal detailing his adventures, but he is to imagine also, about the very book he is reading, that it is such a journal. (The full title of Swift's novel is *Travels into Several Remote Nations of the World, by Lemuel Gulliver.*) The novel thus makes it fictional of itself that it is an account of a traveler's adventures in places like Lilliput, Brobdingnag, and Houyhnhnmland. It too is reflexive. Literary fictions in the form of letters, diaries, and journals are in general reflexive. *Tristram Shandy* makes it fictional of itself that it is an autobiography. Fictionally *A Perfect Vacuum* by Stanislaw Lem is a collection of book reviews (including a review of *A Perfect Vacuum*). Fictionally Beckett's *Malone Dies* is a rambling account of a man's last days scribbled in a notebook on his deathbed.

Reflexivity is a recurring theme in the drawings of Saul Steinberg. The lines constituting figure 3.2 are such that fictionally they have just been inscribed by a rather intense artist seated at a table—and this includes the lines whereby the artist, his table, and his pen are portrayed. Roy Lichtenstein's *Little Big Painting* (figure 3.3) is a larger-than-life-size painting of brush strokes, which represents part of itself as brush strokes. It is fictional of the paint on the canvas that it was put there by four not very careful swipes with a paintbrush.

The Steinberg and Lichtenstein pieces are special. Most paintings and drawings are not reflexive, except in the way that even nonfigurative pictures are. (See §1.8.) It is fictional in Titian's *Venus* that a woman is reclining on a couch, but it is not fictional of the painting or any part of it that *it* is a woman or a couch. *Venus* does not in that way represent itself.

Some cases are unclear. One might be inclined to interpret the fourth-century marble head of Constantine the Great in Rome as

3.2 · Saul Steinberg, *Drawing Table*, 19 × 25¼ inches, ink on paper (1966).
Photograph courtesy of The Pace Gallery, New York.

being such that, fictionally, it—the sculpted block of marble itself—is
the head of Constantine. But I find this construal much less compelling than understanding a doll to make it fictional of itself that it is a
baby. The difference is probably due to the fact that more of the doll's
actual properties are such that fictionally the baby has them. If the
doll is in Decatur, Georgia, fictionally the baby is there. If Chris
cuddles the doll, then fictionally Chris cuddles the baby. But it is not
at all obvious that fictionally Constantine (or his head) is wherever
the marble sculpture is, that fictionally he rides on a truck if the
sculpture does, and so on. The sculpture is eight feet high, but surely it
is not fictional that Constantine's head is that large. It is not the
sculpture's function, at least, to be involved in a game in which fictionally a curator cuddles Constantine if he should somehow manage
to cuddle the block of marble. So the doll corresponds to itself in
many respects in which the sculpture does not; it comes closer to
matching itself, that is (informally), the fictional baby is more like the

doll than the fictional Constantine is like the sculpture. We should not be surprised that because of this the doll is more naturally regarded as representing itself, since (as we saw in § 3.3) a necessary condition for a work's representing a given object is that it correspond, to a certain degree, to the object. But we need not stew over these uncertainties.

3.3 · Roy Lichtenstein, *Little Big Painting*, 68 × 80 inches, oil on canvas (1965). Collection of Whitney Museum of American Art, New York. Purchase, with funds from the Friends of the Whitney Museum of American Art. 66.2.

There are various means by which representations pick out themselves as objects. The usual techniques for referring to other things are available. *A Perfect Vacuum* and the film *Blazing Saddles* refer to themselves by name. If a picture depicts a room with a picture on the wall, whether the depicted picture is the depicting one itself is to be decided in the same way one would decide whether another picture is its object: Did the artist intend it to represent itself? Does it come reasonably close to matching itself? Can spectators be expected to recognize that it prescribes imaginings about itself? Did attention to the picture (when unfinished) guide the artist's hand in (finishing) painting it? It is perfectly possible, in these cases, for one not to realize that the represented work is identical with the representing one. If a moviegoer has forgotten the name of the movie he is watching, he may miss the fact that *it* is the one that, fictionally, the characters go to see when they walk under the marquee advertising *Blazing Saddles*.

We shall be more interested in cases in which the fact that a given thing is identical with the representation or part of it is crucial to establishing that that thing is represented. If (*per impossibile,* perhaps) figure 3.2 had been composed of lines different from the ones that actually compose it, it would represent those other lines rather than the ones it does represent (even if it looked no different from how it actually does). Being part of the work is part of what makes its lines its objects. One can scarcely notice that it represents lines without realizing that the lines it represents are those of the drawing itself. Let's say that figure 3.2 refers to itself *as* itself. *Gulliver's Travels* does also: what makes its words among the objects it represents is in part their presence in the work, and a reader will not notice that words are represented without realizing that those of the text itself are. *Blazing Saddles* and the picture depicting itself hanging on a wall, by contrast, do not refer to themselves as themselves.

Reflexive representations (of both of these sorts) may but need not represent themselves as *representations*. *Little Big Painting* does not; it represents itself as merely an inert brush stroke. But Steinberg's drawing does. Fictionally the lines of the drawing constitute a depiction of an artist seated at a table. This gives us one fictional world nested within another: it is fictional that the lines make it fictional that an artist is seated at a table. In fact we have infinitely many embedded fictional worlds, each of them containing the actual lines of the drawing. Fictionally a man has just drawn those lines, thereby making it fictional that a man has just drawn them, making it fictional that . . . , and so on ad infinitum. It is fictional in *Blazing Saddles* that some of the characters watch a movie, *Blazing Saddles,* which makes it fictional (by implication anyway) that its characters watch a movie, *Blazing Saddles,* which . . . John Barth's "Frame-Tale" consists of the words "ONCE UPON A TIME THERE" on one side of a page, and "WAS A STORY THAT BEGAN" on the other, with instructions to twist the paper and fasten the ends together, forming a Möbius strip.[8]

8. In *Lost in the Funhouse,* pp. 1–2.

So the story reads: ONCE UPON A TIME THERE WAS A STORY THAT BEGAN ONCE UPON A TIME THERE WAS A STORY THAT BEGAN ONCE UPON A TIME . . . ad infinitum. These words (the word types anyway) represent themselves as representations representing themselves as representations representing . . .

Of course representations need not be reflexive in order to establish fictional worlds within fictional worlds. All representation-representations do, whether or not they represent *themselves* as representations (or as anything else). There are pictures of pictures (Matisse's *Red Studio*), stories about stories (Keith Fort, "The Coal Shoveller"), plays about plays (*Hamlet*), sculptures of sculptures (there is a 30 B.C. sculpture of a Roman patrician with busts of his ancestors circa 30 B.C.), films about films (Truffaut's *Day for Night*), novels about novels (Italo Calvino's *If on a Winter's Night a Traveler*), novels about pictures (Oscar Wilde's *Picture of Dorian Gray*), poems about pictures (Keats's "Ode on a Grecian Urn"), novels about films (Manuel Puig's *Kiss of the Spider Woman*), and so on. All representation-representations make it fictional that there is a work that makes various other propositions fictional. It is possible to construe some of them as making it fictional of themselves or parts of themselves that they are such works, but others need not or cannot be so construed. It is not *The Picture of Dorian Gray*–fictional that any part of that novel is a painting of Dorian Gray.

Many reflexive representations represent themselves not as works of fiction but as works of nonfiction. Some represent themselves as biographies, histories, journals, essays (*Tristram Shandy, A Perfect Vacuum, Gulliver's Travels*). Since biographies and the like do not have fictional worlds, such works do not give us nested fictional worlds. Julio Cortázar's story "Blow-Up" is studiously ambiguous between representing itself as fiction or as nonfiction. Beckett's *Malone Dies* is, fictionally, nonfiction for the most part but with interpolations of what seem to be story fragments, works of fiction. Fictionally Malone scribbles (nonfictionally) about his deathbed experiences but apparently tries his hand on several occasions at storytelling. But there are hints that his story fragments are autobiographical and possibly nonfictional, so it is arguable that *Malone Dies* represents itself as entirely a work of nonfiction.

There is a lot of fun to be had with the devices of representation-representation and reflexive representation. But reflexivity, especially, is also of considerable theoretical importance and will play a significant part in the development of my theory.

3.7. THE INESSENTIALITY OF OBJECTS

To be representational is not necessarily to represent something. Not all representations have objects.[9] But the notion of having an object, the possibility of representing something, might still be essential to the concept of the representational. It might be that representationality is to be understood in terms of objects, even though particular representations (unicorn-pictures, ghost-stories) sometimes have none.

I do not think it is. My account in Chapter 1 of what it is for something to be representational made no mention of objects. I shall now defend this omission, arguing against those who would introduce the representing of objects earlier and give them a more central theoretical role.

I am in opposition here to one analogy commonly drawn between representation and language. We have seen that the relation of representing, the relation between representations and their objects (when they have objects), is much like linguistic reference, like the relation names and other referring expressions bear to their referents. Linguistic referring expressions would be promising candidates for models by which to understand representation if representing is central to representation. Our basic building block, one might suppose, should be a pervasive semantic relation which we might call *reference* or *denotation,* and which is best understood by looking at its paradigm instances—reference by linguistic referring expressions. Representing will be construed as an instance of this semantic relation, and the representational will be explained in terms of it.

This program follows the spirit of Nelson Goodman's slogan "Denotation is the core of representation."[10] Unfortunately, a fundamental unclarity in what Goodman means by "denotation" makes it impossible to be sure what his position is. When he speaks of representations "denoting" things, he may have in mind something like what I call "representing," the relation representations bear to their objects. But he may mean instead something akin to *matching.*[11] The

9. Assuming that there are no nonactual entities, that only actual things can be objects of representation. (See §3.8.)

10. *Languages of Art,* p. 5. Goodman uses "representation" both more broadly and more narrowly than I do. It applies, for him, to nonfiction as well as to fiction. And he applies it only to pictures and other (fictional or nonfictional) depictions, excluding works of literature. It is abundantly evident, however, that he considers denotation to be the core of all that I call representation.

11. Here is the evidence in favor of the first interpretation: (a) Goodman speaks of pictures *depicting* or *representing* the things they denote, or being pictures *of* them. To

question is crucial, since there is a fundamental divergence between representing and matching. Let's adopt the first reading for now. Let us take "denotation" to be a relation representations bear to their objects, and which referring expressions also bear to their referents. *War and Peace* and portraits of Napoleon will be said to denote Napoleon, and so will the name "Napoleon Bonaparte" and the phrase "the emperor of France crowned in 1804." Is denotation, so understood, the core of representation?

Goodman agrees that not all representations denote, that representation is not simply a matter of actually denoting something. He has no sympathy for nonactual entities. But he offers hints about how denotation may underlie the representational in a less direct manner:

> Although representation thus depends upon a relationship among symbols rather than upon their relationship to denotata, it nevertheless depends upon their *use* as denotative symbols. A dense set of elements does not constitute a representational scheme unless at least *ostensibly* provided with denotata. The rule correlating symbols with denotata may result in no assignment of any actual denotata to any symbol, so that the field of reference is null; but elements become representations only in conjunction with some such correlation actual or *in principle*.[12]

---

match something is not thereby to be a picture of it or to depict or represent it, in any ordinary sense of these expressions. (b) His examples of denoting pictures—Constable paintings of Marlborough Castle, portraits of Churchill and the Duke of Wellington—are clear cases of representing which are highly unlikely to be instances of matching. All (ordinarily so-called) portraits of Churchill have Churchill as an object, but most glorify or deprecate their object in one way or another, and it is a safe bet that in every case the "Churchill in the picture" differs in some details from the real one, i.e., that the portrait fails to match Churchill. (c) Goodman recognizes the possibility of misrepresenting what is denoted (ibid., pp. 27, 29–30). But misrepresentation is representing *without* matching.

The evidence for the second reading is this: (a) Goodman claims that what a picture depicts, i.e., what it denotes, depends only on its "pictorial properties," i.e. (roughly), "what colors the picture has at what places" (ibid., pp. 41–42). We have seen that this is not true of what a picture represents; titles, intentions, causal relations, or some combination of these come into play. Perhaps what a picture matches depends only on its pictorial properties (given the pictorial system and the nature of the objects to be matched). (b) He assimilates "the relation between a picture and what it represents [i.e., denotes] . . . to the relation between a predicate and what it applies to" (ibid., p. 5). A picture's matching something does seem comparable to a predicate's applying to it, whereas representing is more like the relation between a name and its bearer.

I see no escape from the conclusion that Goodman's notion of denotation hides a serious conflation of representing and matching.

12. Ibid., pp. 227–228; my italics. Novitz, in *Pictures and Their Use*, objects to Goodman's understanding of (pictorial) representation as fundamentally denotative, but for reasons rather contrary to mine.

This is not very explicit. But—taking the denoting in question to be representing—I do not think that it comes even close to the truth. The representational (either in my sense or in Goodman's) is not in any way to be understood in terms of denoting. Representations are not such even partly by virtue of their having a denoting role, either actual or implied or purported or pretended or ostensible or in principle. To be representational is not thereby to belong to a denoting scheme.

The contrast with linguistic referring expressions is telling. Referring expressions are to be understood in terms of their denoting roles. This goes for ones that do not actually denote anything as well as for ones that do; all of them are, let us say, *denotative*. There are several kinds of nondenoting referring expressions. "The only person to climb Mount Everest,"[13] "Grendel," and "Paul Henry O'Mallory" will serve as illustrations.

"The *first* person to climb Mount Everest" denotes someone, but "the only person to climb Mount Everest" does not. The difference is simply that the world happens to contain someone who was the first to climb Everest but not someone who was the only person to do so. The "rule correlating symbols with denotata" does not, I suppose, assign any denotatum to the latter expression. It is not clear that there *is* a rule which applies to "Grendel" and "Paul Henry O'Mallory." (I assume that "Paul Henry O'Mallory" has never been used as a name, not even in fiction.) It is not because denotata purportedly picked out for them happen not to exist that they fail to denote. "Grendel," however, is at least in one sense "ostensibly provided with" a denotatum. We pretend, imagine, make believe that "Grendel," as it occurs in *Beowulf*, names an actual person. No one has even pretended that "Paul Henry O'Mallory" denotes. Yet it is denotative in the sense that it is a member of a class of things—names—that are conventionally assigned denoting roles; it belongs to a repertoire of potential denoters.

There are isolated examples of nondenoting representations that are denotative in similar ways. Suppose that what appear to be dinosaur footprints are discovered in Arizona, and that an artist is commissioned to draw the dinosaur responsible for them. His sketch is so labeled and is displayed in a museum with the footprints. But suppose the prints were not actually made by a dinosaur at all but were carved in rock by an ambitious but frustrated paleontologist. The sketch is like "the only person to climb Mount Everest."

13. Used in what Keith Donnellan calls the "attributive" manner ("Reference and Definite Descriptions").

Gulliver's Travels, and illustrations of Gulliver, are nondenoting but denotative in the way the name "Grendel" is. Perhaps Paul Klee's *Scholar* corresponds to "Paul Henry O'Mallory"; it belongs to a class of things, person-pictures, that often are used to denote.

It should be obvious that representations do not have to be denotative in any of these ways. There could well be a society (much like that in § 2.5) in which artists produce pictures of animals and people—animal-pictures and person-pictures—but never ones portraying actual animals or actual people. None of their pictures have (actual) objects, and there is no provision for making anything an object of a representation. There is no convention whereby attaching a title or other sign to a representation makes it represent some (actual) thing; artists never use anything as a model in producing a representation, let us say. They do not know what representing an object is and so cannot intend a work to represent anything. Drawing a bison is thought of always as *creating, producing* an (imaginary) bison, never as symbolizing or referring to an animal already in existence. (It is no accident that children speak of *making* a giraffe when they draw one.)

A bison-depiction in such a context is not in any way denotative. It does not purport to denote anything in the way that the dinosaur-picture in the museum does, nor is there any sort of pretense that it denotes. Neither is it one of a kind of things which are normally or typically used to denote. Yet certainly it is representational.

The notion of the representational is thus independent of that of denoting. Denotation is not the "core of representation." The failure to recognize this important point is due largely, I believe, to confusion between representing and matching; once these are properly disentangled, there is no excuse for supposing the representational to presuppose or depend on the possibility of representing, the possibility of denoting.

I have not claimed that *literary* representation is possible without provision for representing. Perhaps literary works necessarily consist of linguistic expressions some of which are denotative, and perhaps this means that the works themselves are denotative. But if literary representations are fundamentally denotative, it is because they are literary, not because they are representations. Representation is not to be explained in terms of denotation. The notion of objects of representation is inessential to that of the representational.

In the preceding pages I have assumed that only actual things can be objects of representations, that works represent (denote) only real-world entities. We shall look seriously at this assumption in the following section and in Part Four. But let us consider now what effect dropping it would have on the present question.

The idea that denotation is the core of representation may seem to fare better than it has so far if we are willing to countenance nonactual objects. One might even hope for a simpler account of the representational in terms of denoting than any we have been considering. If representations can have fictitious objects—if, for instance, the bison-picture described in § 2.5 represents a fictional bison—it may look as though every representation will actually denote something.[14] We will not have to worry about potential or purported denotation or denotation in principle or there being provision for denoting even if nothing is actually denoted. This alternative will not tempt Goodman, whose hostility toward fictional entities is notorious. But it may attract some who have managed so far to assuage their ontological qualms.

Even if we do recognize fictitious entities, however, it does not follow that the notion of having objects—fictional if not actual ones—should be taken as basic in explaining representation. The best procedure, in my opinion, would still be to explain representation in terms of games of make-believe and the generation of fictional truths, as I have done, and only then to introduce the idea of objects of representation, relying again on what has been said about games of make-believe and fictional truths. In particular, it will not be reasonable to start with a general semantic relation, denotation, assimilating the relation between representations and their (possibly fictional) objects to linguistic reference, and use it to define the representational. Those who are set on using a linguistic model for representation will not find encouragement in the recognition of fictitious objects.

Let us suppose, for the sake of argument, that *Moby Dick* and *Scholar* have fictional objects. *Moby Dick* represents Ahab (and also Dagoo, the whale, and so on); *Scholar* represents a certain fictional scholar, the "man in the picture." We must now reconsider the supposed analogy between representing and linguistic reference. The relation *Moby Dick* and *Scholar* bear to their fictional objects differs significantly from the relation between referring expressions and their referents. There is ample justification for classifying the representing of *actual* objects with linguistic reference as instances of denoting, but

---

14. Actually, nondenoting representations would still be possible, though rare. "There were ghosts about. The End" seems to be one. (See §3.8.)

we should balk at including the representing of fictional objects in cases like these.[15]

The most striking difference is this: Ahab and the scholar are not independent of the works that represent them. Ahab owes his existence (such as it is) and also his nature to *Moby Dick*. If the novel had been written differently in certain respects, or not at all, he would not have existed, there would have been no such character, or he would not have been as he is.[16] Actual objects of representation, by contrast, exist and are as they are quite independently of the works that represent them, and referents of referring expressions are similarly independent of the referring expressions (except when representations or referring expressions denote themselves). This ought at least to give pause to those who would have us understand the relation between representations and fictitious as well as actual objects on the model of linguistic reference.

Shall we say that *Moby Dick* creates Ahab and, *in addition*, denotes him, and construe at least the denoting on the model of linguistic referring? That would, at best, lessen the utility of the linguistic model, for the representation's creative function would have to be understood separately. Moreover, it is not clear that once we say *Moby Dick* creates Ahab there is any point in going on to say that it denotes him. The addition seems gratuitous. Yet without it there is nothing for the linguistic model to explain. There do not seem to be two distinct functions, creating and denoting, which require independent analyses. What would it be like for a work to create its characters without denoting them? If what is to be explained is a *single* relation, this relation seems insufficiently analogous to linguistic reference to warrant the use of the linguistic model.

It is worth noting that the make-believe theory holds promise for accommodating the "creative" function of representations, whether or not we recognize fictitious entities. Part of the story is that representations "create" by making existential propositions not true but fictional. The rest has yet to be told.

Should representation be understood on the model of linguistic predicates rather than referring expressions? This suggestion goes well

15. We might allow that a representation denotes *immigrant* fictional objects, ones whose homes are in other representations, since immigrants are independent of the representations to which they emigrate.

16. Wolterstorff holds that characters are eternally existing *kinds*, and so are not created but merely picked out by representations (*Works and Worlds*, pp. 134–149). But this identification is objectionable on independent grounds. See Walton, "Review of Wolterstorff."

with the idea that "denotation is the core of representation" if the denotation in question is *matching* rather than representing. Goodman, we saw, can be read with more or less equal justice as construing "denotation" either way. In fact, he explicitly assimilates "the relation between a picture and what it represents to the relation between a predicate and what it applies to."[17]

Objects of representation do not stand to gain a central place in our theory on this proposal, since what a work represents, what it has as objects, is independent of what it matches. But let us pause briefly to consider it anyway.

There is this much analogy at least between predicates and representations: Both indicate, pick out, specify properties.[18] The predicate "(is a) man" indicates the property of being a man. *Scholar* indicates the property of being a man with a certain look, "The Tell-Tale Heart" indicates the property of being a man who kills someone and buries the body beneath his floorboards, and so on. Predicates apply to and representations match whatever there is, if anything, that possesses the properties they pick out.

It is tempting to push the analogy further. Predicates are devices not only for picking out properties but also for attributing them to particular things. This threatens to bring back objects of representation in a central role. But here the analogy breaks down. It is not the function of the bison-picture of §2.5 to attribute the property of being a bison to anything.

People use predicates to attribute properties to things, to say of things that they possess certain properties. I established in §2.3 that such communicative uses are inessential to the representational, that there need be no provision for so using representations.[19] But a representation might be said to attribute a property to something even if it is not used in communication. A picture labeled "Jones's Garden"

---

17. *Languages of Art*, p. 5. The grounds of this assimilation are obscure, especially since so much of what Goodman says suggests that the "denoting" he takes to be the "core of representation" is representing rather than matching and so points toward referring expressions rather than predicates as analogues of representations. Bennett, "Depiction and Convention," has advanced a more explicit theory, based loosely on demystified versions of some of Goodman's remarks, according to which pictures are themselves (nonlinguistic) predicates.

18. Goodman's nominalism bars him from expressing the analogy this way.

19. Bennett takes as fundamental "the role that pictures play in communication." "Pictures are used to make 'sentences' and to enable people to communicate with each other" ("Depiction and Convention," p. 266). His claim is not that this is the most important use of pictures, but rather that it is one without which there would be no pictorial representation at all.

might introduce or specify the singular proposition that Jones's garden has certain properties, without being used to inform anyone about Jones's garden or to perform any other illocutionary actions. Yet it is clear that pictures do not necessarily have the function of specifying singular propositions. There is no provision for using the bison-picture, with or without a caption or title, to introduce a proposition about a particular bison. The job of specifying such propositions is not an essential function of pictorial representation, and hence not of representation in general.

This is not to deny that specifying propositions is central to representation. Representations make propositions fictional, and they specify the propositions they make fictional. But the propositions need not be singular ones, ones about particular things. The bison-picture specifies and makes fictional the (existential) proposition that there is a bison (although its being a "picture of a bison" does not consist merely in its doing this, as we shall see). It does not in any sense attribute the property it picks out to a particular thing.

Not, at least, to any *actual* thing. Shall we say that it attributes that property to a fictitious beast, the "bison in the picture," presuming that there is such a thing? Not in a sense very close to that in which predicates attribute properties to things. What properties a thing possesses is independent of what predicates are attributed to it. But the picture *makes* the picture bison a bison.

We still have the fact that representations, like predicates, pick out properties, even if they do not serve to attribute properties to things. But to say this is to say very little. Lots of things are easily regarded as picking out properties. Works of nonfiction do. The rondo movement of a Mozart symphony might be said to indicate youthful exuberance, the Parthenon stability and order. Expressive works in general can be thought of as picking out the properties they express.[20] Throwing a ball through a hoop in a basketball game could be said to specify the property of scoring a goal, by way of bringing it about that this property is instantiated.

It is not very illuminating to know that representations belong to the enormous and diverse category of specifiers of properties. Nor is it obvious that linguistic predicates deserve to be regarded as especially central or paradigm instances of this class, ones to be taken as models for understanding others, such as representations. What is interesting and important is what is done with the properties that are specified.

20. Goodman holds that a necessary condition for expression is "reference" to what is expressed (*Languages of Art*, p. 86).

The central function of representations is to make propositions involving the properties they specify fictional. One might find an affinity between representations and throwing a ball through a hoop. This action makes it true ("true in the real world") that a goal is scored; *Scholar* makes it fictional ("true in a fictional world") that there is a man of a certain sort. There seems to be no closer affinity between representations and linguistic predicates. The central function of the latter is presumably something like that of being used to inform people of the truth of propositions involving indicated properties. That is a far cry from making propositions fictional.

3.8. NONACTUAL OBJECTS?

Shakespeare's *Julius Caesar* is about a Roman emperor named "Julius Caesar"; Cervantes' *Don Quixote* is about an errant knight who goes by the name of "Don Quixote." One work generates fictional truths about Caesar, the other fictional truths about Quixote. Readers of the novel are to engage in imaginings about Don Quixote, as spectators of the play are to engage in imaginings about Caesar. Don Quixote, it seems, is an object of *Don Quixote* just as Julius Caesar is an object of *Julius Caesar.*

Picasso's *Seated Woman* (1923) is a picture of a certain (unnamed) woman, as his marvelous *Portrait of Stravinsky* (1920) is a picture of Stravinsky. Fictionally the woman is seated with her hands clasped loosely together, and fictionally Stravinsky is doing the same. This woman is an object of the one picture as Stravinsky is of the other.

So it seems. But mustn't something exist in order to be an object of representation, in order for there to be fictional truths about it? Julius Caesar and Igor Stravinsky are real people, but Don Quixote and Picasso's seated woman are not. Some would minimize this difference by claiming that *there are* such entities as Don Quixote and the seated woman, even though they do not *exist*—or that they have a special kind of existence, or exist in a special realm distinct from the "real world." Don Quixote and the seated woman are thus rescued from oblivion to serve as objects of Cervantes' and Picasso's representations.

Such metaphysical contortions are easily ridiculed, but they deserve sympathy and understanding. We need to appreciate and to accommodate somehow in our theory the enormous intuitive urge to deny the undeniable, to make room somewhere in the universe for Don Quixote and his fellow fictions. Recognizing them may do little for the idea that representationality is to be understood in terms of a quasi-linguistic relation of denotation, as I argued earlier, but that is by no means the main ground of their claim for recognition.

The best way to muster sympathy for fictitious objects is to try to do without them. If there is no Don Quixote, there are no fictional truths about him. So perhaps Cervantes' novel makes it fictional merely that *there is* a person whose name is "Don Quixote," who has a squire named "Sancho Panza," who mistakes windmills for giants and flocks of sheep for armies, and so on.[21] It is fictional that all this is true of *someone or other;* the novel does not specify *whom* fictionally it is true of, for the simple reason that there is no one to specify. If there is no (actual or nonactual) person of whom *Seated Woman* makes it fictional that she is clasping her hands loosely together, the painting would seem to make it fictional merely that there is someone or other who is doing so.

If this is right, ordinary claims like

(1) Don Quixote mistook windmills for giants

and

(2) The woman's hands are clasped loosely together,

which sound so similar to ones like

(3) Julius was warned of the Ides of March by a seer

and

(4) Stravinsky's hands are clasped loosely together,

will have to be understood very differently. We can take (3) and (4) almost at face value, apparently, with only the addition of the implicit "in Shakespeare's play" or "in Picasso's portrait" or something to that effect. But (1) and (2) demand drastic reformulation. A first stab would be to gloss (1) as

(5) It is *Don Quixote*–fictional that there is someone named "Don Quixote" who mistook windmills for giants.

This transforms what looks like a statement about a particular thing into one that says merely what *sort* of thing it is fictional that there is.

This analysis is not even remotely adequate. Suppose that the central character of Cervantes' novel did not mistake windmills for giants, but that in an obscure passage one of the characters mentions

21. See Plantinga, *Nature of Necessity,* pp. 159–163.

a remote ancestor of Don Quixote who shares his name and who did mistake windmills for giants. Then, fictionally, there *is* a person named "Don Quixote" who mistook windmills for giants, even though (1), which is "about" *the* Don Quixote, is false. We must be able somehow to distinguish different characters of that name, it seems, and that cannot be done without recognizing characters. A healthy suspicion of the prospects of getting along without fictitious objects is very much in order. A second failing of this analysis is that (5) is in part about the *name* "Don Quixote," whereas (1) uses but does not mention it.

The suspicion deepens when we consider cases in which it is not known whether a given work has an actual object or not. We may have no idea whether or not an aboriginal cave painting or a contemporary sketch portrays a real person. But this uncertainty may scarcely matter; our experience need not depend in any fundamental way on which we suppose to be the case. To describe the uncertainty as uncertainty about which of two drastically different forms the fictional truths generated by the work take would be to make much too much of it. It would seem more faithful to the phenomenology of the experience to allow that we know that the work has an object, that it generates fictional truths about something, and that we engage in the appropriate imaginings about it; what we do not know is just whether the object is actual or merely fictional. When we describe something as a "picture of a person," we need not feel that this claim is radically ambiguous, that it may mean either that there is a person whom the work pictures or something entirely different.

Some representations obviously *do* generate fictional truths just about what sorts of things there are, not about particular (actual or fictional) things. These contrast sharply with *Don Quixote* and *Seated Woman,* as well as with *Julius Caesar* and the portrait of Stravinsky. But the contrast is in danger of being lost if we refuse to allow that *Don Quixote* and *Seated Woman* have fictional objects.[22]

The difference is best understood in light of a corresponding contrast between two sorts of imaginings. I can imagine a squirrel in a tree, or I can imagine merely that there is a squirrel in the tree, that the tree has a squirrel—some squirrel or other—in it. I need not have any particular *actual* squirrel in mind, in the first case, which I am imagining to be in the tree; yet it seems appropriate to describe what I am

---

22. Robert Howell has emphasized this difference ("Fictional Objects," pp. 145–169). See also Fine, "Problem of Non-Existence," p. 104.

doing as imagining a particular squirrel. My imagining is likely to be accompanied by a visual image of a squirrel, although this too is unnecessary. In the second case, when I merely imagine the tree to be squirrel infested, I do not imagine a particular squirrel in the same sense. And although my imagining may be accompanied by an image of a tree, together with the understanding that the tree is besquirreled, it cannot, it seems, be accompanied by an image of a squirrel. To add a squirrel-image to the tree-image would be to imagine a particular squirrel.

The nature of this difference is elusive. All squirrels are *particular* ones, and no doubt this holds for my imaginary world as well as for the real world. So to imagine that some squirrel or other resides in the tree is, surely, to imagine that there is a *particular* squirrel there, some particular squirrel or other. But to imagine this is not to imagine of a particular squirrel—one that I can pick out, identify, refer to—that it is in the tree. *That*, it is tempting to say, is what I do in the first case. And now we are in hot water again. If, when I imagine a squirrel, I can identify the squirrel that I am imagining, there must really *be* such a squirrel to be identified, even if it is not an actual one.

A representation may prescribe imaginings of either kind. This Very Short Story

(A) George was an old and almost worn out ghost who lived in the rundown mansion on Spruce Street. *The End*

prescribes imaginings "about a (particular) ghost." A story that goes

(B) There were ghosts about. The old rundown mansion on Spruce Street was home for some of them. *The End*

does not. It asks us to imagine a haunted house, one that is ghost infested, to imagine merely that there is some ghost or other, perhaps more than one, haunting the house. Story (A) is a story "about a ghost," but I hesitate to describe (B) this way, for (it seems) there is no particular (fictional) ghost which it is about.

The ghost in (A) has a name, whereas none of the ghosts in (B) do. (At least the reader is not told their names.) But this is not the crucial difference. We might expand (B) thus:

(B') There were ghosts about. The old rundown mansion on Spruce Street was home for some of them, including one named "George," no doubt, since at that time all ghosts were called George. *The End.*

We are again asked to imagine only that there is a ghost satisfying a certain description, one who is old and almost worn out and lives in the mansion on Spruce Street, and who bears the name "George." Moreover, if (A) were changed to

(A') He was an old and almost worn out ghost, living in the rundown mansion on Spruce Street. *The End,*

it would still prescribe imaginings "about a particular ghost."

It is not fictional in (A) that there is *only one* ghost named "George" living in the mansion. For all we know there might be lots of them; nothing in the story indicates otherwise. We could expand (A) to make it explicit that George is not unique:

(A") George was an old and almost worn out ghost who lived in the rundown mansion on Spruce Street. He shared his abode with two other ghosts, both of them also named "George," who were also old and almost worn out. *The End.*

But there still seems to be a particular (nonactual) ghost which the story is about, one that is referred to by the first occurrence of "George" in the story and by the pronoun "he."

What happens if we alter (B) to make it fictional that there is a *unique* ghost fitting a certain description?

(B") There were ghosts about. The old rundown mansion on Spruce Street was home for some of them. A light was on in the attic. A ghost must have gone up there—only one, since ghosts like to be alone in attics. *The End.*

Shall we say that (B") is "about a particular ghost" (the one in the attic), that it prescribes imaginings "about a particular (nonactual) ghost"? I am inclined not to. The story still makes it fictional only that some ghost or other has a certain collection of properties, now including the property of being the only one in the attic. Intuitively we seem still not to know *which* ghost is the one in the attic, although that again implies that if we did know this, there would *be* a (nonactual) ghost which we know about. I expect that in some contexts the contrary construal of (B") would be reasonable. In any case, making it fictional that there is a unique *F* is not necessary for "representing a particular *F*," even if it is sufficient.

The contrast between (A) and (B) has pictorial analogues. Compare a picture (X) showing a fish or several of them swimming in a lake, and a picture (Y) of a fishy lake, one which obviously (let us assume) contains fish, although no fish are actually shown. Both pictures make it fictional that there are fish in a lake. But (X), it seems, represents one or several particular fish and (Y) does not. (It is less easy to say whether a picture showing a fisherman in the process of landing a catch but not the fish represents a particular fish, although it clearly does not *depict* one.)

Don Quixote and *Seated Woman* are like story (A) and picture (X), and so are *Julius Caesar* and the portrait of Stravinsky. They do not make fictional, ask us to imagine, just that there is something or other of a certain sort. When we say that Don Quixote mistook windmills for giants or that Picasso's seated woman is clasping her hands, we seem to have in mind a particular (fictional) person: *the* Don Quixote of Cervantes' novel and *the* seated woman in Picasso's painting. We do not yet have a viable alternative to the idea that *there are* fictitious entities, nonactual objects of representations, an alternative that would prevent the collapse of the distinction between *Don Quixote, Seated Woman*, story (A), and picture (X) on the one hand, and representations like story (B) and picture (Y) on the other.

I will work toward such an alternative in Part Four. But it is now possible to sketch a way of understanding the difference between representations of the two sorts which seems to me to render less pressing the need to recognize fictitious objects. The difference lies not in what fictional truths the representations generate, I suggest, but rather in the games of make-believe that are to be played with them.

When a viewer sees picture (X), it is fictional in her game that she sees and thereby identifies a (particular) fish. But it is fictional in the game one plays with picture (Y) merely that one sees a fishy lake and perhaps infers that there must be fish in it. Although the reader of story (A) does not, fictionally, *see* a ghost, it is fictional that he knows about one, that he has *de re* knowledge of a ghost. This is not fictional of the reader of story (B); fictionally, he knows only that there are ghosts in the mansion. If story (A) has a narrator, it may be fictional that the reader is told about a ghost by him, that the reader knows it as the ghost the narrator speaks of. If there is no narrator, it will still be fictional that the reader knows of a ghost, although it may be indeterminate how fictionally he knows of it.

This is not a difference in the worlds of the works. It is fictional in both stories and both pictures just that there is something or are things—ghosts or fish—of a certain sort. The difference is in what is fictional about the appreciator, and these fictional truths belong not to the work worlds but to the worlds of the appreciators' games.

This difference is not the essential one, however. When one sees picture (X), not only is one to imagine that one sees a fish, but one is to imagine this from the inside. This means, in part, that one is to imagine *seeing* a fish, and thus *knowing* about one. (See § 1.4.) The reader of (A) imagines knowing about a ghost, not just *that* he knows about one. The viewer of (Y) and the reader of (B) engage in no such imaginings. The games appreciators play, the games that are to be played with the works, are thus different in a way that goes beyond any difference in what propositions are fictional in the game worlds. Not only is the appreciator of (A) or (X) to imagine certain propositions, but he is to imagine them in a certain manner.

To imagine a ghost or a fish or a squirrel is, I suggest, to imagine knowing about a (particular) ghost or fish or squirrel. (Perhaps it is, more specifically, to imagine this from the inside.) So we can say (as I did originally) that representations "about a particular ghost" are ones that serve as props in games in which one is to imagine a ghost.[23]

We can now appreciate the similarity between representations about actual things and ones that seem to be about merely fictional ones. The reader of *Don Quixote* imagines knowing about an errant knight of that name, as the reader of *Julius Caesar* imagines knowing of a certain Julius Caesar. On viewing either *Seated Woman* or the portrait of Stravinsky, one imagines seeing and thus identifying a particular person. Although in two of these cases one *actually* knows about a particular person and in the other two one does not, there being no one to know about, in all of them one imagines doing so. All four representations thus go beyond merely making it fictional that there is someone of a certain sort.

We can see also why it may not especially matter whether or not a cave painting has an (actual) person for an object, or whether we think it does. The difference consists in whether we are to imagine of some actual person that we see him. But in either case we are to imagine seeing someone.

We have managed to hold off, at least temporarily, the demands of fictitious objects of representation for recognition. The crucial question, so far, is whether imagining a ghost, for instance, requires that

23. If a picture prescribes imagining a fish and to imagine a fish is to imagine (oneself) seeing a fish, it prescribes an imagining about oneself. Doesn't this put the viewer in the work-world? No. There is no particular person such that the picture mandates imagining about him or her; the person who is to be imagined seeing a fish is different for each viewer. (Compare "you" used in novels such as Calvino's *If on a Winter's Night a Traveler* to refer to the reader.) The picture does seem to prescribe imagining, to make fictional the proposition that *someone* sees a fish, however. I treat worries like this in §6.5.

there be a (fictional or imaginary) ghost for one to imagine. Certainly imagining that one sees a ghost does not, and it seems unlikely that imagining seeing a ghost should. But the case is by no means closed.

It may be best for now, however, to assume that fictitious entities *do* exist. A premature embrace of (what I take to be) the correct ontological position may be more seriously distorting than acceptance of an incorrect one. We must be sure that our alternative gives a clear view of the sources of the powerful inclination to reify fictions against our better judgment, and that it provides viable ways of doing the theoretical work fictitious entities are called on to do in theories that recognize them. The reader will have noticed that in accepting statements such as "It is fictional that Gregory discovered the bear hiding in the underbrush" and "It is *Tom Sawyer*-fictional that Tom attended his own funeral," we appear committed to there being fictitious entities: a bear such that fictionally Gregory discovered it and a person referred to as Tom who, fictionally, attended his own funeral. This commitment will be removed in Chapter 10, where statements like these will be ruled out as ill formed. We will have to explain what is meant by their everyday relatives such as "In *Tom Sawyer* Tom attended his own funeral," why they do not represent a commitment to a fictional Tom, why it is so difficult to get along without speaking in this way, and why this does not matter as far as the ontological question is concerned. Until then I will continue to speak in this way, pretending that there are such things as Tom Sawyer and fictitious bears.

4

The Mechanics of Generation

The greatness of critics like Bazin in France and Agee in America
may have something to do with their using their full range of
intelligence and intuition, rather than relying on formulas.
Criticism is an art, not a science, and a critic who follows rules
will fail in one of his most important functions: perceiving what
is original and important in *new* work and helping others to see.
                                                    —Pauline Kael,
                                          I Lost It at the Movies

4.1. PRINCIPLES OF GENERATION

How do we decide what is fictional in a given representation? As we all know, interpretation even at this basic level is frequently uncertain and subject to dispute. Is it fictional that Hamlet
suffers Oedipal guilt? Is it fictional that Macbeth really sees a dagger
or just that he hallucinates one? What, fictionally, is the expression
worn by the Mona Lisa?

Representations generate fictional truths by virtue of their features—the marks on the surface of a painting, the words of a novel,
occurrences on stage during the performance of a play—in accordance with applicable principles of generation. Some disagreements
about what is fictional derive from the failure of one party to notice
crucial features, and are sometimes resolved when these are pointed
out. But many disagreements persist. It is not because anyone has
failed to notice some of the words in Shakespeare's play that Hamlet's
Oedipality is a matter of dispute. There is uncertainty and disagree-
ment, in many cases, about what principles of generation are applicable to a given work.

In this chapter we will observe what we can about the principles of
generation in effect for representations of various kinds. My aim is
not to settle particular interpretive questions; many of them do not
admit of definitive resolution in any case. But we may hope to
improve our understanding of the disputes by clarifying the principles
on which conflicting interpretive claims rest. Beyond that, we will
want to see how the particular forms which the machinery of genera-

tion take accord with the conception of the overall nature of the institution of representation I am developing. This will involve not only observing what principles of generation are at work but also reflecting on why we have the ones we do.

Critics and appreciators rarely have definite principles explicitly in mind, even when they are confident about what fictional truths a work generates; nor do artists consult formulas in order to fashion works so as to make them generate the fictional truths they want generated. Often it just strikes us that, given the words of a novel or the paint on a stretch of canvas, such and such is fictional. Insofar as we do have reasons, what we are conscious of being guided by is a diverse assortment of particular considerations which seem somehow reasonable in one or another specific case.

But rules can operate beneath the surface, and superficial diversity sometimes obscures underlying order. Is there a relatively simple and systematic way of understanding how fictional truths are generated, a limited number of very general principles that implicitly govern the practice of artists and critics? I doubt that any experienced critic will consider this a live possibility. I do not think it is a live possibility. But some theorists have sought such general principles and have made at least tentative suggestions as to what they are.[1] (In the background are worries about how there could be even as much agreement as there is, how we could learn to extract fictional truths from new works as confidently as in many cases we do, unless there is at some level a reasonably simple relationship between features and fictional truths.) Our examination of these suggestions will reinforce the suspicion that the search is in vain, and will foster a healthy respect for the complexity and subtlety of the means by which fictional truths are generated.

The observations of this chapter are not to be construed as contributions to an understanding of the nature of fictionality, of what it is for a proposition to be fictional. We have already dealt with that question. A proposition's fictionality consists in a prescription to imagine it. Our present interest is in the means by which such prescriptions are established, the machinery of various familiar representational genres for generating fictional truths. It is one thing to explain what it means to signal a left turn and quite another to observe how, in a particular cultural context, one goes about doing

1. "Which states of affairs are to be reckoned as included within the world of a given work of art? . . . In pursuing the answer to this question I shall be looking for a general rule, a principle." (Wolterstorff, *Works and Worlds*, p. 115.)

so. Our present task is analogous to the latter. In our society one can signal a left turn either by activating suitably placed blinking lights or by extending one's left arm. There could be conventions whereby left-turn signals—in the very same sense of the phrase—are effected by throwing red balloons into the street or barking like a dog. The contingent means by which fictional truths are generated in one or another social context have no bearing on what it means for a proposition to be fictional. I suspect that failure clearly to separate the two has encouraged the futile hope that there is, that there must somehow be, a simple and systematic way of understanding the mechanics of generation.

Although our present focus is on the generation of fictional truths, we must keep in mind that the interest and significance of representational works of art does not reside in them alone. The critic or appreciator needs to be sensitive to a work's features—the look of a painting, the sound of a poem—apart from their contributions to the generation of fictional truths. There are also the overall themes, morals, admonishments, insights, and visions for which a work's fictional truths are in part (*only* in part) responsible. How much emphasis is accorded one or another fictional truth is also significant, as we shall see, and so is the manner in which fictional truths are generated, including what principles of generation are operative in particular cases. The machinery of generation is not just a means of cranking out fictional truths; it and its operation are open to inspection by the appreciator, and are not infrequently more interesting than the fictional truths that result. Much of the artistry of the painter's or novelist's work consists in the means he discovers for generating fictional truths.

4.2.   DIRECT AND INDIRECT GENERATION

Fictional truths can be generated either *directly* or *indirectly*. I call directly generated ones *primary* and indirectly generated ones *implied*.

Goya's *No Se Puede Mirar* from *The Disasters of War* shows the bound victims of an execution by firing squad and the muzzles of guns pointing at them. It does not show the soldiers wielding the guns; they are outside the picture frame. Yet there can be no doubt that there are soldiers (or anyway people) holding the guns. We know that there are because of the position of the guns. It would be perverse, a willful misinterpretation, to maintain that the guns are hanging in midair.

The fact that fictionally the guns are pointing at the prisoners is more than a reason for believing it to be fictional that soldiers are wielding them; it *makes* this so. The position of the guns is responsible for the presence of the soldiers in the picture world; it is fictional that there are soldiers because it is fictional that there are guns positioned as they are. The former fictional truth is thus dependent on, implied by, the latter; it is generated indirectly.

At the end of Joseph Conrad's novel *The Secret Agent* Mrs. Verloc commits suicide by jumping from a cross-Channel ferry. Nowhere in the novel is it said in so many words that she does this. But her suicide is clearly indicated in the following passage, together with the fact, established earlier, that she was traveling to the Continent:

> Ossipon, as if suddenly compelled by some mysterious force, pulled a much-folded newspaper out of his pocket. The Professor raised his head at the rustle.
> "What's that paper? Anything in it?" he asked.
> Ossipon started like a scared somnambulist.
> "Nothing. Nothing whatever. The thing's ten days old. I forgot it in my pocket, I suppose."
> But he did not throw the old thing away. Before returning it to his pocket he stole a glance at the last lines of a paragraph. They ran thus: *"An impenetrable mystery seems destined to hang for ever over this act of madness or despair."*
> Such were the end words of an item of news headed: "Suicide of Lady Passenger from a cross-Channel Boat." Comrade Ossipon was familiar with the beauties of its journalistic style.[2]

The fact that fictionally this headline appeared in a newspaper shortly after Mrs. Verloc had embarked for the Continent (together with certain other circumstances) makes it fictional that Mrs. Verloc committed suicide. It is fictional that she jumped from the boat because it is fictional that the headline read as it did;[3] the latter fictional truth implies the former.

Fictional truths on which others are based may themselves depend on still more basic ones. The fact that fictionally the newspaper contained the revealing headline is probably implied by the fact that fictionally the narrator reported that it did. That fictionally there are

---

2. *The Secret Agent*, p. 249.
3. This is not to say that fictionally it is because of the headline that she jumped. Nor is the world of Goya's print a peculiar one in which the existence of soldiers depends on the existence and position of guns.

guns aimed at the prisoners may be implied by the fact that fictionally there *appear* to be guns so aimed. It may not be easy to find incontrovertible examples of *primary* fictional truths, ones generated directly by marks on canvas or words on paper rather than via the generation of others. But it will be convenient to assume, temporarily (see § 4.4), that there must be such, that every representation generates a core of primary fictional truths that depend on no others, and that are responsible, indirectly, for whatever other fictional truths it generates.[4]

Fictional truths breed like rabbits. The progeny of even a few primary ones can furnish a small world rather handsomely. We are usually entitled to assume that characters have blood in their veins, just because they are people, even if their blood is never mentioned or described or shown or portrayed. It is fictional in *La Grande Jatte* that the couple strolling in the park eat and sleep and work and play; that they have friends and rivals, ambitions, satisfactions, and disappointments; that they live on a planet that spins on its axis and circles the sun, one with weather and seasons, mountains and oceans, peace and war, industry and agriculture, poverty and plenty; and so on and on and on. All this is implied, in the absence of contrary indications, by the fact that fictionally they are human beings.

Many such implied fictional truths are generated more or less by default, and many are of no particular interest (although if it were fictional that people did *not* have blood in their veins or births or ambitions, *this* fictional truth would be noteworthy). Some indirectly generated fictional truths are needed as background, even if they are not to be focused on. We have seen how a novelist can, economically and without undue emphasis, make it fictional that a large industrial city in an island nation with democratic and imperialist traditions and so on is the setting for various events simply by arranging for it to be fictional that they occur in London. The latter fictional truth implies all the others.

Implied fictional truths are by no means invariably or even typically relegated to the background, however. Sometimes the most prominent and significant ones are generated indirectly. A few offhand remarks by a character or a telling gesture may establish, elegantly and precisely, crucial characteristics of his personality or motives. Fictional truths of central interest in a portrait—ones concerning mood, tension, repose, resignation—may be implied by fictional

4. Some fictional truths depend partly on others and partly on features of the work, independently of their generation of other fictional truths.

truths about the topography of the sitter's face. Indeed, implied fictional truths may vastly overshadow those on which they depend. The latter sometimes have little or no significance apart from what they imply; we may not attend to or even notice them while marveling at their progeny. Readers of a novel may be struck powerfully by a character's determination or insecurity or optimism without being able to say, or caring, what fictional truths concerning his actions or words or others' comments about him are responsible for it. Even close inspection of a painting may fail to reveal which fictional truths about the lay of a person's face imply fictional truths, themselves utterly obvious, about his expression or mood—or indeed whether the latter are implied by the former at all rather than generated in some other way. It is clearly misleading to say that, in general, appreciators *infer* implied fictional truths from those on which they are based. Sometimes the very indirectness of its generation gives a fictional truth prominence, especially when it would be easy to generate it more directly; a little coyness in constructing representations, here as elsewhere, whets the appetite and focuses attention.

Implication is close to indispensable for the generation of certain fictional truths in certain media. How can silent movies portray sounds, or paintings and still photographs movement? In Sternberg's *Docks of New York* the sudden rising of a flock of birds establishes that a shot has been fired, with no help from a soundtrack.[5] It may be fictional in a picture that someone is running or jumping because it is fictional that both of her feet are off the ground simultaneously, in a configuration most unlikely for someone who is not running or jumping.

In addition to warning against taking directly generated fictional truths to be, in general, either more important or more obvious than indirectly generated ones, or supposing that their discovery is less inferential, we must be careful not to identify primary fictional truths with ones that are made "explicit" in the work nor to presume that implied ones are presented "implicitly." We shall see that the fictionality of what a novel explicitly "says" or a picture explicitly "shows," if it is fictional at all, may well depend on the fictionality of propositions the work expresses only "implicitly." (See § 4.4.) By "indirectly generated" fictional truths I mean simply ones that depend on other fictional truths; "primary" or "directly generated" ones do not. Let's not jump to conclusions about what else goes with being primary or implied.

5. Arnheim, *Film as Art*, p. 107.

Our investigation of the machinery by which fictional truths are generated will have to take account of principles of two different kinds: principles of direct generation, which say simply that if a work has or contains certain words or marks or whatever, such-and-such propositions will be fictional, and principles of implication, which specify what fictional truths are implied given the core of primary ones. Let us look first at principles of implication.

4.3.   PRINCIPLES OF IMPLICATION

What determines which fictional truths imply which others? Given a representation's core of primary fictional truths, how do we decide what else it generates? Are there simple and comprehensive principles of implication to go by? Two such principles have been proposed (in various formulations) and discussed fairly extensively, especially in connection with literary representations: the *Reality Principle* and the *Mutual Belief Principle*.[6] Both will turn out to be seriously inadequate when measured against the subtleties and complexities of actual implications. Nevertheless, many implications do conform to one or the other of them, and recognizable variants are at work in some other cases.

The Reality Principle

> Fairy-stories . . . are . . . stories about Fairy, that is *Faërie*, the realm or state in which fairies have their being. *Faërie* contains many things besides elves and fays, and besides dwarfs, witches, trolls, giants, or dragons: it holds the seas, the sun, the moon, the sky; and the earth, and all things that are in it: tree and bird, water and stone, wine and bread, and ourselves, mortal men, when we are enchanted.
>
> J. R. R. Tolkien, "On Fairy-Stories"

The basic strategy which the Reality Principle attempts to codify is that of making fictional worlds as much like the real one as the core of

6. Beardsley, *Aesthetics*, pp. 242–247, and Woods, *Logic of Fiction*, pp. 64–65. More thorough developments of the two principles are to be found in Lewis, "Truth in Fiction," and Wolterstorff, *Works and Worlds*, although their ways of setting up the problem are rather different from mine; in particular, they do not draw the distinction between (what I call) primary and implied fictional truths in the way that I do. Ryan, "Fiction, Non-Factuals, and Minimal Departure," discusses a principle akin to the Reality Principle.

primary fictional truths permits. It is because people in the real world have blood in their veins, births, and backsides that fictional characters are presumed to possess these attributes. Depressing piano keys is understood to have the same effect in fictional worlds that it has in the real one, so long as nothing in the directly generated fictional truths indicates otherwise. So when in Eisenstein's silent film *Potemkin* it is fictional that a person steps on the keys of a piano, it is implied that fictionally piano sounds are produced. A likely corollary of the Reality Principle is that implications follow the lines of what would be legitimate inferences in the real world: If we could legitimately infer q from p, we can legitimately infer the fictionality of q from the fictionality of p, since the latter fictional truth will imply the former.

Here is a working formulation of the Reality Principle (RP):

If $p_1, \ldots, p_n$ are the propositions whose fictionality a representation generates directly, another proposition, q, is fictional in it if, and only if, were it the case that $p_1, \ldots, p_n$, it would be the case that q.

The interpreter is to ask what the real world would be like if the propositions whose fictionality is generated directly were true: What else would be true if they were? The answers give the propositions whose fictionality the primary fictional truths imply. I understand the counterfactual "Were it the case that $p_1, \ldots, p_n$, it would be the case that q" along Stalnaker-Lewis lines, to mean, approximately, that a possible world in which $p_1, \ldots, p_n$ are true and q is also is more like the real world than any possible world in which $p_1, \ldots, p_n$ are true and q is false.[7] Hence the charge to the critic to minimize differences between fictional worlds and the real one. Readers who prefer to understand counterfactuals in other ways will take the Reality Principle (let's call it RP) as formulated to validate different implications and may want to make corresponding adjustments in the formulation.[8] But it will not be necessary for our purposes to go very far into the details of how exactly the Reality Principle is to be construed.

It is important to note that what is implied, according to RP, depends on the body of primary fictional truths as a whole, not on

7. Stalnaker, "Theory of Conditionals"; Lewis, *Counterfactuals*.

8. Some may think that were a person to step on the keys of a piano, it would be only *likely* or *probable* that piano sounds would be emitted. They might preserve the intuition that it is fictional in *Potemkin* that such sounds positively *were* emitted by adopting something like Charles Karelis' "Probability Hardening" principle ("The Las Meninas Literature," p. 112).

just one or several selected members of it.[9] This is as it should be. A particular fictional truth is rarely if ever sufficient by itself to establish the fictionality of any other proposition; its expected implications can be canceled or defeated by other fictional truths. Ordinarily the fact that fictionally a character has human parents implies, in accordance with familiar laws of nature, that fictionally the character is human and not a frog or an insect or a rhinoceros or a pumpkin. But this implication is blocked in Ionesco's *Rhinoceros,* Kafka's *Metamorphosis,* and numerous fairy tales. The text of *Metamorphosis* indicates specifically that Gregor is an insect (after his transformation), even though his parents are human. We will go wrong if we look at particular fictional truths in isolation and ask what things would be like were they true, in order to decide what fictional truths are generated indirectly.

Does this mean that the appreciator or critic must begin the task of interpretation by compiling an exhaustive list of the work's primary fictional truths, and only then proceed to trace their implications? Obviously we *do not* do this, and we cannot be expected to. There is no assurance that the primary fictional truths are finite in number or finitely specifiable, nor that they are all accessible to any ordinary examination of the work.[10] Moreover, whether a particular fictional truth belongs in the list of primary ones is sometimes a very tricky question, and may have no definite answer.

Usually a small subset of the primary core is particularly responsible for a given implication, even if it is not sufficient by itself, and when a fictional truth depends on other indirectly generated ones, it usually rests especially on one or several of them (which of course depend in turn on primary ones). The fact that fictionally someone steps on the keys of a piano, whether or not this is primary, may be said to imply prima facie that fictionally piano sounds are emitted. The implication would be defeated by, for instance, a shot of the innards of the piano showing that the strings are missing, but in the absence of such interference, it goes through. Although the fact that fictionally someone steps on piano keys does not guarantee that fictionally piano sounds are emitted, it shifts the burden of proof to any who would deny it.

9. See Wolterstorff, *Works and Worlds,* p. 128.

10. A picture may have primary fictional truths that only microscopic analysis would reveal, and it may be that nothing short of absolutely precise discrimination of its features would reveal all of its primary fictional truths. See Goodman, *Languages of Art.*

What appreciators and critics do is, roughly, to focus on a selection of fictional truths that the representation seems unquestionably to generate, without worrying about whether it generates them directly or indirectly and without presuming that they exhaust the primary core, and to note their prima facie implications. One can often be reasonably sure that nothing in the core of primary fictional truths defeats them. This requires sensitivity to the work as a whole but nothing like a complete inventory of the primary fictional truths. There are many details concerning the clothing worn by characters in *Potemkin* that viewers will not have noticed when they judge that fictionally piano sounds are emitted. But they can be reasonably confident that none of these fictional truths or the primary ones they are based on—nor any fictional truths about the color of the piano or the exact force (beyond a certain minimum) with which the keys are depressed—interfere with the implication.

So it would seem to be the following rule of thumb, sanctioned by RP, that primarily guides critical practice:

> The fictionality of $r_1, \ldots, r_n$ (whether generated directly or indirectly) prima facie implies the fictionality of q if, and only if, were it the case that $r_1, \ldots, r_n$, it would be the case that q.

Suggestions along the lines of the Reality Principle have been faulted for authorizing an unwarranted proliferation of fictional truths.[11] It appears to force on us far more fictional truths than critics do or should recognize.

It is usually assumed that a contradiction entails everything, and often that a proposition counterfactually implies whatever it entails. It follows quickly that, according to RP, if there is a contradiction among the propositions whose fictionality a work generates directly, everything will be fictional in it. It is hard to avoid the conclusion that everything is fictional in any work in which contradictory propositions are fictional, whether they are primary or not. This is disconcerting. Although it is fictional, arguably, in *False Perspective* (figure 1.2) that a woman is and is not within reach of a man whose pipe she is lighting, it seems entirely unreasonable to suppose that fictionally the woman is at the same time throwing confetti out the window, or that the water under the bridge is not water but blood, or that there are

---

11. For example by Parsons, *Non-Existent Objects*, pp. 177–178, and Wolterstorff, *Works and Worlds*, pp. 117–118.

goblins on Jupiter. Moreover, if everything is fictional when contradictions are, *False Perspective* and H. G. Wells's novel *The Time Machine* will contain precisely the same fictional truths.

Several responses are available. We might find a way of construing counterfactuals so that not all of those with contradictory antecedents turn out to be true. (It is not intuitively obvious that "If a woman is and is not within reach of a man, there would be goblins on Jupiter" should be counted true.) We might reformulate the Reality Principle to block undesired implications.[12] Or we might learn to live with the consequences of the principle as it stands.[13] (After all, shouldn't we expect contradictory fictional worlds to be exotic?)

The danger of excessive proliferation is not limited to contradictory fictional worlds, however. The real world is a very big place. If fictional worlds are as much like it as their primary fictional truths allow, most of them will include most of it. So the world of even—or rather especially!—the sketchiest story or picture will turn out to be vastly richer, vastly more detailed, than anyone would have dreamed. It will be fictional in "Goldilocks and the Three Bears" that Tenzing and Hillary achieved the first ascent of Mount Everest and Neil Armstrong the first landing on the moon. Every detail of Marco Polo's adventures, of the San Francisco earthquake and fire, of the Watergate scandal, of countless other exciting, poignant, tragic, and mundane real-life dramas will belong to the world of "Three Blind Mice."[14]

Rather than banishing all this clutter from fictional worlds, I propose to ignore it. We need to recognize enormous differences in the importance of a work's various fictional truths, in any case. Some are emphasized and highlighted; others remain in the shadows. There

---

12. This is Wolterstorff's strategy in *Works and Worlds*.

13. As Lewis proposes in "Truth in Fiction." This is not as hard as it seems when we realize that of the fictional truths generated by a given work, some may be emphasized more than others. Still, among the fictional truths we will have to tolerate is the fact that it is *False Perspective*-fictional that the woman is not holding a candle, as well as the fact that fictionally she is.

14. Before celebrating the story's newly discovered excitement, we will realize that Marco Polo's adventures recur repetitively in the world of nearly every work, and that they are buried in a vast array of excruciatingly boring episodes also borrowed from real life, such as my most recent visit to a grocery store. Also, no credit is due the artist or the work, so there is no cause for admiration.

A narrower conception of counterfactuals than Lewis' (one such that their truth requires some significant connection between the antecedent and the consequent) or an appropriate reformulation of RP could block this mass immigration from reality, but not without our backing off from the idea that similarities between fictional worlds and the real one are to be maximized.

are major and minor characters, central events and peripheral ones. Needless to say, what is major or central *in a novel* (or picture, or whatever) need not be what would be most significant in the course of history, were the events of the novel actually to transpire. Nor do I have in mind what *fictionally* is more or less significant. In a story about a peasant family living in a great kingdom, it may be fictional that the king is, for good or ill, a central figure in the course of history, that the fate of nations depends on him; and it may be fictional that the peasants are insignificant from a historical perspective. Yet the peasants may be central to the story and the king peripheral. The story may be primarily about the peasant family, with the king serving only as part of the setting in which they live their lives. Charles Kinbote is a central character, the narrator and main protagonist of Nabokov's *Pale Fire,* but it is fictional that he is an insignificant buffoon. Representations do not just present us with a collection of fictional truths; they order and arrange them for us, focusing on some more than others. To pay undue attention to the latter at the expense of the former can be as much a distortion of the work as getting the fictional truths wrong. (Part of the point of Tom Stoppard's *Rosenkrantz and Guildenstern Are Dead* is that it reverses the emphases of *Hamlet,* making minor characters major and major ones minor.)

So we can safely admit Marco Polo, the San Francisco earthquake, Watergate, and all the rest into the world of "Three Blind Mice," provided that we acknowledge their position in the deep background of the story. They will not bother us if we leave them alone. *False Perspective* and *The Time Machine* are enormously different even if they generate exactly the same fictional truths; they differ in which of their fictional truths they highlight.

Some prefer devising a way of excluding unimportant fictional truths entirely to declaring them thoroughly deemphasized.[15] I have no strenuous objection to the former, but I favor deemphasis. On my suggestion we need not even imagine that there is a sharp break somewhere between those features of the real world that are related closely enough to the action of a story to be included in its fictional world and those that are not; and we can easily recognize the finest variations in degree of emphasis and deemphasis. It would be considerably more awkward to retreat to a meta-level and speak of its

15. Routley opts for including only very limited chunks of the real world in fictional ones, "enough to encompass the material the work alludes to or relies upon . . . , enough to enable the story to be understood and avert certain misunderstandings, and no more" (*Exploring Meinong's Jungle,* p. 542).

being more and less plausible that a given real-world truth is or is not included in the fictional world.

This solution may save the Reality Principle some embarrassment. But it poses another question beyond that of what fictional truths a work generates: What determines which of a work's fictional truths are important and which are not? A lot can be said on this score, no doubt, but I would not expect or demand a systematic answer to this question any more than to the question of how the mechanics of generation work.

The reprieve for the Reality Principle is only temporary. We shall see shortly that it must sometimes give way to the Mutual Belief Principle. But more serious objections to both of them are waiting in the wings. Let us keep in mind James Thurber's satirical warning against indiscriminate application of the Reality Principle.

> "I don't think for a moment that Macbeth did it . . . I don't think for a moment that he killed the King," she said . . . "Who do you suspect?" I asked . . . "Macduff," she said, promptly.
>
> "Oh Macduff did it, all right . . . Do you know who discovered Duncan's body? . . . Macduff discovers it . . . Then he comes running downstairs and shouts, 'Confusion has broke open the Lord's anointed temple' and 'Sacrilegious murder has made his masterpiece' and on and on like that . . . All that stuff was rehearsed . . . You wouldn't say a lot of stuff like that, offhand, would you—if you had found a body? . . . You wouldn't! Unless you had practiced it in advance. 'My God, there's a body in here!' is what an innocent man would say."[16]

The Mutual Belief Principle

A storyteller, in a culture in which it is universally and firmly agreed that the earth is flat and that to venture too far out to sea is to risk falling off, invents a yarn about bold mariners who do sail far out to sea. No mention is made in the story of the shape of the earth or the danger. That would be unnecessary, the teller thinks, for he and his audience assume the earth in the story to be shaped as they believe it is in reality. All take it to be implied that fictionally there is, somewhere in the vast ocean, a precipice to nothingness.

Must we, on authority of the Reality Principle, correct their understanding of the story along with their geography? The propositions

16. "The Macbeth Murder Mystery," pp. 81–82.

whose fictionality is generated directly are (I will suppose) such that their truth would not affect the shape of the earth; the earth would (still) be roughly spherical, as it actually is, not flat. So, according to RP, it is fictional that the earth is spherical and that there is no danger of falling off. But to insist on this, to wrench the story from its original context and force on it an interpretation neither the author nor the most perceptive of his intended listeners could have divined, would seem contrived and gratuitously uncharitable. And to do so would ruin a good adventure story; the tale (let us assume) depends on the danger for its dramatic effect. Better to go along with the misconception about the shape of the earth for purposes of understanding and appreciating the story, and allow that fictionally the earth does have a dangerous edge.

In making implied fictional truths depend on facts of nature, the Reality Principle loosens the artist's control over them. If he happens to be mistaken about the relevant facts, his fictional worlds will not turn out as he intends. This would be unfortunate in many instances, since artists whose works are worth experiencing at all can be expected to have good judgment about what sorts of fictional worlds are likely to be interesting or valuable. Why not give the artist a free hand in constructing fictional worlds, rather than permitting chance in the form of unknown facts of nature to help shape them?

The unattractiveness of construing the flat-earth story as the Reality Principle would dictate suggests that principles giving the artist more reliable control over what is fictional than it does are indeed at work. Lewis and Wolterstorff both suggest alternatives to (their versions of) the Reality Principle with something like this in mind. Lewis' second principle bases implications on what is "overtly" believed in the work's community of origin rather than on the real world as it actually is.[17] Wolterstorff's bases them on what the author "assumes the bulk of his intended audience" believes about the real world.[18] Here is a Mutual Belief Principle (MBP) patterned after Lewis' proposal:

If $p_1, \ldots, p_n$ are the propositions whose fictionality a representation generates directly, another proposition, q, is fictional in it if and only if it is mutually believed in the artist's society that were it the case that $p_1, \ldots, p_n$, it would be the case that q,

which sanctions its own rule of thumb:

17. "Truth in Fiction," p. 273.
18. *Works and Worlds*, pp. 123–124.

The fictionality of $r_1, \ldots, r_n$ (whether generated directly or indirectly) prima facie implies the fictionality of q if and only if it is mutually believed in the artist's society that were $r_1, \ldots, r_n$ true, q would be true.

(Something is "mutually believed" in a society if, roughly, most members of the society believe it, most of them believe that most of them believe it, most believe that most believe that most believe it, and so on.)[19]

Why must the belief be mutual? Why not require just that the relevant counterfactual be believed widely in the artist's society whether or not people are aware that others believe it, or only that the artist himself believe it? Either of these options would make fictional worlds insufficiently accessible to appreciators and give an unfair advantage to critics who happen to be mind readers. The first would also take fictional worlds out of the artist's control, insofar as he must guess what others believe. Hence the need for beliefs of a more social sort.

MBP directs us to extrapolate so as to maximize similarities between fictional worlds and the real world not as it actually is but as it is or was mutually believed to be in the artist's society.[20] If in the society in which the flat-earth story is told and heard it is mutually believed that the earth is flat, the story implies that fictionally the adventurers are in danger of falling off the edge, the actual sphericity of the earth notwithstanding. Our superior geographical knowledge need not ruin the excitement for us.

MBP needs refinement. In paintings, fictional truths about characters' physical characteristics imply fictional truths about their personalities, moods, and other psychological states. But it is arguable that none of us, and almost no one in any artist's society, possesses very detailed *beliefs* about what a person's personality or mood would be like were he to have a certain expression on his face. We are nevertheless able to *recognize* personalities and moods when we perceive a person's expression (though we may not notice the relevant details of his expression). MBP might be revised to base some implications on the propensities of members of the artist's society to recognize moods from physical expressions, for instance, rather than on their beliefs about the connections between them. I will not try to devise a better

19. I use Schiffer's phrase "mutual belief" in place of Lewis' "overt belief." See Lewis, "Truth in Fiction," p. 272; Lewis, *Convention,* pp. 52–60; Schiffer, *Meaning,* pp. 30–42.
20. At least it does so given the Stalnaker-Lewis account of counterfactuals.

formulation, however. MBP can be taken to stand for a class of plausible principles according to which implications depend on one or another feature of the cognitive makeup of members of the artist's society. It is a crude first attempt, but it will serve well enough to contrast principles of this sort with the Reality Principle and others.

Is the Mutual Belief Principle an improvement over the Reality Principle? Certainly its results are more palatable, in more than a few instances, and the practice of interpreters seems in significant respects to presuppose it. Critics rarely undertake extensive investigations into the sometimes esoteric facts of nature on which, according to RP, many fictional truths depend, but they do research the social contexts in which works were produced, including the beliefs of the artist and his cohorts.

There are good reasons why we should expect implications to be governed by something more like MBP than RP. MBP not only gives the artist better control over what is fictional; it also, in many cases, gives appreciators easier access to it. Appreciators are often in a better position to determine what the artist's society mutually believes than what is true—especially when they belong to that society. The result is that MBP fits better than RP into a conception of representations as vehicles whereby artists guide the imaginings of appreciators, one according to which the artist arranges for his work to make certain propositions fictional in order to encourage appreciators to imagine them, and the appreciator endeavors to imagine what is fictional in order to imagine as the artist meant him to.[21] Of course when both parties share the same misconceptions about reality,[22] artists may succeed perfectly well in directing appreciators' imaginings even if RP is in effect. What the appreciator then takes to be fictional will be what the artist thought he made fictional, and in imagining it the appreciator will be imagining what the artist meant him to. But then the notion of what is *actually* fictional would seem idle. What would be the point of the theorist's insisting that what the artist succeeds in getting the appreciator to imagine, what both take to be fictional, is not really so, not really what the work prescribes the appreciator to

21. There can be no doubt that this is an important purpose of representations, even though, as we saw in Chapter 2, what it is to be a representation, a work of fiction, is not to be explained in such terms.

22. Or if appreciators know what the artist thought was fictional, even if they realize he was mistaken, and then endeavor to imagine not what they take to be fictional but what they take the artist to have thought fictional. Here also the notion of what is really fictional would seem idle.

imagine—*if* the whole purpose of the operation is for the artist successfully to direct the appreciator's imaginings?

Nevertheless, it is by no means obvious that MBP (or some variant) always or even usually takes precedence over RP. MBP is not even applicable to natural representations—clouds, stumps, patterns of stars. In tracing their implications we must, presumably, either go by the mutual beliefs of the community of viewers rather than those of the artist's society or else revert to the Reality Principle. Natural representations are not vehicles whereby artists seek to direct the imaginings of appreciators.[23] But even representations that are such are arguably governed sometimes by RP rather than MBP. It seems to me, moreover, that quite apart from the frequency with which it gives better results, RP plays a more fundamental role in our thinking about representations.

I find it particularly reasonable to prefer RP to MBP when fictional truths having to do with morality are at stake. This suggestion is not unrelated to Hume's contention that, although in treating a work from a previous age we should be tolerant of and make allowance for "innocent peculiarities of manners" and "speculative opinions" with which we no longer agree, and not permit them to detract from the work, we should not tolerate ideas of "morality and decency" we find vicious or perverse. "I cannot, nor is it proper I should, enter into such sentiments," he says, "and however I may excuse the poet . . . I never can relish the composition."[24] Perhaps we are to go by something like the mutual beliefs of the artist's society in tracing implications concerning "factual" matters but by the truth insofar as we can ascertain it when it comes to matters of morality. We must be prepared to assume it to be fictional that bloodletting cures disease, that the sun revolves around the earth, that people think with their hearts, if such is mutually believed in the artist's society and the directly generated fictional truths fail to indicate otherwise, but not that the only good Indian is a dead one or that slavery is just and torture in the service of tyranny humane. Certainly things are not as simple as this, but I expect that many of us will have sympathies in this direction.

If, in a story from a fascist society in which it is firmly and mutually believed that mixing of the races is evil and its repression a moral necessity, it is fictional that people of different races strike up a friendship and are punished by the authorities for doing so, must we set aside our own contrary moral convictions even for the limited purposes of understanding and appreciating the story? Must we allow the story to imply that fictionally the friendship is immoral and its oppression justified? It is by no means evident that we must.[25] Refusing to go along might ruin the story for us, to be sure.[26] But we may be quite willing to have it ruined; we may find it impossible to enjoy going along with such reprehensible sentiments anyway. It is arguable that the story itself is morally perverse in a way that destroys it "aesthetically."

Is it simply that we are unable or unwilling to bring ourselves to imagine propositions we take to be morally perverse, even if we recognize that they are fictional? (Compare the difficulty of bringing oneself to push pins into a photograph or painting of a loved one, notwithstanding a full realization that doing so will harm nothing but the paper.)[27] One might attempt to salvage the Mutual Belief Principle by arguing that it is indeed fictional in the story that the friendship is evil and the punishment just, as that principle decrees, but that we simply cannot stomach complying with the prescription to imagine this. (Some might put this by saying that we are unable or unwilling to take a "purely aesthetic" stance in this case.) But it is equally reasonable, it seems to me, to conclude that there is a "convention," rooted perhaps in the difficulty of imagining what we consider perverse moral doctrines to be true, whereby we are not obliged to do so, a convention making something like RP operative in cases involving morality. Is it that interpretive questions are independent of moral issues and care needs to be taken not to confuse the two, or rather that moral considerations sometimes have interpretive consequences? I do not think that there are good grounds on which to decide.

25. The plausibility of applying one or the other principle to this story may of course depend on features of the example which I have not specified. It may make a difference whether the thought that racial mixing is evil is a central "moral of the story," or whether it is more a vehicle for a study of personalities and human nature, or a backdrop for an adventure involving the danger of punishment from the gods.

26. But it might not. The point of the story might depend on its being fictional that some or all of the characters *consider* racial mixing to be evil but not on its being fictional that they are right. We need not hesitate to accept the former fictional truth.

27. "There needs but a certain turn of thought or imagination to make us enter into all the opinions which . . . prevailed [in the polite writings of another age or country] and relish the sentiments or conclusions derived from them. But a very violent effort is requisite to change our judgment of manners, and excite sentiments of approbation or blame, love or hatred, different from those to which the mind from long custom has been familiarized. And where a man is confident of the rectitude of that moral standard by which he judges, he is justly jealous of it, and will not pervert the sentiments of his heart for a moment in complaisance to any writer whatsoever" (Hume, "Standard of Taste," p. 22).

Some have cited psychoanalytic interpretations foisted on works of unsuspecting pre-Freudian artists as test cases for choosing between principles like RP and MBP.[28] But the bearing of one's choice of principle on such interpretations is far from clear-cut. Let us assume that psychoanalytic theory is basically correct and that behavior such as that which fictionally Hamlet exhibits would, in the real world, justify a diagnosis of severe Oedipal conflict. Were someone to behave thus (and were all of the propositions whose fictionality *Hamlet* generates directly true), he would be Oedipal. Is it then fictional that Hamlet is Oedipal, even though Shakespeare and his fellow Elizabethans were blissfully unaware of Freudian theory? RP would seem to yield a positive answer and MBP a negative one.

But the committed Freudian will surely respond that although Shakespeare and his cohorts knew nothing of Freud, they might have or must have realized unconsciously the truth of much of Freudian theory. *Hamlet* itself may be cited as evidence that Shakespeare did: How could anyone have written that play without an intuitive awareness of the dynamics of Oedipality? The fact that audiences respond to the play may be taken to indicate their intuitive understanding of basic tenets of Freudian theory. Once we go this far, it does not seem farfetched to suppose that Shakespeare and his compatriots realized, implicitly of course, that their understanding of Oedipality was shared by others. Shakespeare must have expected audiences to respond; audiences must have realized that Shakespeare deliberately, if unconsciously, arranged for Hamlet's Oedipality. Soon we have the required mutual belief. So a partisan of MBP might accept the Freudian interpretation of *Hamlet* after all.

The interpretive issue may come down to a question of how to construe MBP: whether mutual beliefs held consciously and explicitly should take precedence over ones held unconsciously. But I suspect that much of the resistance to Freudian interpretations is based on dissatisfaction with Freudian theory itself—either on doubts about the premise that Hamlet's behavior would, in the real world, indicate Oedipality, together with acceptance of the Reality Principle, or on doubts about whether this conditional proposition was mutually believed (unconsciously) by the Elizabethans.

Even if we are sometimes prepared to endorse the implications sanctioned by the Reality Principle over those sanctioned by the Mutual

28. Lewis, "Truth in Fiction," p. 271. See also Wolterstorff, *Works and Worlds*, pp. 120–121.

Belief Principle in cases of conflict, I suspect that the reverse is more often true. Nonetheless, RP figures more importantly in interpretive practice. How is this?

Often there is no conflict. When the relevant mutual beliefs are true, the two principles have the same consequences. And critics who share these beliefs, true or not, will come to the same conclusions whichever principle they employ. We are likely to share the mutual beliefs of the artist's society when it is our own. So our interpretations of works from our own culture are likely to be the same whether we base extrapolations on (what we take to be) facts of nature or on mutual beliefs.

Usually in such cases we go by facts of nature. We tend to take RP as our guide, in practice, when we can get away with it, even if we are prepared to opt for something more like MBP should a conflict arise. Why do we assume that Prince Mishkin and Moll Flanders have blood in their veins? Because that is the way people are—real people and so (ordinarily) fictional ones. That is our ready answer, even if we can be pushed to hold mutual beliefs rather than biological facts responsible for the implication (by being asked whether it would still be fictional that these characters have blood in their veins if we turned out to be mistaken in thinking that real people do). In advising painters how to portray psychological traits by means of physical ones, Leonardo specified what he took to be facts about connections between the two, not beliefs about them (or recognitional capacities):

It is true that the face shows indications of the nature of men, their vices and temperaments. The marks which separate the cheeks from the lips, the nostrils from the nose, and the eye-sockets from the eyes, clearly show whether men are cheerful and often laugh. Men who have few such marks are men who engage in thought. Men whose faces are deeply carved with marks are fierce and irascible and unreasonable. Men who have strongly marked lines between their eyebrows are also irascible. Men who have strongly marked horizontal lines on their foreheads are full of sorrow, whether secret or admitted.[29]

It is only when the results of applying the two principles are likely to differ, typically when we treat works from cultures other than our own, that we are apt to feel the need to replace RP with MBP. Only

29. Leonardo da Vinci, *Treatise on Painting*, quoted in Baxandall, *Painting and Experience*, p. 59.

then do we look to people's beliefs about reality rather than reality itself in tracing implications.

Moreover, the Reality Principle remains in the picture even in cross-cultural contexts when the Mutual Belief Principle guides our extrapolations. Our stated purpose in appealing to MBP is likely to be to recapture a way of understanding the work which members of the artist's society might have achieved using RP. We want to understand Shakespeare from an Elizabethan perspective and Javanese Wayang Kulit (shadow puppet) performances from a traditional Javanese one. I do not mean that we aim to duplicate exactly the (or a) way in which particular people actually understood these works. We may, for instance, hope to be more perceptive in certain respects than some or all of the original audiences were. What we are after is something of an idealization of their understandings—understandings that we might think of them as having striven for. But we do seek to step into Elizabethan or Javanese shoes, to adopt their point of view in some ways, and from *that* standpoint to achieve the best understanding of their works we can manage. The Elizabethans and the Javanese, treating works of their own culture, will have based many of their extrapolations on reality, as best they were able, given the limitations of their knowledge. In order for us to recapture their interpretations or ones they might ideally have arrived at, we must appeal not to reality as *we* believe it to be but to *their* conception of it; we must ourselves use something like MBP. The main rationale behind the employment of the Mutual Belief Principle is to reproduce results that the Reality Principle might have yielded, given the beliefs that are mutual in the artist's society.

But it is not just the results that we are after. The process of using the Reality Principle to obtain them is important too. It is not that we coldly ascertain what was mutually believed in order to figure out what propositions are fictional, which we then proceed to imagine. We imagine sharing those beliefs, believing as the artist's society mutually does or did, and applying RP from that standpoint. We then endorse the results of this imagined application of RP, which coincide approximately with the results of MBP; we extrapolate on the basis of the real world as we imagine taking it to be.

Why this persistent attachment to the Reality Principle? Consciously basing one's extrapolations on RP rather than MBP can have certain advantages. We are not yet in a position to appreciate them fully, but here is the central idea: Appreciators participate in games of make-believe using representations as props. A pervasive and especially important form of participation consists in its being fictional of the appreciator, in his game, that he investigates reality in certain ways. This is fictional by virtue of the manner in which he actually investigates the world of the work. The process of discovering what is fictional in the work makes it fictional of him in the game that he discovers what is true. RP is especially conducive to such participation, since investigations of fictional worlds in accordance with it mirror investigations of the real world.

One quick illustration will have to do for now. On reading a story, Loretta notes that it is fictional that a character, Andy, behaves in certain antisocial ways. She infers that fictionally Andy suffers from an inherited neurological disorder, basing her extrapolation on the Reality Principle, for she thinks that behavior of that sort in a real person would indicate such a disorder. But others suggest that actions of the kind in question, in similar circumstances, are rather to be explained by traumatic childhood experiences, or by chemical imbalances in the brain induced by eating bad mushrooms. Loretta visits a medical library to research the matter. She comes away convinced of her original opinion about the innate neurological basis of antisocial behavior of the relevant variety, and reaffirms her original interpretation of the story.

In reading the story and reflecting on it, Loretta plays a game of make-believe. It is fictional in her game that she notes Andy's antisocial behavior and infers that he suffers from an inherited neurological disorder. Even her library researches are easily integrated into the game, for what she does there is just what she would do to confirm a diagnosis of a real person. Fictionally she consults the latest published findings of leading experts on behavioral disorders to see what light they might shed on Andy's condition.

Things do not go as smoothly when the Mutual Belief Principle is operative. Mabel reads the story and notes that fictionally Andy behaves antisocially. Using MBP, she infers it to be fictional that he is possessed by the devil, for she takes it to be mutually believed in the author's society that such behavior is indicative of possession by the devil. To confirm this inference Mabel consults appropriate historical archives. She comes away convinced that the author's society did indeed mutually believe as she thought they did, and she reaffirms her interpretation of the story.

Mabel, like Loretta, plays a game of make-believe. When she determines that fictionally Andy is possessed, it is fictional in her game that she determines this, and fictionally it is on the basis of Andy's antisocial behavior that she thinks he is possessed. But her historical research does not fit easily into the game. Her attempts to ascertain what was believed in the artist's society about the causes of antisocial behavior, while disregarding how misinformed or prejudiced or self-deceived she (an advocate of modern science and a debunker of old superstitions) thinks their beliefs were, is so unlike diagnosing a real person that it would be awkward to understand her investigation to be, fictionally, an investigation of the causes of Andy's behavior.

Mabel does participate significantly in her game, however. As a result of her archival research she takes it to be fictional that there is a devil who sometimes possesses people and makes them behave anti-socially. And she understands it to be fictional in her game that *she* believes this. She imagines herself believing it. Thus she imagines herself in the shoes of members of the artist's society. Much of her subsequent effort to decide, in accordance with MBP, what, fictionally, is the cause of Andy's behavior is incorporated in her game. She must decide what Andy's problem is, given the picture of human nature which it is now fictional that she holds. Fictionally she reflects on the evidence in light of that picture and arrives at the conclusion that Andy is possessed. But her actual religious convictions and scientific beliefs have been left out of the game, along with her reasons for holding them and the process by which she arrived at them. The historical researches are needed to determine what world view it is to be fictional that she accepts, the shape of the shoes she is to imagine herself in. But this process—her investigation of the beliefs, however batty, of the artist's society—does not itself count easily as fictionally coming to adopt that world view. Loretta can transpose more of what is true (and what she knows to be true) about herself into the world of her game than Mabel can.

The trade-off between the two principles, then, is something like this: The Mutual Belief Principle, understood as the determiner of what fictional truths are implied, gives the artist better control over what is fictional and his immediate audience better access to it, and it better facilitates the use of representations by artists to direct the imaginings of appreciators. The Reality Principle, used by the appreciator to ascertain what fictional truths are implied, makes for richer and more natural participation in his games of make-believe. It is not surprising that both principles should have a significant place in the practice of reputable critics.

When the use of RP can be expected to yield results which accord with MBP, we have it both ways. This occurs, typically, when members of a cognitively homogeneous culture appreciate representations created by the artists among them.

Some readers may have become impatient with my patience with the Reality and Mutual Belief Principles, having noticed counterexamples to them—vast numbers of counterexamples, perhaps. We must remember that our interest in the mechanics of implication goes considerably beyond assessing the validity of these principles. But it is time to look at the counterexamples. We will concentrate first on cases in which it seems evident that certain fictional truths are implied by certain others, but the implication is not sanctioned by either RP or MBP. In § 4.5 we will note examples of the opposite kind: implications that seem not to hold, but ought to according to RP or MBP or both.

Other Implications

> The man who knows how to use a gun is, by movie convention, the man without an ass.
>
> Pauline Kael, *I Lost It at the Movies*

Here are some examples of implications not sanctioned by either the Reality Principle or the Mutual Belief Principle.

(a) Any child can draw a witch. Depicting a woman with a black cape, conical hat, and long nose will usually do the trick. A broomstick, a black cat, and a full moon are clinchers. The fact that fictionally there is a witch is implied by the fact that fictionally there is a woman with a black cape, conical hat, and long nose. But it is not the case that were there (in the real world) a long-nosed woman decked out in black cape and conical hat, even one with a broomstick and a black cat under a full moon, there would be a witch. Nor is this mutually believed in the child's society. Such a person would most likely be a housewife dressed up for a Halloween party, and we all realize this. Even if we take the entire body of propositions whose fictionality the picture generates directly, it is probably neither true nor mutually believed that, were they all true, there would be a witch. Neither the Reality Principle nor the Mutual Belief Principle allows the implication that fictionally there is a witch to go through. Yet there is no question that it does go through. The picture unmistakably depicts a witch.

(b) A line drawing accompanying James Thurber's story "The Unicorn in the Garden" portrays a horselike animal with a single horn in the middle of its forehead. It is obvious (even without help from the story or its title) that, being a unicorn, it is white.[30] But unicorns are mythical beasts, as we all know. If there were in the real world a horselike single-horned animal, it would most likely not be white, and probably no one believes otherwise. (Most similar animals have darker coloration.) It is unquestionably fictional that the animal is white, but neither of our principles condones the implication.

(c) Recall the suicide of Mrs. Verloc on her voyage to the Continent in Conrad's *Secret Agent*. The newspaper headline, "Suicide of Lady Passenger from a cross-Channel Boat," informs the reader of her death. But how can we jump so irresponsibly to the conclusion that she was the victim? We have some additional circumstantial evidence, to be sure. We know that Mrs. Verloc was distraught after having killed her husband, and was afraid of the gallows. Earlier she had contemplated drowning herself in the Thames. Ossipon had abandoned her on the train and stolen her money. But little if any of this additional evidence is needed to establish the fact that fictionally it was Mrs. Verloc who jumped from the ferry. And even this evidence would, in a real case, stand in need of confirmation; there could easily have been another suicidal passenger crossing the Channel the same night. It is doubtful at best that, were a newspaper to carry that headline in those circumstances, it would have been Mrs. Verloc who had jumped (or even that it would have been more likely than not that it was she), and it is no less doubtful that this counterfactual is mutually believed. Yet there is no doubt whatever that, fictionally, the suicide was hers.

(d)   Slithergadee

> The Slithergadee has crawled out of the sea.
> He may catch all the others, but he won't catch me.
> No you won't catch me, old Slithergadee,
> You may catch all the others, but you wo—[31]

The Slithergadee did catch the boastful speaker, and we relish his downfall. We know that it caught him because the boasting stopped abruptly in midword. But what an insanely rash inference! The

---

30. The drawing does not portray the animal as being white by virtue of the whiteness of the paper. See Walton, "Categories of Art."

31. Silverstein, "Slithergadee."

speaker might suddenly have remembered an important appointment or spilled his coffee or swatted a mosquito or hiccoughed; even an attack by a tiger escaped from a circus would be more likely than sudden obliteration by a sea monster called a Slithergadee. The *most* likely explanation for the interruption, in a real-world case, would be that the speaker is reciting a poem which ends in midword!

(e) Readers of fantastic literature accept the most outrageous absurdities on the say-so of narrators and other characters. When in *The Hobbit* various characters speak of a ring that makes its wearer invisible, we unhesitatingly, and rightly, take it to be fictional that they are speaking truly, that there is such a ring.

(f) Saint Sebastian can be identified in medieval and Renaissance depictions by the arrows protruding from his body. But untold thousands of people have died in a similar manner. How can we assume that the depicted victim is Sebastian? A halo, when present, rules out some candidates—General Custer, for instance—and so do details of setting and clothing. But such hints are hardly necessary. Scarcely more than the fact that fictionally someone is pierced by arrows is required, in medieval and Renaissance Christian art, to establish without a shadow of doubt that fictionally the person in question is Saint Sebastian.

(g) In addition to his familiar studies of Renaissance iconography, Panofsky spoke of "a fixed iconography" in silent films of the early twentieth century which "informed the spectator about the basic facts and characters":

> There arose, identifiable by standardized appearance, behavior and attributes, the well-remembered types of the Vamp and the Straight Girl . . . , the Family Man, and the Villain, the latter marked by a black mustache and walking stick. Nocturnal scenes were printed on blue or green film. A checkered tablecloth meant, once and for all, a "poor but honest" milieu; a happy marriage, soon to be endangered by the shadows from the past, was symbolized by the young wife's pouring the breakfast coffee for her husband; the first kiss was invariably announced by the lady's gently playing with her partner's necktie and was invariably accompanied by her kicking out with her left foot.[32]

Obviously the purpose of so many examples is not simply to demonstrate the inadequacy of RP and MBP. But it is clear that those

32. Panofsky, "Style and Medium," p. 254.

principles leave huge portions of accepted critical practice unaccounted for. They do not even come close, either separately or together, to providing a systematic, comprehensive account of the mechanics of implication. It is important to realize how far short of that goal they fall, and also how they fall short of it, how many and how various are the implications they fail to accommodate. Many of the particular forms that implications take will interest us quite apart from their bearing on the fate of RP and MBP.

Some of the examples suggest variants of one or the other principle. Several trade on well-known myths or legends. Although it is neither true nor mutually believed in Thurber's society that were one to come across a single-horned horselike animal it would be a white unicorn, there is a legend mutually recognized in that society in which it is arguable that this is fictional. A principle according to which mutually recognized legends take the place of reality or mutual beliefs may be what grounds the implication in Thurber's sketch.

But it is doubtful that principles modeled straightforwardly on RP and MBP will capture the role myths and legends play in many implications. Although it is fictional in a mutually recognized legend that there are witches and that they have long noses and wear conical hats, it is much less clearly fictional in it that, were there a woman of that description, she would be a witch. Is it part of the legend that there are no Halloween parties, or that nonwitches never dress thus, or even that genuine witches outnumber impostors?

Examples (c), (f), and (d) have more to do with reality as it is or as it was believed to be in the artist's society than with myths or legends, but they accord with neither RP nor MBP: A newspaper headline announcing a suicide from a cross-Channel ferry together with the fact that a certain Mrs. Verloc, in a suicidal frame of mind, was making the crossing at the time would point in her direction, even though this would be far from conclusive. The information that a given person died in a barrage of arrows would be at least a very meager reason in favor of the supposition that he was Saint Sebastian. Stopping suddenly in midword makes it a hair less improbable than it would otherwise be that the speaker was the victim of a monster from the sea. These evidence relations, or the fact that they are mutually believed to be such, clearly have something to do with the success of the implications. But the *strength* of the evidence seems hardly to matter. It is rather its salience, the obviousness of the fact that it is evidence, however insubstantial, that enables the implication to go through. If a person's boasting of immunity from a Slithergadee is abruptly interrupted, the thought of his having been caught by some such monster comes naturally to mind, even though the interruption is a vanishingly insignificant reason to accept that that actually happened.

If even the flimsiest evidence relation can ground implications, provided it is reasonably conspicuous, one should expect there to be implications involving no evidence relation at all (neither actual nor believed), but merely a sufficiently salient connection or association of some other sort. There are such, of course. Sometimes the association holds only within a given representational tradition, and sometimes it is established by representations themselves. The iconography of silent films which Panofsky describes consists (in part, at least) of conventions specific to the genre to the effect (approximately) that when certain propositions are fictional, certain others are as well. There is an elaborate set of codes in Peking Opera whereby costumes and makeup indicate character types; a white face, for instance, indicates treachery or cunning. Such conventions are not usually specified or established explicitly, except after the fact by commentators such as Panofsky; they develop with the tradition and are learned by appreciators through exposure to it. Some have roots in more "natural" connections. It is a convention of the Renaissance that arrows in a body identify it as Saint Sebastian's. The implication holds not so much because Sebastian died in a barrage of arrows, or was believed to have, as because that is the way he is traditionally portrayed. But the convention no doubt arose mainly as a result of the facts (or mutual beliefs) about the circumstances of his death. The source of the understanding in certain French cartoons that to portray a person wearing a bowler hat and carrying an umbrella is to make him an Englishman is probably a myth or joke associating Englishmen with bowler hats and umbrellas, or possibly a mutual belief that the two generally go together.

Some implications are less comfortably thought of as "conventional" and depend less obviously on precedents but still have little or nothing to do with evidence relations (actual or believed or legendary). As in the case of metaphors, we get the point, for one reason or another, sometimes without knowing why we do. I expect that viewers of portraits easily understood that people portrayed as larger than others were to be considered more important, even before this device became conventional.[33] Moviegoers manage to decipher

33. Probably the size of the portion of the canvas used to depict a person, as well as the size he is portrayed as being, affects how important fictionally he is. Also, by depicting someone as being large or devoting a lot of canvas to him, the artist may be saying that he really is important, as well as making it fictional that he is.

devices for indicating dreams, flashbacks, and flashforwards—smoke, fuzzy focus, change from color to black and white, characters' mentioning previous or subsequent events (as when in a film of *Anna Karenina* Vronsky says, "I must meet Anna at the train station" just before a cut to the train station)—without relying on very specific precedents in other works. We know what creators of representations are up to, that a large part of their job is to make propositions fictional. When an artist has arranged for a work to generate fictional truths that in one way or another call attention to some further proposition, it is often apparent that his reason for doing so was to make this proposition fictional as well. There is likely to be an understanding approximately to the effect that when this appears to have been the artist's objective, the salient proposition is fictional, its fictionality being implied by the fictional truths that call attention to it.

We saw earlier that the Mutual Belief Principle accords better than the Reality Principle with the role of representations as vehicles by which artists direct appreciators' imaginings. Appreciators can more easily succeed in imagining what is fictional, what representations enjoin them to imagine, when the Mutual Belief Principle is operative, and in doing so they are more likely to be imagining as the artist meant them to.

But the MBP is by no means uniquely suited to this purpose; it can be achieved more straightforwardly and no less effectively in other ways. All that is needed are clear understandings shared by artist and appreciator as to what features of the work generate what fictional truths (provided the relevant features are controllable by the artist and ascertainable by the appreciator). There is no particular reason why anyone's beliefs about the real world should come into play. As far as implications are concerned, simple conventions to the effect that whenever such and such is fictional, so and so is as well, serve nicely—a decree concerning movies of the 1920s, for example, that if it is fictional that a family eats on a checkered tablecloth, it is fictional that it lives in a "poor but honest" milieu. If such understandings are achieved without explicit decrees, so much the better. They can be based on almost any conspicuous connection between the implying and the implied fictional truths. A salient mutual belief to the effect that if such and such were the case so and so would be also is but one of many such connections.

I mentioned another significant objective that a principle of implication may further: that of encouraging and enriching the appreciator's participation in her game of make-believe. RP is especially suited to this purpose, we noted, though MBP manages to retain much of RP's advantage in this respect. This objective is largely abandoned, however, insofar as implications are based on principles unlike either RP or MBP.

Loretta judges it to be fictional that Andy suffers an innate neurological disorder, on the basis of fictional truths about his antisocial behavior. When she does so, it is fictional in her game that she judges Andy to suffer this condition, from his antisocial behavior. Fictionally his behavior (and surrounding circumstances) constitutes her reason for believing that his neurological system is defective. Assuming that Loretta is right in using RP to interpret the story and in the implication she finds in it, it is fictional that her reason is a good one, that Andy's antisocial behavior is indeed a good indication of a neurological disorder.

This much is true of Mabel also. When, using MBP, she takes fictional truths about Andy's behavior and circumstances to imply that fictionally he is possessed by the devil, it is fictional in her game that she judges from Andy's antisocial behavior that he is possessed by the devil (although she would never make such an inference in real life); fictionally the former is her reason for believing the latter. If Mabel is right in using MBP and in the implication she finds in the story, it is fictional that her reason is a good one—that Andy's antisocial behavior is indeed a good indication of possession by the devil.

But when Robert, examining a woodcut attributed to Dürer, notes that it portrays arrows piercing a man's body and infers (contrary to both RP and MBP) that fictionally the body is Saint Sebastian's, it is not fictional in his game that the arrows are a significant part of his reason for identifying the person as Sebastian, nor is it fictional that they constitute good grounds for doing so; fictionally they provide only the most negligible indication that the body is Sebastian's. It is not fictional that Sebastian was the only person in history (or the only saint in history) to die from a barrage of arrows. It *is* fictional in Robert's game, I would claim, that he knows the body to be Sebastian's. But there probably is no answer to the question of how, fictionally, he identified it or what his grounds are. The world of his game is incomplete in this respect. The actual inference he makes about what is fictional and his reasons for thinking it fictional stand outside his game; only his conclusion affects what is fictional in the game.

Likewise, it is not fictional in "Slithergadee" that the abrupt interruption of the speaker is by itself reasonable grounds on which to accept that the Slithergadee got him, nor is it fictional in the reader's game that this is his reason for accepting it, even if it is unquestionably fictional that the monster did get him and that the reader knows (somehow or other) that it did.

The case of the checkered tablecloth is less clear-cut. A convention that whenever it is fictional that people eat on checkered tablecloths it is also fictional that they live in a poor but honest milieu may, but need not, be accompanied by an understanding that, fictionally, anyone who uses a checkered tablecloth lives in such a milieu. It need not be fictional that there is any nomological or evidential connection at all between checkered tablecloths and honest poverty, and it may be fictional that there is no such connection. So when a viewer infers, quite legitimately, the one fictional truth from the other, it may well not be fictional that he infers the milieu from the tablecloth.

4.1 · Pablo Picasso, *Women Running on the Beach*, $13\frac{3}{8} \times 16\frac{3}{4}$ inches, oil on plywood (1922). Musée Picasso. Copyright © ARS N.Y. / SPADEM, 1989. Photo © R.M.N.–SPADEM. Used in 1924 for curtain of the ballet *Le Train Bleu*.

The mechanics of indirect generation have turned out—to no one's surprise, I should think—to be very disorderly. Implications seem not to be governed by any simple or systematic principle or set of principles, but by a complicated and shifting and often competing array of understandings, precedents, local conventions, saliences. Sharply divergent principles, answering to different needs, are at work in different cases, and it seems unlikely that there are any very general or systematic meta-principles for determining which is applicable when. Experience and knowledge of the arts, of society, and of the world will sharpen the critic's skills. But in the end he must feel his way.

The following description of Picasso's *Women Running on the Beach* (figure 4.1) illustrates nicely the diversity of devices by which fictional truths can be implied—in this case a single fictional truth or group of them in a single work. Picasso's objective is not just to establish the fictionality of the proposition that the figures are moving (or moving quickly), however, but also to convey a "sense of motion." He does this by establishing that fictional truth many times over in many different ways.

> We find that the forward thrust of the two figures becomes irresistible because of a combination of calculated distortions acting in concert. The lead is given by a greatly enlarged arm stretched forward and pointing in the direction that the girls are running. This is backed up in every detail by flowing hair and garments, elongated clouds and the empty horizon between beach and sky across which they run. But the most telling feature is the haptic tension between the pointing hand and the much smaller foot almost left behind in the haste of the leading figure. We are presented, in fact, with a powerful make-believe, strengthened by a multiplicity of devices both plastic and psychological, such as the appearance of reluctance in the companion to be carried along at such a pace, which acts as as foil.[34]

4.4. THE MECHANICS OF DIRECT GENERATION

Is the machinery of direct generation any more orderly than that of implication? Lest anyone be tempted to suppose that it is, that representations establish their primary fictional truths in relatively simple and predictable ways and that things get messy only when it comes to extrapolating from them, let us look briefly at a few instances of direct generation. A quick survey will suffice for this purpose. But we

---

34. Penrose, "In Praise of Illusion," p. 267.

will have occasion later to examine some of the examples more closely. Again, the particulars of the means by which fictional truths are generated in various kinds of cases will be of interest in their own right.

It is evident that the principles of direct generation for verbal and pictorial representations differ greatly, but one might look for consistency within each of these modes. Do literary works *say* what is to be made fictional and pictorial ones *show* it? This suggestion is easily undermined, even without capitalizing especially on the fuzziness of the notions of saying and showing. In rejecting it we will see why in § 4.2 I resisted identifying directly generated fictional truths with those the works make *explicit*.

Any inclination to suppose that the propositions whose fictionality a literary work generates directly are simply the ones its words express, given the language in which it is written, dissipates quickly.[35] Many of these propositions are not fictional at all, most obviously in the case of works with "unreliable" narrators (such as Ford's *Good Soldier*), and when they are fictional their fictionality is often implied rather than primary. It is fictional that someone (the narrator) utters the words of the text, in many cases, and, if the narrator is "reliable," this implies the fictionality of what the words express. Is it always fictional at least that someone utters the words in question: Does *this* constitute the core of primary fictional truths? No. Sometimes it is fictional merely that someone thinks those words without uttering them, or that they express his fantasies or dreams or desires. Sometimes, perhaps, there is no narrator and it *is* simply what is expressed by the text (taken perhaps in one or another nonliteral manner) whose fictionality is generated directly. It is not uncommon for readers to be very uncertain which of these alternatives obtains.

Ordinarily there is nothing analogous to narrators in pictures and other depictions, so ordinarily we do not have to worry about untrustworthy ones. Do pictures generate directly the fictionality of whatever is *shown* in them? Can we assume that if a man is shown, it is a primary fictional truth that there is a man, although it will probably be only implied that he has blood in his veins or a brother in Vienna? No. Rousseau's painting *The Dream* shows an elephant, a pair of tigers, and a snake charmer in a jungle scene, in the midst of

---

35. Even if that were so, direct generation would be no more simple or systematic than the semantic rules by which those propositions are determined. Moreover, it is obviously not just the literal meaning of the text that needs to be taken into account but also metaphors, irony, and so on.

which the dreamer sleeps. But it is fictional not that there is an elephant and so on, but merely that the dreamer dreams that there is. And it is fictional neither that she sleeps in a jungle nor that she dreams of doing so, though it would seem that this state of affairs is "shown." In the dinner scene of Ingmar Bergman's *Hour of the Wolf* (figure 8.12) we see a dinner party through the eyes of a neurotic artist, Borg. The faces of the diners are shown monstrously distorted, but it is fictional merely that this is how they appear to Borg, not that they *are* monstrously distorted. What is shown in *Rashomon,* in its several conflicting portrayals of the incident in the forest, is what happened according to the testimony of various witnesses. Their testimony cannot all be true. (See § 8.7.)

The notion of what a picture "shows" is open to some manipulation. Does Duchamp's *Nude Descending a Staircase* show a series of ladies following one another down the stairs, rather than successive stages of a single one? Does Benozzo Gozzoli's *Dance of Salome and the Beheading of John the Baptist,* which portrays Salome dancing, the beheading of John, and Salome presenting the head to Herod, all within the same frame, show these events occurring simultaneously? We could insist on answering negatively in order to accommodate better the hypothesis that what is shown is fictional (and that these fictional truths are primary). But this would merely transfer the perplexities of ascertaining a depiction's primary fictional truths to the question of what it "shows." What would be the grounds for denying that *Nude Descending* "shows" a parade, if not that this is not what it represents, that it is fictional that there is only a single woman on the staircase? So how could an appeal to what it shows assist the task of determining what it makes fictional?

When in response to these negative observations we look to see how direct generation does work, we are treated to a veritable variety show. Artists use every trick in the book and more. Some techniques are more or less traditional; others are strikingly ad hoc. (One is reminded of the impromptu utilization of unconventional props in children's games.) Some, even some ad hoc ones, leave no doubt about what is fictional; others keep us guessing forever. Some require familiarity with the genre to be understood, or familiarity with one or another aspect of the outside world. Artists are no less inventive in devising ways of getting fictional truths generated than they are in choosing what fictional truths to generate.

There is a convention in Central Javanese theater that (fictionally) the witch Rangda is flying, when two attendants cross bamboo poles in front of her. It is traditional, in many cartoons, to put characters' unspoken thoughts in dotted-line balloons. Manuel Puig's use of italics to indicate unspoken thoughts in *Heartbreak Tango* is no less transparent, but as far as I know there are no precedents for it. Large letters, in cartoons and in captions for silent films, sometimes mean that a character speaks loudly. Musical sounds are conveniently portrayed by bits of musical notation—emitted, for instance, from the mouth of a trumpet. Film music and music in opera and dance often contribute subtly but effectively to the generation of fictional truths— helping to establish, for example, that fictionally a character is nervous or cocky or ecstatic.[36] Sometimes music makes it fictional that there is music, that a band is playing, for instance. How do we decide whether it does or not? If, in a film, the visually depicted scene includes a band that appears to be playing, the sound track will probably make it fictional that music is heard. If the scene is that of a sheriff's posse chasing bandits in the desert, it will not.[37] Common sense is our guide.

One could argue with some credibility that the personalities or personal lives of movie actors, or the public's image of them, affect what is fictional about the characters they portray; we have a tendency to read our impression of the actors into their characters. This can be understood as an instance of RP or MBP in operation. But it is clearly illegitimate to allow them to operate similarly in Shakespearean theater, for instance. We are not to attribute to Hamlet what we think we know about Laurence Olivier's life offstage.

In his film *La Roue* Abel Gance uses accelerating montage, an increase in the rate of alternations between shots, to indicate the increasing speed of a locomotive.[38] This is not a clear instance of *direct* generation, however. The acceleration of the montage consists

---

36. Such fictional truths may be generated only with the assistance of fictional truths about the character's actions and circumstances. To the extent that this is so, the former fictional truths are implied. But the generation is probably direct as far as the music's contribution is concerned; that is, it is probably not by generating any other fictional truths that the music contributes to their generation. We might call this "partial implication."

Generating fictional truths is not the only function of music in these arts, and probably not the main one. It "sets the tone" for a work or a scene, and this is not simply a matter of generating fictional truths. Sometimes music underscores or reinforces fictional truths generated by other means, and it may give appreciators premonitions, which may or may not turn out to be right, of what is to be made fictional later.

37. In *Blazing Saddles*, music that seems at first to be a mere accompaniment to the movie is incorporated in the fictional world when we suddenly come across a band set up in the desert.

38. See Bazin, *What Is Cinema?*, I, 25.

in the increasing frequency of sharp discontinuities in successively generated fictional truths. So the fact that fictionally the locomotive accelerates depends on other fictional truths. But not simply on what other fictional truths are generated; it depends on the order in which they are generated. The order of the film images thus contributes to the generation of this fictional truth directly, not by virtue of its contribution to the generation of other fictional truths. In any case, we have here a device for generating fictional truths which, though surely obvious enough to the viewer, does not fit neatly into any very general scheme or principle of generation.

It is difficult to say, in many simpler cases, whether a fictional truth is primary or implied. One might assume that a halo in the portrayal of a saint makes it fictional that a ring of light hovers above his head, and that this implies that fictionally he is a saint. But viewers in a different frame of mind might prefer to take the halo at less than face value, denying that fictionally there actually is a ring of light and understanding the character's sainthood to be established more directly by the white ellipse on the canvas. Note, however, that it is only because the ellipse is such as might be taken by literal-minded viewers to portray a ring of light that it indicates sainthood.[39]

Do motion lines in cartoons portray air streaming around and behind the moving object, thereby implying that fictionally it is moving? Or do they make it fictional merely that the object is moving? Concentric arcs around a bell may serve to make it fictional that the bell rings. Do they do so by making it fictional that there are sound waves emanating from it, or more directly? Some artists distort human figures for expressive purposes (which may but need not involve the generation of further fictional truths). We might say either that fictionally the person's body is distorted in such and such a manner, and that this fictional truth has certain expressive consequences, or that the expressive purpose is served merely by the fact that the figure is painted *as though* it were to be made fictional that the body is distorted.[40]

---

39. One might count this an instance of what I will call *ornamental* representation. It may be merely fictional that it is fictional that there is a ring of light above the saint's head, and that may be why it is fictional that he is a saint. (See § 7.6.)

40. "Miró produced very powerful images of savage violence, of which *Head of a Woman,* 1938, is perhaps the most extreme. To obtain this effect he has used contrasts of colour, an entirely illogical scale of proportions and arbitrary distortions of the human form. There is nothing of illusionism in his methods; yet we are presented with an image of terror and aggression, a nightmare, childish and grotesque, at which we might wish to laugh were not its primitive strength so overwhelming." (Penrose, "In Praise of Illusion," p. 270.)

In general, when it is clear that the main reason for the presence of what seems to be a certain fictional truth, perhaps a primary one, consists in its implication of others (or, for instance, in its achieving a certain expressiveness), and when the implying fictional truth itself is anomalous or unrealistic or out of place in one way or another, it may be reasonable to think of it as dropping out after it has done its job— to think of the fictional truths which seem to depend on it as arising simply from what would ordinarily have generated it.[41] This is not the only available option, however. We might accept the anomalous implying fictional truth but declare it unemphasized, not to be dwelt on. Or, in some cases, we might think of the implying and implied fictional truths as belonging to different fictional worlds. Often, no doubt, there is no choosing among these alternatives.

It would appear from observations in this section that the pouring of the foundations of fictional worlds is no more orderly than the erection of their superstructures; the mechanics of generation are soggy to the core.

As a matter of fact, it is time now to expose the fiction that there must necessarily *be* a core to support the superstructure. The various fictional truths generated by a work may be mutually dependent, none of them generated without assistance from others. There may be no primary fictional truths.[42] How does it all get started? The words or color patterns of the work are *suggestive* of certain fictional truths, some of which, in this tentative status, lend support to one another sufficient to remove the tentativeness. The interpreter must go back and forth among provisionally acceptable fictional truths until he finds a convincing combination.

4.5.   SILLY QUESTIONS

Anyone capable of composing the following lines would surely qualify as a poet of the first rank:

41. The case of the motion lines is a little different from the others. There is no anomaly in the idea that fictionally there is air streaming around the moving object. Indeed that is probably fictional in any case, implied by the fact that fictionally the object is moving rapidly in an air-filled environment. But if the lines are understood to portray directly the movement of air, there would be some pressure to allow that it is fictional in the appreciator's game that he *sees* it. One way to avoid this is to deny that it is by virtue of generating fictional truths about the movement of air that the lines make it fictional that the object is moving. Still, it is because we can understand how the lines *might* portray moving air that they serve so naturally to portray motion.

42. Here I am indebted to William Taschek.

Had it pleased heaven
To try me with affliction, had they raised
All kinds of sores and shames on my bare head,
Steeped me in poverty to the very lips,
Given to captivity me and my utmost hopes;
I should have found in some place of my soul
A drop of patience. But alas . . .[43]

How did Othello, a Moorish general and hardly an intellectual, manage to come up with such superb verse on the spur of the moment, and when immensely distraught? Apparently he is to be credited with an almost unbelievable natural literary flair; at least this would appear to be a consequence of either the Reality Principle or the Mutual Belief Principle. And isn't it peculiarly inappropriate for Othello to make such a grandiloquent speech in such distressing circumstances? Why does he flaunt his literary skills so pompously? Why do other characters take no notice of his peculiar manner of discourse, or of his astounding literary talent?

Why do all thirteen of the diners in Leonardo's *Last Supper* line up in a row on the same side of the table? So that we, the viewers of the painting, should be able to see all of their faces, of course. No doubt that was Leonardo's reason for painting them so, for making it fictional that they are configured as they are. But what, fictionally, are *their* reasons for arranging themselves thus? It isn't fictional that they want to accommodate us or Leonardo, or that they are posing for a portrait. Must we suspect that they are fearful of facing one another—of kicks under the table or bad breath? Or is it fictional that there is nothing unusual, nothing remarkable or noteworthy about their crowding together on one side of the table? Is it, fictionally, the custom to sit thus at a communal meal? How did such a peculiar custom arise? Could it be fictional that that is not their custom, that diners normally sit on both sides of a table, but fictional also that their departure from the norm on this occasion is not noteworthy, not in need of explanation? None of the alternatives is very attractive.

It is fictional in William Luce's play *The Belle of Amherst* that Emily Dickinson is an extraordinarily shy person who keeps to herself.[44] Yet she is onstage throughout the play, speaking constantly. Hers is the only role called for in the script; the actress playing it must

43. Shakespeare, *Othello*, act 2, sc. 2.
44. This is clear from what, fictionally, Dickinson says, and is reinforced by what we know about her real life.

command the attention and interest of the audience for the duration of the performance while portraying an unusually shy and retiring character. How can it be fictional that Dickinson says all that she does, all of what Julie Harris actually says while impersonating her, yet fictional that she is not gregarious? Is it fictional that all *that* is not *much*? Is it fictional that Dickinson is and is not gregarious? That she is and is not shy?

These are silly questions. They are pointless, inappropriate, out of order. To pursue or dwell on them would be not only irrelevant to appreciation and criticism but also distracting and destructive. The paradoxes, anomalies, apparent contradictions they point to seem artificial, contrived, not to be taken seriously. We don't take them seriously. Ordinarily we don't even notice them.

Contrast fictional worlds containing paradoxes that we do take seriously. Hogarth's *False Perspective* (figure 1.2), Escher's prints, Flann O'Brien's *At Swim-Two-Birds* (see § 5.3, note 18) all highlight their anomalies, and appreciators relish them. It is not silly to ask how a person leaning out of a second-story window could light a pipe for a friend on a distant hill; or how the water in M. C. Escher's *Waterfall* can be flowing uphill and down simultaneously, as it seems to be; or how a character could give birth to her author's son. These questions may have no good answers, but that is just the point. To ignore them is to miss the point. Other works contain paradoxes that are painful, legitimately disturbing, and that constitute aesthetic defects. Mistakes in perspective can be distressing,[45] and so might a character in a novel whose actions unaccountably conflict with his personality (as established by an "omniscient" narrator). The questions raised in such cases may be entirely in order, not silly at all. They may make the work look silly.

Othello, The Last Supper, and *The Belle of Amherst* are not science fiction or metaphysical fantasies; neither are they defective, by virtue of the anomalies one can, if one chooses, dig out of them. How Othello could have uttered verse worthy of Shakespeare is not a question of focal interest, a puzzle to intrigue and entrance, nor is it an irritating intrusion on the appreciator's experience, indicative of a blemish in the play. From the perspectives of appreciation and criticism, it is just silly.

We are reminded of dreams that seem perfectly normal and ordinary while they are being dreamed but manifest paradoxes when the

---

45. Perspective mistakes need to be differentiated from alternative kinds of perspective, although the distinction is by no means sharp. And "mistakes" vary in their seriousness.

dreamer tries to reconstruct them afterwards. Joan dreams of paying repeated visits to a man who seems sometimes to be her father and sometimes her boss (and it is clear that her father is not her boss). Who *is* the man in her dream? Do the father and the boss alternate appearances in it? But it may be part of the dream that all of the visits are to the *same* person. Is that person someone with (possibly incompatible) characteristics of each, but identical to neither? But Joan *does* dream of visiting her father, not just someone like him, and also her boss. Does the recipient of her visits change his identity periodically (whatever that might mean)? The breakfast conversation will be baffling. But the dream experience itself was not. The paradoxes did not intrude during the dream, however inescapable they seem in the bright light of day. Only at breakfast does Joan think something was amiss. Even at breakfast, moreover, Joan may feel that the anomalies have little to do with the true character of her dream or what is important about it, that dwelling on them can only interfere with an understanding of it.[46] One can appropriate the dream for purposes of paradox mongering, but to do so is to refuse to comprehend it on its own terms.

Dreams like this are by no means unusual, and neither are representations in which one can uncover pointless paradoxes by asking silly questions. In countless English-language novels everyone everywhere speaks English: French taxi drivers, Burmese peasants, Roman soldiers. Renaissance paintings portray ancient personages in Renaissance dress and settings, and contemporary theatrical productions sometimes forgo period costumes in favor of blue jeans. People ride on buses in stories of Balinese Arja theater set in the thirteenth century. Opera characters sometimes spend their last moments singing (of all things!), while in excruciating pain and as life and strength ebb away—and singing exquisitely. The most minimal disguises, transparent to the least perceptive member of the audience and from the farthest gallery, may nonetheless fool other characters.[47] (Is it fictional that those characters are blind or stupid?) Narrators in literary works—and not just "omniscient" ones—tell of events they could not possibly know about. (How could anyone know that "they lived

46. Joan's association of her boss with her father may be a central "meaning" of the dream, which might be brought out by questions about the identity of the man she visits. But this does not mean that the *paradox*, the difficulty of finding a logically coherent reading of the dream world, is of any significance.

47. In *The Awful Truth* (Leo McCarey, 1937) Irene Dunne disguises herself as Cary Grant's sister: "The other people at the party . . . don't recognize her in her flimsy disguise because of the necessities of plot and comic form" (Braudy, *The World in a Frame*, p. 109).

happily ever after"? And how could even an "omniscient" narrator report this in the past tense?) The mirror in Rubens' *Toilette of Venus* (figure 4.2) shows *us* what according to the laws of optics Venus should see in it; yet it is fictional, presumably, that this is what she does see in it. (See § 8.7.) Few works are safe from the determined paradox monger. With a little cheek and a suspension of charity the impish critic can find what look like embarrassing questions to ask

4.2 · Peter Paul Rubens, *Toilette of Venus*, 48¾ × 38⅝ inches, panel (c. 1613–1615). Sammlungen des Regierenden Fürsten von Liechtenstein.

about even the most staid, ordinary, and straightforwardly "realistic" representations.

There is a lot of variety here. Some silly questions are sillier than others. Artificial anomalies vary in both artificiality and paradoxicality. In some cases one might hope to get away with observing merely that the fictional world differs astonishingly from the real one. There is nothing *paradoxical* in that, nor in the fictionality of propositions whose truth would be most unlikely or even impossible. It is fictional that Burmese peasants speak English, that Oedipus wears blue jeans, that there were buses in the thirteenth century; these fictional worlds are thus unlike the real one. So what? But reality (or what is mutually believed about reality) exerts its influence on fictional worlds in ways that clash, if we allow them to, with recognized fictional truths. Is it fictional that English is the world's only language? Rarely can we insist comfortably that it is, especially if it is fictional, as it may well be even in a novel written entirely in English, that foreigners and natives fail to understand one another and that translators travel with traders and diplomats. But if Burmese is the language of Burma, how (fictionally) do uneducated Burmese peasants manage to learn English? How did the ancient Greeks acquire the technology for making blue jeans? Surely such evenly woven and identically constructed garments could not have been produced by hand (except by virtue of truly extraordinary skill and concentration—which would themselves demand explanation). If they did possess this technology, why were they still riding in chariots and throwing spears at one another? Tensions emerge from differences between fictional worlds and the real one when we insist on asking the wrong questions.

The anomalies consist in dissonances among fictional truths each of which, considered separately, appears to be generated in a normal and ordinary manner, by virtue of principles that are in other contexts unobjectionable. Individually innocent fictional truths are uncomfortably paradoxical in combination. The source of the dissonances can often be seen to lie in divergent demands made on the artist; diverse objectives he may be pursuing and constraints he may be working under may interfere with one another.

Sometimes the need to make a fictional world accessible to the intended audience conflicts with a desire to make it reasonably "realistic," reasonably like the real world. *A Tale of Two Cities* puts English words into the mouths of French characters so that English readers will understand, although if it weren't for that, one would expect Dickens to have had his French characters speak French, as the French normally do. Constraints inherent in the medium sometimes make it difficult to generate combinations of fictional truths that might otherwise be desired. Leonardo wanted to establish fictional truths concerning the faces of all thirteen diners at the Last Supper. Perhaps he would have preferred it to be fictional that they surround the table in the ordinary manner, but he sacrificed the latter for the sake of the former. This example, like the previous one, involves consideration of the appreciator's relation to the fictional world, although the question is not one of the accessibility of fictional truths. Leonardo's choice was dictated, no doubt, by the desire to make it fictional in viewers' games that they see the fronts rather than the backs of the diners. Similar considerations are at work in *The Belle of Amherst* and in the case of Rubens' optically exotic mirror. It is for the audience's sake that Emily Dickinson talks as much as she does; it is so that fictional truths about her can be generated, and so that viewers can, fictionally, learn about her. Essentially the same body of fictional truths might be generated in other ways, without making Dickinson so loquacious. Someone else might occupy the stage in her stead and give the audience a detailed account of her thoughts and actions, while Dickinson herself (fictionally) remains in the woodwork. No doubt Luce had reasons for letting Dickinson tell her own story. Given that choice, the conflict with her shyness is hard to avoid. Othello's peculiarly elaborate language is demanded by the style in which the play is written and by Shakespeare's desire to provide superb verse for the pleasure of his audience, which in this case took precedence over considerations of "realism."[48]

Declaring a question to be silly does not answer it; it is an excuse, however legitimate, for not answering it. Perhaps our silly questions should not arise in the course of ordinary interaction with the work, but they are fair game for the theorist, standing as he does somewhat apart from appreciation and criticism and observing them from without. In any case, suppose one simply insists, pigheadedly, on asking about Othello's literary talent, the disciples' peculiar seating arrangement, and Emily Dickinson's verbosity. Silly or not, what are the answers to these questions?

Many have no definitive answers, and answers of different sorts will seem reasonable in different cases and to different observers. If the questions do not much matter within the institution of representation, we will not be surprised if that institution fails to provide answers to be discovered from without. Still, if one insists on responding to the questions, how is one to do so?

It may be best to defuse some paradoxes by disallowing fictional

48. Here is a conflict of a different sort among an artist's objectives: "In *Queen Christina*, the famous final close-up apparently has the wind blowing in two directions at once, one to get the boat under way and the other to arrange Garbo's hair to the best advantage" (Halliwell, *The Filmgoer's Companion*, under "Boo-Boos," p. 97). This anomaly does and should bother the viewer, it seems to me, although it would be unreasonable to dwell excessively on it.

truths responsible for them. The generation of fictional truths in what seems otherwise to be a perfectly normal manner may be blocked simply by the fact that they clash with others. When Oedipus and other ancient personages are portrayed in contemporary dress, we can deny that what the actors wear is, fictionally, what the characters do, thereby undercutting questions about how the ancients managed to manufacture blue jeans. We can simply refuse to count the actors' clothing as props, even though the same clothing on the same actors would undoubtedly serve as props in a play about Chicago street gangs. What *does* Oedipus wear, if not blue jeans? Probably no very specific fictional truths about his clothing are generated, although it may be reasonable to assume it to be fictional that he dresses appropriately for his culture and station. The world of the play performance is probably incomplete in this regard, just as black-and-white drawings are incomplete with respect to color.

If the silliness of a question convinces us that the generation of otherwise acceptable fictional truths should be blocked, it may be unclear where in a chain of implications the block should come. Given that fictionally Emily Dickinson says all of the particular things she does say, it would seem to be implied that fictionally she speaks a great deal on those occasions, that fictionally she ordinarily or frequently speaks much, and that fictionally she is a rather talkative person and not at all shy. The fact that it is fictional, for other reasons, that she *is* shy will dissuade us from drawing this last conclusion and may suggest that the series of extrapolations should have been cut short earlier. But it is uncertain where the line should be drawn.[49]

What about Othello? Most of us will probably prefer not to allow that fictionally Othello is a great literary talent, and even to affirm that fictionally he is not. But this only shifts the paradox. Is it fictional that Othello lacks special literary talent and yet is capable of improvising superb verse while distraught? Shall we deny that fictionally

---

49. These blocks differ significantly from those mentioned in § 4.3. The fact that fictionally, in a silent movie, someone steps on piano keys may imply that fictionally piano sounds are emitted. But the fact that fictionally the piano has no strings, generated later by a shot of the innards of the piano, would block the implication. Still, it is fictional that it appeared as though piano sounds would be produced when the keys were stepped on, and it was fictional that one would be justified in supposing that they were. But it is not fictional even that Oedipus appears to be wearing blue jeans when the actor portraying him does. It is as though the clash between the actor's blue jeans and the fact that fictionally Oedipus lived in ancient Greece changes the rules of the game, so that the implication does not even get off the ground. In the case of the piano, the explanation for the blocked implication lies within the fictional world, we might say; in the case of Oedipus, it is to be found in the principles whereby the fictional world is determined.

Othello's words "Had it pleased heaven / To try me with affliction" . . . are superb verse, even though it is manifestly true that they are? Or shall we go so far as to deny that fictionally those are Othello's words? Perhaps it is fictional, rather, that Othello utters an unspecified vernacular paraphrase of the words Shakespeare's actor enunciates. Shall we say, similarly, that it is not usually fictional in opera that people sing, though performers portray speech by singing? Is it fictional in English novels that Burmese peasants speak what would be Burmese translations of the English words attributed to them? There is something to be said for these proposals, especially with regard to opera and English novels. But there will be some strain in refusing to allow that the words spectators of *Othello* hear from the actor's mouth, with his particular inflections and emphases, are to be imagined to be spoken, in just that manner, by Othello.

An alternative strategy is to declare offending fictional truths deemphasized, rather than disallowing them. (We noted that differences in emphasis among fictional truths must be recognized in any case.) It is not easily denied that fictionally, in *The Last Supper,* the diners are lined up on one side of the table. But this fictional truth is an unimportant one, one that is not to be dwelt on or even noticed particularly. Its position in the shadows may be taken to mean that it does not have the implications that might otherwise be expected. Perhaps we are not to infer it to be fictional either that the diners are seated peculiarly, or that it is customary in their culture to sit thus, or that one or the other of these explanations holds. Or we might admit some such implied fictional truths but declare them deemphasized also. In any case, questions about the disciples' motives for arranging themselves on the same side of the table will be inappropriate.

Sometimes it may be best to accept and even emphasize fictional truths that clash with one another, but to mute the clash by disallowing the fictionality of their conjunction. It may be important in Joan's dream that on Monday she visits a man who is her father (and who is not also her boss), that she visits the same person on Tuesday, and that the person she visits on Tuesday is her boss. Each of these three propositions may be fictional, and each may have considerable significance in the dream. But that does not force the fictionality of their contradictory conjunction; we need not accept that fictionally Joan visited a man on Tuesday who was and was not identical with someone she visited on Monday. (Nor must we deny the fictionality of the proposition that conjunctions of true propositions are true.)

The specifics of how one chooses to treat these examples do not much matter. I have mentioned various possibilities mainly to show that plausible options are available. There are reasonable ways of escaping or softening anomalies like those we have discussed, if anyone insists on dredging them up by forcing silly questions to the fore. We can explain why the anomalies do not and should not give rise to a sense of paradox. And we can understand how normal-seeming fictional worlds can seem so normal despite (ostensible) paradoxes lurking within, why the works that house them differ so strikingly from Hogarth's *False Perspective* and other representations that, willingly or otherwise, wear paradoxes on their sleeve.

I have added a few wrinkles to my earlier observations about the mechanics of generation. One is that there is a principle of charity at work. The generation of fictional truths is sometimes blocked (if not merely deemphasized) just, or primarily, because they make trouble—because they would render the fictional world uncomfortably paradoxical. But usually more than charity is involved. Recognition of a question's silliness, and so of one reason for disallowing or deemphasizing fictional truths that give rise to it, may depend on awareness of various demands to which the artist must respond. A decision to disallow anomalous fictional truths is especially plausible when it is evident that there are other reasons for the presence in the work of the features that appear to generate them—when, for instance, they are needed to make the fictional world accessible to the audience, or to enhance appreciators' games of make-believe. Since it is in order to keep the audience's interest and generate fictional truths about Emily Dickinson that Julie Harris talks so constantly in her performance of *The Belle of Amherst,* we need not presume that she does so in order to make it fictional that Dickinson is talkative. This can be understood as an instance of the influence of what the artist seems to have intended to make fictional on what is fictional. (See § 4.3.) If there is another ready explanation for the artist's inclusion of a feature that appears to generate a given fictional truth, it may not seem that he meant especially to have it generated. And *this* may argue against recognizing that it is generated.

4.6. CONSEQUENCES

The machinery of generation is devised of rubber bands and paper clips and powered by everything from unicorns in traces to baking soda mixed with vinegar. Sometimes the mechanism works astonishingly "well"—not infrequently by the most unexpected means—

yielding easily recognizable and all but indisputable fictional truths. When it breaks down, artists improvise crude or elegant or surprising or ingenious fixes, or else welcome the resulting ambiguities and capitalize on them in one way or another. For purposes of divining fictional truths there is no substitute for a good nose: a combination of imagination and common sense, leavened within limits by charity and informed by familiarity with the medium, genre, and representational tradition to which the work in question belongs as well as by knowledge of the outside world—all of this combined, of course, with sensitivity to the most subtle features of the work itself.

This is the picture that emerges even from the relatively simple examples treated in this chapter. A thorough examination of critics' wrestlings with complex representations, of their attempts not just to answer particular isolated questions of interpretation but to put together coherent and convincing readings of a work as a whole, would but deepen our appreciation of the vagaries of generation. I will not undertake any such examination. But we should note one kind of consideration unlike any mentioned so far—one that bears significantly on the generation of fictional truths.

Ascertaining a work's fictional truths is only one part of the critic's job, but it is fundamental. Overall themes, "meanings," morals, what a work says to us about our lives, depend to a considerable extent on the fictional truths it generates (though we must not forget the importance of the degree of emphasis accorded various fictional truths, the means by which they are generated, and aspects of style not reducible to any of the above). But the reverse is sometimes true as well. Decisions about what is fictional must be sensitive to feedback from one's overall assessment of the work. One way of supporting a judgment about a character's actions or motivations is to show that it fits a Marxist or a psychoanalytic "reading" of the work as a whole better than alternatives do, and that this reading is also plausible on independent grounds. (Compare: What the scientist accepts as data may depend on what theory he otherwise finds reasonable.) This too goes into the mix of determinants of what is fictional.

It is time to face the consequences of the disorderly behavior of the machinery of generation. There is nothing to fear—nothing, at least, that we do not have to live with anyway, quite apart from the representational arts. But several qualms are likely to occur to certain readers, and may even encourage the conviction that there *must*, somehow, be more regularity in the process of generation than we have found. Some may wonder how we could ever manage to learn and apply "rules" that are as complex and unsystematic as those governing the generation of fictional truths seem to be, how we could ever pronounce on what is fictional and what is not with any assurance at all. Some may worry that there will not be any justification for considering attributions of fictional truths right or wrong unless their generation can be shown to rest on a relatively simple set of principles. (Those who are skeptical about the truth or falsity of interpretations anyway might take the chaos we have observed as confirmation.) Finally, it may appear that fictionality is not a "natural kind" and hence not a proper pillar on which to erect a theory of anything, that what is meant in calling a proposition fictional will vary from case to case, if different fictional truths are generated in such different manners.

This last worry, especially, need not detain us long. Fictionality is not *defined* by the principles of generation; it consists rather in prescriptions to imagine. The variety lies in the means by which such prescriptions are established. Although fictional truths are generated in very different ways, the result is the same in every case: propositions that are to be imagined.

How can we manage to master such complex rules? One line of response will be familiar to readers of Wittgenstein. I will sketch it briefly for the benefit of others. It is an inescapable fact that many concepts are applied without the aid of rules or formulas; otherwise language would be impossible. How do we decide whether something is *sweet smelling,* or *red?* We sniff or look, and it just seems to be so or not. When we do have something like rules to go by (for deciding whether something is *square,* or a *mammal,* for instance), they merely link the concept in question to others. Eventually we come down to concepts that we apply without rules ("My reasons will soon give out. And then I shall act, without reasons").[50] So there need be no pressure to explain the ability to recognize fictionality by supposing that we know, that we have somehow learned the relevant principles.[51] A work just strikes us as generating certain fictional truths when we experience it in its context (broadly conceived).[52] The principles are more reconstructions of our judgments about what is fictional than guides for making them.

It is true that we often base our judgments on particular conscious

50. Wittgenstein, *Philosophical Investigations,* pt. 1, § 211.

51. Even if we do somehow, or in some sense, "know" the relevant principles, it need not be assumed that we learned them from scratch. People may have natural or innate propensities to accept certain principles of generation, or to do so given certain other experiences.

52. Our impression of what is fictional can be mistaken, however, as can our impression of what is red. We don't have ready formulas for deciding when a mistake has been made, but additional experiences or information may enable us to recognize that that is so.

considerations, on facts about the work or its predecessors or the outside world that seem relevant in particular cases; and we can frequently say *something* about how a given fictional truth is generated and why we judge it to be so. (Recognition of fictionality appears to differ from recognition of colors and smells in this respect.) But this is no reason to suppose that we must have learned or otherwise acquired comprehensive rules for deciding what is relevant and how, which guide us in particular cases (unless this means no more than that we act in accordance with such rules).[53] Nor need we suppose that our ability to recognize a particular device by which fictional truths are generated depends on our having come across the "same" or "similar" devices previously. Given what we know and the experiences we have had, we simply "go on" identifying fictional truths in new cases. ("If I have exhausted the justifications I have reached bedrock, and my spade is turned. Then I am inclined to say: 'This is simply what I do.'")[54]

There is a sense, then, in which our opinions about what is fictional cannot ultimately be justified. Is this grounds for denying that they can be correct or incorrect, true or false? Only if we are prepared to deny that *any* of our judgments can be true or false, correct or incorrect—and I am not. (I allow that truth and falsity may be "relative to" a language or a "conceptual scheme" or whatever. See § 2.7.)

These are large issues that have received much discussion and deserve more.[55] But the present worries about judgments of fictionality can be alleviated by a more specific comparison—one that is revealing in any case. I doubt that anyone seriously supposes that there are simple and systematic "rules" for making and interpreting metaphors. Metaphors opportunistically take advantage of whatever resources happen to be available, whatever works: contextual features of the most diverse sorts, associations, shared myths and experiences, natural propensities, unexplained saliencies, even nonsemantic attributes of the language used, the sounds of words. (I doubt that "beeswax" in "It's none of your beeswax" would have come to mean "business" if it were not for the lexical similarity.) Sometimes we can say something about how particular metaphors work, why we and others take them as we do. Sometimes their operation is almost completely mysterious. In any case it is clear that we are unable to specify

53. On this point see Walton, "Linguistic Relativity."
54. Wittgenstein, *Philosophical Investigations*, pt. 1, § 217.
55. The reader may especially want to consult Kripke, *Wittgenstein on Rules and Private Language.*

comprehensive formulas for understanding them, and it is certain that the principles on which they are based are enormously complex, context sensitive, and constantly changing. The machinery of metaphor is no more orderly than that of generation.

But metaphors *do* work. They can, of course, be highly ambiguous, frustratingly or delightfully vague, suggestive in conflicting directions. Sometimes their "meaning" is almost entirely up for grabs, and this may be deliberate and desirable. But in many cases we understand them (or what is said by means of them) well enough. Metaphors, perfectly fresh ones included, can be effective and indeed precise tools of communication.

The unruly behavior of the machinery of generation makes life hard for critics. But it is no threat to the theorist; it presents the artist with exciting opportunities; and it is a rich source of fascination for the appreciator.

There is much more to appreciation of representational works of art than observing the operation of this machinery and reflecting on its results, however.

PART TWO

Appreciating Representations

Don't take it as a matter of course, but as a remarkable fact, that pictures and fictitious narratives give us pleasure, occupy our minds.
—Ludwig Wittgenstein,
Philosophical Investigations

From the wildness of my heart I cannot exclude the question whether railway-engineers, if they had been brought up on more fantasy, might not have done better with all their abundant means than they commonly do.
—J. R. R. Tolkien,
"On Fairy-Stories"

We now know what representations are. It is time to ask what they are for. What is the point of the institution of fiction? Why do people bother to make up stories and tell them to one another? Why don't we summarily dismiss *Anna Karenina* and *La Grande Jatte* and *Hamlet* as "mere fiction" and as such irrelevant to our lives in the real world? It is a fact—a remarkable one—that we appreciate representational works of art. We are moved, fascinated, entranced by them, sometimes almost hypnotized, even when we are perfectly aware of their mere fictionality. Why? And what is the nature of our appreciative experiences?

We know better than to expect a single comprehensive answer to these questions, or a simple one. Different works are appreciated in many different ways and valued for many different reasons. Nevertheless, there is a central kind of appreciative stance, a role played by the appreciator, that is common to many of the diverse experiences that can be called appreciation, and most others are best thought of as variations of it or understood otherwise in terms of it. Explaining this role is the main task of Part Two. In doing this I will barely begin the job of accounting for the appeal and power even of relatively simple representational works of art. I will not pursue psychological dimensions of the question, for instance, and many philosophical matters will be left dangling also. But I will lay a foundation on which further investigation can be built.

The reader will not be surprised to learn that comparisons with the playing of children's games of make-believe will figure importantly in our inquiry. The basic appreciative role consists, in a word, in *participating* in a game of make-believe in which the appreciated work is a prop.

5

Puzzles and Problems

What relations hold between the real world and fictional worlds? In what ways do appreciators interact with fictional characters? This question is misleadingly framed. If, as I claim, there are no fictional characters, nothing can bear any relations to them or interact with them. But posing the question in this form will bring out several puzzles whose trail will eventually lead to an account of the basic appreciative stance and suggest explanations of the importance fiction has for us. For now I will speak, especially blatantly, as if fictional characters do exist and possess ordinary sorts of properties, as if they are people and are tall or short, rich or poor, old or young, male or female, and so on.

Our prereflective thoughts about what links can obtain between the real world and fictional ones are strangely schizophrenic. On the one hand, fictional worlds and their contents seem insulated or isolated in some peculiar way from the real world, separated from it by a logical or metaphysical barrier. That, indeed, is why we call them different *worlds*. From our position in the real world we cannot rescue Robinson Crusoe from his island or send flowers to Tom Sawyer's relatives grieving at his funeral. Willy Loman, in Arthur Miller's *Death of a Salesman*, cannot tell us his troubles, nor can we give him advice. A Frankenstein monster may threaten with destruction any character who has the misfortune of sharing its world, but we in the real world are perfectly safe from it.

On the other hand, we seem to be in *psychological* contact with characters, sometimes even intimate with them. We have epistemological access to fictional worlds; we know a great deal about what happens in them. Often we are privy to characters' most private thoughts and feelings. And we respond to what we know, apparently, in many of the ways in which we respond to what we know about the real world. We worry about Tom Sawyer and Becky when we learn that they are lost in a cave. We sympathize with the plight of Willy Loman. We are terrified of the Frankenstein monster. Fictional characters cause real people to shed tears, lose sleep, laugh, and scream.

Is the barrier between worlds a selective one, then, physically opaque but psychologically porous? Does it for some reason allow psychological links between appreciators and characters while preventing physical contact? This is not a comfortable picture of the situation. Physical and psychological relations are too closely intertwined for one to expect a barrier to be thus selective. We must look more carefully both at the notion that physical interaction across worlds is somehow blocked and also at the notion that psychological interaction is not. In many children's games there does not even appear to be such an asymmetry. When Monica plays dolls, she is as capable of feeding her baby and rocking it to sleep as she is of loving it and being concerned about its welfare.

5.1. RESCUING HEROINES

Henry, a backwoods villager watching a theatrical performance, leaps to the stage to save the heroine from the clutches of the villain and a horrible death. Henry is mistaken, of course, if he thinks he can save the *actress*. She is not in danger. But the character she portrays is in danger and does need saving. Can Henry help her, despite the fact that he does not live in her world?

Suppose that, if the performance proceeded according to plan, the villain would tie the heroine to railroad tracks and a passing train would do her in. This is to be portrayed as follows: Two parallel two-by-fours on the stage floor represent the railroad tracks. The actor playing the villain places the actress playing the heroine on the two-by-fours and wraps a rope around her body. The curtains close, and the passing of the train is indicated by sound effects. If Henry rushes to the stage and removes the actress from the two-by-fours before the sound technician brings the train through, hasn't he saved the heroine? Or he might cause such a commotion that the performance has to be canceled entirely. This prevents the performers from portraying the heroine's death. And since what happens in the fictional world is just what is portrayed as happening, Henry seems to have prevented the heroine's death.

Henry needn't be naive about the play; he needn't think it is the real-world actress who is in danger and try to save *her*. Suppose he knows perfectly well that what he is watching is a play, and that only a fictional woman is in danger. But suppose he feels so strongly that such an innocent and beautiful damsel ought to be spared, even in fiction, that he intervenes in her behalf. If he knows what he is doing, he may simply pull the plug on the sound equipment, thereby diverting the train and saving the heroine.[1]

The principle of this example can be generalized. Since real-world novels, plays, paintings, and so forth are what determine what happens in fictional worlds, we can affect fictional worlds to whatever extent the nature of novels, plays, and paintings is within our power. We can destroy an evil picture man, not with a dagger, perhaps, but with a paintbrush—by painting a dagger through him and an expiring look on his face. Painters, authors, and other artists are veritable gods vis-à-vis fictional worlds.[2] The physical isolation of fictional worlds from the real world seems to have vanished.

There is an air of trickery about all this. If it is so easy to save characters in distress, why don't we do so more often? One possible answer is that jumping on the stage or otherwise interfering with the performance is *inappropriate,* a violation of the conventions of theater. But no conventions prohibit an author, playwright, or painter from sparing his characters; it is his prerogative to decide their fate. And anyway, would we let mere conventions deter us from saving a life?

Perhaps fictional lives do not matter in the way real ones do; we do not regret merely fictional suffering, and we feel no obligation to prevent it. But this flies in the face of the psychological links that we do seem to have to fictional characters, the fact that we sometimes do, apparently, care very much about them. We are distressed at the plight of Tom and Becky in the cave; we feel for Willy Loman; we hope fervently that the hero will arrive in time to rescue the hapless heroine. And we may pass moral judgment on a character who is in a position to help but does not—even while we ourselves sit glued dumbly to our seats!

Is our concern for the heroine a fake, a sham? If we really do blame the villain for mistreating the heroine, shouldn't we blame even more the author who put him up to it? But we may have nothing but praise

1. I am supposing that the theatrical event Henry tangles with is not a performance of a written play, an instance of a play (type) that might have other instances as well, but is entirely improvised on the spot. Sabotaging a particular performance will do nothing to help the heroine of a play type. That would require tampering with the text.

2. It is arguable, however, that altering a painting or novel does not affect what happens in the fictional world but rather creates a new work and a new fictional world to go with it.

for the author, even while purporting to bemoan the calamities he allows to befall his characters. It is not hard to find reasons for secretly wishing the heroine ill. Watching fictional suffering can be thrilling, instructive, cathartic. And we may think that if the heroine does not suffer, the work will be insipid, a namby-pamby, everyone-lives-happily-ever-after affair. We appreciate and admire tragedies and hope the work will turn out to be one, even though this means disaster for the heroine. (Compare a person watching a bullfight whose selfish desire to be entertained overcomes his natural compassion for the bull.)

But do we ever suffer even the slightest pangs of conscience for allowing our desire for a valuable aesthetic experience to interfere with our concern for a character in distress? It hardly seems that we consider intervening on behalf of the heroine but fail to act when our selfish urges get the best of us; we do not think of intervention as a live alternative. This is no ordinary instance of mixed motives, of conflicting interests or desires.

Some will be impatient for the theory developed in Part One to rescue us from these embarrassments. It does suggest an easy way of dealing with Henry's challenge to the supposed physical isolation of fictional worlds from the real world, and one which I endorse. But this success will force to the fore uncomfortable questions about our psychological involvement with fictional worlds.

We must be careful to distinguish fictionality from truth, even though the same words may be used in attributing either. The question of whether Henry saves the heroine when he leaps to the stage upsetting the performance just before her fate is sealed divides into two: Is it true that he saves her? Is it fictional that he does? The answer to both is no. It is not true that the heroine is in danger or even that she exists, so it cannot be true that Henry saves her. And it is not fictional that Henry exists, let alone that he saves anyone. There is no understanding whereby his unplugging of the sound effects, for instance, makes it fictional that he saves the heroine.[3] What *is* true is that Henry makes it fictional that the heroine survives. He arranges things in such a way that this fictional truth is generated. But doing this is not *saving* the heroine, either really or fictionally. To save someone is to make it true, not just fictional, that she survives. Henry does not make this true; neither is it fictional that he does.

Other examples can be treated in a similar fashion. A painter or author can arrange for it to be fictional that an evil man dies, or that

---

3. Except, possibly, in an unofficial game of make-believe. (See § 10.4.)

everyone lives happily ever after. But in doing so he does not kill the evil man or give everyone eternal bliss, nor is it fictional that he does.

This bears out our original impression that fictional worlds are somehow insulated from the real world. What happens in fictional worlds—what fictionally is the case—can indeed be affected by what happens in the real world. But one person can save another only if they live in the same world. *Cross-world* saving is ruled out, and for similar reasons so is cross-world killing, congratulating, handshaking, and so forth.

We must be careful how this isolation is described. It *can* be fictional that a real person such as Henry saves a heroine or destroys a villain or congratulates a hero. For as we have seen, real people can exist in fictional worlds. Suppose Henry is not just a spectator of the play but also a character in it; one of the actors portrays him. Obviously, then, it might be fictional that Henry saves the heroine— depending, of course, on what the actor portraying him does onstage. Or Henry might do the acting himself; he might play himself. In that case whether it is fictional that he saves the heroine will depend on what he does in his role as an actor. Either way, it may be fictional that Henry rides heroically to the rescue.

This might appear to constitute a major breach in the barrier between worlds. But the appearance is deceiving. It would be misleading to express the point by saying that real people *can*, after all, save fictional heroines. That is easily taken to mean that real people are such that fictionally they can save heroines, which is usually not true. Every actual person is such that it *can* be fictional that he saves a heroine. But this does not mean that it *is* fictional that he can do anything at all. Moreover, even when it is fictional that Henry can and does save the heroine, the interaction between them occurs entirely within the fictional world. It happens that Henry, besides "existing" in the fictional world and in that world saving the heroine, exists also in the real world. But he does not reach over *from* the real world to the fictional one to save the heroine; he doesn't need to, since he belongs to the fictional world also. Cross-world saving, interaction *between* worlds, remains excluded.

5.2.   FEARING FICTIONS

The plot [of a tragedy] must be structured . . . that the one who is hearing the events unroll shudders with fear and feels pity at what happens.

                                                        Aristotle, *Poetics*

If the gulf separating fictional worlds physically from the real world is as unbridgeable as it seems, it may be hard to make room for psychological interaction across worlds, for the apparent fact that real people fear Frankenstein monsters, pity Willy Loman, admire Superman, and so on. We feel a psychological bond to fictions, an intimacy with them, of a kind we ordinarily feel only toward things we take to be actual, things that are not (or are not thought to be) isolated physically from us. To allow that mere fictions are objects of our psychological attitudes while disallowing the possibility of physical interaction severs the normal links between the physical and the psychological. What is pity or anger which is never to be acted on? What is love that cannot be expressed to its object and is logically or metaphysically incapable of consummation? We cannot even try to rescue Robinson Crusoe from his island, no matter how deep our concern for him. Our fear of the Frankenstein monster is peculiarly unfounded if we are destined to survive no matter what—even if the monster ravishes the entire world!

Let's reconsider. *Do* we have psychological attitudes toward characters and other mere fictions? We do indeed get "caught up" in stories; we frequently become "emotionally involved" when we read novels or watch plays or films. But to construe this involvement as consisting of our having psychological attitudes toward fictional entities is to tolerate mystery and court confusion.

Here is an example of the most tempting kind: Charles is watching a horror movie about a terrible green slime. He cringes in his seat as the slime oozes slowly but relentlessly over the earth, destroying everything in its path. Soon a greasy head emerges from the undulating mass, and two beady eyes fix on the camera. The slime, picking up speed, oozes on a new course straight toward the viewers. Charles emits a shriek and clutches desperately at his chair. Afterwards, still shaken, he confesses that he was "terrified" of the slime.

Was he terrified of it? I think not. Granted, Charles's condition is similar in certain obvious respects to that of a person frightened of a pending real-world disaster. His muscles are tensed, he clutches his chair, his pulse quickens, his adrenaline flows. Let us call this physiological-psychological state *quasi-fear*. But it alone does not constitute genuine fear.

The fact that Charles describes himself as "terrified" of the slime and that others do as well proves nothing, not even if we assume that they are being truthful and, indeed, expressing a truth. We need to know whether this description is to be taken literally. We do not take

Charles literally when he says, "There was a ferocious slime on the loose. I saw it coming." Why must we when he adds, "Boy, was I scared!"? Charles might try (seriously or otherwise) to convince us of the genuineness of his fear by shuddering and declaring dramatically that he was "really terrified." This emphasizes the intensity of his experience, but that is not the issue. Our question is whether his experience, however intense, was one of fear of the slime. It may have been a genuinely emotional experience. He may even have been genuinely frightened, as we shall see. But he was not afraid of the slime.

It is conceivable (barely) that a naive moviegoer should take the film to be a live documentary, a news flash portraying a real slime really threatening him and all of us. Such a viewer would be afraid, naturally. But Charles is not naive. He knows perfectly well that the slime is not real and that he is in no danger. How then can he fear it? It would not be far wrong to argue simply as follows: to fear something is in part to think oneself endangered by it. Charles does not think he is endangered by the slime. So he does not fear it.[4]

That fear necessarily involves a belief or judgment that the feared object poses a threat is a natural supposition which many standard theories of emotion endorse.[5] There are dissenting opinions, however, which need to be taken seriously. I will argue that being afraid is in certain respects similar to having such a belief, in any case, and that Charles's state is not relevantly similar to that of believing that the slime endangers him; hence he does not fear it.

But let us assume, temporarily, that to fear something is, in part, to think oneself endangered by it. There will be objections even so. Could it be that Charles *does* think he is in danger from the slime, that he believes it to be real and thus a real threat? Even if he is fully aware that it is purely fictitious, he might also, in a different way or on a different "level," believe the contrary. It has been said that in cases like this, one "suspends one's disbelief," or that "part" of a person believes something that the rest of him disbelieves, or that one finds oneself accepting what one nevertheless knows to be false.

One possibility is that Charles *half* believes that there is a real danger and that he is at least half afraid.[6] To half believe something is

---

4. Our question is whether Charles fears for himself. Fear for someone else plausibly involves the belief that that other person is in danger.

5. On some accounts fear *is* in part a belief or judgment of danger. Others take it to be a feeling caused by such a belief, or merely accompanied by it. See Farrell, "Recent Work on the Emotions."

6. All "stage presentations are to produce a sort of temporary half-faith" (Coleridge, *Selected Poetry and Prose*, p. 396).

to be not quite sure that it is true, but also not sure that it is not true. If a child is told that his house is haunted but is uncertain whether the remark is meant seriously or in jest, he may half believe that it is haunted. If he does, he will be half afraid of the ghosts that may or may not inhabit it.

But Charles has *no* doubts about whether he is in the presence of an actual slime. If he half believed and were half afraid, we would expect him to have *some* inclination to act on his fear in the normal ways. Even a hesitant belief, a mere suspicion, that the slime is real would induce any normal person seriously to consider calling the police and warning his family, just in case. Charles gives no thought whatever to such courses of action. He is not *uncertain* whether the slime is real; he is perfectly sure it is not. Moreover, the fear symptoms that Charles does exhibit are not symptoms of a mere suspicion that the slime is real and a queasy feeling of half fear. They are symptoms of the certainty of grave and immediate danger and sheer terror. Charles's heart pounds violently; he gasps for breath; he grasps the chair until his knuckles are white. This is not the behavior of a man who basically realizes that he is safe but suffers flickers of doubt. If it indicates fear at all, it indicates acute and overwhelming terror. To compromise, to say that Charles half believes he is in danger and is half afraid, does less than justice to the intensity of his reaction.

One who claims that Charles believes he is in danger might argue not that this is a hesitant or weak or half belief but rather that it is a belief of a special kind—a "gut" feeling as opposed to an "intellectual" one. Compare a person who hates flying. In one sense Aaron realizes that airplanes are (relatively) safe. He says, honestly, that they are, and he can quote statistics to prove it. Yet he avoids traveling by air as much as possible. He is brilliant at devising excuses. If he must board a plane, he becomes nervous and upset. Perhaps Aaron believes, at a "gut" level, that flying is dangerous, despite his "intellectual" opinion to the contrary. And he may really be afraid of flying.

But Charles is different. Aaron performs *deliberate* actions that one would expect of someone who thinks flying is dangerous, or at least he is strongly inclined to perform such actions. If he does not actually decide against traveling by air, he has a strong inclination to do so, and once aboard the airplane he must fight a temptation to get off. But Charles does not have even an inclination to leave the theater or call the police. The only signs that he might really believe he is endangered are his more or less automatic, nondeliberate reactions: his throbbing pulse, his sweaty palms, his knotted stomach, a spontaneous shriek.[7] This justifies treating the two cases differently.

Here is one way of characterizing the difference: Deliberate actions are done for reasons; they are done because of what the agent wants and what he thinks will bring about what he wants. There is a presumption that such actions are reasonable in light of the agent's beliefs and desires (however unreasonable the beliefs and desires may be). So we postulate beliefs or desires to make sense of them. People also have reasons for doing things they are inclined to do but, for other reasons, refrain from doing. If Aaron thinks flying is dangerous, then, assuming that he wants to live, his actions or tendencies thereto are reasonable. Otherwise they probably are not. So we legitimately infer that he does believe, at least on a "gut" level, that flying is dangerous. But we do not have to make the same kind of sense of Charles's automatic responses. One doesn't have reasons for things one doesn't *do,* like sweating, increasing one's pulse rate, involuntarily knotting one's stomach. So there is no need to attribute beliefs (or desires) to Charles that will render these responses reasonable. Thus, we can justifiably infer Aaron's ("gut") belief in the danger of flying from his deliberate behavior or inclinations and yet refuse to infer from Charles's automatic responses that he thinks he is in danger.

Could it be that at moments of special crisis during the movie—when the slime first spots Charles, for instance—Charles "loses hold of reality" and *momentarily* takes the slime to be real and really fears it? These moments are too short for Charles to think about doing anything; so (one might claim) it is not surprising that his belief and fear are not accompanied by the normal inclinations to act. This move is unconvincing. In the first place, Charles's quasi-fear responses are not merely momentary; he may have his heart in his throat throughout most of the movie, yet without experiencing the slightest inclination to flee or call the police. These long-term responses and Charles's propensity to describe them afterwards in terms of "fear" would need to be understood even if it were allowed that moments of real fear are interspersed among them. Furthermore, however tempting the momentary-fear idea might be, comparable views of other psychological states are much less appealing. When we say that someone "pities" Willy Loman or "admires" Superman, it is unlikely that we have in

---

7. Charles *might* scream *deliberately.* But insofar as he does, it is probably clear that he is only pretending to take the slime seriously.

mind special moments during her experience of the work when she forgets, momentarily, that she is dealing with mere fiction and feels flashes of actual pity or admiration. Her "sense of reality" may be robust and healthy throughout the experience, uninterrupted by anything like the special moments of crisis Charles experiences during the horror movie. Indeed, it may be appropriate to say that someone "pities" Willy or "admires" Superman even when she is not watching the play or reading the cartoon. The momentary-fear theory, even if it were plausible, would not help us with cases in which one apparently has other psychological attitudes toward fictions.

Let's look at challenges to the supposition that fear necessarily involves a judgment of danger and that emotions in general have cognitive dimensions. Is it possible that Charles fears the slime even without taking himself to be endangered by it?

Charles's case and others like it are themselves thought by some to show the independence of fear and other emotions from beliefs, but the treatment of these cases is often distressingly question begging.[8] Charles *is* afraid, it is assumed, and he does not think he is in danger. So fear does not require such a belief. One then cooks up a weaker requirement so as to protect the initial assumption: Fear requires only imagining danger, it is said, or the idea of danger vividly presented. (The fuzziness of the line between imagining and believing adds to the confusion.)

The question begging rests implicitly, no doubt, on an assumption that taking Charles to fear the slime, as he says he does, is the natural or ordinary or commonsense or pretheoretically more plausible position, and that it wins by default or at least is to be preferred in the absence of substantial reasons to the contrary. This assumption is unwarranted. One will understandably hesitate to second-guess Charles's assessment of his own psychological condition. But the nature of his assessment is by no means self-evident, and is itself part of what is at issue. To take him literally and straightforwardly when he testifies to being afraid of the slime is dangerously presumptive. His saying this no more establishes that he thinks he is afraid than the fact that children playing a game of make-believe say "There is a monster in the basement!" shows them to believe that a monster is in the basement. If asked whether he has had any really terrifying experi-

8. I have in mind some (not all) of the recent literature narrowly focused on Charles's "fear" and on the experience of being "moved" by Anna Karenina. The reader can trace much of it back through the references in Hyslop, "Emotions and Fictional Characters," and Morreall, "Enjoying Negative Emotions in Fiction."

ences in the last decade, Charles might well omit mention of his confrontation with the slime. Or he might cite it in a parenthetical spirit, as though it does not really count. ("Well, only in watching a movie.") Initial intuitions are not all on one side, and neither side bears disproportionately the burden of proof.

Patricia Greenspan has undertaken a more substantial reconsideration of standard views about links between emotions and beliefs.[9] Frances, let's suppose, was once attacked by a rabid dog. As a result of this traumatic experience she "exhibit[s] fear in the presence of all dogs," including lovable old Fido, "even though she knows full well that Fido has had his rabies shots and is practically toothless anyway." Frances genuinely fears Fido, Greenspan suggests, as Aaron fears flying, and she avoids the dog when she can. But it is awkward to attribute to her the belief that Fido is dangerous. For one thing, she is perfectly happy to allow friends and loved ones to play with him. (Does she judge Fido to be dangerous to her but not to anyone else?)[10]

Part of the problem is that the notion of *belief* (or *judgment*) is far from clear. It may even be that beliefs do not constitute a natural kind, that no refinement of the ordinary notion has a legitimate place in a sophisticated theory of mind. If so, the question of whether emotions require beliefs will be ill formed.[11] But we do not have to settle these larger issues in order to diagnose Charles's condition. Even if Frances fears in the absence of a belief in danger, this hardly suggests that Charles does. Frances exhibits deliberate behavior characteristic of fear while Charles, we saw, not only does not but has not even the slightest tendency to. Frances "give[s] in to [her] immediate urge to sidestep any unnecessary encounters with Fido"; she flees "when [Fido] approaches, out of fear."[12] Fear is *motivating* in distinctive ways, whether or not its motivational force is attributed to cognitive elements in it. It puts pressure on one's behavior (even if one resists). (If sky divers and mountain climbers *enjoy* fear—not just danger—they nevertheless have *inclinations* to avoid the danger.) To deny this, to insist on considering Charles's nonmotivating state to be

9. "Emotions as Evaluations." See also Kraut, "Feelings in Context."

10. Perhaps Aaron too fears without thinking himself endangered?

11. Greenspan holds that emotions do require appropriate "evaluations" of their objects—"pro- or con-attitudes" ("Emotions as Evaluations," p. 163). Perhaps Charles lacks an attitude or "evaluation" necessary for fearing the slime, but these notions are no clearer than that of belief.

12. Ibid., pp. 164 and 162. Kraut, who argues that emotions do not require beliefs, appears also to allow action a role in their analyses ("Feelings in Context," p. 645).

one of fear of the slime, would be radically to reconceive the notion of fear. Fear emasculated by subtracting its distinctive motivational force is not fear at all.

The issue is not just one of fidelity to a deeply ingrained pretheoretical conception of fear. The perspicuity of our understanding of human nature is at stake. The "fear" experienced by Charles, whose munching of popcorn is interrupted by a wave of quasi-fear sensations, and that experienced by Frances, who flees from Fido, or Aaron, who, with his teeth gritted in determination, manages to go through with an airplane flight, are animals of different kinds. To assimilate them would be to emphasize superficial similarities at the expense of fundamental differences. A creditor might as well accept payment in fool's gold.[13] We will do better to assimilate genuine fear and genuine emotions generally to belief-desire complexes. (This does not imply that emotions are not "feelings.") If fear does not consist partly in a belief that one is in danger, it is nevertheless similar to such a belief (combined with a desire not to be harmed) in its motivational force, and perhaps in other ways as well.

My claim is not that Charles experiences no genuine fear. He does not fear the slime, but the movie might induce in him fear of something else. If Charles is a child, he may wonder whether there might not be real slimes or other exotic horrors *like* the one in the movie, even though he fully realizes that the movie slime itself is not real. He may genuinely fear these suspected actual dangers; he may have nightmares about them for days afterwards. And he may take steps to avoid them. *Jaws* caused a lot of people to fear sharks, ones they thought might really exist, and to avoid swimming in the ocean. But this does not mean they were afraid of the fictional sharks in the movie. If Charles is an older moviegoer with a heart condition, he may be afraid of the movie itself or of experiencing it. Perhaps he knows that excitement could trigger a heart attack and fears that the movie will cause excitement—by depicting the slime as being especially aggressive or threatening. This is real fear. But it is fear of the depiction of the slime, not of the slime depicted.

Several commentators willing to agree that Charles does not fear

13. Lamarque, "How Can We Fear and Pity Fictions?" points out that a condition like that Charles is in *may* be motivating in certain ways. Some viewers bury their faces in their hands or even flee the theater rather than face the horrors on screen. But this behavior is easily explained by a fear of the depiction or of experiencing it, or merely by a prediction that one will find the experience unpleasant. In any case, it is clear that viewers often do not behave in these ways or have any inclination to, even when they are said to be "afraid of the slime."

the slime have tried to understand his experience as one of actual fear with a different object. Peter Lamarque takes him to fear the *thought* of the slime (or the "sense" of a description of it).[14] That he *might* fear this thought, or the experience of thinking it, is evident; the Charles with a heart condition does. But Lamarque does not have in mind such special circumstances. What we call "fear of the slime" by ordinary appreciators fully aware of its fictitiousness is in general, he thinks, fear of the thought. I see no advantage in this suggestion. The reasons for denying that Charles fears the slime apply equally to the thought. Apart from special circumstances, as when he has a heart condition, he does not consider the thought dangerous or treat it as such, nor does he experience even an inclination to escape from it. Moreover, his experience simply does not feel like fear of a thought; characterizing it as such flies in the face of its phenomenology. And it is the *slime,* not a thought, that Charles so inevitably and unabashedly describes himself as afraid of. The original intuition, for what it's worth, is that the slime is the object of Charles's fear. Lamarque's proposal abandons that intuition and *also* fails to recognize our reasons for denying it. In § 7.1 we will understand Charles's experience in a way that does full justice to its phenomenology and accommodates easily the normal ways of describing it, yet does not have him (literally) fearing the slime or, necessarily, anything at all.

If I am right about Charles, skepticism concerning other psychological attitudes purportedly aimed at fictitious objects is in order as well. We should be wary of the idea that people literally pity Willy Loman or grieve for Anna Karenina or admire Superman while being fully aware that these characters and their sufferings or exploits are purely fictitious. It is not implausible that pity involves a belief (or judgment, or attitude) that what one pities actually suffers misfortune, and admiration a belief that the admired object is admirable, but the normal appreciator does not think it is actually the case that Willy suffers or that Superman is admirable. Perhaps it is more reasonable to think of these emotions as merely *akin* to such beliefs (together with appropriate desires), in particular in their motivational force. But the spectator who "pities" Willy, especially, would seem not to feel the motivational force in question; she feels no inclination to commiserate with him or to try to help him. It is less clear what one must believe about someone in order to grieve for him or what moti-

---

14. Ibid. Of course the thought may well be a *cause* of one's fear, even if it is not its object. See also Clark, "Fictional Entities"; Mannison, "On Being Moved by Fiction"; Novitz, "Fiction, Imagination, and Emotion"; Skulsky, "On Being Moved by Fiction."

vational force may be intrinsic to grief. But grief, as well as pity and admiration, would seem to require at the very least awareness of the existence of their objects. It is arguable that for this reason alone appreciators cannot be said actually to pity Willy or grieve for Anna or admire Superman.[15]

Like the slime movie, *Death of a Salesman, Anna Karenina,* and Superman comics may induce in appreciators genuine emotions of the *kind* in question. *Anna Karenina* fosters genuine sympathy for real people in unfortunate situations like Anna's; this is part of what is important about Tolstoy's novel. But to consider the experience commonly characterized as "pity for Anna" to be merely pity for real people "like" her (or a determination or inclination conditionally to feel pity toward people in like situations) does not do it justice.[16] It is no accident that we speak of sympathizing with or grieving for *Anna.*

A call for skepticism is no place to stop. We need a positive account of appreciators' experiences, a well-articulated alternative to literal-minded acceptance of ordinary claims that they "pity Willy," "grieve for Anna," "fear the slime," and so on. This I will provide in § 7.1. The success of the alternative will bolster the grounds for skepticism. But it is more than evident already that the legitimacy of such literal mindedness is not to be taken for granted.

5.3. FICTIONALITY AND OTHER INTENTIONAL PROPERTIES

> I prefer to exist in comic strip form rather than in real life, because my chances for happiness are greater.
>
> Woody Allen

Our difficulties in trying to sort out the ways in which fictional worlds and the real world are and are not connected demonstrate the inadequacy of the theoretical tools I have utilized so far. I have brought into play the notion of fictionality, distinguishing the question of whether it is fictional that Henry saves the heroine or Charles fears the slime from that of whether it is true. But I have considered only fictionality in work worlds, not fictionality in games of make-believe. And I have not made use of the account of fictionality developed in

15. People do seem to *fear* things of whose existence they are doubtful, such as a tornado that *might* occur. What is called fear of a (possible) tornado might better be thought of as fear that there will be a tornado, that is, as *de dicto* rather than *de re* fear, together with imagined *de re* fear.

16. See Charlton, "Feeling for the Fictitious"; Clark, "Fictional Entities."

Chapter 1. So far in this chapter fictionality has been thought of simply as a property of propositions, as analogous to being believed or desired or hoped for or denied.

The comparison of fictionality with such other intentional properties accords nicely with our feeling of physical isolation from fictional worlds. We cannot kiss or kick or save something that is believed or wished or said or denied to exist but does not; neither can we interact in any of these ways with something that exists only fictionally. The comparison also bears out my contention that we do not fear or envy or worry about characters whom we know to be merely fictional. If it is believed by someone that an assassin is after me, and I know for sure that nothing of the sort is true, we do not suppose that I might nevertheless be afraid of the believed-to-exist assassin. I can hardly envy a wished-for rich uncle, realizing that he is only wished for. If it is asserted, or denied, that there is someone on top of Mount Everest with acute appendicitis and I know that there is not, I will not and cannot worry about this nonactual person or feel sorry for him.

But the comparison of fictionality with being believed or desired or claimed fails entirely to bring out the disconcerting difference that seems to obtain between physical relations across worlds and psychological ones, the *impression* we have, even if it is illusory, that things known to be merely fictional are objects of our psychological attitudes. Why isn't it even tempting to think that we might pity a claimed-to-exist mountaineer with appendicitis without believing in him ourselves? Why don't we find ourselves in states that are at least very like pity, or describe ourselves as feeling "sympathy" when we contemplate such claims? (Perhaps occasionally we do—when we *imagine* with a certain vivacity the claims to be true. This takes us back to fictionality.)

It is clear that there is something special about fictionality, as contrasted with other intentional properties. The observation, made in §§ 1.5 and 3.8, that we have a strong inclination to think of fictionality as a species of truth even though we know better, sums it up. We somehow regard what only fictionally exists as being real and what only fictionally occurs as actually taking place, whereas we comfortably take what is merely believed or desired or said to exist or occur to be just that.

The psychological bond we feel to fictions is a dramatic symptom of this inclination, but there are others. One is the simple propensity to speak of "fictional worlds." The notion that fictions belong to worlds *different* from ours does, to be sure, reflect a conception of them as "distant" from us. But why do we think of fictions as belonging to "worlds" at all—as though they have a place (or places) *somewhere* in reality, however remote they may be from the actual world? It is significant that there are no very comfortable analogues of the notion of fictional worlds corresponding to most other intentional operators. If a novel makes it fictional that someone attends his own funeral, we are likely to express this by saying that "in the world of the novel" someone *does* attend his own funeral. But if Jones claims to be a genius, we are not likely to say that he *is* a genius "in the world of his claim(s)." And we rarely if ever speak of something's being the case "in the world of" someone's wishes, or belief, or denial. What fictionally is the case is naturally thought of as being the case in a special realm, a "world," in a way in which what is claimed or believed or desired to be the case is not.[17] The ordinary conception of "fictional worlds"—worlds different from the real one but worlds nevertheless—is a device to paper over our confusion about whether or not (mere) fictions are real.

Our conception of fictional worlds and our propensity to think of them as parts of reality are what give rise to worries about how Lady Macbeth can have children without having a definite number of them, or how it can be utterly impossible for us to discover how many she has. It is hard to imagine taking seriously analogous puzzles about what is said or believed or wished for. We may think that someone has children without having any idea how many she has. A person may wish to have children without wishing specifically for some definite number of them. There is no puzzle here; the incompleteness of "worlds" (shall we say?) of belief, desire, and so on is not even noteworthy. Why is it puzzling that fictionally Lady Macbeth has children without its being fictional that she has two, or that she has three, or more, or fewer? Because we think of fictionality as a kind of truth: If it is *true* that someone has children, it must be true of some definite number that that is the number of her children.

Often we do not even bother to mention explicitly that the "world" in which something is the case is a fictional one. We talk about what is fictional as though it is true "in the real world," as though it actually is the case. Instead of saying, "In the world of Defoe's novel, Robinson Crusoe survived a shipwreck," or "In the novel, Crusoe survived

---

17. Some philosophers have found it convenient to introduce notions of belief worlds, perceptual worlds, and so on. But these worlds, however useful they may be for technical purposes, do not capture the imagination in the way that fictional worlds do. This fact needs to be explained.

a shipwreck," we are likely to say *just* "Robinson Crusoe survived a shipwreck." "In the novel" and other colloquial fictional operators are commonly and comfortably omitted when there is no danger of misunderstanding.

This practice might be dismissed as nothing more than a shortcut to speed conversation were it not that we rarely take similar shortcuts with other intentional operators. Phrases such as "it is believed that," "it is wished that," "Jones wishes that" are not often left implicit. Even when it is clearly understood that one is speaking about Jones's wishes, it would be peculiar at best to say merely "A golden mountain will appear on the horizon," meaning that Jones wishes that a golden mountain would appear on the horizon. Occasionally "it is believed that" or "he says that" is omitted, but only in fairly special circumstances—ones that plausibly involve fictionality. (See § 6.3.) I know of no ordinary situations in which one might say, "Smith robbed the bank" as an abbreviation for "It is denied"—or "It is denied by Jones"—"that Smith robbed the bank."

Any doubts about the significance of this disanalogous treatment of fictional and other operators vanish in light of a related but even more striking peculiarity of German. In German, a sentence or clause, *p,* is ordinarily in the indicative mood when the speaker is committing himself to its truth and in the subjunctive mood when he is not; *p* is indicative when it is simply asserted and when it occurs in contexts like "I know that *p*," "I claim that *p*," and "He knows that *p*." It is subjunctive in contexts like "I wish that *p*," "I doubt that *p*," "It is believed that *p*," "He says that *p*." But fictional statements are a striking exception. The indicative is used in contexts like "In the story, *p*," even though the speaker is *not* committing himself to the truth of *p* ("In der Geschichte hat Robinson Crusoe einen Schiffbruch überlebt"). The indicative is used also when "In der Geschichte" is omitted but understood ("Robinson Crusoe hat einen Schiffbruch überlebt"). Indicative fictional statements obviously cannot be considered elliptical for their subjunctive variants—and not just because they are not shorter; the subjunctive variants are incorrect.

When we say, "Tom Sawyer was lost in a cave" (rather than "In the story, Tom Sawyer was lost in a cave"), or a German equivalent using the indicative, we are speaking just as we would if we were referring to an existing person named "Tom Sawyer" and saying of him that he (really) was lost in a cave.

Theorists are not bound to treat fictional entities in the way colloquial speech does, of course. But we do need to provide an explanation for the strangely persistent inclination to think of fictions as sharing reality with us which is reflected in colloquial speech. And our feelings of intimacy toward them must somehow be squared with the obvious physical isolation of fictional worlds from the real world. The observation that being fictional is in some ways like being believed or desired or claimed to be the case is inadequate on both counts. It only heightens the mystery.

The notions of fiction and reality are a rich source of witticisms, many of them deriving from the seemingly schizophrenic attitude toward fictionality we have been examining. Woody Allen's stated preference for fictional existence is one.[18] The joke trades on a deliberate conflation of the notions of fictionality and truth. Altered as follows: "I prefer to exist in (the world of) someone's desires (beliefs, denials) rather than in real life, . . . because my chances for happiness are greater," it falls flat. Deliberately conflating being true with being desired or believed or denied is just silly.

It is time to bring to the table more of the results of Part One and to develop them further. A proposition is fictional in the world of a work, we recall, just in case there is a prescription that it is to be imagined by appreciators. This brings us, as appreciators, into the picture in a way in which we are not in the case of (other people's) beliefs and wishes and claims. *We* are to imagine that Willy Loman lost his job, that Superman rescues people from tall buildings, and so on. Such imaginings are part of our games of make-believe, games that have their own fictional worlds distinct from work worlds. And these imaginings go with imaginings about ourselves. When we imagine Willy losing his job, we also imagine knowing about it. It is a mistake to think of appreciators as mere spectators of work worlds, observers from the outside of what is fictional in them. That leaves out our *participation* in games in which representations are props. A close look at the nature of this participation will go a long way toward extricating us from our difficulties.

---

18. In Flann O'Brien's *At Swim-Two-Birds* a writer creates characters for a novel, including one so ravishingly beautiful that he cannot resist ravishing her. She becomes pregnant by him and produces a son, a person of the "quasi-illusory sort." Resenting the author's dictatorial control, the bastard son (who inherited his father's literary talents), with help from the other characters, turns the tables on the author by writing a story about him in which he is arrested, tortured, charged with various crimes, and put on trial.

6

Participation

[The actor] on a stage plays at being another before a gathering
of people who play at taking him for that other person.
                                              —Jorge Luis Borges,
                                              "Everything and Nothing"

6.1. PARTICIPATION IN CHILDREN'S GAMES

Participants in games of make-believe need to be distinguished from mere onlookers. A minimal condition for participation
in a game is considering oneself constrained to imagine the propositions that are fictional in it. Participants consider the rules or principles of generation to apply to themselves. Onlookers, observing the
game from without, do not think of themselves as subject to its rules;
the fictionality of a proposition is not taken to be a reason for *them* to
imagine it. (They may take great interest in the game, however. They
may study it and its props thoroughly, learning what is fictional,
which fictional truths imply which others, what principles of generation are operative, and in many ways analyzing and explaining the
game and assessing its significance.)

The roles children play in their games usually go far beyond satisfaction of this minimal condition for participation. Typically they are
themselves props, reflexive ones: they generate fictional truths about
themselves. This is an immensely significant feature of children's
games, and one we will do well to bear in mind when we think about
representational works of art and the games people play with them.

Children are almost invariably characters in their games of make-
believe; the imaginings they engage in are partly about themselves. It
is fictional of a child playing dolls or house that he bathes a baby or
makes a bed or cooks spaghetti. In a game of cowboys and Indians it
is fictional of some of the participating children that they are cowboys, of others that they are Indians, of all that they ride around on
horses and perform assorted heroic deeds. Even when a child pushes a
toy truck too small actually to ride in across the floor, it is probably
fictional that he is driving it.

Such fictional truths about the participants are typically generated by the participants themselves. It is because Chris actually places a doll in a plastic bread box that, fictionally, he bathes a baby. It is by virtue of the fact that children "gallop" around the house that, fictionally, they ride horses in the Wild West. The participants are props as well as objects.

They are in these respects like stumps which make it fictional of themselves that they are bears. In fact the mere presence of participants in the vicinity of stumps or dolls or other such reflexive props makes it likely that they will function similarly. Props, especially reflexive ones, have a strong propensity to reproduce their kind. If Gregory and Eric declare a stump to be a "bear," it is natural, indeed all but inevitable, that they will understand things around it to be props also. If the stump's existence makes it fictional that it is a bear, we almost automatically take its possession of various properties to make it fictional that it is a bear of a certain sort—a large or ferocious one, one that is rearing up or sitting on its haunches. This holds for relational as well as nonrelational properties. The fact that the stump is on a hill makes it fictional that the bear is on a hill. If the stump is surrounded by poison ivy, it is probably fictional that the bear is in the midst of a poison ivy patch. These relational facts are as much facts about the hill and the poison ivy as they are facts about the stump. The hill and the poison ivy generate fictional truths; they are props. The hill, by virtue of having the stump on it, makes it fictional that the bear is on a hill. In this way props beget props.

Props thus begotten are almost always reflexive. It is fictional of the actual hill that the bear is on *it*. It is the actual patch of poison ivy in which, fictionally, the bear cavorts. Much of the rest of the stump's surroundings are similarly drawn into the game: hawks or airplanes flying overhead, the clouds in the sky, even a squirrel that lands momentarily on the stump and quickly ("frantically") scurries away. There are limits, of course. Termites in the stump or skyscrapers and freeways nearby may be ignored. It may be too disruptive to allow that fictionally the bear is termite infested, or has an urban habitat.

People, too, even mere onlookers, are drawn into the game and enlisted as reflexive props. If the stump is ten yards in front of Gregory, this fact about Gregory makes it fictional that the bear is ten yards in front of him; likewise if it is not Gregory but his mother who strays dangerously close to the bear.

Comparing participants to the stump and other reflexive props that it recruits such as the hill and the poison ivy is fine as far as it goes.

But the comparison ignores much of what is important about participants' roles in their games. There is the obvious point that *actions* Eric and Gregory perform vis-à-vis the stump make it fictional that they perform actions vis-à-vis the bear (often but not necessarily the same ones). If Eric comes across the stump suddenly, fictionally he comes suddenly across the bear. Other of his actions may make it fictional that he catches sight of the bear through the trees, or feeds it, or jumps on its back. He may yell "Watch out!" thereby fictionally warning Gregory of the danger.

A participant differs from the stump and many of its progeny also in being a primary focus of interest. It does not especially matter that the particular stump and poison ivy patch in Eric's and Gregory's game are the ones they are. Different ones (with similar properties) would serve just as well. But that it is Gregory and Eric who are reflexive props does matter—notably to Gregory and Eric. Reflexive props can be mere instruments in a game of make-believe, or they can be objects of interest in their own right. Participants fall into the latter category. I suggested that self-illumination is a key function of games of make-believe and other imaginative activities. The role of participants as reflexive props has a lot to do with the effectiveness of games of make-believe in this regard. Imaginings about oneself plausibly contribute to self-understanding; hence the value of fictional truths about the participants, of their being given prescriptions to imagine about themselves. But it is also important, as we shall see, that such fictional truths be generated by the participants themselves, that the participants be props.

Participants are in some ways better likened to actors playing themselves in theatrical events than to the stump, the hill, and the poison ivy patch. A game of make-believe bears comparison to a play or movie about Ronald Reagan in which the part of Reagan is taken by Reagan himself. Reagan is a reflexive representation, generating by his actions as well as his presence fictional truths about himself. No doubt he will be a focus of interest as well.

But this comparison too is severely limited. Onstage actors perform for audiences, but children playing make-believe games usually do not. Onlookers, if there are any, may be ignored; the children are not staging a spectacle. They play the game for the sake of playing it, for themselves. The point of an ordinary play about Reagan, no matter who does the acting, is to entertain or edify or illuminate spectators. The point of Eric's and Gregory's game is to entertain or edify themselves or to provide themselves with insight—insight partly about themselves. Eric and Gregory are the interested parties as well as the objects of interest.

The means by which Reagan is referred to and thus made an object of representation are very different from those by which Eric and Gregory are. The character Reagan plays bears his name; the theatrical event corresponds substantially to him (it may be fictional that the character was a Hollywood movie actor who continued his career as the fortieth president of the United States); the author may have inserted an explanatory footnote in the script. These are just the sorts of circumstances which in other cases establish that an actor portrays an actual person other than himself. In our example it happens that the person to whom they point is the actor himself. The fact that Reagan is the actor has little if anything to do with making him the object of representation. An understudy who takes over his role would portray Reagan just as surely as Reagan himself did. But it is because Gregory is a player in the game of make-believe that he is also its object. If Sam should take his place in the game, it would be fictional that Sam, not Gregory, confronts a bear in the woods. Since Gregory's representing role in his game is what makes him the object of representation, one can hardly fail to realize the identity of object and prop as one might in the case of the play about Reagan.

Participants in games of make-believe are thus props, objects, and imaginers all three, intimately combined in one neat package. They prescribe imaginings—imaginings that are about themselves by virtue of the fact that they themselves do the prescribing—and it is to themselves that they issue the prescriptions.

Not only is the participant to imagine about himself; he is to do so in a first-person manner, in the sense illustrated in § 1.4. Eric does not just imagine of someone whom he knows to be himself that that person confronts a bear and stands his ground, or flees, or whatever. He imagines *confronting* the bear and standing his ground or fleeing. And he imagines this *from the inside*. (We might say that he "imaginatively confronts a bear.") In general, participation involves imagining, from the inside, *doing* and *experiencing* things: imagining bathing babies, riding horses, driving trucks.

Even this does not fully capture the participant's experience, however. It omits the place of his actual activities in the content of his imaginings. His coming upon a stump, his dunking a doll, his "galloping" astride a stick are themselves reflexive props in the game and objects of his imaginings. He imagines of his sighting a stump that *it* is an instance of his sighting a bear, of his dunking the doll that in doing this he is bathing a baby, and so on.

Suppose Reagan watches from the audience as an understudy, taking his part, portrays the president making a speech. Reagan imagines that Reagan is giving a speech, and he realizes, probably, that the person he is imagining is none other than himself. He imagines, moreover, of the actor's performance that it is an instance of his—Reagan's—speaking. But this self-imagining is not done in a first-person manner; he is probably not *imagining giving a speech,* and he is certainly not imagining from the inside doing so. He might, of course, retreat into a reverie, prompted by the performance, and imagine thus. But *this* imagining, though from the inside, will not be an imagining of the actor's actions that *they* are an instance of his giving a speech. Participants in games of make-believe, being at once reflexive props and imaginers, imagine of the actual representing actions that they are instances of their doing things, and they imagine this from the inside.

6.2. APPRECIATORS AS PARTICIPANTS

We should expect viewers of paintings and films, spectators of plays, readers of novels and stories to participate in the games in which these works are props much as children participate in games of cops and robbers, cowboys and Indians, dolls, and mudpies. They do. There are differences, to be sure—important ones. But they must not be allowed to obscure the underlying similarities. Appreciation of representational works of art is primarily a matter of participation.

It is not *only* as participants that we are interested in representations, however. Critics and historians of the arts, insofar as they are not appreciators also, may be more onlookers than participants. And even appreciation does not always involve participation, as we shall see. My suggestion is that the primary or central instances of appreciation do, and that those which do not are nevertheless to be understood largely in terms of participation.

Given my earlier conclusion that representations have the function of serving as props in games of make-believe, it can hardly be controversial that appreciators normally participate in the minimal sense of considering themselves subject to the "rules" of make-believe, constrained to imagine as the works prescribe. What is not so obvious, but of very considerable importance, is that viewers and readers are reflexive props in these games, that they generate fictional truths about themselves. Many of their actions, like those of participants in children's games, are reflexive props as well. And as in the case of participants in children's games, it is in a first-person manner that appreciators are to, and do, imagine about themselves; they imagine, from the inside, doing things and undergoing experiences.

Support for thinking of appreciation in this way will come gradually. In the present section I present some preliminary considerations in its favor. But its strongest confirmation will consist not in direct arguments but in its contribution to a systematic and satisfying overall picture of representation, and its capacity to unravel puzzles, resolve paradoxes, and penetrate mysteries.

In § 1.4 I observed that imagining something (in the sense we are interested in) seems to involve, perhaps necessarily, imagining (oneself) believing or knowing it. So an appreciator who participates in a game in the minimal sense of imagining what is fictional will engage in self-imaginings as well. It should not be surprising that, when the appreciator recognizes that p is fictional and imagines believing or knowing that p, as well as p itself, it is fictional that he believes or knows that p. This fictional truth can be understood to be generated

6.1 · Willem Van der Velde the Younger, *The Shore at Scheveningen*. Reproduced by courtesy of the Trustees, The National Gallery, London.

by his realization that p is fictional (or possibly by his imagining as he does). Thus the appreciator is a reflexive prop in his game.

But appreciators' roles as reflexive props go much further than this, although in different ways for works of different kinds. *Gulliver's Travels* makes it fictional of itself that it is the journal of a certain ship's physician, Lemuel Gulliver. It is almost inevitable that in reading it, one should understand it to be fictional that one is reading such a journal. The novel, itself a reflexive representation, thus draws people into games of make-believe in much the way that Eric's and Gregory's stumps do.

The museum goer who looks at Willem Van der Velde's landscape *Shore at Scheveningen* (figure 6.1) in the normal manner makes it fictional of himself that he is looking at a group of sailing ships approaching a beach on which there is a horse-drawn cart. The painting is not a *reflexive* prop like *Gulliver's Travels*, but it too draws the appreciator into a game. Here is a quick consideration in support of this claim: The viewer—let's call him Stephen—might well remark, on examining the painting, "I see several sailing ships," and in much the same spirit as that in which he might say, "There are several sailing ships offshore." If, as seems likely, the latter is to be understood as prefaced implicitly by something like "It is fictional that," probably the former is to be understood similarly, as the assertion that fictionally he sees several sailing ships. It would seem that in making either of these remarks Stephen is expressing a truth. So it seems to be fictional not only that there are several sailing ships offshore but also that Stephen sees them. His looking at the picture makes this fictional of himself.[1]

Stephen does not belong to the fictional world of the painting, of course, as the ships do, and a reader of *Gulliver's Travels* is not a character in the novel as Napoleon is a character in *War and Peace*. We need to recall the distinction between work worlds and game worlds, between the worlds of novels, pictures, and plays and the worlds of games of make-believe in which these works are props. Appreciators belong only to the latter. It is fictional in the game the reader plays with *Gulliver's Travels*, not in *Gulliver's Travels* itself, that she reads the journal of a ship's physician, and it is fictional in the viewer's game with *Shore at Scheveningen* that he sees ships offshore. The world of an appreciator's game includes fictional truths gener-

1. We will later discover that "I see several sailing ships" may not be best understood as short for "It is fictional that I see several sailing ships." But our reasons will *reinforce* the idea that fictionally the speaker sees several sailing ships.

ated by all of its props, by the appreciator as well as by the work, and by relations among them. The work world includes only fictional truths generated by the work alone. It is *Shore at Scheveningen*–fictional that there are ships offshore, that there is a horse cart on the beach and a dog swimming in the surf. When Stephen contemplates the painting, it is fictional in his game that all this is so and in addition that he *sees* ships offshore and a dog in the surf. His game world is an expansion of the work world.

There is nothing unusual about having distinct fictional worlds, one included within the other. Illustrations in novels and performances of plays, like appreciators, add to one fictional world to form a larger one. A picture of Raskolnikov illustrating Dostoevski's *Crime and Punishment* combines with the text to establish a world in which not only is it fictional that Raskolnikov killed an old lady and otherwise acted as the novel has him acting, but also it is fictional that he has the appearance the picture portrays him as having.

What needs to be shown in order to establish that appreciators are reflexive props in their games of make-believe? That certain principles of make-believe are in force, ones whereby a person's reading of *Gulliver's Travels,* for instance, makes it fictional that she is reading the journal of a ship's physician, and whereby in looking at *Shore at Scheveningen,* Stephen makes it fictional that he sees ships. What principles are in force is a matter of what principles participants recognize or accept or take to be in force. This recognition or acceptance can be implicit, as we have seen; principles need not be stated or formulated. Games launched by stipulation ("Let's say that stumps are bears") include principles that are unthinkingly, automatically assumed to be in force (that larger stumps "count as" larger bears, for instance). But there need not be even an initial stipulation; children do not begin by saying, "Let's let this be a baby," each time they play dolls. The reader of *Gulliver's Travels* and the viewer of *Shore at Scheveningen* do not start their games with stipulations, and their understandings about the relevant principles of make-believe are almost entirely implicit.

Let us recall, also, that games of make-believe need not be social affairs. Appreciators' games are usually rather personal. Although the work that serves as a prop is publicly recognized and appreciated by many, each appreciator ordinarily plays his own game with it. There are exceptions to this, but what is important now is simply that games of make-believe can be personal; they can be played and even recognized by only a single person. So my proposal does not require anyone other than the appreciator himself to recognize the relevant principles of make-believe.

What needs to be shown, then, is that the reader of *Gulliver's Travels,* for example, recognizes or accepts, at least implicitly, a principle whereby her reading of the novel makes it fictional that she reads a ship's physician's journal, a principle according to which, given her actual reading, she is to imagine herself reading such a journal. We need to establish that Stephen accepts a principle whereby, given his observation of *Shore at Scheveningen,* he is to imagine himself looking at ships, a horse cart on the beach, and so on. I suspect that the painting causes more qualms than *Gulliver's Travels* does, so I will concentrate now on it.

Not only is Stephen likely to remark that he sees ships offshore when he views Van der Velde's beachscape, but he may also make comments such as: "I think I detect a trace of joy in the expression of the man on the cart, but he is too far away to see clearly"; "A seventh and an eighth ship are barely visible on the horizon"; and "Look, there's a dog swimming in the surf." It seems undeniable that Stephen thinks of himself, imagines himself, to be looking at a beach, ships in the ocean, and so on. And there is good reason to suppose that he understands this imagining to be called for, prescribed, by his experience of looking at the painting. His act of imagination is not a deliberate or reflective one, but is triggered more or less automatically by his perception of the painting. He is simply disposed to think of himself as seeing ships, without deciding to do so, when he sees the painting. This is just the sort of disposition which suggests implicit recognition of a principle of make-believe. If a child who comes across first a small stump and later a large one, both of which are "bears" in his game, is disposed automatically to imagine that he came across first a small bear and then a larger one, it will probably be reasonable to regard him as recognizing, implicitly, a principle correlating the size of "fictional bears" with that of the corresponding stumps. Stephen's tendency to imagine himself seeing ships when he looks at the picture is grounds for attributing to him acceptance of a principle whereby his seeing the picture makes it fictional that he sees ships.

Support of a different kind can be derived from other remarks people make when looking at depictions, ones involving demonstratives: Stephen says, "That is a ship," pointing toward a ship-depiction on the canvas. A person viewing a painting, film, or theatrical event may remark, while gesturing appropriately: "That child looks distressed"; "This is the king's armor"; "Someone is hidden in the shadows over there." It is not easy to see how such comments can be understood except on the hypothesis that the viewer is a reflexive prop in a game of make-believe, that he participates verbally in such a game. (This argument, unlike the preceding one, has no obvious analogues applicable to literary representations.)

Consider Stephen's "That is a ship." This is clearly a perfectly appropriate thing for a viewer of *Shore at Scheveningen* to say, provided that he points in the right direction. Stephen would be open to correction had he said, "That is not a ship," while indicating the same spot on the canvas. The most obvious explanation of this appropriateness would be that Stephen is asserting something true. Assume for the moment that he is. What truth is he asserting? Before looking for an answer, we should note that it would not be appropriate for a reader of a novel about a ship to make an analogous comment. The reader of *Moby Dick* will not in a similar spirit remark "That is a ship" while pointing toward the following passage or some part of it: "She was a ship of the old school, rather small if anything; with an old-fashioned claw-footed look about her. Long seasoned and weather-stained in the typhoons and calms of all four oceans, her old hull's complexion was darkened like a French grenadier's, who has alike fought in Egypt and Siberia. Her venerable bows looked bearded. Her masts . . ."[2]

What does Stephen mean? Certainly he is not pointing out an actual ship; his words require a less straightforward interpretation. Should we regard them as preceded implicitly by "It is fictional that," or more colloquially "It is true in the picture that"? Is Stephen claiming that the proposition his words express is fictional?

But what proposition is this? His words appear to express a proposition about a particular thing, about something he indicates by pointing and saying "that." The suggestion is that he is asserting of this thing that fictionally it is a ship. But what thing? The painting, or the portion of it at which his finger is aimed? Is he claiming it to be fictional that *this* is a ship? If so, his claim is false. No part of the canvas is such that fictionally it is a ship. Pictures, as we have seen, do not ordinarily represent themselves. This suggestion clashes with our assumption that Stephen is expressing a truth.

Does the demonstrative refer to a fictitious entity (assuming that there are such), one of the "ships in the picture"? Pointing to the relevant marks on the canvas might be a convenient way of indicating which fictitious thing one has in mind. Is Stephen saying either that

2. Melville, *Moby Dick*, chap. 16 ("The Ship").

this thing is fictionally a ship, or that it really is one? But then why is it not appropriate to point to the text of *Moby Dick* and declare "That is a ship"? If there is an "object in the picture" which fictionally (or actually) is a ship, there is an "object in the novel" which is such also. Why shouldn't the reader specify this fictional object by pointing to an appropriate part of the text and assert that fictionally (or actually) it is a ship?

There seems no other reasonable candidate for the referent of "that." If Stephen is attributing fictionality to a proposition, it must not be a proposition about something picked out by his demonstrative. Is he claiming it to be fictional merely that there exists a ship? But then why did he use the demonstrative? (This proposal is inadequate, in any case, for reasons that are clear from § 3.8.)

Maybe Stephen is not attributing fictionality to anything. Could it be that "that" refers to the painting or part of it, and that Stephen is claiming this to be a ship-*representation*? Is "That is a ship" short for "That is a ship-representation"? This again leaves us in the dark about why a reader does not point to *Moby Dick* and say "That is a ship." *Moby Dick* is a ship-representation too, to which one can refer by pointing. Granted, the picture and the novel are different kinds of representations. "That is a ship" might conceivably mean "That is a *picture* of a ship (a ship-picture)." But then we need an explanation of why "ship" should sometimes abbreviate "picture of a ship" but never "novel about a ship."

It is time for a more radical proposal. Perhaps Stephen is neither referring to anything nor attributing fictionality to anything. We may even have been too hasty in assuming that he is asserting something true, or anything at all. Things fall neatly into place if we suppose that Stephen is merely *pretending* to refer to something and to claim it to be a ship. This frees us from the supposition that his demonstrative actually picks anything out, or even that there is anything to which he pretends to refer. He only *pretends* that there is something which he refers to and calls a ship. Yet his use of "that" is easily explained. In pretending, one copies the behavior one pretends to be engaging in. In pretending to refer, one naturally uses words and gestures—demonstratives and pointings, for instance—that are ordinarily used in referring.

We are freed also from the obligation to find a truth that Stephen asserts, or for that matter a falsehood, or even a proposition, true or false, that he pretends to assert. "That is a ship" does not express a proposition; Stephen only pretends that it does.

Stephen is not trying to fool anyone, of course, when he pretends.

The sense of "pretense" relevant here is to be explained in terms of make-believe. In saying "That is a ship," Stephen makes it fictional that he is referring to something and claiming it to be a ship. This is a fictional truth about Stephen, one that belongs to the game he plays with the picture. He is a reflexive prop in that game. To pretend, in the sense in question, is to participate verbally in a game of make-believe.

We do have to make sense of the appropriateness of Stephen's remark and the corresponding inappropriateness of "That is *not* a ship" said while indicating the same part of the canvas. It was in order to explain this that we provisionally accepted the idea that Stephen was saying something true. But it can be explained by the fact that it is *fictional* that Stephen expresses a truth, whereas to say "That is not a ship" would be, fictionally, to express a falsehood. It is usually appropriate to act so as fictionally to speak the truth. Granted, one might respond, "That's true," to Stephen's utterance; or "Not so" if he should say, "That is not a ship." But these responses may be acts of pretense themselves; it may be fictional that one pronounces Stephen to have spoken the truth, or to have spoken falsely.

It is possible that Stephen is really asserting something, in addition to pretending to do so, and what he really asserts may be true. In § 10.3 we shall consider what it is that he might really be asserting. Answering this question will be much easier than it seemed earlier. We now realize that there is no reason to expect his assertion to be about something he refers to by "that." Stephen's pretense already sufficiently explains his use of the demonstrative.

Why is it inappropriate for the reader of *Moby Dick*, pointing toward certain parts of the text, to remark, "That is a ship"? Because the games we play with novels are of a different kind from those we play with pictures. It is not fictional of the reader that he sees a ship, or that there is one before him. (Probably it is fictional, instead, that he hears told of a ship.) So pointing to the text does not make it fictional that one points to a ship.

6.3.   VERBAL PARTICIPATION

There is no denying the pervasiveness of verbal participation in children's games. "Stick 'em up!" says a child pretending to rob a bank. His getaway is foiled when another child shouts, "Stop, thief!" and fictionally carts him off to jail. "Careful! There's a bear in the thicket behind you," Eric exclaims, fictionally warning Susan of a dangerous bear.

We should expect appreciators to participate verbally in their games with representational works of art as well. Nothing is more natural than for Stephen to pretend to point out a ship by remarking, "That is a ship," and we should not be surprised if, in saying things like "There are several ships offshore," "Gulliver was captured by the Lilliputians," and "Ivan was furious with Smerdyakov," it is sometimes fictional that one is recounting events or reporting on states of affairs. We shall see in Chapter 10 that this mode of participation is more common than one might suppose, and that the possibility of participating verbally underlies much of our discourse concerning representations even when we are not actually doing so. Let us note now that insofar as such discourse constitutes verbal participation, insofar as what is said is said in pretense (however "serious" it might also be), one puzzle broached in § 5.3 evaporates.

Why do we so often say simply, "There are several ships offshore," or "A society of six-inch-tall people was living in a strange land," when what we seem to mean is merely that this is so in the world of *Shore at Scheveningen* or in *Gulliver's Travels?* We may be pretending to assert seriously what we say. One would hardly expect a person pretending to claim that there really are several ships offshore to say, "There are ships offshore *in the world of the picture.*" Again, pretenders copy the behavior they pretend to be engaging in, and they tend to avoid blatantly displaying the fact that they are just pretending. "There are ships offshore" is exactly what we should expect a person to say if he is playing a game of make-believe in which, fictionally, he remarks on the presence of ships offshore. If a German speaker, in uttering "Robinson Crusoe hat einen Schiffbruch überlebt," is pretending to assert that a certain Robinson Crusoe survived a shipwreck, naturally he uses the indicative mood, the mood of assertion. He speaks as he would if he were actually asserting this.

Not all discourse about representational works of art is pretense (even in part), however. Surely critics delivering dry lectures of academic commentary and esoteric analysis are not usually engaging in make-believe. Yet fictionality operators are commonly omitted even then. "That is a ship" might well be said in even the most sober criticism, when the speaker cannot easily be construed as pretending to point out an actual ship. This should be taken as a hint that make-believe is somehow in the background in critical discourse about representations even when the speaker is not actually engaging in it; what the critic is analyzing or commenting on, after all, is something whose function is to serve as a prop in games of make-believe. We shall see in § 10.2 how this is so.

Fictionality operators are not the only ones that are sometimes left implicit, although they are omitted more commonly than most.

> On Iki Island . . . the fishermen are killing the dolphins annually now . . . [The] fish catch of the region is declining, and so the fishermen, cursing their luck, blame the dolphins. It doesn't matter that the area is over-fished, or that pollutants dumped by industry have destroyed breeding grounds, or that worldwide fish catches are down as a consequence of man's rapaciousness. On Iki, as elsewhere throughout the world, the dolphins are to blame—and so are put to death.[3]

Obviously we are not to understand the writer herself to be claiming that the dolphins are to blame or that the overfishing and pollution don't matter. She is saying or suggesting that the fishermen claim or believe this (or perhaps that they act as though they do). But the omission of "They believe (claim) that" is not a mere abbreviation. The paragraph loses its heavy irony when such phrases are inserted. ("It doesn't matter that the area is over-fished, they believe [claim], or that pollutants dumped by industry have destroyed breeding grounds . . . The dolphins are to blame, they think [say]—and so are put to death.") The writer of the original version is not just using an economical form of words to describe the fishermen's beliefs or assertions; she is describing them by pretending to endorse the ideas she attributes to them (no doubt with exaggeration).

This suggests a general account of irony (one variety of irony anyway) in terms of pretense. To speak ironically is to mimic or mock those one disagrees with, fictionally to assert what they do or might assert. Irony is sarcasm. One shows what it is like to make certain claims, hoping thereby to demonstrate how absurd or ridiculous it is to do so.[4]

> Call this a govment! why, just look at it and see what it's like. Here's the law a-standing ready to take a man's son away from him—a man's own son . . . Oh, yes, this is a wonderful govment, wonderful.[5]

3. Fundraising letter for Greenpeace USA, signed "Susan Fountain, For the men and women of Greenpeace" (undated).
4. Clark and Gerrig propose an account of irony along these lines in "Pretense Theory of Irony."
5. Pap, in Twain, *Huckleberry Finn*, chap. 6, p. 49.

Pap is mimicking, mocking, sneering at those who do seriously call it a government and a wonderful one, although he does not specify who they are.

In Garcia Marquez's story "The Incredible and Sad Tale of Innocent Erendira and Her Heartless Grandmother," Erendira escapes in the middle of the night from the tent where her tyrannical grandmother kept her. But

> [she] hadn't taken five steps outside the tent when she came across the photographer, who was lashing his equipment to the carrier of his bicycle. His accomplice's smile calmed her down.
>
> "I don't know anything," the photographer said, "I haven't seen anything and I won't pay for the music."[6]

Rather than claiming seriously that he did not see the escape or know about it, the photographer is indicating, demonstrating, what he will say later to the grandmother. He might be understood to be mimicking the assertion he intends to make, pretending (or pretending to pretend?) to claim that he did not witness the escape, as a means of assuring Erendira that he will say this to the grandmother. Hence the omission of "I will tell her that."

One might indicate that those who postulated the existence of a planet "Vulcan" believed it to have mass M by saying simply, "Vulcan had mass M." Here too there may be a hint or more of mimicry.

It is not easy to find cases in which phrases like "Jones wishes that" and "It is doubted that" are omitted but might plausibly be said to be understood. One does not say "Gold will rain from the sky" as a way of asserting that Jones wishes gold would rain from the sky. This may be because there is no actual or envisioned serious utterance of that sentence for the speaker to mimic. His point is not one that could naturally be made by pretending to assert that gold will rain from the sky, thereby showing what Jones does or might actually assert.

Although the propensity to omit certain operators is often explained by the fact that the speaker pretends seriously to assert what he says, such pretense can occur even when the operators are present. This is so in some instances of reported speech. In cases of direct quotation ("He said, ' . . . '") the quoter indicates what words the quoted person used by uttering them himself. But he may also show, demonstrate, what the other person claimed (seriously) by means of his words and the attitudes he expressed, by pretending to make that

6. "Innocent Erendira," pp. 40–41.

claim or express those attitudes himself. This will be evident when the quoter mimics or mocks the quoted person's tone of voice, inflection, emphases. In quoting a person indirectly ("He said that . . . ") one does not use the very words he did. But it may be fictional that one endorses a certain thought, thereby indicating that the quoted person, using his own words, endorsed it. Such participation may occupy less than whole sentences, even a single word or phrase. In saying, "Tom proposed that President X, 'the greatest president of the century,' should have his image carved in Mount Rushmore," one may be pretending to tout X as the greatest president of the century, thus portraying the quoted person as doing so. The scare quotes or an obviously exaggerated, sarcastic tone of voice serve both to make it clear that the speaker is engaging in this pretense and to betray it, to indicate that one is *only* pretending. (See § 11.1.)

"He said that" and "he said" are also devices of betrayal, when there is pretense to betray. But sometimes the pretense is not betrayed in this way; one may say merely, "Vulcan has mass *M*," or "X was the greatest president of the century," perhaps pretending to assert it seriously, as a way of indicating what someone else asserted or believes.

The games of make-believe in which one participates verbally, in these last cases, are ones that have no connection with representational works of art or works of fiction. They illustrate the pervasiveness of our propensity to engage in make-believe, and they point toward the account of existence claims I will propose in Chapter 11, many of which have nothing to do with such works. But more needs to be said about the ways in which appreciators participate in their games with pictures, novels, plays, and films—and the ways in which they do not.

6.4. RESTRICTIONS ON PARTICIPATION

So far we have readers and spectators of representational works of art participating in activities analogous to children's games of make-believe. Some may still be uncomfortable with the analogy. An adult curled up in an armchair with a novel or standing transfixed before a painting seems hardly to be participating in a game in the way children do when they play dolls or gallop around the house straddling sticks. Appreciators are passive, reflective, and "distanced," it may seem, while children are active, physical, and involved.

We have seen already that in addition to participating in games of make-believe, appreciators observe fictional worlds to which they do not belong, the worlds of the works they appreciate. Children are usually concerned only with the worlds of their games. If props like dolls and sticks have worlds too, ones analogous to work worlds, they are not often very interesting.

But beyond this there are significant differences in the nature and extent of children's and appreciators' participation. The participation of appreciators is restricted in ways in which that of children is not. We need to look carefully at these restrictions, both because they are important in themselves and to counteract their tendency to obscure the justice of the basic analogy between appreciation and the playing of children's games. It is essential to see the differences as differences of degree.

It may be fictional of Lauren, when she plays with dolls, that she bathes or feeds or dresses a baby. No one fictionally bathes or feeds or dresses a child while viewing Rubens' *Helene Fourment and Her Children*. It may be fictional in a game of dolls that a baby is hugged or carried or praised or reproved, or left at home while Lauren goes shopping, or discovered under a sofa, and so on and on, depending on what Lauren or other children actually do with or to the dolls. Nothing a viewer does with or to a picture will, ordinarily, make it fictional that he treats a child in any of these ways. By carrying a doll to her friend's house, Lauren fictionally takes a baby there. Moving Antoine Gros's *Napoleon at Eylau* from the Louvre to the Metropolitan Museum would not count as fictionally transporting Napoleon and a number of his troops (not to mention the building and fields shown in the background) across the Atlantic. It is fictional in any normal game played with the painting that Napoleon is at Eylau, no matter where the painting is. Games played by spectators of paintings are restricted in two ways, compared with children's games: There are fewer sorts of actions such that it can be fictional that the spectator performs them. And fewer actions which the spectator might actually perform are easily interpretable as contributions to the game, as generating fictional truths. Games played by appreciators of plays, poems, novels, and other works are restricted in similar ways, although the details vary from case to case.

Some restrictions are due to the nature of the props. Picking up a doll by its arms is naturally understood as fictionally lifting a baby by its arms. But Rubens' painting does not have similarly graspable "arms." Other restrictions may be more conventional. It is, I suppose, a convention of traditional theater that spectators are not to jump onto the stage, and that if one should do so, he is not to be understood as fictionally saving anyone or as fictionally doing anything at all. We could easily understand having a principle of generation whereby talking in a certain tone of voice in front of a painting counts as fictionally talking to a baby, or a principle on which by kissing a certain spot on a canvas one makes it fictional that one kisses a baby. But it is not the function of works like Rubens' painting to serve as props in games of this kind. (Such participation may be expected in games with religious icons, however.)

Children's games have limitations also, though usually less extensive ones. It is not easy, in a game of stump bears, for Eric to arrange for it to be fictional that a bear chases him home or that he scares one away by banging on pots. The stump just will not cooperate. (Of course he could abandon the prop and merely imagine such occurrences.) Lauren might, fictionally, hold a child while it practices walking, but without a fancy mechanical doll, she cannot very conveniently make it fictional that a child learns to walk on its own.

The limitations on appreciators' games do not prevent them from being immensely rich and varied. The participation of the spectator of Vermeer's *Girl Reading Letter by Open Window* (figure 8.8) goes far beyond his fictionally observing a girl reading a letter. It may be fictional that he notices her reflection in the window, or fails to notice it; that he glances in passing at the fruits in the foreground, or studies them intently; that he identifies them or counts them; that he examines the expression on the girl's face for clues about the content of the letter. He may, fictionally, point to the drape hanging over the window or to ornaments on the chair in the corner. It may be fictional that he remarks on what he knows, or discusses with someone what might be in the letter or where the fruit might have grown. It is fictional of the reader of *Gulliver's Travels* not only that she reads the journal of a ship's physician about a series of adventures in strange lands, but also that she reads quickly or slowly, with rapt attention or indifference, that she skims over details or commits them to memory. In both cases there will be psychological participation: it will be fictional that the appreciator has thoughts and feelings, opinions and attitudes of one or another sort concerning what he or she sees or reads about.

We have noted sharp contrasts between the activity of appreciating *Girl Reading Letter* or *Gulliver's Travels* in normal ways and that of children playing dolls and similar games of make-believe. There are many intermediate cases, however—games with some but not all of the restrictions imposed on the former activities. Some of them are games of standard, established, traditional kinds; others are improvised and ad hoc. Consideration of these intermediate cases and of the ease with which restrictions on participation in appreciators' games can be relaxed will encourage regarding the differences as differences of degree.

Sculptures often allow for games that are in some ways less restricted than the ones we play with pictures. To walk behind a portrait is probably not to make it fictional that one walks behind a person. But this is fictional, probably, when one walks behind (around) Michelangelo's *David*. Caressing a sculpture of a person—or even a painting— can easily be understood as fictionally caressing a person, even if convention does not sanction this understanding and snippy museum guards discourage the behavior. It is almost impossible not to regard throwing darts at a portrait or sticking pins into it as fictionally attacking the person portrayed. (It is not easy to bring oneself to stick pins into the portrait of a loved one.) The Richard J. Daley exhibition at the Feigen Gallery in Chicago in 1968 included *Tattered Image* by James Rosenquist, a pink-and-white plastic picture of Daley slit vertically into ribbons. Spectators shoved their fists through the picture, of course, fictionally punching Daley. Children sometimes treat pictures like dolls or teddy bears, feeding picture tigers and taking them to bed with them, for example, or sitting on pictures of fire engines in order to ride on them. These are unconventional games to play with pictures, but they are easily understood.

Several of these examples are altered versions of games ordinarily played with representations; they are like those normal ones except for the addition of certain sorts of overt physical participation. It would be hard to account for the naturalness of the variants if the normal games did not themselves involve some participation of the kind that occurs in games of dolls and other such children's games. How could it be so obvious that to put one's fist through *Tattered Image* is fictionally to punch Daley if it were not already fictional, just by virtue of the fact that the person is standing in front of the picture that she is standing in front of Daley, if she were not already participating in a game of make-believe? The activities of appreciating representations in normal ways are best seen as truncated variants of children's games of make-believe.

Why do we put up with the restrictions? We could, after all, be down on the floor playing dolls instead of looking at pictures and reading novels. It must not be assumed that restrictions on appreciators' games are disadvantages, that it is always or even usually better to play games that allow for more extensive participation. There are benefits in the limitations.

Appreciators' games are typically less physical than children's but more reflective, more contemplative. The restrictions on physical participation shift the emphasis to psychological participation. The convention that prevents Harry (Henry's more sophisticated brother) from leaping to the defense of a damsel in distress may result in his reflecting more deeply on her predicament; he does not interrupt his reflections to intervene, nor do worries about whether he should (fictionally) intervene intrude. Since the game is such that it cannot be fictional that he intervenes, it is likely to involve a richer collection of fictional truths about his thoughts and feelings. He also has ample opportunity for actually reflecting on what, fictionally, he thinks and feels.

A second advantage that limitations on appreciators' participation may have is that of expanding the contributions the artist makes to their games. Much of what is fictional in appreciators' games is determined by the work appreciated and by the artist responsible for it. But the artist's role can conflict with participation. If by writing or painting in a certain way an artist is to arrange for it to be fictional in appreciators' games that an accused murderer stands ramrod straight, defiantly, before a judge throughout his trial, the games can hardly be ones in which an appreciator can make it fictional that he badgers the accused into confessing, or helps him to escape, or disrupts the courtroom. Artists make valuable contributions to our games; we benefit from their experience, wisdom, and insight. But we must accept corresponding restrictions on our own participation.

The advantages are not all on one side. Playing a game in which the participants themselves, not artists or prop makers, are responsible for the principal fictional truths is like exploring or experimenting on one's own. In some ways and in some situations this is better than relying on a wise teacher.

To allow that restrictions on participation are sometimes desirable is not to diminish the role of the participation that does occur. What is important is not simply the fact that fictionally an accused murderer comports himself in a certain manner at his trial, for example—a fictional truth for which the artist is responsible—but the fact that fictionally the appreciator sees him comport himself that way or knows that he does, and has thoughts or feelings of one or another sort about his doing so. *These* fictional truths are generated by the appreciator and the artist in collaboration, by the appreciator's participating in a game in which the artist's work is a prop.

One common kind of limitation on appreciators' participation has not yet been mentioned. When it is violated or suspended or just absent, we have what I will call an "aside to the audience."

6.5.   ASIDES TO THE AUDIENCE

It is fictional that the viewer of *La Grande Jatte* sees people strolling in a park. But it is not fictional that they see him. The spectator of a performance of Ibsen's *Hedda Gabler* fictionally hears Hedda speak, but it is not fictional that she addresses him or speaks to him. It is not commonly fictional, in our games with representational works, that characters notice or respond to us, or that we exchange glances with them or hold conversations with them.

But there are exceptions. "I don't know if you happen to take Old Doctor Gordon's Bile Magnesia, which when the liver is disordered gives instant relief, acting like magic and imparting an inward glow?"[7] Thus does the narrator of P. G. Wodehouse's *How Right You Are, Jeeves,* speak to the reader. If the actor playing Balthasar looks toward the spectators in delivering the following lines, it is fictional that Balthasar addresses them:

Romeo: So shalt thou show me friendship. Take thou that.
  Live and be prosperous, and farewell good fellow.

Balthasar [aside]: For all this same, I'll hide me hereabout.
  His looks I fear, and his intents I doubt.[8]

Caravaggio's Bacchus offers a drink to the viewer. The first Western, *The Great Train Robbery* (figure 6.2), ends with a shot in which a bandit aims a revolver at the camera and fires. There are occasions in film and theater when a character suddenly turns to the spectator to ask advice or appeal for sympathy.[9] There is the First World War recruitment poster captioned "Uncle Sam Needs You!" Let us speak

---

7. Wodehouse, *How Right You Are, Jeeves,* p. 85.
8. Shakespeare, *Romeo and Juliet,* act 5, sc. 3.
9. For example in *Tom Jones* (Tony Richardson, 1963) and *The Magic Flute* (Ingmar Bergman, 1976).

of "asides to the audience" (or just "asides")[10] in cases like these (altering somewhat the usual application of this phrase).

Asides are not always easy to diagnose. The presence of second-person pronouns or "Dear reader" in a literary work is no sure indication. (Nor is it necessary—witness the *Romeo and Juliet* exam-

6.2 · Edwin S. Porter, *The Great Train Robbery*, still (1903). Museum of Modern Art / Film Stills Archive, 11 W. 53rd Street, New York City.

ple.) The author can *actually* address the reader, as Apuleius does in *The Golden Ass:* "In this Milesian Tale, reader, I shall string together a medley of stories, and titillate your agreeable ears with a merrily whispered narrative, if you will not refuse to scan this Egyptian paper written with a subtle pen of Nilotic reeds,"[11] and as Thackeray

10. There are what are called asides which are not to the audience, as when Balthasar speaks his lines gazing at the sky, but they won't concern us now.

11. Apuleius, *The Golden Ass*, p. 31.

appears to do in *Vanity Fair*.[12] Groucho Marx stops in the middle of *Animal Crackers* to remark (approximately): "Well, the jokes can't all be funny. You gotta expect that once in a while." If the reader is actually being addressed, occurrences of "you" in the text need not indicate that it is fictional that he is.

But in instances like these we might attribute the words to a fictional storyteller. We might understand it to be fictional in the game played by the reader of *Vanity Fair* that he is addressed by a storyteller, who then proceeds to tell his tale of harrowing villainy and complicated crime. This gives us an aside after all.[13]

In epistolary novels second-person pronouns are likely to "refer" not to the actual reader of the novel but to the character to whom the letter is written; it may not be fictional that the novel reader is addressed. But perhaps the reader of *Lord Jim* is to imagine himself to be among the friends to whom Marlow recounts his experiences.

John Barth gives us an especially intriguing example in the following paragraph:

> The reader! You, dogged, uninsultable, print-oriented bastard, it's you I'm addressing, who else, from inside this monstrous fiction. You've read me this far, then? Even this far? For what discreditable motive? How is it you don't go to a movie, watch TV, stare at a wall, play tennis with a friend, make amorous advances to the person who comes to your mind when I speak of amorous advances? Can nothing surfeit, saturate you, turn you off? Where's your shame?[14]

The actual reader of Barth's story may well feel himself the target of this tirade. If it is "from inside a fiction" that he is being addressed, this presumably means that it is fictional that he is addressed, and we have an aside. (We will just have to swallow the paradox that fictionally the speaker recognizes the fiction within which he speaks.)

But this paragraph is to be understood as occurring within quotations, for Barth continues: "Having let go this barrage of rhetorical or at least unanswered questions and observing himself nevertheless in midst of yet another sentence he concluded . . . "[15] So it is not fictional in my game with "Life Story" that the words "The reader! You,

12. See the passage quoted in § 7.6.

13. See § 9.6. It may of course be *both* fictional and true that the reader is addressed. And it may be the actual author who fictionally addresses him.

14. "Life Story," p. 123.

15. Ibid., p. 124.

dogged, uninsultable, print-oriented bastard" are directed to me, but rather, apparently, that they are part of a story. It is merely fictional that there is an aside. It is "Life Story"–fictional that there is a story such that it would be fictional in games played by its readers that they are addressed.

There are other possibilities, however. It may be that (to speak intuitively) it is the actual reader of Barth's story, you or I, who is addressed from inside the story within the story. Here are a couple of stabs at what this might mean: (a) It is fictional in my game with "Life Story" that I read a paragraph quoted from a story and that in doing so I play a game in which fictionally I am addressed. Again, it is only fictional that there is an aside, but it is fictional that there is an aside directed to *me*. (b) In reading "The reader! You, dogged, uninsultable, . . . " I am really playing a game, one distinct from the game I play with the story as a whole, in which it is fictional that I am addressed. So the paragraph taken alone really does contain an aside directed to me. But it is "Life Story"–fictional that this paragraph, together with its aside, occurs in a story and is directed to whoever should read *that* story.

We do not encounter quite the same difficulties in identifying asides to the audience in the visual arts. It is hard to imagine a viewer of a painting confusing its being fictional that Bacchus or a bandit notices him or offers him a drink or aims a gun at him with the painter's actually doing so. There are other difficulties, however; we will come upon one shortly. But let's focus on relatively unproblematic cases first.

Asides can be singular or plural. It is fictional in the game played by a viewer of *The Great Train Robbery* that a bandit aims a gun at him alone. But Balthasar may speak to the audience as a whole. We might think of the spectators of *Romeo and Juliet* as participating in a single joint game of make-believe, one in which it is fictional that Balthasar addresses them all collectively. But it is usually best to understand each individual spectator of a movie as engaging in his own private game. (The darkness of the theater encourages this also.) It is fictional in the game each spectator of *The Great Train Robbery* plays that a gun is aimed directly at him, but it is not fictional in any game that a gun is aimed directly at all of the spectators at once. This highlights a significant difference between film and theater: An actor on stage cannot aim a gun at or establish eye contact with each spectator simultaneously; an actor in film can.

Asides can be plural even if the games of make-believe are individual. When Dostoevski's Underground Man says, "And so, in the end, ladies and gentlemen, it's best to do nothing at all!"[16] it is not fictional in any normal game that he is addressing all of the actual readers of *Notes from the Underground* collectively. It is fictional in each reader's game that he addresses a group of people to which the reader belongs.

Asides are not rare, but in many contexts they are special. One is taken aback by Bacchus' offer of a drink. It is disconcerting, if pleasantly so, to go to a movie and be recognized from the screen. There is something surprising, striking about many asides. They mark an important shift in one's relation to the fiction.

Some will say that asides "bring the appreciator into the fiction," that we suddenly feel ourselves included in a fictional world in a way in which normally we are not. Asides do involve appreciators in the worlds of their games: it is fictional that the reader or spectator is noticed or addressed or offered a drink or threatened. But appreciators belong to their game worlds anyway, even without any such device. The naturalness of asides—our readiness to understand that fictionally someone notices or speaks to us, even if we are surprised that this should be fictional—supports this claim. When it is fictional that someone looks in a certain direction or uses second-person pronouns, why do we so readily understand it to be fictional that he notices or addresses *us* unless it is fictional already that we are there to be noticed or addressed?

But if we do belong to our game worlds anyway, why should there be anything special or remarkable about asides? Part of the answer lies simply in the fact that being recognized or addressed in real life marks a significant change in one's social situation. (Think of a student suddenly called on in class or a lecturer picking out someone in the upper gallery and speaking specifically to him.) One feels included in a manner one wasn't previously. An aside makes it fictional that the appreciator is included similarly. This change may be important, but it doesn't consist in the appreciator's suddenly being drawn into a fictional world to which until then he did not belong.

The special poignancy of many asides is to be explained in part, however, by restrictions against them. In many contexts they are deliberately avoided; sometimes they are more or less explicitly forbidden. Hence, for example, the usual instructions to novice film actors not to look at the camera. Michael Fried has documented

16. *Notes from the Underground*, p. 120.

Diderot's condemnation of most asides (to the audience) in theater and painting as in poor taste, and the preference of painters such as Jean-Baptiste-Siméon Chardin and Jean-Baptiste Greuze for figures absorbed in what they are doing and oblivious to everything else, notably refusing to acknowledge the beholder's presence.[17] Asides are especially striking when they are unexpected or forbidden, of course. The surprise is sometimes not unlike that which attends the violation of other conventions: a small patch of color in an otherwise black-and-white sketch, for instance.

(Diderot seems to think of the beholder as belonging to a fictional world together with the characters, even when they do not recognize him. In explaining why in a painting of Susannah and the Elders no one is offended by Susannah, who "covers herself with all her veils" from the Elders' view while exposing "herself entirely to the eyes of the beholder," he observes: "It is the difference between a woman *who is seen* and a woman who exhibits herself."[18] Although, as Fried notes, the woman in Greuze's *Jeune Fille Qui Pleure Son Oiseau Mort* is "wholly absorbed in [an] extreme state and oblivious to all else," Diderot remarks that "soon one catches oneself conversing with this child and consoling her" and reports what he remembers having said to her on various occasions: "There, there, my child, open up your heart to me.")[19]

Not all asides are equally special or equally disconcerting. Subjects of portraits can "look at the viewer" without raising eyebrows. There is nothing especially noteworthy about the fact that the gentlemen in Hans Holbein's painting *The Ambassadors* appear to be looking out at us. The most obvious explanation is that in portraiture, or portraiture of certain kinds, there is no restriction against asides; they may even be more or less obligatory.[20] Hence the unremarkableness of the fact that fictionally the ambassadors notice us. But *The Ambassadors* can be understood not to involve asides at all. It may be expected in portraits of certain kinds that the sitter will be made to "look straight ahead," to focus, as it were, on the spot where viewers will stand. And

17. Fried, *Absorption and Theatricality*. "[The leading actors] arrive with careful, measured steps; they seek applause, they depart from the action; they address themselves to the audience; they talk to it and become dull and false" (Diderot, *Discours,* quoted and translated in Fried, p. 95).

18. Quoted and translated in Fried, *Absorption and Theatricality,* p. 97; my italics.

19. Fried, *Absorption and Theatricality,* pp. 58–59.

20. "More nakedly and as it were categorically than the conventions of any other genre, those of the portrait call for exhibiting a subject, the sitter, to the public gaze; put another way, the basic action depicted in a portrait is the sitter's presentation of himself or herself to be beheld" (ibid. p. 109).

because this is expected, it may *not* be understood to be fictional that the sitter notices the viewer. He looks in the direction he does not because he has caught sight of the viewer (so to speak), but simply because that is the way portraits of that kind are painted. (I do not think there is a definitive answer as to which of these two construals of works like *The Ambassadors* is correct.)

Asides make for moments of interaction, within the appreciator's game world, between him and one or more of the work's characters. But only moments. The interaction remains severely limited. It is rarely fictional that the appreciator carries on an extended conversation with a character, or that he and a character make eyes at each other or exchange more than a glance or two.[21] There is an obvious practical reason for these limits. When the artist constructs her work, she determines, once and for all, what fictionally her characters say and do. But different appreciators will behave differently in front of the work; what fictionally they say and do, what they choose to attend to and how, what they mutter under their breath will vary greatly, and some will behave in ways the artist did not foresee. So the artist cannot fit her characters' responses to what, fictionally, the appreciator says or does. She cannot customize the work for the game any particular appreciator might play with it.[22] If fictionally Papageno, in Bergman's rendition of Mozart's opera, appeals to the appreciator for sympathy, it may be fictional that the appreciator willingly complies, or that he brushes off the request with disdain, or that he ignores it. What should the artist (Mozart or Bergman) have Papageno do now? Should he make it fictional that Papageno breaks down in tears of gratitude, or that he spits in the spectator's eye? Rather than risk an inappropriate reaction (or an appropriate one, if the artist prefers it to be fictional that the character responds inappropriately), the interaction is cut off.

Cutting off interaction after an aside can be awkward. If care is not

21. Italo Calvino's *If on a Winter's Night a Traveler* is a long, extended aside; it is fictional in the reader's game that he is addressed constantly during his reading. But there still is little *interaction*. It is not often fictional that the reader and narrator respond very much to each other or that they converse together. Even when it is fictional that the reader speaks and the narrator replies, it is the words of the text, not what the reader actually says, that determine what fictionally he says. When Calvino writes: " 'I prefer novels,' she adds, 'that bring me immediately into a world where everything is precise, concrete, specific . . .' Do you agree? Then say so. 'Ah, yes, that sort of book is really worthwhile' " (p. 30), he is putting words into the reader's mouth. Contrast children's games: It is because Gregory actually says, "Watch out for the bear!" that fictionally he says this.

22. This can be done in improvisational theater. It is no accident that improvisation and audience participation often go together. There is also interactive fiction for computers.

taken to do it cleanly, it may be unclear when the aside ends. We may be uncertain, for example, whether it is fictional that Papageno deliberately ignores whatever response we make to his request, or whether it merely fails to be fictional that he acknowledges it. It may seem better, simpler, to have no interaction at all, not to allow it to be fictional that the appreciator is noticed or addressed in the first place. Hence, the restriction against asides.

One effect of this restriction and of limitations on participation generally is to give the appreciator a kind of objective, "distanced" perspective on the world of his game. Questions about what fictionally others think of him, how they do or might react to him, what might be demanded of him recede into the background, as do questions about how fictionally he might or should try to influence events. Indeterminacy concerning certain aspects of his place in the game world typically goes with the restrictions. Nothing much is to be said about why the strollers in *La Grande Jatte* fail to notice me (assuming it to be fictional that they do not notice me—not just not fictional that they do). It is not fictional that they deliberately ignore me, or that they absentmindedly overlook me. We will not comfortably affirm that, fictionally, they are too preoccupied with other things to notice me, or that the explanation is none of the above. Some such answers may be less artificial than others.[23] Even so, the question is out of place, silly. The appreciator does not ask why fictionally no one pays any attention to him. And it is not fictional that he wonders why no one does or that he tries to come up with an explanation.

Since convention forbids Harry to come to the assistance of the unfortunate heroine (prevents it from being fictional that he does), there is probably no saying what, fictionally, his reason for not doing so was; neither, I think, is it fictional that the thought of intervening simply did not occur to him. (After all, it is fictional that he is desperately concerned about her plight and feels deeply for her.) There is little room for questions about whether he ought to get involved or how he might do so or what people would think of him if he did or if he didn't. It won't be fictional that he kicks himself afterwards for not helping, or makes excuses for his inaction, or feels guilty or justified. (Harry may reflect on whether, in real life, he would or should go to the aid of a woman in similar straits. But this is different.)

23. Not all such questions dissolve in indeterminacy. Why don't the men in Pieter Brueghel's *Parable of the Blind* notice the viewer? Because they are blind, obviously. It may be fictional in a viewer's game with *Une Jeune Fille* that the girl does not see him because she is absorbed in her grief. (But it probably is not fictional that the viewer *would* have been noticed if the men weren't blind or the girl weren't absorbed in grief, or for that matter that he would not have been noticed even in those circumstances.)

The appreciator is thus encouraged to concentrate on fictional truths about what the characters are up to, the predicaments they find themselves in, and what they think and feel. It is important, also, what fictionally he thinks and feels about them, but in abstraction, to a certain extent, from how they do or might affect him. (Charles's confrontation with the slime, involving an aside as it does, is unusual in this respect.) This allows the appreciator a kind of empathy with the characters, an ability to look at things more purely from their points of view, from a perspective relatively uncontaminated by his own personal concerns.

The "objectivity" of this perspective contributes, no doubt, to the impression some may have that appreciators do not ordinarily belong to fictional worlds at all, that—in the absence of asides anyway— they merely observe from without. This impression is mistaken, but we can think of the appreciator as having, usually, a rather "sketchy" or "ghostly" presence in the world of his game, in light of the restrictions on his role in it and the indeterminacy that often results from them. Asides disturb this "objectivity" momentarily and reduce the indeterminacy. They do not introduce the appreciator into a fictional world he did not previously or would not otherwise belong to. But they do give him a slightly fuller presence in the world of his game.

6.6. SEEING THE UNSEEN

Another objection has been waiting impatiently in the wings. It is time to call it onstage.[24]

It is fictional in the Creation panels of Michelangelo's Sistine Ceiling, and so in viewers' games of make-believe as well, that God creates the earth and the planets and that there is no one else present (no humans anyway) to witness these momentous events. How, then, can it be fictional in the viewer's game that *he* witnesses them? Is it fictional that the Creation is observed by no one and also observed by him? These depictions seem wholly unlike works that clearly do serve up contradictory fictional truths: Escher's *Waterfall*, Hogarth's *False Perspective*, stories about time travel and circle squaring (although in

24. Charles Karelis and others have raised this objection in conversation. See also Wolterstorff, *Works and Worlds,* p. 325, and Karelis, "The Las Meninas Literature." The issues here are obviously related to Berkeley's claim that one cannot conceive a tree "existing by itself, independent of, and unperceived by any mind whatsoever," on the grounds that if one conceives it, it is not mind independent (*Three Dialogues,* pp. 163–164). See Williams, "Imagination and the Self," and Peacocke, "Imagination, Experience, and Possibility."

the latter cases the contradictions are fictional in the work world as well as the world of the appreciator's game). The Creation panels evoke scarcely any sense of paradox.

When we view a painting or film depicting people dressing or undressed, bathing, or making love, is it fictional that we watch these activities? Often it is implied that the person in question is entirely proper, modest, even shy—someone who would never allow herself to be seen in those circumstances. Can it also be fictional that she allows us to see her so? Why doesn't she react to our presence? Why is she not embarrassed? Could she really be unaware of our prying eyes? Is she blind? Surely it is not fictional that we are spying through a keyhole or a convenient knot in the wall or a one-way mirror. Must we worry that a cough will betray our presence? Shouldn't *we* be ashamed to be peeping as we are?

When an indoor scene is staged or filmed, the viewer's point of view is, in many cases, too distant to be within the room. Is it fictional that she sees through the wall? That it is transparent? That the wall (the "fourth wall") is missing?

It is fictional in some literary works that certain horrible events transpire which no one lives to tell of. Yet there may be a narrator who, fictionally, tells the reader about these events. How can this be?

When we read epistolary novels, it is fictional that we read letters written by one character to another, sometimes very personal and private ones. It may be fictional that a given letter was burned immediately after it was received and that no one but the sender and the recipient ever saw it. How then can it be fictional that *we* read it?

The embarrassments pile up if we let them. But we need not let them. The reader's sense of déja vu points to the proper response. The questions that are supposed to embarrass us are, in varying degrees, *silly,* like those examined in § 4.5.[25] They are largely if not entirely irrelevant to appreciation and criticism. It would be inappropriate to stew over them, or even to raise them without tongue in cheek. Like many other silly questions, they arise from the demands of appreciators' access to fictional worlds. The pictorial mode is chosen for the portrayal of the Creation in order to give the appreciator the experience of fictionally observing it ("Now I realize what it must have been like"). The cost—if it is a cost—is the nominal clash with the fact that fictionally the Creation is unobserved, a clash that is to be ignored.

___

25. Not entirely silly, perhaps. The viewer of the Sistine Ceiling can, with an effort, summon a sense of paradox. Viewers of painted nudes *do* sometimes feel a certain embarrassment. Some filmmakers insist that their cameras respect walls and other opaque barriers.

However these clashes are to be treated, the mere fact that there are such, that (silly) questions can be posed, hardly constitutes a challenge to my claims about appreciators' participation in games of make-believe. Apparent paradoxes arising from cases like that of Michelangelo's ceiling are of a kind that would be with us anyway, as we know from § 4.5, even if we did not recognize this participation. We are no worse off recognizing it.

Will the proper treatment of the silly questions, if not their mere existence, uncover a challenge? Several possible ways of answering them—if anyone insists on answers—are evident from § 4.5. We could defuse the apparent paradoxes by declaring certain of the offending fictional truths deemphasized, or by considering them not to be generated at all. One option, to be sure, would be to deny that it is fictional in one's game that one witnesses the Creation, or sees the lady in her bath, or reads the private letter. But there are other perfectly reasonable options, and this suffices to take the wind out of the sails of the objection.[26] I am partial to the idea that although it is fictional that we see the Creation and also fictional that nobody sees it, the conjunction of these propositions is not fictional; it is not fictional that there is and is not a witness to the Creation. Some may prefer deemphasis of one or another of the trouble-making fictional truths. Pictures are inherently props for use in visual games of make-believe. That fictionally the viewer of the Sistine Ceiling observes the Creation follows almost automatically from the fact that it is represented pictorially.[27] This may be a reason to take this fictional truth for granted, if it is not exploited or emphasized in one way or another, a reason to consider it deemphasized.[28]

My reply to the objection is no more than that. I have certainly not established in this section that pictures are props in games in which fictionally we perceive things or that appreciators in general participate in games of make-believe; my defense of these claims comprises this entire study. Here I have merely shown how little one who accepts them on other grounds need worry about the objection raised.

---

26. The tinge of (fictional) embarrassment which the viewer of a depiction of a lady in her bath might feel suggests, at least, that it is fictional that he sees her, that declaring that fictional truth blocked is not the best way of defusing the paradox. A reader of a novel describing a lady's bath is unlikely to feel even the tinge; it is not fictional that he sees her.

27. The viewer must at least be "playing the game," of course.

28. There may be reasonable solutions consisting in assigning the fact that fictionally the viewer observes the Creation and the fact that fictionally it is unobserved to different fictional worlds. Or one might regard the fresco as an "ornamental" representation in relevant respects, in the sense to be introduced in § 7.6.

7

Psychological Participation

We have barely scratched the surface, so far, of the ways in which appreciators participate in games with representational works. This participation is almost always partly physical, as we have seen, notwithstanding the restrictions noted in § 6.4. Fictionally we see ships, read journals, listen to eyewitness reports, and sometimes discuss what we see or read or hear about. But there are important psychological dimensions to our participation as well. Actions of seeing and reading and talking are themselves partly psychological. When we contemplate *Shore at Scheveningen* or read *Gulliver's Travels,* it is fictional not just that our eyes are aimed in certain directions—toward ships or people or the pages of a journal—but also that we notice things, that we make discoveries and acquire beliefs. Often it is fictional that we look *for* things of certain kinds, or that we are surprised or relieved or excited or bored by what we see or read. Verbal participation is not just a matter of fictionally mouthing certain words. Fictionally we tell people things, expecting them to believe what we say, or at least to understand. It is fictional, ordinarily, that our various verbal and visual actions involve intentions, expectations, desires, hopes, and beliefs of the kinds that attend similar actual actions.

Although children's games of make-believe are typically more physical than those of appreciators, it is obvious that they too have significant psychological dimensions. Fictionally Chris hopes his baby will fall asleep when he puts it to bed. It is fictional that Dan, an Indian setting out on his first buffalo hunt, feels a mixture of excitement and fear.

But in appreciators' games psychological participation tends to outrun and overshadow physical participation. This accounts for the apparent asymmetry in our relations with fictional characters, the fact that we seem psychologically intimate with them but physically cut off from them. There is not really any such intimacy. It is only fictional, not true, that we feel for Willy Loman or detest Iago. But it is not even fictional that we come to Willy's assistance or tell Iago off—or even attempt to do so. (There is no such apparent asymmetry between Chris's physical and psychological access to his baby when he plays dolls.) Isn't it strange that there should be pity or anger in appreciators' games without the possibility of acting on these emotions in normal ways? But there isn't. It is not fictional of the appreciator that he *cannot* assist Willy or harm Iago; possibly it is fictional that he can. The point is just that it cannot be fictional that he *does*.

Recognition of the psychological role appreciators play in their games will contribute significantly to our understanding of the nature of fiction and its importance in our lives. It lies at the heart of the experience of being "caught up in a story." It will enable us to account for what has been misleadingly called the suspension of disbelief without supposing that appreciators lose touch with reality when they are immersed in a work of fiction. It will contribute to the resolution of the chief aesthetic question about fiction, the question of why we do not dismiss novels and stories and other such works as *mere fiction* and thus unworthy of serious attention.

7.1. FEARING FICTIONALLY

I put my face close to the thick glass-plate in front of a puff-adder in the Zoological Gardens, with the firm determination of not starting back if the snake struck at me; but, as soon as the blow was struck, my resolution went for nothing, and I jumped a yard or two backwards with astonishing rapidity. My will and reason were powerless against the imagination of a danger which had never been experienced.

Charles Darwin

It is high time we looked in again on Charles, whom we left in the theater quaking with quasi fear as the green slime bore down on him from the screen. We know that he is not really in danger. He knows this too, and he is not really afraid (not of the slime, anyway). His condition needs attention nevertheless. What *is* the nature of his experience? We must account for it in a way that will explain why it seems so natural, so nearly obligatory, for him and others to describe it as fear of the slime. Our account must do justice to the important connections that surely obtain between his experience and an experience of actual fear.

The main component of the answer has been anticipated: Charles is participating psychologically in his game of make-believe. It is not true but fictional that he fears the slime. So of course he speaks of himself as being afraid of it. His speaking thus may itself constitute participation—verbal participation—in his game. It is fictional that he is afraid, and it is fictional that he says he is.

In many ways Charles is like a child, Timmy, playing a game of make-believe with his father. The father pretends to be a ferocious monster who cunningly stalks him and, at a crucial moment, lunges "viciously" at him. Timmy flees screaming to the next room. The scream is more or less involuntary, and so is the flight.[1] But Timmy has a delighted grin on his face even as he runs, and he unhesitatingly comes back for more. He is perfectly aware that his father is only playing, that the whole thing is just a game, and that only fictionally is there a vicious monster after him. He is not really afraid. But it is fictional that he is afraid. Fictionally the monster attacks; fictionally Timmy is in mortal danger and knows that he is; and when he screams and runs, it is fictional that he is terrified. Likewise, when the slime raises its head, spies the camera, and begins oozing toward it, it is fictional in Charles's game that he is threatened. And when as a result Charles gasps and grips his chair, fictionally he is afraid.

What makes it fictional that Charles is afraid? Facts about Charles himself. He is an actor, of a sort, in his game, as well as an object; he is a reflexive prop generating fictional truths about himself. In this respect Charles, and Timmy also, are like actors portraying themselves in ordinary theatrical events, like Ronald Reagan playing Ronald Reagan in a stage play.

But there are crucial differences. Charles represents himself *as* himself, and Reagan does not. This goes with the fact that Charles can hardly fail to realize that the person he represents is himself, whereas Reagan might conceivably think he is playing the part of someone else who shares his name. The fact that it is *Charles* who is quivering in the theater is what makes it fictional that it is *he* who fears the slime. But it is not Reagan's identity that makes it Reagan whom he is impersonating. (See § 3.6.)

Another difference concerns what it is about Charles and Reagan that does the generating. Fictional truths about Charles are generated

---

1. If the scream and the flight are deliberate, they are likely to be self-conscious pretense. If they are deliberate but not self-conscious pretense, probably he *is* afraid.

partly by what he thinks and feels, by his actual mental state. It is partly the fact that he experiences quasi fear, the fact that he feels his heart pounding, his muscles tensed, and so on, that makes it fictional that he is afraid; it would not be appropriate to describe him as afraid if he were not in some such state. This is not true of Reagan playing Reagan. Ordinary onstage actors, whether self-impersonating or not, generate fictional truths by virtue of their acting, their behavior. Whether it is fictional that the character portrayed is afraid depends just on what the actor says and does and how he contorts his face, regardless of what he actually thinks or feels. It makes no difference whether his actual emotional state is anything like one of fear. An actor may find that putting himself into a certain frame of mind makes it easier to act in the required manner. Nonetheless, it is how he acts, not his state of mind, that is responsible for generating fictional truths. If it is fictional that Reagan is afraid, that is so because of his demeanor on stage, regardless of his actual emotional state.

This is how our conventions for (traditional) theater work, and it is entirely reasonable that they should work this way. Theatrical events are put on for audiences. Audiences cannot be expected to have a clear idea of an actor's personal thoughts and feelings while he is performing. That would require being intimately acquainted with his offstage personality and taking into account recent events that may have affected his mood (an argument with his director or his wife, a death in the family). If fictional truths depended on actors' private thoughts and feelings, it would be awkward and unreasonably difficult for spectators to ascertain what is going on in the fictional world. It is not surprising that the fictional truths for which actors onstage are responsible are understood to be generated by just what is visible from the galleries. Acting involves dissembling; actors take pains to hide their actual mental states from the audience.

Charles is not performing for an audience. It is not his job to get across to anyone else what fictionally is true of himself. Probably no one but he much cares whether or not it is fictional that he is afraid. So there is no reason why his actual state of mind should not have a role in generating fictional truths about himself.

It is less clear what makes it fictional in the monster game that Timmy is afraid. He might be performing for the benefit of an audience; he might be *showing* someone—an onlooker or just his father—that fictionally he is afraid. If so, perhaps he is like an onstage actor; perhaps his observable behavior is responsible for the fact that fictionally he is afraid. But there is room for doubt. Timmy behaves as though he is afraid, as an actor would, but he also experiences quasi-fear sensations, as does Charles. And his audience probably has much surer access to his mental state than theater audiences have to those of actors. The audience may know him well, and Timmy probably does not try as hard or as skillfully as actors do to hide his actual mental state. It may be perfectly evident to the audience that he suffers from quasi fear as a result of his realization that fictionally a monster is after him. So it is not unreasonable to regard Timmy's mental state as helping to generate fictional truths.

A more definite account of the situation is possible if Timmy is participating in the game solely for his own amusement, with no thought of an audience. In this case he himself, at least, almost certainly understands his fictional fear to depend on his mental state rather than (just) his behavior. (It is possible that at the same time observers understand his behavior alone to be responsible for his fictional fear. The child and the observers may recognize different principles of generation.) Suppose Timmy is an undemonstrative sort who does not scream or run or betray his "fear" in any other especially overt way. His participation in the game is passive. Nevertheless he does experience quasi fear when fictionally the monster attacks, and he still would describe himself as being afraid (although he knows full well that there is no danger and that his "fear" is not real). Certainly in this case it is (partly) his quasi fear which generates the fictional truth he expresses when he says that he is afraid.

My proposal is to construe Charles on the model of this undemonstrative child. Charles may, of course, exhibit his "fear" in certain observable ways. But his observable behavior is not meant to show anyone else that fictionally he is afraid. It is likely to go unnoticed by others, and even Charles himself may be unaware of it. No one, least of all Charles, regards his observable behavior as responsible for the fact that fictionally he is afraid.

Charles's quasi fear is not responsible for the fact that fictionally it is the *slime* that he fears (not by itself anyway), nor even for the fact that fictionally he is afraid rather than angry or excited or merely upset. What is? The details will probably depend on what one takes actual fear to consist in. But Charles's realization that fictionally the slime is bearing down on him is likely to be central.

Recall the familiar and not implausible accounts of fear that go approximately like this: To be (really) afraid of a tornado, for instance, is to have certain phenomenological experiences (quasi fear) as a result of knowing or believing that one is endangered by the tornado. What makes the state one of *fear* rather than anger or excitement is the belief that one is in danger, and what makes the tornado its object is the fact that it is the tornado that one takes to be dangerous.

It is clear enough what to say about Charles if this is what fear is: He experiences quasi fear as a result of realizing that fictionally the slime threatens him. This makes it fictional that his quasi fear is caused by a belief that the slime poses a danger, and hence that he fears the slime.[2]

Fear may not *require* a belief that one is in danger. In § 5.2 I treated sympathetically the suggestion that Frances fears poor old Fido without judging him to be dangerous. If she does, the account of fear I have just sketched will not do as a *definition*. But many instances of fear may still consist partly in a belief in danger. Quasi fear caused by a belief that one is threatened by a tornado may constitute fear of the tornado, even if it is possible to fear a tornado without so believing. It is fictional that Charles, as we understand him, believes that the slime poses a danger; the fear that, fictionally, he has for the slime is thus unlike Frances' fear of poor old Fido. So we can still say that the fact that Charles is quasi-afraid as a result of realizing that fictionally the slime threatens him is what generates the truth that fictionally he is afraid of the slime, while allowing that this fictional truth *could* be generated in other ways.

(I have suggested thinking of fear in general as a state akin to that of a certain belief-desire complex, in its motivational force at least. This includes cases in which the person believes that he is in danger as well as ones in which he does not. The fact that fictionally Charles believes himself endangered by the slime and has a normal desire not to be harmed implies that fictionally his behavior is subject to the

---

2. Certain aspects of quasi fear are sometimes caused directly by the stimulus rather than by the belief that fictionally one is in danger. The sudden appearance of a looming shape on the screen is startling, quite apart from any beliefs it may engender about what is fictional. Even so, if it is fictional that one is afraid, one's realization that fictionally one is in danger probably plays a part in making it so. It is evident in many cases that quasi fear is caused partly or wholly by the realization that fictionally one is in danger. There may be nothing startling or shocking about the images themselves. Yet a progressively intensifying tingling in the spine may accompany the gradual realization of the incredible danger in which fictionally one finds oneself.

Why does the realization that fictionally one is in danger produce quasi fear when it does? Why does it bring about a state similar to one of real fear, even if the person knows he is not really in danger? The answer does not matter for our purposes, but a Darwinian explanation may be available. Psychological participation in games of make-believe is of great value to us. Probably it has survival value. So evolutionary pressures may be responsible for our being organisms of a kind susceptible to quasi emotions in situations in which they might enrich our psychological participation in games of make-believe.

relevant motivational pressure, that fictionally he is inclined to try to escape the slime, even though he is not actually so inclined.)

There is a lot of room for refinement in our understanding of the nature of fear and in our account of what makes it fictional, in Charles's case and others, that one is afraid. What seems nonnegotiable is that Charles does, fictionally, fear the slime. Given that he is participating in a game of make-believe in the first place, one in which it is fictional that he watches as the slime turns on him, it would be nearly unthinkable to deny that, when he recoils, it is fictional that he does so in horror. His recoiling is not deliberate. But he might shriek deliberately or exclaim, "Yikes! Here it comes!" blatantly playing along with the fiction. The ease with which he might slip into such willful participation suggests that the shriek or the exclamation should be regarded not as suddenly inaugurating a new game but as a natural continuation of a game already in progress.[3]

We must not stop with the recognition that it is fictional in Charles's game that he fears a slime. This fictional truth is surrounded by others which, together with the manner in which all of them are generated and also the manner in which Charles imagines what is fictional, give it, and Charles's psychological role in his game generally, an extraordinary air of realism.

It is fictional not just that Charles is afraid, but that his fearful experience has a certain character and progresses in a certain fashion. These more specific fictional truths depend largely on the character and progress of his quasi-fear sensations. If it is fictional that his fear is overwhelming, or that it is only momentary, this is so because his quasi-fear sensations are overwhelming or are only momentary. Fictionally his fear grows more or less intense or becomes almost unbearable or finally subsides, as his quasi-fear feelings change in these ways.

Since it is Charles's actual state of mind, his beliefs about what is fictional (probably) and his feelings of quasi fear that generate fictional truths about his fear of the slime, it is by attention to his actual state of mind that he is aware of these fictional truths. His realization that fictionally he is afraid is based largely on introspection, just as his

---

3. We can also invoke an argument like one used in § 6.2. That Charles *imagines* himself fearing the slime is strongly implied by the fact that he readily describes his experience as one of "fear"—once he has a chance to catch his breath. This imagining is triggered more or less automatically by awareness of his quasi-fear sensations. He is simply disposed to think of himself as fearing the slime, when he feels his heart racing, his muscles tensed, and so forth. This is precisely the kind of disposition that suggests implicit recognition of a principle of make-believe, one whereby his experience makes it fictional that he is afraid of the slime. That he accepts such a principle is all that needs to be shown to establish that it is fictional, in his game, that he fears it.

realization that he is really afraid would be. He follows the waxing and waning of his "fictional fear" by looking within himself, much as he would follow the progress of actual fears. Mistakes seem out of the question (assuming he has mastery of the relevant principles of make-believe). Charles enjoys a certain "privileged access" to fictional truths about his fear, as one does to facts about one's real fears.

The realistic nature of Charles's access to fictional truths about his fear of the slime brings in still another class of associated fictional truths. The act or experience of attending to his actual state of mind, whereby Charles ascertains fictional truths about his fear, is inevitably understood to make it fictional that he ascertains facts about his fear of the slime by means of such attention. Further, it will be fictional that he is neurotically attentive to his fearful experience if he attends neurotically to his experience of quasi fear. If he barely notices his quasi fear, it will be fictional that he barely notices his fear. And so on.

Moreover, it is fictional of Charles's actual quasi-fear feelings that they themselves are feelings of (real) fear, and his attendings to his quasi fear are themselves, fictionally, attendings to a fearful experience. The elements of his actual experience that serve as props are objects of his imaginings as well, and they enhance the vivacity of his imaginings in the way that objects generally do. (See § 3.5.) We can see the point of saying that Charles actually experiences his "fictional fear." This must not be taken to mean that there is a special kind of fear—fictional fear—that Charles experiences. But he does actually experience something that, fictionally, is an experience of fear.

Finally—and this point is closely linked to the others—Charles does not imagine merely *that* he is afraid; he imagines *being* afraid, and he imagines this *from the inside*. Imagining in this manner is prescribed, given the nature of his game and his actual experience.

The best way to appreciate the remarkably realistic character of Charles's psychological participation in his game is to contrast a case of a different kind. Recall William Luce's play *The Belle of Amherst*, in which Julie Harris plays Emily Dickinson. Suppose that Dickinson herself—with the help of a time machine or a fortuitous reincarnation—is in the audience. Various happenings onstage generate fictional truths about her state of mind.[4] It is fictional, for example, that

---

4. I am interested now only in fictional truths generated by what happens onstage, ones belonging to the world of the performance. In her capacity as a spectator Dickinson is like Charles; her actual mental state generates fictional truths about herself, ones that may or may not cohere with those Julie Harris generates. Dickinson is in a curiously ambiguous position, but not an uncommon one. It is much like having a dream in which one watches oneself "from the outside."

she dislikes public contact and public exposure and experiences severe anxiety in social situations. But Emily Dickinson the spectator has no special intimacy with these fictional truths. Like any other spectator she must observe what Julie Harris says and does onstage in order to determine how fictionally she herself feels. Like other spectators she might be mistaken. It is as though she is watching another person, even though that person, the character portrayed, is herself.

Is it fictional that Dickinson is introspectively aware of her feelings of anxiety? Probably. But this fictional truth is generated in a very roundabout and, we might say, unrealistic manner. It is not generated by actual introspection on her part. Nor is it generated by her non-introspective realization, from her seat in the audience, that fictionally she experiences such feelings. Rather, it is implied by the fact that, because of the happenings onstage, it is fictional that she feels thus and expresses her distress in certain ways. (The Reality Principle comes into play: anyone who felt thus and expressed it so would be introspectively aware of his or her anxiety.) Dickinson must infer from Harris' performance and from fictional truths that it generates that fictionally she, Dickinson, is introspectively aware of her anthropophobic feelings. That is not how a person knows that he himself has introspective knowledge; it is a lot more like determining this about someone else.

Furthermore, nothing is such that, fictionally, *it* is Dickinson's anxiety; certainly none of her actual feelings are. Nor is anything Dickinson actually does or experiences such that fictionally it is an act or experience of introspective awareness. She does not actually experience her "fictional anxiety." And it is not from the inside that she imagines feeling anxiety. (Not, at least, as part of her game with the performance. Her mind might wander; the performance might trigger a separate fantasy in which she does imagine this from the inside. But her imagining of the behavior on stage—Harris'—that it expresses her anxiety is not an imagining from the inside.)

The situation is much the same if Dickinson herself should replace Julie Harris in the title role. She still must judge from her external behavior, from what spectators could observe, whether or not it is fictional (in the performance and in authorized games) that she experiences severe anxiety in a social situation, and she might easily be mistaken about how she looks to spectators. It is still as though she is considering herself "from the outside," from the perspective of another person.

Charles's situation is dramatically different. It is not as though

Charles is confronting another person, a fictional version of himself, but rather as though he himself actually fears the slime. Fictional truths about his fear, especially the fact that fictionally it is *his,* are portrayed to him with extraordinary vivacity. Charles feels himself to be intimately involved with the slime, to be part of the fictional world of his game.

Charles's experience is typical of appreciators who participate psychologically in their games. We are beginning to see how fictional worlds can seem to us almost as "real" as the real world, even though we know perfectly well that they are not. We have begun to understand what happens when we are emotionally "involved" in a novel or play or film, what it is to be "caught up in a story."

Now that we have a reasonably clear positive picture of the character of Charles's experience, we can reaffirm with renewed confidence our denial that he fears the slime. The fact that it is fictional that he fears it does not automatically rule out his actually doing so, since fictionality and truth are not incompatible. But that fictional truth, generated in approximately the manner I suggested, preempts the phenomenological and verbal data which might be explained by taking his fear to be actual. It leaves little incentive to so take it, even if we ignore the absence both of a belief that the slime endangers him and of an inclination to escape. This point is strengthened by the fact that our reasons for considering it fictional that Charles fears the slime do not depend on denying that he actually does. It is not just that we can manage to fill the gap left by that denial. What fills the gap is something we have on hand anyway.

Must we declare Aristotle wrong in decreeing that tragedies should evoke fear and pity? Not unless we naively insist on a literal-minded reading of his words. They are better construed in a spirit not entirely detached from that in which we are to understand Charles's exclamation, "Boy, was I scared!"

7.2.   PARTICIPATING PSYCHOLOGICALLY

The case of Charles and the slime is but an illustration of the important psychological roles appreciators play in their games of make-believe. We do not actually pity Willy Loman or grieve for Anna Karenina or admire Superman, I have suggested, nor do we feel contempt for Iago or worry about Tom Sawyer and Becky lost in the cave. But it is fictional that we do. It is fictional, when we appreciate

novels, plays, films, and paintings, that we feel compassion, exaspera-
tion, indignation, and so on, as it is fictional that Charles fears the
slime. And these fictional truths are generated in a similar manner—
in part by our actual states of mind.

The slime movie is rather special in that it contains what I earlier
called an aside to the audience; fictionally the slime notices Charles
and goes after him. So naturally it is fictional that he is afraid. It is
unusual in works of some kinds for appreciators to be "brought into"
the fiction in this way, as we have seen, for it to be fictional that
someone notices them or speaks to them or threatens them. There is
no need to treat the responses of appreciators to works without asides
in a fundamentally different manner from their responses to works
with them, but the particular psychological attitudes which it is fictional that one has are likely to be different. Fictionally one may fear
for someone else, if not for oneself. A spectator of the shower scene in
Hitchcock's *Psycho* probably does not fictionally take *himself* to be in
danger or fear for himself.[5] Fictionally he is aware of danger to someone else (the character played by Janet Leigh), and his shrieks are
fictionally shrieks of fear for her.[6]

One can admire or detest or pity or worry about someone without
being noticed by her, and it can easily be fictional in the absence of
anything like an aside that an appreciator does so. This is not to deny
that asides are sometimes involved. If it is fictional that someone
looks at me pleadingly, or with contempt, this may make it more
likely that I will fictionally pity or hate her. Still, the latter can be
fictional when the former is not.

What makes it fictional of an appreciator that he pities or hates or
admires or worries about someone? How are these fictional truths
generated? The details will depend on what we think constitutes
actual emotions of these kinds, but our discussion of Charles suggests
some possibilities. Certain features of one's mental state that are typical of these emotions—what we might call quasi pity or quasi hate,
for instance—are likely to play a role. In some cases the fact that
fictionally one pities or detests or admires someone is probably generated by the fact that one experiences the quasi emotion as a result of
being aware of an appropriate fictional truth about her. Perhaps some
instances of (actual) pity consist in quasi pity caused by a belief that

---

5. But see the discussion later in this section of identifying with a character.

6. An aside is not necessary for one fictionally to fear for oneself, however. One does not
have to be noticed in order really to feel threatened, and it can be fictional that one is in
danger without its being fictional that one is noticed.

the person pitied suffers misfortune. Realizing it to be fictional that Anna Karenina suffers misfortune, it is fictional that we are aware of her suffering, and we experience quasi pity as a result. This, perhaps, is approximately what makes it fictional that we pity her. (If it is possible to pity someone without judging him or her to suffer, it may be possible fictionally to do so as well.) That fictionally one detests Iago, admires Superman, or worries about Tom and Becky may in some instances be generated by quasi hate, quasi admiration, or quasi worry resulting from the realization that fictionally Iago deceived Othello about Desdemona, that fictionally Superman can do almost anything, that fictionally Tom and Becky are lost in a cave.

What is quasi pity? What are quasi worry, quasi admiration, and so on? By analogy with the case of Charles's "fear," they ought to be constellations of sensations or other phenomenological experiences characteristic of real emotions, ones that the appreciator who "pities Anna" or "admires Superman," for instance, shares with people who really pity or admire real people. It is not hard to specify sensations characteristic of fear—intense fear, anyway. But other quasi emotions are more elusive. Quasi admiration may seem especially hard to put one's finger on. What does it *feel* like to admire someone?

We need not look for anything especially distinctive about quasi admiration. Fictionally admiring someone may be distinguished from fictionally having other emotions by something other than the character of the quasi emotion (by its cause, for example; perhaps by what one believes to be fictional, and hence what it is fictional that one believes).

But admiration may seem not always to involve any particularly notable phenomenological experiences at all. There may be a swelling sensation, or a feeling of one's breath being taken away. But there need not be. Pity sometimes involves tears and the sensations of crying, but not always. Indeed, these emotions are not always occurrent; it may be true that one pities or admires someone when one is not even thinking about her. Probably they can also be unconscious. It isn't obvious, for that matter, even that fear always has definite phenomenological components; it is not always easy to say what constitutes quasi fear.

There is a problem here. But it is not so much a problem for my account of the appreciation of works of fiction as one for theories of emotion. What are admiration and pity? Believing that someone is admirable or that she suffers misfortune is not *sufficient* for admiring or pitying her (whether or not it is necessary); one can hold such beliefs without experiencing the emotion.[7] Perhaps the emotions involve mere dispositions to feel in certain ways, or dispositions to react in certain ways to certain stimuli, dispositions of which one may or may not be aware, or nonintrospectable feelings, or certain physiological states. Whatever it is that combines with the appropriate belief to constitute the emotion (in those instances in which such a belief is involved), I suggest that some such state or condition, or one that is naturally taken to make it fictional that the appreciator is in such a state or condition, helps to make it fictional that one admires or pities someone. We can call it quasi admiration or quasi pity, but we will not insist that it must be a phenomenological experience. Let us keep our conception of quasi emotion flexible enough to accommodate any reasonable theory of emotion.

I have emphasized the separation between our actual mental lives and the mental lives we lead in the worlds of our games of make-believe. But although they are distinct, there is substantial overlap between them. We do not actually grieve for Anna Karenina, feel disgust for Iago, or fear the slime when it is fictional that we do; but many other ways in which fictionally we think and feel are ways in which we really do so. There is no bar to such overlap with respect to thoughts and feelings that are not directed at purely fictional objects.

Emily Dickinson, being an actual person, can be an object of actual pity. One may really feel disgust for Ivan the Terrible or empathize with Julius Caesar. It may also be fictional that one feels thus toward these real people when they are characters in fiction. On reading *War and Peace,* a real-life admirer of Napoleon may fictionally admire him as well. Similar correspondences are possible and indeed common in the case of *moods,* which seem not to be directed toward objects at all. It may be fictional that one is in a solemn or agitated or joyful or gloomy or contemplative mood when it is also true that one is.

Not only do our actual feelings and what fictionally we feel coincide; frequently they tend to be linked closely together in several important ways. The reasons for which, fictionally, a reader of *War and Peace* admires Napoleon may be imported from the real world. He may take what he knows or believes about Napoleon's real-life exploits to be fictional, by virtue of the Reality Principle or the Mutual Belief Principle of implication, even if the novel does not mention them. And the fact that he actually admires Napoleon for

7. We might recognize degenerate senses of "admire" and "pity" in which the relevant belief is sufficient. It will be fictional that one admires or pities someone, in such a degenerate sense, merely if it is fictional that one holds the belief. No quasi emotion is required.

these exploits makes it likely, perhaps almost inevitable, that it will be fictional that he does. In addition to encouraging the viewer fictionally to feel disgust for Ivan, Eisenstein's *Ivan the Terrible* may induce actual disgust in her, either by informing her of Ivan's real-life cruelty, if she takes the film to be historically accurate, or by presenting familiar historical facts in a vivid manner. The same quasi disgust (tenseness, nausea) may do double duty, partially constituting one's actual disgust as well as contributing to the generation of the fact that fictionally one is disgusted. Tears coursing down the cheeks of a viewer of *Ivan the Terrible* as, fictionally, she grieves for Ivan's victims may also be tears of genuine grief. (The tears may be causally overdetermined, caused independently by what she knows about the victims, and also by her realization of what fictionally is true of them.)

One might almost suppose that a person's actual moods are simply carried over into the fictional world, that for it to be fictional that one is grouchy or contemplative is simply for one to be grouchy or contemplative. I prefer to say that the appreciator's experience of the work must be a significant cause of his mood. Grouchiness arising from a (real) domestic quarrel should not be thought of as belonging to the game of make-believe played with the work. But it is clear that a work may really put an observer in a cheerful or gloomy mood, and thereby make it fictional that he feels thus. And I doubt that it can be fictional that an appreciator is relaxed and cheerful while he is actually tense and grouchy.[8] (If his grouchiness is excluded from the fictional world, it may be indeterminate what, fictionally, his mood is.)

We have scarcely sampled the diversity, subtlety, and complexity of feelings, attitudes, sentiments, and passions appreciators can, fictionally, experience. It may be fictional that the reader of a novel feels a mysterious attraction toward someone he despises and fights to resist it. It may be fictional that an appreciator feels vaguely uneasy about a situation without realizing why; that his anger for someone is tinged with respect or his sympathy with resentment; that he is surprised at the depth and persistence of his antipathy to something; that he finds himself strangely unmoved by certain tragic events and feels guilt for his lack of concern; and so on and on. There do seem to be some limits, however. Ordinarily we would not expect appreciators fictionally to feel embarrassment or shame or jealousy or pride, or for

---

8. Unless this fictional truth is generated by a passage (in a novel like Calvino's *If on a Winter's Night a Traveler*) such as: "You, dear reader, are relaxed and joyous."

it to be fictional that one is hurt by an unsympathetic remark or grateful for a favor, or that one takes offense at an insult. This is because of restrictions on appreciators' roles in their games. (See § 6.3.) Because of them it is unlikely to be fictional that the appreciator is in an embarrassing situation, or that he does something for which he might feel ashamed, or that someone does him a favor or insults him.[9] There are fewer such limits in audience-participation theater and works with especially elaborate asides, and fewer still in children's games. But even when common restrictions on participation are not suspended, the mental lives we lead in the worlds of our games of make-believe can be, in many respects, almost as rich, varied, and subtle as our actual ones.

It is not just while actually confronting representations that we participate in games in which they are props. An appreciator's game—psychological aspects of it especially—often continues long after she has closed the book or left the theater or gallery. The example of Charles's experience of the horror movie might be misleading in this regard. It is only while Charles is actually watching the movie that fictionally he fears the slime. This is because only then is it fictional that the slime threatens him. But in many cases reading or viewing a work is just the beginning of a long, extended, psychologically rich game of make-believe, especially when one's psychological participation is not dependent on the immediacy of anything like asides. One may ponder the events of Anna Karenina's life for days or even years after finishing the novel. One may brood over a Rouault face. Bosch's monsters, once seen, may long continue to haunt. A short poem may take months to digest. Such meditations consist in part in the continuation of psychological participation. The reader of *Anna Karenina* continues, fictionally, to contemplate Anna's situation and to feel for her. Frequently it is fictional that our feelings or attitudes change as we reflect. It may be fictional that the appreciator's understanding of a character deepens, that grief is replaced by anger and eventually by acceptance, that rage is transformed gradually into something approaching sympathy, that what started as a vague undercurrent of uneasiness becomes a dominating anxiety. Many of the works we consider *great* have the capacity to set in motion complex, persisting games of make-believe of this sort.

An important aspect of our emotional reaction to works of art that

9. It may be fictional that the appreciator feels shame or guilt for saying or thinking certain things, if not for his overt actions, or that he is embarrassed *for* someone else.

I have not mentioned is the experience of "identifying with" a character. What is it for a spectator of *King Lear* to identify with Lear in his disappointment and disillusion at Goneril and Regan's betrayal? The identification does not consist in its being fictional of the appreciator that he feels betrayed; it is not fictional that Goneril and Regan betray *him* (not in an authorized game anyway). Still less does it consist in his actually feeling betrayed by them. I suggest that the spectator engages in imaginings that are not part of his authorized game but occur along with it. He imagines himself to be in Lear's shoes, to have been deceived by his daughters and to feel the intense pain of betrayal. (Whether he imagines himself to *be* Lear and to have been deceived by Goneril and Regan or just to be in a situation like Lear's is a question we need not decide. See § 1.4.) These subsidiary imaginings may be more or less subliminal; perhaps they are not occurrent. But they are an important part of one's experience of the work and one's later meditations on it. Of course we identify with real people as well as with fictional characters. My not very surprising suggestion is that this too involves imagining oneself in the shoes of the person identified with.

It should be emphasized that my denial that Charles fears the slime has by no means led to a conception of appreciation of representational works of art as an unemotional experience. The experience of fictionally fearing a slime or grieving for Anna Karenina may itself be counted an emotional one, although one's emotion is not fear of a slime or grief for Anna. And it is clear from the recent discussion that many works play on and with our actual emotions in a complex variety of ways. I will have more to say on this score in § 7.5. But let us look first at other issues that require distinguishing clearly between our psychological games of make-believe and our actual mental lives.

7.3.   PARADOXES OF TRAGEDY

> It seems an unaccountable pleasure which the spectators of a
> well-written tragedy receive from sorrow, terror, anxiety, and
> other passions that are in themselves disagreeable and uneasy.
> David Hume, "Of Tragedy"

Thus does David Hume express what we might call the classic paradox of tragedy. How is it that appreciators eagerly seek the painful experiences they know to expect from works of tragedy, and indeed enjoy them? We now know that tragedies do not induce actual sorrow and terror in spectators—not, anyway, in most of the instances in which one might think they do. (Anxiety is a different matter.) But this does not dissolve the paradox. It *is* considerably overrated, as we shall see. But not for this reason.

It is true that the pleasure (if that is the right word) we take in tragedies depends, not infrequently, on its being *only* fictional that we feel sorrow or terror; in many cases we would not enjoy actually feeling the way it is fictional that we feel. Sometimes, of course, appreciators find even the experience of *fictionally* feeling sorrow or terror unpleasant. People sometimes avoid such experiences, refusing to watch *Psycho,* choosing lighthearted spoofs over heavy-handed tearjerkers or even genuinely moving tragic masterpieces. There is no particular mystery here. We might conclude simply that the experience of *fictionally* feeling sorrow or terror is neither "in [itself] disagreeable and uneasy," as Hume takes actual sorrow and terror to be, nor necessarily enjoyable. Sometimes we like it and sometimes we don't.

But the paradox remains. Some representations arouse *actual* sorrow or terror—sorrow for actual people they remind us of, terror of horrors we think we might actually face—or an objectless mood of anxiety, and it would appear that we sometimes seek and enjoy these experiences. Moreover, as Hume observes, people apparently take delight in nonfictional reports of actual suffering and horror, reports they accept as true. He mentions Cicero's "pathetic description of the butchery made by Verres of the Sicilian captains." "The sorrow here is [not] softened by fiction," he notes, "for the audience were convinced of the reality of every circumstance."[10] The notion of make-believe does not help to explain the enjoyment of genuine experiences of negative emotions.

Cases like these no doubt strike us as much less paradoxical than they did Hume, operating as we do with a more complex picture of human psychology. Attributions of mixed and conflicting feelings or attitudes (perhaps but not necessarily on different levels of consciousness) are accepted easily. We scarcely blink at the idea of a person's being fascinated by what repulses him, of enjoying pain as an expiation for guilt, of self-deception, of masochism. A simple (too simple)

10. Hume, "Of Tragedy," p. 224.

solution would be to say that appreciators recognize benefits which certain painful experiences produce—deepened awareness of themselves and their situations or whatever—and that they undergo the experiences for the sake of these benefits, like taking castor oil. What Hume calls pleasure might be the satisfaction of seeing these benefits obtained. The solution is not this easy, of course. But there would seem to be more than enough fancy psychologizing in the air to provide a solution.

As far as emotions directed toward objects are concerned, the puzzle largely evaporates with the recognition of a simple but central confusion. Hume's characterization of sorrow as a passion that is "in [itself] disagreeable" is very much open to question. What is clearly disagreeable, what we regret, are the things we are sorrowful *about*— the loss of an opportunity, the death of a friend—not the feeling or experience of sorrow itself. It is undesirable for there to be circumstances in which sorrow is appropriate. But given that such circumstances obtain, sorrow *is* appropriate, and one may well welcome it. One may *want* to experience sorrow, and may find a certain enjoyment or satisfaction in the fact that one does experience it. To be sorrowful is not, in general, to be sorry about being sorry, and it is entirely consistent with being glad about *that*.

There is nothing paradoxical, then, in wanting to experience the tears one sheds over the butchery described by Cicero or in taking pleasure or comfort in one's grief for the victims. Even if appreciators did really feel sorrow for Anna Karenina or Willy Loman, willingly and with pleasure, even if I am wrong in claiming that they don't, we do not have a paradox on our hands. There would be no tension between even the deepest regret for the fate that Anna suffers and an eagerness to read the novel and the enjoyment of it. Avoiding it or refusing to enjoy it will not help Anna. Given that she suffers as she does, it would seem fitting and appropriate, the least one can do, to pay attention to her predicament and to grieve for her. One may feel satisfaction amidst one's tears in doing this much.

Granted, real grief, like the experience of fictionally feeling sorrow, *can* be painful or unpleasant, and sometimes we do avoid it; sometimes we absent ourselves from funerals or avoid what we fear might be bad news. But there is nothing in the notion of sorrow or grief to make it surprising that the opposite is sometimes true, that we sometimes seek and enjoy the experience of real sorrow. Much of Hume's paradox thus evaporates without help from the fact that it is only fictional that the appreciator feels sorrow. (We may still need some fancy psychologizing to explain the enjoyment of negative moods.)

When we consider the appreciator's attitudes toward the object of her sorrow rather than her supposed enjoyment of the experience of sorrow itself, we encounter a more compelling puzzle, one anticipated in § 5.1. It can be resolved easily enough, but only on the supposition that appreciators participate psychologically in games of make-believe.

Arthur appreciates tragedies, but he finds happy endings asinine and dull. In watching a play he hopes that it will end tragically. He "wants the heroine to suffer a cruel fate," for only if she does, he thinks, will the play turn out to have been worth watching.[11] But at the same time he is caught up in the story and "pities the heroine," "sympathizes with her plight." He "wants her to escape." Indeed his feeling of "pity" and his "desire for the heroine's survival" constitute an important part of his appreciation of the tragedy, if that is what it turns out to be. Are we to say that Arthur is *torn* between opposite interests, that he wants the heroine to survive and also wants her not to? This does not ring true.

Contrast a genuine case of conflicting desires. In watching a bull-fight or a neighbor's marital squabble one might secretly (or otherwise) hope for blood, expecting to find a disastrous denouement entertaining. This desire need not exclude genuine sympathy for the victim or victims and a desire that it or they not suffer. But there will be a tension between the two, each qualifying and diminishing the other. Moreover, one's sympathy is likely to color one's hopes for the worst with guilt. Arthur is not like this. Both of his "conflicting desires" may well be wholehearted. He may hope unreservedly that the work will end in disaster for the heroine, and he may with equal singlemindedness "want her to escape such an undeserved fate." He may be entirely aware of both "desires" and yet feel no particular conflict between them. He need not experience the slightest pangs of guilt for "wishing the heroine ill," notwithstanding his most heartfelt "sympathy for her."

The solution, of course, is that Arthur does not actually sympathize with the heroine or want her to be spared; it is only fictional that he

---

11. "Some people—and I am one of them—hate happy ends. We feel cheated. Harm is the norm. Doom should not jam. The avalanche stopping in its tracks a few feet above the cowering village behaves not only unnaturally but unethically" (Nabokov, *Pnin*, pp. 25–26).

does. What he really wants is that it be fictional that she suffer a cruel end. He does not have conflicting desires. Nor, for that matter, is it fictional that he does.

7.4.   SUSPENSE AND SURPRISE

I've seen [*West Side Story*] about five thousand times maybe. And I always end up in tears.

Leonard Bernstein

I've never used the whodunit technique, since it is concerned altogether with mystification, which diffuses and unfocuses suspense. It is possible to build up almost unbearable tension in a play or film in which the audience knows who the murderer is all the time . . . I believe in giving the audience all the facts as early as possible.

Alfred Hitchcock

Knowing What Is Fictional and Fictionally Knowing What Is True

It is fictional of appreciators that they know or fail to know various things, that they have certain beliefs, expectations, suspicions, hunches; that they make guesses; that they are ignorant or uncertain; that what they believe or assume or surmise proves later to be true, or false; that they are or are not surprised at how things turn out. Often what fictionally one knows or believes is just what one really knows or believes to be fictional. It is when Charles realizes that fictionally a green slime is on the loose that it becomes fictional that he realizes that a green slime is on the loose. And his uncertainty about what fictionally the slime might do, or his surprise at what fictionally it does do, makes it fictional that he is uncertain about or surprised at the slime's behavior. But what we know to be fictional and what fictionally we know sometimes come apart. This fact has important consequences.

One problem it helps to solve is that of why works last as well as they do, how they manage so often to survive multiple readings or viewings without losing their effectiveness.[12] Suspense of one kind or another is a crucial ingredient in our experience of most works: Will Jack of "Jack and the Beanstalk" succeed in ripping off the Giant

12. David Lewis pointed out the relevance of my theory to this problem.

without being caught? Will Tom and Becky find their way out of the cave? Will Hamlet ever get around to avenging the murder of his father? How will Othello react when he finds Desdemona's handkerchief? What is in store for Julius Caesar on the Ides of March? Will Godot come?

How can there be suspense if we already know how things will turn out? Why should Tom and Becky's plight concern or even interest a reader who has read the novel previously and knows perfectly well that they will find their way out of the cave? One might have supposed that once we have experienced a work often enough to become thoroughly familiar with the relevant features of the plot, it would lose its capacity to create suspense, and that future readings or viewings of it would lack the excitement of the first one. In many cases this does not happen. *Some* works do fade quickly from exposure. The interest of certain mysteries lies largely in the puzzles they pose for the reader. We try to figure out "who done it" from a succession of clues. Once we know the answer, there is no puzzle to be solved, and little point in rereading the story. Familiarity with any work alters our experience of it in certain ways, no doubt. But the power of many is remarkably permanent and the nature of their effectiveness remarkably constant. In particular, suspense may remain a crucial element in our response to a work almost no matter how familiar we are with it. One may "worry" just as intensely about Tom and Becky while rereading *The Adventures of Tom Sawyer,* notwithstanding one's knowledge of the outcome, as a person reading it for the first time would. Lauren, listening to "Jack and the Beanstalk" for the umpteenth time, long after she has memorized it word for word, may feel much the same excitement when the Giant discovers Jack and goes after him, the same gripping suspense, that she felt when she first heard the story. It is a notable commonplace that children, far from being bored by familiar stories, frequently beg to hear the same ones over and over again. Some adult traditions—ancient Greek theater, Javanese Wayang Kulit—have a relatively fixed repertoire of standard, well-known plots, which nevertheless remain alive and exciting for the audiences.

The manner in which a familiar story is told can be of considerable interest. We may value a fresh reading or performance, a new way of presenting an old plot. But this observation scarcely dents the puzzle. Appreciators are usually interested in the story itself, not just in how it is told. An innovative presentation of a tale is not invariably or even usually more powerful than a skillful but unsurprising one. The appreciator does not look merely (if at all) for novel nuances of intonation, wording, staging, or even new twists in the story line. He is typically interested in and gripped by the central features of the plot, even if he already knows what they are. Lauren feels the tension of Jack's predicament; that is the focus of her interest, notwithstanding her knowledge of the outcome. Her experience is one of suspense, and it is not suspense about how the reader will enunciate the words of the story or about what words he will use in telling it.

None of this is surprising in light of the present theory. Although Lauren knows that fictionally Jack will escape from the Giant, as she listens to still another rereading of "Jack and the Beanstalk," it is fictional that she does not know this—until the reading of the passage describing his escape. Fictionally she is genuinely worried about his fate and attentively follows the events as they unfold. It is fictional in her game during a given reading or telling of the story that she learns for the first time about Jack and the Giant. (Probably it is fictional that someone whose word Lauren trusts is giving her a serious and truthful report about a confrontation between a boy and a giant.) It is the fact that fictionally she is uncertain about the outcome, not actual uncertainty, which is responsible for the excitement and suspense of her experience. What she actually knows to be fictional does not, in this case, affect what it is fictional that she knows to be true. The point of hearing the story is not to discover fictional truths about Jack's confrontation with the Giant but to engage in a game of make-believe of a certain sort. One cannot learn, each time one hears the story, what fictionally Jack and the Giant do, unless one always forgets in between. But one can participate each time in a game, and that is what appreciators do. The value of hearing "Jack and the Beanstalk" lies in having the experience of being such that fictionally one realizes with trepidation the danger Jack faces, waits breathlessly to see whether the Giant will awake, feels sudden terror when he does, and finally learns with admiration and relief how Jack chops down the beanstalk, sending the Giant to his doom.

Why play the same game over and over? In the first place the game may not be exactly the same each time, even if the readings are the same. On one occasion it may be fictional that Lauren is paralyzed by fear for Jack, overwhelmed by the gravity of the situation, and emotionally drained when Jack finally bests the Giant. On another occasion it may be fictional that she is not very seriously concerned about Jack's safety and that her dominant feelings are admiration for his exploits, the thrill of adventure, and a sense of exhilaration at the final outcome. But even if the game is much the same from reading to reading, the tension and excitement of fictionally not knowing how things will turn out may be present each time.

The puzzle about reexperiencing works, the question of why repeated exposure does not rob a work of its power, applies to music as well as to the (obviously) representational arts. Indeed, it is especially acute there; our tolerance and even zest for repetition are often greater in music than in theater, film, and literature (aside from poetry). Adults as well as children listen to the same pieces of music, even the same recordings, over and over, often with *increasing* enjoyment. We easily understand a person's deciding against seeing a certain movie because she has seen it previously. But "I've already heard it" would be an exotic reason for forgoing a performance of a Handel oratorio or a Brahms symphony.

A central thesis of Leonard Meyer's *Emotion and Meaning in Music* is that "affect or emotion-felt is aroused when an expectation—a tendency to respond—activated by the musical stimulus situation, is temporarily inhibited or permanently blocked."[13] The appreciation of music derives largely, he claims, from frustrations of expectations about how the music will proceed. In the case of a deceptive cadence, listeners expect the tonic to follow the dominant, and they experience "affect" when it does not. This may be an accurate description of the experience of the first-time listener, but what about the listener who knows the piece well, having heard it many times before—well enough, let's say, to be able to play it from memory or write it down? Such a listener can hardly be said to expect the tonic to succeed the dominant; she fully realizes in advance that the cadence will be "deceptive." Yet she may appreciate the "deceptiveness" of the cadence as much as or more than a novice listener would. It may "sound surprising" to her.[14]

My explanation will have been anticipated. It is *fictional* that the listener expects the tonic, regardless of what she actually expects, and it is fictional that she is surprised to hear the submediant or whatever occurs instead. (This makes the music a prop in a game of make-believe and hence representational in our sense, in much the way that nonfigurative painting often is. See § 1.8.)

I have focused on the question of *re*experiencing representations, of why works do not go stale with repeated exposure. But the point is

13. *Emotion and Meaning in Music*, p. 31.
14. Meyer treats this objection in "On Rehearing Music," pp. 42–53.

larger than this. An appreciator may know how a story will end even before hearing or reading it for the *first* time, without this knowledge ruining the suspense. He may have been told by others; he may have seen a review; the work may be billed as a tragedy or a fairy tale and he may know how works of that kind end; the author may be one whose heroes invariably come to grief; one might sneak a look at the last chapter before reading from the beginning. Advance knowledge about the plot gained in these ways usually does not affect what it is fictional that we know, so it does not prevent it from being fictional that we are in suspense or surprised.

So far so good. But epistemological aspects of appreciators' experiences—what fictionally they know or believe or suspect or conjecture as well as the suspense and surprise that fictionally they experience, and how these are related to their actual knowledge, beliefs, suspicions, conjectures, suspense, and surprise—can be far more complex, and fascinating, than is evident from the examples considered so far.

Lauren and other appreciators know to be fictional something that fictionally they do not know. Sometimes the reverse is true.

We read in the first paragraph of Conan Doyle's "Adventure of the Empty House" that "the public has already learned those particulars of the crime which came out in the police investigation,"[15] so probably it is fictional of the reader that she already knows much of what Watson goes on to describe. Fictionally she knows all along that it was Colonel Moran who murdered Ronald Adair, but she may not learn until the final pages of the story that it is fictional that she knew this (although she knew all along that fictionally she knew the identity of the killer), and she may have (really) been in suspense until then about who, fictionally, the murderer was. A story that begins: "Listen again to the exploits of our ancestors" makes it fictional that what follows is a *re*telling of the events in question, and fictional in the reader's game that he has heard about them before. This is fictional on a *first* reading of the work, let alone a second or a seventeenth; it is fictional even of the first-time reader that he has prior knowledge of the ancestors' exploits—even if he does not know what the exploits of which fictionally he has knowledge are. On rereading the story one neither actually experiences suspense or surprise, nor is it fictional that one does. (It may, however, be *fictional that it is fictional* that the appreciator is surprised or in suspense: that is, it may be fictional in his game that, as he is told again of adventures he already knows

15. "The Adventure of the Empty House," p. 483.

about, he plays a game in which fictionally he learns of them for the first time.)

Stories like those just mentioned are unusual. In most cases it is to be understood that fictionally the speaker (narrator) is addressing an audience who does not have prior knowledge of what he says, that he is giving them new information. (In real life the very act of saying something frequently implies that it is new to the auditors; so it is not surprising that the fact that fictionally such and such is said should, in many cases, make it fictional that those listening do not already know it. Sometimes the latter fictional truth is indicated more explicitly, as when fictionally the speaker says or shows by the manner in which he speaks that he expects his audience to be surprised at the events he recounts.)

It is usually fictional of the spectator of a film or play, no matter how often she has seen it before, that she is watching the events of the plot for the first time. It can hardly be fictional that the viewer of *Othello* is watching, again, the same particular events—Desdemona's dropping her handkerchief, Othello's ranting—that she observed on a previous occasion! If during the early scenes it is fictional that she knows that Othello will kill Desdemona, it is fictional that she knows this by some means other than having previously seen him do so.

The tendency of many still pictures—landscapes and others that depict unchanging states rather than fleeting moments of ongoing events—is in the opposite direction. We can easily regard a person viewing Cézanne's *Montagne Sainte-Victoire* for the second or seventieth time as fictionally looking again at a mountain he has seen before. It is equally reasonable to think of him, when he first sees the painting, as fictionally glimpsing the mountain for the first time. Here, alone among our recent examples, it is plausible that whether fictionally it is for the nth time that one experiences something depends on whether one is experiencing the work for the nth time.

I have emphasized the independence of what we know to be fictional and what it is fictional that we know. But they can correspond, of course. Sometimes our knowledge of how a story will go makes it fictional that we know the characters' fate in advance; sometimes it does not. Whether it does or not depends largely on the manner in which our information about the story was acquired, on whether our acquiring it as we did reasonably counts as fictionally learning of events before they happen.

In discovering the story's outcome by reading a review or from the fact that it is billed as a tragedy one may not be engaging in a game of make-believe at all. If the reader has experienced the work previously, or sneaked a premature look at the last chapter, he probably was not then playing the game that he plays later when he experiences the work again or in full. So we can comfortably deny that his acquiring this knowledge makes it fictional in the later game that he learns of the characters' fates, and we can deny almost as comfortably that his possession of this knowledge makes it fictional that he knows what their fates will be.

The more interesting cases, however, are ones in which our fore-knowledge is based largely on evidence internal to the work and is acquired as we experience the work in the normal manner. The story-teller may, following Hitchcock's recommendation, plant telltale clues in the early chapters or scenes, deliberately giving away the denouement. It may be that appreciators are *supposed* to have advance knowledge of the outcome, of what later chapters or scenes will make fictional, and this knowledge may be acquired in the course of engaging in an authorized game of make-believe. Even so, it is sometimes awkward to think of the appreciator as fictionally possess-ing prior knowledge of the adventures later to be portrayed.

Sunset Boulevard (Billy Wilder, 1950) opens with a flash-forward showing the protagonist's body floating in a swimming pool, and then proceeds to relate the story from its beginning. The viewer's experi-ence is like that of the novel reader who looks at the last chapter first, except that there is nothing illicit about the sequence, and the advance information is acquired while one is engaged in an authorized game.[16] Gregory was never in doubt about whether Dorothy, the Shaggy Man, and their friends, in *The Road to Oz,* would avoid being made into soup by the Scoodlers, since the chapter in which they fall into the Scoodlers' hands is titled "Escaping the Soup Kettle."[17] Stylistic evidence during the first moments of "Little Red Riding Hood" may make it obvious to Eric that it is a fairy tale of a kind that invariably ends happily, enabling him confidently to predict that Little Red Rid-ing Hood will survive the wolf's evil designs.

The appreciator, in cases like these, is not happily regarded as fictionally possessing foreknowledge of the denouement. A significant

16. Sometimes we see a later event earlier in a film without being able to understand it. This does not give anything away, although it may arouse curiosity and provoke guesses. When the same scene occurs again in a context in which we do understand it, it seems right, inevitable, fated to happen; we feel *as though* we knew all along that it would happen, even though we didn't. (It is not fictional that we knew it would happen, and we did not know it would be fictional that it would.)

17. Baum, *Road to Oz,* chap. 9.

reason for this (not in itself a conclusive one) is that there is likely to be no good answer to the question of *how*, fictionally, the appreciator comes to know how things will turn out. Is it fictional, when Susan watches *Sunset Boulevard*, that she knows what end the protagonist will come to, as she witnesses various events in his life, *because she has already seen his body face down in the swimming pool?* Is it fictional that she (or the character) took a spin in a time machine? (It is fictional at the beginning of the film that she sees the protagonist's body, and it is fictional later that she sees him alive, but this does not have to make it fictional that she sees him alive after seeing him dead, nor that she learns about his death before it happens.) How, fictionally, might Eric have managed to predict Little Red Riding Hood's escape? Certainly it isn't fictional that he inferred this from the fact that she is a heroine of a fairy tale; fictionally she is not a character in a fairy tale. To be sure, it *can* be fictional that an appreciator knows something even if it is indeterminate how fictionally he found out. But this indeterminacy makes it less natural than it would otherwise be to take it to be fictional that he knows.

Suppose Eric predicts the outcome of the story in a different way. He is struck by the wolf's evil demeanor, as it is described early in the story, and also by Little Red Riding Hood's pluck and the concern and competence of the hunter. He then judges on the basis of *these* observations that, fictionally, the wolf will hatch an evil plot but that it will be foiled. We need have no qualms, in this case, about allowing it to be fictional that Eric foresees the wolf's attempt on Little Red Riding Hood's life and her escape. Here we can easily say how, fictionally, Eric learns what he knows: it is fictional that he predicts the outcome on the basis of the wolf's evil demeanor, the girl's pluck, and the hunter's concern and competence. (In *this* case Eric's knowledge of the outcome of the story, supporting as it does the fictional truth that he knows what will transpire, may tend to lessen the suspenseful excitement of his experience; once he makes his actual prediction, it is not even fictional that he is uncertain about the outcome, and it is not fictional later that it surprises him.) The reader of *Moby Dick* realizes from the very beginning that fictionally Ishmael lived to tell about the disasters he witnessed. And it is fictional of the reader that he knows Ishmael survived. How, fictionally, does he know this? By hearing of the disasters from Ishmael himself.

What are we to say if Eric's grounds for predicting what, fictionally, will happen to Little Red Riding Hood are mixed, if he judges partly on the basis of fictional truths about the characters' intentions, personalities, and abilities, and partly from the fact that the story is a tale of a sort that invariably has a happy ending? Is it fictional, then, that he knows what Little Red Riding Hood's fate will be? Neither we nor Eric himself may be able to say. There may be no fact of the matter, nothing even for the gods to know.

Suspense and Surprise in the Static Arts

Notions of "suspense" and "surprise" have their most obvious applications in the "time" arts: literature, theater, film, and music. But there are parallels in the "static" arts as well. Appreciation of paintings and still photographs sometimes involves the excitement of fictionally, or actually, being surprised or being in suspense.

Still pictures can portray dilemmas, predicaments, and difficulties about whose resolution the viewer fictionally wonders or worries. It is fictional in John Copley's *Watson and the Shark* (1778) that a youth floundering in the sea is threatened by a shark while people in a boat try to rescue him. Will they succeed? Will he escape? Fictionally we observe his plight with concern and trepidation, scarcely daring to hope that he will make it. Our "suspense" involves no genuine uncertainty about what is fictional, of course—not in this case because we already know, but because we know that there is nothing further to know. The entire picture is plainly before us; there are no subsequent scenes to wait for. (And we can be reasonably sure that no as yet unnoticed details of the painting will give away the result.) It is fictional neither that the boy will be rescued nor that he will not be, and we realize that this is so. Situations in which fictionally the appreciator is in suspense but is not actually so are by now familiar. What is new in this example is that it never will be fictional that we learn (with relief or surprise or dismay or whatever) how things turn out. The painting is in this respect like a novel that ends without revealing the dcnouement, leaving the reader hanging. But the first-time reader of such a novel may not realize until the end that it will not be fictional that he lcarns the outcome. The viewer of the painting knows this all along.

Sometimes there are genuine surprises in store for the viewer of a still picture, as there are for appreciators of films and novels. We may be astonished to see what fictional truths are generated: that fictionally there is a gigantic apple completely filling a room (René Magritte, *The Listening Chamber*), or that fictionally there are beasts of certain incredible varieties (Bosch). Pictures from genres in which we expect idealized portrayals of nobility can surprise us by generating fictional truths about peasants and mundane details of ordinary life. Contemporary viewers of 1950s movies may be startled by the dress styles and automobiles of that decade, by what is fictional about what people wear and the cars they drive.

These surprises occur at the moment of one's initial contact with a work, but others occur only afterwards. Pictures, like novels, films, and plays, are experienced over a period of time, and the appreciator's discoveries, including unexpected ones, can come later as well as earlier. A hidden but startling feature of a picture may go unnoticed at first. Careful examination of what appears to be a placid scene of a couple walking in a park might, to the viewer's astonishment, reveal a gun hidden in the shrubbery. Suspense (*actual* suspense about what is fictional) will occur if the viewer suspects that a surprise may be in the offing before it comes.[18] Surprises like these are not repeatable indefinitely, if at all. Magritte's room-filling apple and Bosch's monsters no longer astonish us once we are familiar with them. If we already know that there is a gun in the bushes in an otherwise ordinary landscape, we will not be surprised to find it.

Is it fictional, again and again, that we are surprised, even if we are not really? No doubt, in some instances, but probably not in others. We have anticipated one questionable kind of case. It is not unreasonable to think of the veteran viewer of *The Listening Chamber* as fictionally observing a room-filling apple that he has seen many times before. If he is so regarded, we might best consider it fictional that he is *not* surprised at what he sees, although it may be fictional that he still marvels at it. This interpretation of his game will be nearly unavoidable if, as is likely, he is not (actually) startled, if he feels no quasi surprise.

Even when the viewer really is surprised at what is fictional, it may not be fictional that he is surprised. (This goes for both the "time" arts and the "static" ones.) Peasants, chickens, dogs, and children with dirty faces are ordinary and unsurprising features of our world. They are likely to be equally ordinary and unsurprising inhabitants of fictional worlds also; it is likely to be fictional that they are perfectly ordinary. This may be so even when their *portrayal* is astounding—as it may be in works of kinds that usually eschew such mundanities. Granted, people are sometimes surprised by what is not surprising,

---

18. Fried emphasizes the importance of the fact that certain features of Thomas Eakin's painting *The Gross Clinic* are not readily visible, and are noticed only after one has spent some time studying it (*Realism, Writing, Disfiguration*, pp. 10–11, 59–61).

and when the first-time viewer of a painting is amazed to see chickens and dirty children portrayed, it *might* be fictional that perfectly ordinary, unsurprising chickens and children surprise him. This supposition will be strained, however, if the viewer recognizes immediately that it *is* fictional that the chickens and children are unsurprising, which strongly suggests that fictionally he recognizes immediately that they are unsurprising, even if he continues to be astonished at what is fictional. The viewer's actual surprise at what is fictional may thus be disengaged from his game of make-believe. This does not mean that it is unimportant or irrelevant aesthetically. The artist may have meant to shock, and his success may be a crucial part of what is exciting about the work. But what is shocking is precisely the portrayal of things which, fictionally as well as actually, are unsurprising—their portrayal in a work of a kind in which that is not done. What is shocking is the work's "realism," in one sense of this much abused expression.

Fictional worlds obviously do not always agree with the real one with respect to what is surprising and what is to be expected. Fairies, goblins, metamorphoses of people into animals, all of which would be astonishing in our world, are fictionally, in fairy tales, perfectly ordinary. The frequency of the portrayal of such things in these works probably does play a role here; it may encourage us to consider it fictional that they are commonplace, and may also make us less inclined to consider it fictional that we are surprised by them (partly by making it less likely that we will experience quasi surprise).[19] It is fictional in many portrayals of nudes that nudity is ordinary and unremarkable (or at least it is not fictional that it is remarkable), and it is usually not fictional in viewers' games that they are surprised by it. (Manet's *Déjeuner sur l'Herbe*, which depicts an unclothed woman in the company of fully dressed men, is a well-known exception.) This also is due in part, I suggest, to the fact that, although we do not often expect to see real people unclothed, painted and sculpted depictions of unclothed people are common.

But other considerations come into play as well. It is arguable that by portraying in a matter-of-fact manner things or events that in the

19. We may have in the back of our minds a notion of a single, large fictional world to which the many fairy tales we have heard contribute. Since we are aware of many other cases in which it is fictional, in this comprehensive fairy tale world, that a person is transformed into an animal, we easily take it to be fictional that another such occurrence is not surprising and does not surprise us. Our background conception of this large fictional world may then influence what we take to be fictional in the world of each particular fairy tale and the game we play with it.

real world would be fantastic and incredible, some works make it fictional that they are perfectly ordinary. The reactions of characters in the work are often telling. It is plausibly fictional, in Magritte's *Memory of a Voyage* and in appreciators' games, that there is nothing out of the ordinary about the lion resting on the floor, since it is fictional that the man standing next to it takes no notice. The wonder evident on the faces of the crowd in Leonardo's *Adoration of the Magi* helps to ensure that fictionally the infant's birth is extraordinary.

The complexities of appreciators' responses to representational works of art may by now seem overwhelming, even when only epistemological aspects of their responses are considered—ones having to do with knowledge, suspense, and surprise. Critics are often interested in relations between "what we (the readers) know" and "what characters know": Sometimes we know what characters do not; sometimes they know what we do not; sometimes we share their knowledge and their ignorance.[20] This way of describing the situation is a considerable oversimplification. "What readers know" is ambiguous, we now realize, between what they "know" qua participants in their games of make-believe and what they know qua observers of a fictional world (the work world or the world of their games), between what it is fictional that they know and what they know to be fictional. The critic will want to compare what (fictionally) a character knows with both of these, in addition to comparing them with each other. He will want to consider also to what extent the appreciator's actual knowledge, ignorance, suspense, and surprise are integrated into his game of make-believe and to what extent they are independent of it, the roles they do and do not play in generating fictional truths, and what is or is not fictional about them. Even if one's actual epistemological states do not influence those one fictionally enjoys, the counterpoint between the two, the respects in which they do and do not correspond, and how this changes over time, can be significant.[21]

But this is only the beginning. We have seen that appreciators may or may not know what it is that fictionally they know. There is the difference between what is, fictionally or actually, unusual or surprising and what, actually or fictionally, surprises the appreciator, as

20. See, for example, Chatman, *Story and Discourse*, pp. 60–61. (It is obvious that I am not using "suspense" and "surprise" in the senses in which Chatman does.)
21. See Genette, *Narrative Discourse*.

well as what one knows about these and relations among them. There is the possibility of embedded fictional truths, of its being fictional that it is fictional that the appreciator is in a given epistemological state. On top of all this is the likelihood of several kinds of vagueness, ambiguity, obscurity, indeterminacy, undecidability concerning what is true and what is fictional, not to mention changes along these various dimensions during the course of one's experience. The variety of possibilities and their subtlety and complexity are boggling, as befits the preanalytically evident complexity, subtlety, and variety of appreciators' responses to representational works of art.

7.5.   THE POINT OF PARTICIPATION

Why do we care about Anna Karenina and Emma Bovary? Why do we take an interest in people and events we know to be merely fictitious? We don't; it is only fictional that Anna's fate matters to us, that we are fascinated by the adventures of Robinson Crusoe and admire the exploits of Paul Bunyan. But we do care—in a different way—about the experience of fictionally caring, and we are interested in games in which it is fictional that we follow the fortunes of Emma or Robinson Crusoe or admire Paul Bunyan's deeds. Why? What is to be gained from fictionally caring? What is in it for us? This question is central to an understanding of why we value representational works of art as much as we do.

We have already confronted and partially dissolved the special perplexity attending the appeal that works of tragedy have for us, works that appear to arouse "negative," unwanted feelings. But what are the positive reasons for being interested in representations generally, whether tragic or not? Their job is to serve as props in games of make-believe, games in which we participate. But why have such games? Why do we participate? Even when "positive" feelings are involved, ones we would certainly like to experience, what advantage is there in *fictionally* experiencing them, in fictionally rejoicing or fictionally being elated or content, let alone fictionally being saddened or distraught? What is the point of participation?

The reader will not find anything approaching full-fledged answers here. But a host of promising proposals clamor for consideration. What is the point of engaging in imaginative activities generally? There is a large body of folklore and some serious research on the benefits of dreams, daydreams, and children's games of make-believe.[22] It has been suggested, variously, that such activities furnish opportunities to try out unfamiliar roles, thereby helping us to understand and empathize with people who have those roles in real life and to develop skills needed to assume them ourselves; that they provide safe outlets for the expression of dangerous or socially unacceptable emotions, or purge us of undesirable ones, or help us to recognize and accept feelings that are repressed or just unarticulated; that they assist us in working out conflicts and in facing up to disturbing or unpleasant features of ourselves and our situations; that they give us practice in dealing with situations of kinds we might actually expect to face; and so on. Whatever exactly the benefits of other imaginative activities are, one would expect the appreciator using a novel or painting as a prop in a game of make-believe to enjoy similar ones.

(The benefits received may or may not be our *reasons* for valuing or attending to representational works. On a conscious phenomenological level there may be nothing much more definite than the thought that one's experience of the work is exciting or fun or moving or stimulating or enjoyable. One is not always explicitly aware of gaining insight or wisdom. There may be an evolutionary explanation of why human beings find experiences that do in fact produce insight exciting or enjoyable.)

I will not try to sort out or develop or evaluate these various suggestions. Many very different values are realized, no doubt, from participating in various ways, in games of various sorts, with (and without) props of various kinds. But it is worth noting that the imaginer's own place in her fictional world, her role as a reflexive prop, her imaginings about herself, would seem to be central in a great many diverse instances. It is surely no accident that children are virtually always characters in their games of make-believe, and that (as I suppose) one rarely if ever dreams without dreaming partly about oneself. The experience of fictionally facing certain situations, engaging in certain activities, having or expressing certain feelings in a dream or fantasy or game of make-believe is the means by which one achieves insight into one's situation, or empathy for others, or a realization of what it is like to undergo certain experiences, and so on.

This is no less true of appreciators of representational works of art than of other imaginers. Our own involvement in the worlds of our games is the key to understanding much of the importance representa-

---

22. See, for example, Singer, *Child's World of Make-Believe;* Bettelheim, *Uses of Enchantment;* Sheikh and Shaffer, *Potential of Fantasy and the Imagination;* Rubin et al., *Socialization, Personality, and Social Development;* and of course Freud.

tions have for us. If to read a novel or contemplate a painting were merely to stand outside a fictional world pressing one's nose against the glass and peer in, noticing what is fictional but not fictionally noticing anything, our interest in novels and paintings would indeed be mysterious. We might expect to have a certain clinical curiosity about fictional worlds viewed from afar, but it is hard to see how that could account for the significance of representations, their capacity to be deeply moving, sometimes even to change our lives.

We don't just observe fictional worlds from without. We live in them (in the worlds of our games, not work worlds), together with Anna Karenina and Emma Bovary and Robinson Crusoe and the others, sharing their joys and sorrows, rejoicing and commiserating with them, admiring and detesting them. True, these worlds are merely fictional, and we are well aware that they are. But *from inside* they seem actual—what fictionally is the case is, fictionally, *really* the case—and our presence in them, effected in the enormously realistic manner I described in §§ 7.1 and 7.2, gives us a sense of intimacy with characters and their other contents. It is this experience that underlies much of the fascination representations have for us and their power over us.

We must not underestimate what remains to be done: spelling out the specific ways in which participatory experiences contribute to our lives. But our make-believe theory has made a significant contribution, if only by harnessing our assorted thoughts and intuitions concerning the benefits of imaginative activities generally (and the limited research backing them up) to the question of the value of the representational arts, and facilitating their application by highlighting the respects in which our dealings with representational works are similar to, as well as different from, other imaginative activities. The very fact that we are interested in fiction at all should no longer astonish us. We need not shake our heads in amazement and ask why in the world people bother to read *Anna Karenina* or contemplate Cézanne's *Card Players*, given that the people and events they portray are merely fictional. Recognizing the role of representations as props and the participation of appreciators in games of make-believe takes the edge off the mystery and shows where to look for a fuller account of their value.

But our observations are incomplete in another way. Participation is central, but it isn't everything. The appreciator's perspective is a dual one. He observes fictional worlds as well as living in them; he discovers what is fictional as well as fictionally learning about and responding to characters and their situations. The former perspective also has an important place in appreciation, and sometimes it is dominant. Participation—the notion or thought of participation—remains fundamental. But things are more complex than I have yet indicated.

7.6. APPRECIATION WITHOUT PARTICIPATION

> You are about to begin reading Italo Calvino's new novel, *If on a winter's night a traveler*. Relax. Concentrate. Dispel every other thought. Let the world around you fade.
>
> Italo Calvino, *If on a Winter's Night a Traveler*

We have explored the considerable dimensions of appreciators' participation in games of make-believe, noting that they not only recognize and comply with prescriptions to imagine but also themselves serve as reflexive props, generating by their actions and thoughts and feelings fictional truths about themselves, and imagining accordingly. Thus do appreciators immerse themselves in fictional worlds. They are carried away by the pretense, caught up in the story.

Such immersion is not equally part of all appreciation, however. Sometimes appreciators participate scarcely at all. Some representations positively discourage participation, especially the psychological participation that would constitute the experience of being caught up in the story. That experience is perhaps the aim of much "romantic" art, broadly speaking, but works of certain other kinds shun it as sentimental excess, deliberately "distancing" the appreciator from the fictional world. Representations sometimes hinder even the imagining of what is fictional. In doing so they effectively undercut appreciators' roles as reflexive props. For if one does not imagine a proposition, it is unlikely to be fictional that one knows or believes it; and if one imagines it with minimal vivacity, one is unlikely to have the experience of fictionally being concerned or upset or relieved or frightened or overjoyed by the fact that it is true.

But appreciation without participation *is* appreciation. Works that limit our involvement in fictional worlds include acknowledged masterpieces, and they can be in their own way enormously provocative, entrancing, satisfying. Appreciation in such cases is something of a spectator sport; our stance is more akin to that of an onlooker than a participant in games of make-believe, although what we "observe" is not someone's actually playing a game but rather the kind of game that might be played. We step back and examine the prop, contemplating the games it might inspire and the role it would have in them. We may marvel at a work's suitability for use in games of certain sorts; we may be fascinated by the combination of fictional truths it generates (this amounts to an interest in the work world); we may admire the artist's skill and ingenuity in devising ways of generating fictional truths; we may delight in the devices by which participation is inhibited. Even in such "distanced" appreciation, however, the *thought* of the work's serving as a prop in a game of make-believe is central to our experience. Appreciation is not, in general, to be identified simply with participation, still less with the kind of participation that constitutes being "caught up in a story." But as far as representational aspects of appreciated works are concerned, the notion of participation is fundamental; appreciation not involving participation is nevertheless to be understood in terms of it.

One obvious way in which works sometimes discourage participation is by prominently declaring or displaying their fictionality, betraying their own pretense. Calvino's *If on a Winter's Night a Traveler* does this especially blatantly.[23] So does Thackeray in *Vanity Fair:* "I warn my 'kyind friends,' then, that I am going to tell a story of harrowing villainy and complicated—but, as I trust, intensely interesting—crime. My rascals are no milk-and-water rascals, I promise you . . . And as we bring our characters forward, I will ask leave . . . not only to introduce them, but occasionally to step down from the platform, and talk about them."[24] Even the phrase "Once upon a time" is in effect an announcement that what follows is fantasy.

I noted in § 1.1 the tendency of explicit reminders of the falsity of a proposition to lessen the vivacity with which we imagine it. We are not likely to imagine very vividly that we are being told truths about actual events, when we read a story, if (and while) it forces on our attention the fact that it is a just a story, that it is intended as a prop for games of make-believe rather than a report of actual events, that what it says is not true. The fact that *If on a Winter's Night a Traveler* and *Vanity Fair* are mere fictions is certainly not news to the reader, but emphasizing it, compelling the reader to dwell on it, restrains his imagining otherwise. The works of Saul Steinberg that depict not only certain objects but also the drawing of those objects (figure 3.2) call attention to the fact that the objects are merely pictured, and to that extent interfere with the viewer's imagining himself to be seeing real things.

23. P. 3; see the passage quoted at the beginning of this section.
24. Pp. 78–79. See also the passage cited in § 6.5 from Barth's "Life Story."

A similar effect can be achieved simply by focusing attention on the work itself, on its physical properties apart from their role in generating fictional truths, or on the process by which it was made. Deliberate slashes in paintings or areas of canvas left bare are vivid reminders that what we see is only a piece of painted canvas, and encourage us to examine the physical painting itself rather than using it as a prop in a game of make-believe, thus "destroying the illusion."[25] The cubist techniques of Braque and Picasso sometimes have the effect of restraining participation, and so does the multiplicity of Mona Lisas in Andy Warhol's *Mona Lisa* (1963). Literary works sometimes refer to themselves (even without reminding us that they are mere fiction) or discuss the telling of the story in a way that distracts from the story told: "We're going to tell it slowly, what happens in the middle of what I'm writing is coming already . . . And after the 'if' what am I going to put if I'm going to close the sentence structure correctly? But if I begin to ask questions, I'll never tell anything."[26] Even when the telling is not a subject of discussion, gratuitously flowery or alliterative or otherwise self-conscious language may take on a life of its own, calling attention to itself at the expense of the things described— even more so when a measure of near nonsense makes it unclear what sort of game is appropriate, what fictional truths are generated: "It's rare that there is a wind in Paris, and even less seldom a wind like this that swirled around corners and rose up to whip at old wooden venetian blinds behind which astonished ladies commented variously on how unreliable the weather had been these last few years. But the sun was out also, riding the wind and friend of the cats, so there was nothing that would keep me from taking a walk."[27]

Participation can be important even when it is hindered or limited. The bicycle seat and handlebars of Picasso's *Bull's Head* (figure 7.1) inevitably draw attention to themselves and to the fact that they are (bronze) bicycle parts, distracting the viewer from their representational function and probably interrupting the participatory experience of fictionally looking at a bull. The seat and handlebars compete with the bull, to some extent. But what is remarkable about this work is how well these familiar forms can serve as props, and it is by using them as such that the viewer appreciates this. Certainly one is not expected to lose oneself in the fictional world to any considerable extent, to partake more than nominally of the experience of fic-

25. The paintings of John Marin, for instance. See Rose, *American Art since 1900*, p. 52.
26. Cortázar, "Blow-Up," p. 102.
27. Ibid., p. 102. Beckett's writing has a tendency in this direction also.

tionally fearing a ferocious charge or fictionally admiring the bull's bravery or fictionally regretting its forthcoming fate in the ring. One's focus is more on the fact that games can be played with the work than on the experience of playing them. But unless one tastes the game, unless one participates at least to the extent of fictionally recognizing the bull, one will not realize how surprisingly well adapted the bicycle parts are for use as a prop.

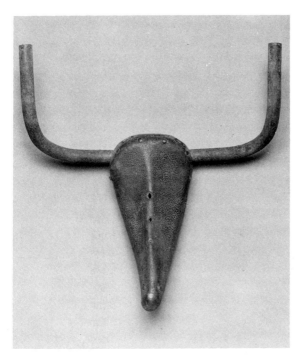

7.1 · Pablo Picasso, *Bull's Head,* $16\frac{1}{2}$ × $16\frac{1}{8}$ × $5\frac{7}{8}$ inches, bronze (1943). Copyright © ARS N.Y. / SPADEM, 1989. Photo © R.M.N.–SPADEM.

The conspicuous brush strokes of Van Gogh's *Starry Night* call attention to themselves and to their record of the process by which paint was applied to the canvas, possibly intruding on the viewer's participation in his game. The prop is seductive, however—more so than *Bull's Head*—and the appreciator probably uses it as such more extensively. One can ignore the brush strokes enough to lose oneself in the fictional world. But a part of one's interest, again, consists in appreciation of the way the brush strokes work together to make a

7.2 · Italian fabric design (late fifteenth or early sixteenth century). Richard Glazier, *Historic Textile Fabrics* (London: Batsford / New York: Scribner's, n.d.).

If poeta el pittor Vanno di pare
Et tira il lor ardire tutto ad un segno
Si come espresso in queste carte appare
Fregiare dopre & d'artificio degno

Di questo Roma ci puo essempio dare
Roma ricetto dogni chiaro ingegno
Da le cui grotte oue mai non saggiorna
Hor tanta luce asi bella arte torna

7.3 · *Master of the Die*, grotesque (early sixteenth century). B. 82 Kupfer-
stichkabinett SMPK, Berlin. Photo Paulmann-Jungeblut Berlin.

viable prop, and this requires both attention to the paint and participation in the game. Continuous single-minded participation, concentration on the visual surroundings in which one fictionally finds oneself, is easier, for example, for viewers of *Girl Reading Letter by Open Window* (figure 8.8) by Vermeer, who in the interest of "realism" disguised his own painterly activity and rendered inconspicuous the physical properties of the paint. Frank Stella remarked that in sixteenth-century Italy "projective reality was the goal of painting and . . . the job of the artist was to effect successful self-effacement, both of his personality and his craft. This, it seems obvious, is the nature of pictorial illusionism—to make the action surrounded and created by painting seem real, and to make the creator of that action and activity seem remote."[28]

Participation is not everything, however, even in the case of Vermeer and sixteenth-century Italian painting. The viewer will inevitably stand back, momentarily, from her game and marvel at how well the prop is suited to its role, whether or not she notes the specific means it employs.

Ornamental patterns composed of figurative forms (flowers, shells, leaves, vines), such as in figure 7.2, can be so compelling as designs as to preempt serious participation in games of make-believe.[29] Nominal participation is easy, but the games are scarcely absorbing. (Ornamental uses of depictions of human forms have a harder time suppressing participation, all the more so when the depictions are prominently three-dimensional. See figure 7.3.) Again, we are interested partly in the relation between the work's physical properties and its possible role in make-believe. But we are struck not so much by the suitability of independently notable or conspicuous marks for use as props as by the way in which forms that can serve as props combine to produce a riveting, visually interesting pattern. We think of the depictions as the material from which otherwise significant forms are constructed, rather than the reverse. Still, nominal participation would seem necessary for appreciation of the coincidence of the two functions.

Even nominal participation is unimportant in the case of icons used as traffic signs. No one stops to get involved in the world of figure 7.4, fictionally to study the (picture-) pedestrians' dress or demeanor or gait, or gaze into their eyes, or reflect on their station in life, or

28. Stella, *Working Space*, p. 40.
29. David Hills suggested examples of this sort.

whatever. Losing oneself in the fictional world is out of the question. The driver simply gets the message and takes the advice. Nevertheless, it is because the icon obviously could be used as a prop in a game of a certain sort—one in which the observer fictionally sees people crossing a street—that it is easily understood to carry the message it does. We recognize it as a viable prop even if we are not tempted to use it as such. (Many philosophical examples are fictions with a further purpose that can often be achieved with little or no participation on the part of the reader.)

Do these latest examples prescribe imaginings at all? To the extent that a work discourages imagining (let alone engaging in more intimate forms of participation) or accomplishes its evident purposes apart from anyone's doing so, it may seem not to have the function of prescribing imaginings, of serving as a prop in games of make-believe, and so not to qualify as a representation in our sense. We do not expect a sharp division between possessing the function of prescribing imaginings and lacking it; the notion of function and the line between imagining something with minimal vivacity and its merely occurring to one are both fuzzy. But a certain degree of built-in discouragement is clearly compatible with this function. If one says, "Imagine that p (of course it isn't true)," the parenthetical reminder may lessen the liveliness of the imaginings but does not cancel the request to imagine. "Let's pretend that the Russians are coming, but keep in mind that it is only pretense" is genuinely a proposal to engage in pretense. Nevertheless, some apparent representations may issue no serious directives to imagine the propositions that appear to be fictional in them.

7.4 · School crossing sign.

A chair is something with the function of being sat on. Chess sets are, by definition, to be used in playing chess. But there are *decorative* or *ornamental* "chairs" and "chess sets," ones that lack the normal function. They share something of the form of ordinary chairs or chess sets but are not meant or expected to be used as such, being too weak to support a sitter or too uncomfortable or too small, perhaps, or too valuable to risk injury or loss. They are for the eyes only. We refer to them as "chairs" or "chess sets" only in quotes; they are not actually such. Nevertheless, we think of them in terms of the functions which genuine chairs and chess sets serve. Our experience of an ornamental "chair," as we view it in a glass case, is informed by the thought of its being used as a seat, even if we realize it is not to be so used. One squirms if it appears uncomfortable or relaxes if it looks comfortable.

There are similarly nonfunctional "representations," ones that are merely "decorative" or "ornamental." Just as the fragility of its construction may make a "chair" unsuitable for use as a seat, references in a story to its fictionality may to some extent render it unsuitable for use as a prop. But such references allow and even demand thinking of it in terms of such use. The vase-and-plant–depiction of figure 7.2, which probably serves only minimally and intermittently as a prop in games of make-believe, may recall the possibility of fuller, more elaborate games. The notion of make-believe remains fundamental to our understanding of "ornamental" representations, even if they are not really representations, as the notion of being sat in is fundamental to the understanding of ornamental chairs. (Traffic sign icons are something of a special case. It is their function to serve as props only insofar as that is necessary to understand their instructions. One does not engage in contemplative reflection on them, informed by the thought of their being used in make-believe.)

In what way is one's experience of an ornamental chair informed by the thought of its being used as a seat? It is likely that one *imagines* its being so used, or at least that one imagines its function to be that of serving as a seat. And it is likely that the ornamental chair actually possesses the function of prescribing *these* imaginings, of serving as a prop in games of make-believe in which one is to imagine that its function is to be sat in. The ornamental chair may make it fictional that it is a genuine chair; it may be a reflexive representation representing itself as a chair.

Representations that are partly or wholly ornamental may likewise be understood to represent themselves as representations. Their function, if it is not especially to prescribe imaginings about people or fairies or flowers or whatever they may appear to represent, may be to prescribe imagining that that is their function. Fictionally appreciators may take the work to be a person-representation or a flower-representation and reflect on what it would be like to use it as such; they may imagine doing so. Reminders that one is not really seeing flowers or learning about people do not interfere with *these* imaginings, nor does attention to the medium or material. Appreciators imagine of the object that it is composed of the material it actually is composed of—paint on canvas, words on paper—and that its job is to generate fictional truths about fairies or flowers or people.

This reflexivity is explicit in some of our examples. *Vanity Fair* is partly about itself, representing itself as a story whose author announces that it is to be about "harrowing villainy and complicated crime." Figure 3.2 depicts the lines of which it is composed as a recently drawn depiction of a man sitting at an easel—with the twist that the depicted man is the one who drew the lines. Other cases are not so explicit. Takeoffs on children's stories about fairies and frogs and princesses can be understood to represent themselves as being children's stories about fairies and frogs and princesses. We (adults) may not be especially caught up in the fairyland, but we may pretend, imagine that we are, or at least imagine that we are supposed to be. When in *If on a Winter's Night a Traveler* we read, "Relax. Concentrate. Dispel every other thought. Let the world around you fade," we are to imagine that we are to lose ourselves in the fictional world of *If on a Winter's Night a Traveler*, although in reminding us that that work is his new *novel* and that there is a real world around us, Calvino inhibits our losing ourselves in it. In viewing an ornamental flower or vine design we may not imagine much participation beyond fictionally seeing flowers or vines, but we may imagine that it is the function of the design to be used at least in such minimal games. Insofar as it does prescribe *this* imagining, it represents itself as a representation.

Reflexive representations are of course representations. So although ornamental chairs may not be genuine chairs, ornamental representations are genuine representations. Their ornamentality merely alters what they are representations of.

Ornamental representations, like representation-representations generally, present us with fictional worlds in which other fictional worlds are embedded. (See § 3.6.) *Vanity Fair* establishes a world in which there is a novel *(Vanity Fair)* which establishes a world in which Amelia Sedley and Becky Sharp confront and interact with various rascals. It is fictional that it is fictional that they do.

Embedding a fictional world within another one puts it at a certain emotional "distance" from us. The couple who "look at us" from their portrait on the wall of the artist's studio in Velázquez's painting *Las Meninas* do so less insistently and command less of our attention than the man in the doorway does; the depicted frame separates them from us. Consider a story that ends with the hero waking from a bad dream. The reader, on realizing that it is fictional (in the story) only that it is *fictional* (in a dream) that monsters were chasing him, not that they really were, heaves a sigh of (fictional) relief.[30]

This might seem strange. The fact that it is only fictional that it is fictional that *p* does not make *p* any less true than it would have been were *p* actually fictional. The world of a dream within the world of a story is no less real than the world of the story.[31] Why shouldn't we be as concerned about what happens in the former as we are about what happens in the latter?

The answer, of course, is that if *p* is fictional we imagine it to be true, whereas if it is merely fictional that *p* is fictional we imagine only that *p* is to be imagined to be true. Our participation is in the first-order game of make-believe. In participating in it we may imagine that there is another game which we could participate in; we might even imagine participating in another one. But imagined participation is not actual participation, and imagined participation, let alone imagining merely that there is a game to participate in, does not constitute involvement in a fictional world. We stand apart from the internal fictional world and observe it through its frame.

Things are not usually as simple as this, however. I have suggested construing various works as ornamental representations insofar as they inhibit or interrupt certain imaginings, as works which fictionally prescribe these imaginings. But the inhibitions are usually partial and the interruptions temporary. We *do* imagine ourselves seeing lights reflected on the water when we contemplate Van Gogh's *Starry Night;* we do imagine learning about the lives of Amelia Sedley and Becky Sharp as we read *Vanity Fair.* We lose ourselves in these fictional worlds, to a considerable extent, even if the work limits our involvement and occasionally brings us back to reality.

30. Borges' story "Tlön, Uqbar, Orbis Tertius," is a case of the opposite kind: at first the world of Tlön seems deeply embedded in other fictional worlds, but it becomes, or is revealed to be, less and less so as the story progresses.

31. If both are unreal. But the contents of the story-dream might be actual even if those of the story are not.

Do we simply forget about or ignore the primary, framing fictional world, and think of the internal one as though it were primary, as though it were the world of the work? Do we illicitly use the work as a prop in a way in which it is only fictional that it is to be used? Surely not. Surely we are *supposed* to participate in these games. The reader of *Vanity Fair* is supposed to imagine that Becky Sharp marries Rawdon Crawley, not just that imagining this is prescribed. Van Gogh's *Starry Night* prescribes imagining not just that one is to imagine that there are reflections on the water but that there *are* such reflections. To engage in the latter imagining is not to misconstrue or misperceive the work. It is genuinely, not just fictionally, a depiction of light reflected on water.

Let's have it both ways. What is fictional can also be true. It is true as well as fictional that *Vanity Fair* is a novel about Becky Sharp. The novel makes it fictional both that Becky marries Rawdon Crawley and also that it makes it fictional that she does. But we will not want to allow that the two fictional truths belong to the same fictional world. So let us recognize two distinct work worlds, one in which Becky resides and one in which *Vanity Fair* establishes a fictional world in which Becky resides. There are two distinct games to be played with the novel. The reader alternates between them. (To some extent, perhaps, he plays them simultaneously.) It is fictional in the world of one game that he learns about Becky, her marriage, her affair with Lord Steyne, and responds with pity or disgust or admiration or whatever; it is fictional in the world of the other game that the reader examines and reflects on a prop that is to be used in games of the first sort. He alternately inhabits Becky's world and observes it from the outside. *Vanity Fair* is like a chair that is both ornamental and functional, one that is to be looked at with the thought of its being used as a seat in mind, and that is also actually to be used as a seat.

The emphasis in the case of *Vanity Fair* is on the work world in which Becky is actual and on the corresponding game of make-believe. But both worlds and both games are important, and the reader considers the relations between them. Steinberg's joke in figure 3.2 consists in a deliberate confusion of its two functions, a deliberate amalgamation of the two fictional worlds. There is a man in one of its worlds and merely a depiction of a man in the other. But the viewer is to imagine that in seeing the depiction she is seeing the man.

My suggestion that these works be regarded as having two alternate work worlds can be clarified by consideration of a case in which this is even more obviously so. Figure 7.5 depicts Richard Nixon and it depicts an arrangement of magnetic recording tape and reels, but it does not depict both together. It is fictional in one work world that Nixon stares ahead rather grimly; it is fictional in a different one that tapes and reels are deployed in such a fashion as to constitute a picture of Nixon. The viewer engages alternately in two distinct

7.5 · *Newsweek* cover, November 12, 1973. Cover art by Robert V. Engle. Photograph by Matt Sullivan.

games, and these games tend to interfere with each other, to interrupt each other. Their juxtaposition is, of course, the point of the piece.

How extensive is ornamentality? Since it can be partial and can coexist with genuine representationality even in the same respects (an ornamental *P*-representation can be an actual *P*-representation), we might expect traces of it to be widespread. I believe that they are, although detecting them may require considerable subtlety and sensitivity, and there will be the usual plethora of borderline cases. We should suspect ornamentality wherever representation is significantly "stylized." I have elsewhere considered the importance in many works of how they appear to have been produced.[32] (Van Gogh's *Starry Night* is an obvious example.) In many such cases it will be reasonable to think of what is apparent as being fictional.[33] It will be fictional of a work that it was produced or created in a certain manner or with certain intentions or by a person of a certain sort. The world in which this is fictional may exist alongside another one. If the work appears to be a *representation* created in a certain manner, if fictionally it is such, it will be an ornamental representation, a representation-representation. The content of its manifest world will be also the content of a world within its alternate work world.

What is the point of ornamentality? My earlier suggestions (sketchy though they were) regarding the interest of representation made it depend significantly on appreciators' participation in games of make-believe. We are now considering works that inhibit participation, ones that tend to make appreciation a spectator sport. Granted, the game in which participation is inhibited is, on my understanding of ornamentality, embedded in another one in which the appreciator might participate. But the world of this framing game is frequently very sparse, consisting of scarcely more than the work itself together with, by implication, its artist and his creative activity, and inviting minimal participation. To the extent that the representation is ornamental, its "main" characters and events, those we focus on, are likely to live their lives in the world of the internal game, which the appreciator observes from the outside but does not enter; it is fictional of her that she observes only that it is fictional that they live and die, love and hate, succeed and fail. The "emotional distance" that a framing fiction inserts between us and the characters complicates the task of explaining our interest in them.

The characters may inhabit a first-order work world as well as a world within a world, as we have seen; an alternate game of make-believe may bypass the framing fiction and give appreciators the opportunity fictionally to interact with and respond to them. But why have frames at all? Why even dilute the appreciator's participation? Why do artists ever arrange for the inhibition or interruption of participation?

Some critics and appreciators are indeed unsympathetic especially

---

32. Walton, "Points of View" and "Style."

33. At least when the appearance is to be noticed by appreciators. Even so, there may be cases in which one would not want to call what is apparent fictional, although it is not very clear what would distinguish them.

to the more blatant manifestations of ornamentality, regarding them as cheap tricks good for a joke perhaps, but not conducive to aesthetic profundity or greatness. Traditionalists bemoan the tendency of some recent art to turn inward on itself, to make representation its own subject matter, ignoring the big issues of human existence and the human condition in favor of what they consider trivialities and artificiality. But others object to demands for too intensive participation as cheap sentimentality, and welcome the relief afforded by ornamentality. Many works that promote participation most actively, that most effectively engage the appreciator in the fictional world, are, though seductive, anything but profound or great (soap operas? superrealist photographic paintings?). We noted that elements of ornamentality seem frequently to be present in acknowledged masterpieces. It may be that the "distance" afforded by a certain ornamentality makes for less direct but more significant connections with our lives.

We need not take sides in this dispute (no doubt there is some truth in both), and I will not attempt to map the battle lines with any precision. But there do seem to be certain values in ornamentality—in the inhibition of participation, in observation at the expense of participation—which need to be accounted for, whether one considers them more or less important than values they supplant. One may admire the artist's cleverness in devising the prop and designing the game, of course, but the values of ornamentality go deeper than this. Here are a couple of speculations.

If actual participation can have important benefits for us—helping us to clarify our thoughts and come to grips with our feelings about our position in life or whatever—one would expect people to be interested in the means by which participation is promoted and the kinds of participation one might engage in. This interest may be merely theoretical: one might simply want to understand how these things work, given that they are important. But it may also have a practical aspect; one might discover or develop techniques for achieving similar insights (or whatever) on one's own, without the aid of an artist's stimulus. Observation of games of make-believe and of techniques for stimulating participation may be difficult while one is actively participating, while one is caught up in the story. Ornamentality encourages withdrawal to a more "objective" perspective.

The intensity of the participant's experience when she is emotionally involved may hinder "objective" observation of the experience itself as well as of its stimulus. The experience of fictionally detesting a villainous rascal or fictionally grieving for a beloved hero may be so overwhelming that one cannot attend to and fails to notice much about what it is that fictionally one feels and why. No doubt there are benefits in simply having such experiences. But surely it can also be valuable to reflect on them, or on what one might fictionally think or feel were one to participate. Such reflection may make it easier to see connections between possible or actual fictional experiences and actual or possible real-life ones. So it may be desirable to "break the spell" of a representational work, if only temporarily. (It is not surprising that many works encourage alternating between participation and observation.) This reflection need not be as cerebral as it sounds. It may consist not so much in thinking about one's possible participation as in *imagining* it—*imagining* having the experience of fictionally grieving or whatever, *imagining* imagining oneself grieving.

Both of these speculations about the point of ornamentality, of inhibiting participation, retain the centrality of the notion of participation. Appreciators' thoughts or imaginings about participation, if not participation itself, remain fundamental in their experience and crucial to what is valuable about the works appreciated.

PART THREE

Modes and Manners

There are enormous differences among representations. We have had occasion to note some of them in the preceding chapters, but our focus so far has been on similarities, on what paintings, novels, stories, plays, films, and sculptures have in common. That emphasis was necessary in order to separate what is essential to representationality from peculiarities of its particular varieties. But we are now in a position to treat the differences systematically, within the context of a theory of representation in general. Let us now look at what is distinctive about some of the main varieties of representation.

One difference stands out above all others: a difference crudely characterized as between "pictorial" and "verbal" representation, or between "depicting" and "describing," or "showing" and "telling." These expressions are less clear than they seem and, as ordinarily understood, they correspond no more than approximately to any distinction our theory will want to recognize. In Chapter 8 I develop a notion of *depiction* which comprises more than pictures and more than *visual* representations—even some verbal ones. Chapter 9 treats several varieties of verbal representation, among which what I call *narrated* representations are perhaps most distinctive. But narrated representations exclude not only works of nonfiction, which are not even representations in our sense, but also some literary works which are representations. And they include some depictions. There are important variations among depictions and among narrations to be recognized and explored, as well as distinctions which cut across this division. And these two categories are not exhaustive; some representations are neither. We will pay particular attention to various senses in which certain representations might be said to be more *realistic* than others, and also to differences in what might be called *points of view.*

Our account of representation in general shows us where to look for what is special about particular varieties. Knowing that representations have the function of serving as props in games of make-believe, we can examine the nature of the games that works of various sorts are to be used in and the roles they have in them. Most of the differences we will investigate can be explained in these terms.

8

Depictive Representation

In some respects I stand towards [a picture-face] as I do towards a human face. I can study its expression, can react to it as to the expression of the human face. A child can talk to picture-men or picture-animals, can treat them as it treats dolls.

—Ludwig Wittgenstein,
Philosophical Investigations

8.1. DEPICTION DEFINED

We have already observed that pictures are props in games that are *visual* in several significant respects. The viewer of Meindert Hobbema's *Water Mill with the Great Red Roof* (figure 8.1) plays a game in which it is fictional that he sees a red-roofed mill. As a participant in the game, he imagines that this is so. And this self-imagining is done in a first-person manner: he imagines seeing a mill, not just that he sees one, and he imagines this from the inside. Moreover, his actual act of looking at the painting is what makes it fictional that he looks at a mill. And this act is such that fictionally it itself is his looking at a mill; he imagines of his looking that its object is a mill. We might sum this up by saying that in seeing the canvas he imaginatively sees a mill. Let's say provisionally that to be a "depiction" is to have the function of serving as a prop in visual games of this sort.

Why must the viewer imagine of his actual act of looking that *it* is an instance of looking at a mill? Why is it not enough that, on viewing the picture, one simply imagines looking at a mill? Because that would not distinguish depictions from descriptions such as this:

> From the fire tower on Bear Swamp Hill . . . the view usually extends about twelve miles. To the north, forest land reaches to the horizon. The trees are mainly oaks and pines, and the pines predominate. Occasionally, there are long, dark, serrated stands of Atlantic white cedars, so tall and so closely set that they seem to be spread against the sky on the ridges of hills . . . To the east, the view is similar. . . To the south, the view is twice broken slightly—by a lake and by a cranberry bog—but otherwise it, too, goes to the horizon in forest. To the west, pines, oaks, and cedars continue all

the way, and the western horizon includes the summit of another hill—Apple Pie Hill—and the outline of another fire tower. . . in a moment's sweeping glance, a person can see hundreds of square miles of wilderness.[1]

It is plausible that the reader of this passage is to imagine taking in the view from the fire tower, seeing the oaks and pines, the serrated stands of cedars, the vast wilderness, and so on, and to imagine this from the inside. But the reader does not imagine *his viewing of the words of the text* to be a viewing of the pine barrens. His actual visual activity is only the occasion for his imaginings. It prompts and prescribes them but is not their object. This prevents the text from qualifying as a picture. Looking at a picture (in games of the sort in which it is its function to serve) is part of the content of the imaginings it occasions. On observing Hobbema's canvas, one imagines one's observation to be of a mill.

1. McPhee, *The Pine Barrens*, pp. 3–4.

8.1 · Meindert Hobbema, *The Water Mill with the Great Red Roof*, 81.3 × 110 cm, oil on canvas (c. 1670). Gift of Mr. and Mrs. Frank G. Logan. Copyright © 1989 The Art Institute of Chicago.

But our imaginings and our perceptual experiences when we look at pictures are even more intimately connected than this. One does not first perceive Hobbema's picture and then, in a separate act, imagine that perception to be of a mill. The phenomenal character of the perception is inseparable from the imagining which takes it as an object. It is by now a commonplace that cognitive states of many sorts—beliefs, thoughts, expectations, attitudes, desires—enter into our perceptual experiences, that there is no such thing as an "innocent eye," a purely receptive capacity yielding data distinguishable from what one thinks about it, how one interprets it, what one does with it.[2] I do not mean just that thoughts have causal effects on one's experiences, but that the experiences *contain* thoughts. Imaginings also, like thoughts of other kinds, enter into visual experiences. And the imaginings called for when one looks at a picture inform the experience of looking at it. The seeing and the imagining are inseparably bound together, integrated into a single complex phenomenological whole. And, for reasons I am not yet ready to present, they must be thus integrated if the picture is to qualify as a picture.[3] It is this complex experience that is distinctive of and appropriate to the perception of pictures, the experience sometimes labeled "seeing the picture as a mill" or "seeing a mill in the picture."

Why doesn't the novel qualify as a *visual* art? Readers of novels use their eyes, after all, as do viewers of paintings and sculptures. Yes, novels can be read or recited to us; then we use our ears. So isn't the novel an optionally auditory or visual art—a perceptual one in any case? The answer is before us: Novels are not props in perceptual games of the appropriate sorts. When one reads *Madame Bovary* it is not fictional that what one sees is Emma, not even when one looks at passages describing her appearance. Although the reader may imagine seeing Emma, he does not imagine his actual perceptual act to be a perceiving of her, nor is his actual visual experience penetrated by the

---

2. Gombrich's insistence on this is well known. Strawson, while endorsing Kant's claim that "imagination is a necessary ingredient of perception itself," argues that perceptions are "soaked with, infused with, animated by, irradiated by" concepts or thoughts, that thoughts are "alive in them" ("Imagination and Perception," pp. 40, 41, 46). In discussing "seeing as" Wittgenstein speaks of an "amalgam" of seeing and thinking, and he observes that "the flashing of an aspect on us seems half visual experience, half thought" (*Philosophical Investigations*, p. 97). See also Steinberg, "The Eye Is Part of the Mind."

3. To anticipate: If they weren't, our visual game would not be adequately rich and vivid. When one sees an actual mill, the thought that one is seeing a mill is inseparable from the experience of seeing it. If the thought of seeing a mill, one's imagining this, is not part of one's perception of the canvas, one will not vividly imagine this perception to be an experience of seeing a mill.

thought that Emma is what he sees. Thus does depiction differ from verbal representation and from description generally.[4]

To be a depiction is to have the function of serving as a prop in visual games of make-believe in the manner indicated. But we should add that the games must be sufficiently *rich* and *vivid* visually. They are rich to the extent that they allow for the fictional performance of a large variety of visual actions, by virtue of actually performing visual actions vis à vis the work. It will be fictional of the viewer of Hobbema's painting, depending on how he actually looks at it, that he notices the woman in the doorway or that he overlooks her, that he searches the trees for squirrels or examines the wood for worm holes, that he gazes casually toward the fields in the distance or stares intently at them, and so on. A game's (visual) *vivacity* consists in the vivacity with which the participant imagines performing the visual actions which fictionally he performs. Stick figures, iconic traffic signs, and the like provide for visual games of only minimal richness and vivacity. This accounts for the hesitation Wollheim expresses as to whether or not they are pictures, whether we do or do not "see in" them what they are of.[5] We need not be satisfied merely declaring them to be borderline cases. We can specify the particular respects in which our visual games with them, in contrast to those we play with the works of Michelangelo and Vermeer (and even Braque), are attenuated and less than vivid. (See § 8.3.)

Sculptures and theatrical performances are also props in visual games, although the ranges of visual actions which fictionally one performs are somewhat different. Representations of other kinds figure in games involving senses other than sight. When one listens to Haydn's String Quartet, opus 32 (*The Bird*), it is fictional that one hears the chirping of birds. Touching a teddy bear counts as fictionally touching a bear. Theater and film audiences fictionally hear as well as see. Let us broaden our understanding of "depiction" to include representations that are auditory or tactile or otherwise perceptual in the way that paintings are visual. A *depiction,* then, is a representation whose function is to serve as a prop in reasonably rich and vivid perceptual games of make-believe.

There may be *ornamental* depictions, works such that it is fictional that they are to be used as props in perceptual games. (See § 7.6.) I

---

4. The impression that the make-believe theory of depiction gives insufficient weight to the perceiver's visual experience is misconceived. See Schier, *Deeper into Pictures,* p. 24; Wollheim, *Painting as an Art,* p. 361, n.21; Peacocke, "Depiction," pp. 391–392.

5. *Painting as an Art,* p. 60.

doubt that anything commonly called a picture is *purely* ornamental—that it does not also actually have the function of serving in such games—although even partial ornamentality may lessen the game's richness and vivacity. In any case a purely ornamental depiction would not properly qualify as a depiction in my sense. Even so, it would be understood in terms of the notion which is the essence of genuine depictiveness, and it would no doubt share many characteristics symptomatic of the function which it only fictionally possesses.[6]

The depictive *content* of a work is a matter of what or what sorts of things it is fictional (in appropriate visual games) that one sees when one looks at the picture. Fictionally one sees peasants feasting on seeing Breughel's *Peasant Wedding* (one's observation of the picture is fictionally an observation of a feast); thus it is a picture of peasants feasting, in the sense of being a peasants-feasting-picture. (See § 3.1.) A work depicts a particular actual object if in authorized games it is fictional that that object is what the viewer sees.

Depicting an actual object is a species of representing. But not all representing by depictions is depicting; pictures are not *pictures* of everything they represent. To represent something is to generate fictional truths about it. (See § 3.1.) Anthony Van Dyck's *Marchesa Grimaldi* is a picture of the marchesa. But it is not a picture of her feet, although it does represent them; it makes it fictional that she is standing on them, that they are completely obscured by her long gown, and so on. What is lacking is our fictionally *seeing* her feet. (It is fictional, in our games, that we *cannot* see them because they are obscured.) The objects of a representation are determined by what fictional truths it generates on its own. Whether that representing is depicting depends on what sorts of games it authorizes. What it represents can be read off from the work world; whether it depicts what it represents requires attention to the worlds of authorized games, to features of them beyond what they inherit from the work world.[7]

---

6. Depictions that raise the seeing-the-unseen problem might be considered partly ornamental. See § 6.6.

7. Novitz contends that "picture of" never expresses a denotative relation, that a pillar-of-salt picture labeled *Lot's Wife*, for instance, isn't a *picture* of Lot's wife but is merely a picture of a pillar of salt which is used to denote her (*Pictures and Their Use*, pp. 5–6, 18). What is wrong with this proposal is now clear. Pictures can, of course, be used to denote things they do not (denotatively) picture, or even represent. Such cases need to be distinguished from *Lot's Wife*, in which the denoting is *pictorial;* the picture presents Lot's wife in a manner such that it is fictional that we see her (in the form of a pillar of salt) when we see the picture. *Lot's Wife* is in this sense a picture of her, a picture of a person, although it is not a "picture of a person" in the sense of being a person-picture. (Novitz is right in urging that what it is to be *depictive* is not to be explained in terms of denotation.)

My way of differentiating depiction from description is a substantial departure from the usual ones. Depiction is often said to be somehow "natural," whereas description is "conventional" or "arbitrary." There is truth in this observation, but most attempts to ferret it out are seriously distorting. Traditional accounts of the naturalness of depiction speak of resemblances between pictures and what they picture; some even postulate illusions. A picture of a dog looks like a dog, it is said; but the word "dog" means dog only because there happens to be a rule or agreement or convention in the English language to that effect. Charles Peirce's distinction between *symbols,* which denote simply because they are used and understood as doing so, and *iconic* signs, which pick out their referents by virtue of sharing properties with them, is widely and all too often uncritically accepted.[8]

Resemblance theories face obvious and by now familiar difficulties.[9] Hobbema's *Water Mill* looks like what it is—a paint-covered stretch of canvas—not at all like a red-roofed water mill. A portrait of John may resemble his twin brother as much as or more than it does him, but it portrays John and not the brother. John himself looks very much like his brother, and he resembles his portrait as much as it resembles him; yet John depicts neither his brother nor his portrait. A novel about a novel resembles its object more closely than most pictures resemble theirs, but that does not make it a picture of a novel.

Many have noted elements of what might be called "conventionality" in depiction as well as in description. One cannot help being impressed by the variety of established pictorial styles, by the many *different* ways there are of picturing, convincingly, a dog or a person or a building. Some have urged that these are mere differences of "convention," that there are many different pictorial "languages," and that the choice among them is to a considerable extent arbitrary. If this is so, how is it that depiction differs from description by being "natural" rather than conventional, and what becomes of the idea that pictures rely on resemblance in a way words do not? Nelson Goodman contends that pictures are pictures by virtue of certain syntactic properties of the symbol systems in which they are embedded—what he calls "density" and "relative repleteness"—that similarity and naturalness have nothing to do with it.[10]

8. Peirce, *Collected Papers,* vol. 2.

9. Goodman, among others, has detailed the difficulties (in *Languages of Art*). Gombrich (in *Art and Illusion*) provides ammunition, although he resists Goodman's radical conventionalism.

10. *Languages of Art,* chap. 1 and pp. 225–232. There are intimations in Panofsky ("Perspective") of the idea that different systems of perspective are merely different conventions. See Podro, *Critical Historians,* pp. 186–189.

In addition to distinguishing depictions in general from descriptions, we need to explain important differences among them, especially differences of *realism*. "Realism" can mean many things, but resemblance theorists have a quick if crude way of accounting for one variety at least. Similarity has degrees, they point out, and some pictures look more like what they portray than others do. Realistic pictures are ones that look *very much* like what they portray, or ones that present especially convincing illusions. The closer the similarity, the greater the realism.

Conventionalist theories have no equally straightforward way with realism. If we regard pictorial styles as "languages" and resist the idea that some are more "right" or more "natural" than others, if we assimilate differences between Renaissance perspective painting and impressionism and cubism to differences between English and Turkish and Swahili, it is unclear where we will find room for realism. Calling a dog a dog is not a more or less realistic way of referring to it than calling it a *hund* or a *perro*. If cubism simply amounts to a system of conventions—a language different from that used by Vermeer, for instance—how is Vermeer's way of portraying things any more realistic than a cubist one?

Goodman does not flinch. There is no such thing as realism in pictures themselves, he claims, nor are any pictorial styles inherently more realistic than others. What we call realism is just a matter of habituation, of how familiar we happen to be with the conventions of a given symbol system. Pictures judged realistic are merely ones belonging to systems we have learned to "read" fluently.[11]

Goodman's fare is hard to swallow. The fact that pretheoretical intuitions and common sense favor resemblance is not itself of much consequence: intuitions can change and sense can be uncommon. But we need to appreciate from the new perspective the attraction of the rejected one. Goodman offers no insight into the motivations underlying resemblance theories. If they contain as little truth as he claims, why have they often seemed so self-evident as not even to require defense? Why do they persist in the face of obvious difficulties? How could common sense have gone so terribly wrong? The spell cannot be broken without understanding it. As long as the intuitions on which resemblance theories are based remain mysterious, they will retain their potency. A frontal assault designed to suppress them by brute force is bound to be less than fully convincing and to leave the field less than fully illuminated; one will always suspect that the

11. *Languages of Art*, pp. 34–39.

attack seems successful only because its target is blurred, that if we can only put our finger on similarity of the right special sort, the objections will fall away.

Speaking of seeing pictures *as* what they depict may be suggestive of the right sense of "similarity." In any case, "seeing-as" accounts of depiction share much of the intuitive plausibility of resemblance theories and appear to escape many of their problems. The fact that a portrait looks so unlike the sitter in obvious ways does not prevent us from seeing it as a person. We do not see the sitter as his portrait, nor do we see the portrait as his twin brother—at least we are not supposed to. Neither do we see *War and Peace* as a novel or Hobbema's *Mill* as a picture.

Not, anyway, in the sense in which we see pictures as what they depict. "Seeing-as" may not lead us astray in ways that "resemblance" does, but it does not take us very far either. It too needs clarification. It would not be far wrong to say that the problem of the nature of depiction *is,* at bottom, the problem of the nature of the relevant variety of seeing-as.[12]

Wollheim's change of terminology, substituting "seeing-in" for "seeing-as," is welcome.[13] (We do not see a picture "in" most pictures, although we do in one sense see them "as" pictures.) Wollheim does not fully explain what seeing-in amounts to, however. (Nor does he claim to.) Whereas seeing-as is "a form of visual interest in or curiosity about an object present to the senses," seeing-in "is the cultivation of a special kind of visual experience, which fastens upon certain objects in the environment for its furtherance."[14] What is that special visual experience? What is a person doing when she sees a dog in a design? She is participating in a visual game of make-believe. What is special about her experience is the fact that it is penetrated by the thought, the imagining, that her seeing is of a dog (as well as by the realization that it is of a picture). The way in which the design and other objects in the environment further experiences of this kind is by serving as props (and prompters) in visual games in which this imagining is prescribed.

Wollheim emphasizes what he calls the "twofoldness" of the experience of seeing-in, the fact that one attends to the canvas as well as to

12. Hermerén (*Representation and Meaning*) and Wolterstorff (*Works and Worlds*) offer suggestions about how to distinguish the kind of "seeing-as" that constitutes "representational seeing" from other varieties.

13. *Art and Its Objects,* §§ 11–14, pp. 205–226.

14. Ibid., pp. 222, 223.

the picture's representational content. And he insists that these are not two separable experiences but distinguishable aspects of the same one.[15] Both points are easily accounted for when seeing-in is understood as I suggest. The duality consists simply in the fact that one uses the picture as a prop in a visual game: one imagines seeing a mill, and one does so because one notices the relevant features of the canvas. The sense in which these are inseparable aspects of a single experience is given by the mutual interpenetration of the seeing and the imagining that I insisted on earlier. Rather than merely imagining seeing a mill, as a result of actually seeing the canvas (as one may imagine seeing Emma upon reading a description of her appearance in *Madame Bovary*), one imagines one's seeing of the canvas to be a seeing of a mill, and this imagining is an integral part of one's visual experience of the canvas.[16]

The question of the "conventionality" of depiction, despite the hackles it so often raises, is largely a red herring. In § 1.4 we noted how misleading it can be to call principles of make-believe in general arbitrary or conventional—apart from the rare instances in which they are established by stipulation and explicitly borne in mind by participants. Conventionality is incompatible with depictiveness, moreover, if it is understood to imply that the perceiver must explicitly figure out, on the basis of the colors and shapes before her, what a picture is a picture of. This would prevent participation in appropriately visual games of make-believe. (See § 8.2.) But many of the issues commonly disputed in debates about whether depiction is essentially "conventional" are irrelevant. We need not worry about how much or how little the principles linking pictures and their contents vary from culture to culture, tradition to tradition, or style to style; in what senses they could or could not have been different; how easy or difficult it is to change them; whether they are learned—by unconscious absorption or explicit instruction or otherwise—or are innate. Are the principles biologically grounded, as Wollheim thinks

15. *Painting as an Art*, pp. 46–47.

16. Schier objects to the seeing-in account of depiction thus: Projecting an image of one's grandfather onto a stone in the way that one sees afterimages on a wall counts as seeing the grandfather in the stone, he claims, but that does not make the stone a depiction of the grandfather—not even if runic instructions on it call for such projection (*Deeper into Pictures*, p. 17). The answer lies in the requirement that the actual seeing of the picture must be an *object* of representation and so of the perceiver's imagining, not just a prop and a prompter. The perceiver imagines seeing the grandfather, but he does not imagine his looking at the stone to be his looking at the grandfather. Properly spelled out, the seeing-in account survives.

the capacity for picture perception is, or cultural artifacts, as Goodman contends? I am sure they are some of both. The proportions do not matter. Evidence that chimpanzees understand pictures or can be trained to, or that natives of an isolated tribe do not understand them without special prompting, is beside the point. What is important for depiction is how the principles are used—whether they are used in appropriately visual games of make-believe—not how they or the ability to use them thus is acquired or who does or does not possess it.

Some think conventionality compromises the perceptual character of depiction.[17] It doesn't—except on the supposition that conventions are to be used in explicitly figuring out what a depiction is of. Suitably internalized, the principles of make-believe guide the imaginings that inform one's perceptual experience; one *perceives* depictions in accordance with them. These "conventions," if you like, thus promote rather than inhibit the experience of engaging in perceptual games of make-believe, wherein the perceptual character of depiction resides. It is not because Goodman's conventionalist theory postulates conventions that it fails to make depiction sufficiently perceptual. The fault lies with its contention that the presence of conventions satisfying certain syntactic criteria *suffices* for pictoriality. Insofar as such conventions can be integrated into appropriately visual games of make-believe, they are not incompatible with pictoriality. Indeed they are conducive to it, as we shall see.

One respect in which talk of "seeing-as" and "seeing-in" points in the right direction is in the emphasis on viewers' visual actions. Traditional disputes about the role of resemblance in depiction concern similarities between pictures and the things they picture. We will do better to look for similarities in a different place—between *lookings* at pictures and *lookings* at things, between the acts of perception rather than the things perceived. The process of investigating the "world of a picture" by examining the picture is analogous in important ways to the process of investigating the real world by looking at it. Visual examinations of picture men and picture mountains, to speak loosely, are like visual examinations of real men and real mountains. The resemblances we find here do not lie at the heart of depic-

17. "Walton's view holds that there is a conventional link between the appearance of the picture and what we are led to make-believedly see, and therefore does not require that we bring a special kind of perceptual capacity to bear on the appearance of the picture" (Wollheim, *Painting as an Art,* p. 361, n.21). (I do not without reservation regard the links to be "conventional.")

tion, but they are closer to it than are resemblances between pictures and things.

Certain analogies between visual investigations of pictures and visual investigations of things of the kinds they depict are closely linked to the perceptual games in which the former are, fictionally, the latter. Examining these links will do much to clarify the account of depiction I have offered. It will also help us to appreciate the intuitions on which resemblance theories are grounded and to see just where they go wrong.

But we will also discover that there is more to Goodman's density and repleteness requirements than pretheoretical intuitions would allow. As a matter of fact, many of the startlingly diverse proposals about the nature of depiction various theorists have advanced will be seen to converge on ours. Features taken to constitute part or all of the essence of depiction will turn out to be symptoms of the one that matters: having the function of serving as a prop in rich and vivid perceptual games of make-believe.

We will approach these matters by considering an objection: People can play whatever games of make-believe they like with a given prop, the objector proposes. Couldn't we simply choose to play appropriately visual games with verbal texts? Couldn't we stipulate, for instance, that reading a description of Emma in *Madame Bovary* is to count as fictionally scrutinizing her, and so on? But surely this would not transform the novel into a picture, not even if it were understood to have the function of serving in such games.[18] Nor would it be a picture, it seems, if the relevant principles were internalized so that we engaged in the visual games automatically, without figuring things out.

The answer is that we are *not* free to play any game we like with a given prop. It would be awkward at the very least to play visual games with texts as props, in the manner suggested, and next to impossible to use them for visual games of any significant richness and vivacity. Some things are better suited than others to serve as props in games of certain kinds. A tree makes a fine mast on a pirate ship. A tunnel or a watermelon would make a terrible one. A game of pirates in which to crawl through a tunnel or to eat a watermelon is fictionally to climb a mast is unlikely to be at all rich or vivid. (What would count as fictionally swaying with the mast in the wind, or fictionally grabbing a spar to keep from falling, or fictionally scanning the horizon for merchant vessels?) Flaubert's text is singularly

18. Schier offers an objection like this one (*Deeper into Pictures*, p. 23).

unsuited to a game in which visually examining it in various ways is, fictionally, visually examining Madame Bovary. (If we did manage somehow to play the appropriate visual game with it, our experience of the text would be so radically different from what it actually is that we need have no qualms about considering it then to be a depiction.)

In general, what we call pictures make much better props in visual games than verbal descriptions would.[19] This is because looking at pictures is analogous to looking at things in ways in which looking at verbal descriptions is not. The analogies make it easy to imagine, and to imagine vividly, of one's various visual examinations of pictures that they are examinations of things of the kinds portrayed. Hence it is natural that these imaginings should be prescribed, and that pictures should have the function of issuing such prescriptions.

The analogies in question do not hold equally for all kinds of pictures. Because of these differences the visual games in which painted canvases of various kinds are props vary in richness and vivacity and in other significant respects. This will enable us to distinguish between pictures that are more and less "realistic," in some senses of this extraordinarily slippery term. It will also help to illuminate differences among pictorial styles that are not easily regarded as differences in realism.

8.2. LOOKING AT PICTURES AND LOOKING AT THINGS

In what ways is looking at pictures like looking at things? I do not mean to compare the visual sensations or phenomenological experiences which viewers of pictures and observers of things enjoy. (It is not obvious how *this* comparison could be separated from a comparison between the visual characteristics of pictures and the visual characteristics of things. Both would amount to comparing *how pictures look* with *how things look*.) The analogies I am interested in hold between the process of inspecting pictures to ascertain what is fictional and the process of inspecting reality to ascertain what is true, between visual investigations of picture worlds and visual investigations of the real world.

Peter is a spectator of Hobbema's *Mill*. Mildred observes an actual scene of the kind the painting portrays—a red-roofed mill near a cluster of large trees with ducks in a pond and peasants in the

---

19. I will qualify this in § 9.1.

background—from a position corresponding to the point of view of the painting, from the left bank of the river some two hundred yards downstream from the mill. The process by which Peter ascertains that fictionally there is a red-roofed mill near a cluster of large trees and so on corresponds in important ways to the process by which Mildred determines that there is actually a red-roofed mill near a cluster of large trees and so on.

Some points of analogy are obvious. Both investigations are visual ones; Peter and Mildred both use their eyes. And the two investigations yield corresponding kinds of information—information about visual characteristics of the world of the picture in the one case, and information about visual characteristics of the real world in the other. Peter discovers the redness of the mill's roof, the size and approximate number of trees, the presence of peasants, ducks, and so on in the picture world; Mildred discerns similar features of the real world. (More precisely, Peter ascertains the *fictionality* of propositions whose *truth* Mildred ascertains.) Neither is likely to learn the marital status of the (fictional or actual) peasants or their taste in wine or the names of their siblings.

There is also a correspondence in the *order* in which the two observers acquire their information. A quick glance at the painting may reveal that fictionally the mill has a red roof and a peasant is carrying a long tool silhouetted against the bright field. A longer look will reveal that the tool is a hoe and that a woman is hidden in a dark doorway. Perhaps only after careful and extended scrutiny of the picture will Peter discover knots in the wood of the mill, subtleties of the woman's facial expression, or warts on her hand. The sequence is "realistic." Mildred is likely to notice the red roof before noticing that the peasant's tool is a hoe, and only after that pick out knots in the wood or warts on the woman's hands.

Already we are beginning to see why it is so natural for the viewer of the painting—as he notices that fictionally there is a mill with a red roof, a woman hidden in the shadows of the doorway, knots in the wood—to imagine himself looking at an actual mill and observing that it has a red roof, that there is a woman in the doorway, and so on.

How unique are the analogies so far? Robert reads a story about a red-roofed mill. He uses his eyes to learn about the fictional mill, of course. But much of the information he acquires about it is likely to be nonvisual. The story might tell him that the peasant was born in Haarlem and has three children, that one of her children is asleep inside the building, that she is thinking about the price of grain. And it may neglect to specify the color of the mill's roof or to mention the trees surrounding it. If it does concentrate on visual features of the scene, this information may be presented in an unlikely order. Robert may learn first of a wart on the woman's hand and only much later of the mill's prominent red roof. It may be as awkward for him to imagine his reading to be his visually examining a scene of the kind described as it is to imagine crawling through a tunnel to be climbing the mast of a pirate ship.

But consider a story that provides only visual information about a scene and presents it in a sequence in which an observer might actually learn it. An author may "write from life"; he may sit in front of a mill and simply record what he observes over his typewriter as he observes it. Alain Robbe-Grillet comes to mind:

> Now the shadow of the column—the column which supports the southwest corner of the roof—divides the corresponding corner of the veranda into two equal parts. This veranda is a wide, covered gallery surrounding the house on three sides. Since its width is the same for the central portion as for the sides, the line of shadow cast by the column extends precisely to the corner of the house; but it stops there, for only the veranda flagstones are reached by the sun, which is still too high in the sky. The wooden walls of the house— that is, its front and west gable-end—are still protected from the sun by the roof (common to the house proper and the terrace). So at this moment the shadow of the outer edge of the roof coincides exactly with the right angle formed by the terrace and the two vertical surfaces of the corner of the house.
>
> Now A . . . has come into the bedroom by the inside door opening onto the central hallway.[20]

Investigating the world of the novel by reading *this* passage will be much like visually inspecting an actual house surrounded by a veranda, in the respects mentioned so far.

But other correspondences between looking at pictures and looking at the world are more difficult to duplicate in a verbal medium. Some have to do with why it is that we make discoveries in the order that we do. It is because the red roof in the painting is more obvious, more striking visually than the knot in the wood, that it is likely to be noticed first. This may well be true of the actual scene. But if, in reading a story, one learns that fictionally a mill has a red roof before

20. Robbe-Grillet, *Jealousy*, p. 39.

learning fictional truths about a knot in the wood, one does so because of the order in which the sentences of the story occur, not because the red roof springs from the pages and forces itself on our attention. Detecting the knot does not require a closer examination of the text than detecting the red roof does. One just reads the sentences as they come. Also, the viewer of the painting, like the spectator of life, has some choice about what he looks at when. If Robert reads the story in the normal manner, from the beginning to the end, he makes no similar decisions; the author determines the order of his discoveries for him.

We can easily understand how a viewer of Hobbema's painting who is struck by the prominent red patch in the canvas and learns from it that fictionally the mill has a red roof, might imagine this experience to be one of being struck by the red roof of a (real) mill. It would be much less natural to imagine of one's methodically reading on in a story that *that* is an experience of being struck by a mill's red roof. Searching deliberately for marks on the canvas that would portray squirrels in the trees is more easily imagined to be looking deliberately for (actual) squirrels than is perusing sentences in a text in the order the author chose even if one learns from the sentences that fictionally there are squirrels in the trees. It is no wonder that our games of make-believe are not ones that call for imaginings of the latter sort.

There is a certain open-endedness to the task of visually investigating our (real-world) surroundings. There seems always more to be learned by examining things more closely or more carefully. Likewise, one can continue more or less indefinitely discovering fictional truths in Hobbema's painting: details about the grain of the wood, the expressions on the peasants' faces, the precise dimensions of the building and the pond in front of it. But there is a definite limit to what fictional truths can be learned by perusing a description (although one may always continue reflecting on and digesting what one has learned). One can *finish* reading a novel, but there is no such thing as completing either the task of examining a painting or that of visually investigating the real world. One does not stop to *contemplate* a text, as one does a picture. One simply reads each sentence and goes on to the next, and the next, until one comes to the end.

This point is not as clear-cut as it may first appear. There are limits to how closely we can look at a picture and to our powers of discrimination. The limits can be extended by the use of magnifying glasses and microscopes, in theory perhaps indefinitely. But the "information" in pictures often runs out even before optical instruments come into play. The image dissolves into blobs of paint or black dots, and it becomes clear that closer looks will not reveal anything more about the fictional world.[21] (This happens sooner for pictures of some kinds—tapestries, mosaics—than for others.) It is significant that approximately when we see the information running out, we no longer see the picture as what it portrays; we no longer see in it a mill or a bowl of fruit or a person. As long as one examines a picture in a manner normal for depictions of the kind in question, one does not exhaust the fictional truths it generates. No normal examination of Hobbema's painting reveals all of the fictional truths that can be extracted from it; there is always more to be found. In this respect looking at the picture in the normal manner is like looking at life.

The open-endedness of the task of "reading" pictures is related to the fact that the experience of *seeing-as* or *seeing-in* is not a momentary occurrence but a continuous state. One continues to see a mill in a picture for a period of short or long duration. But there seems to be no comparable continuous state connected with descriptions. Does one see an inscription of the word "elephant" as meaning elephant for thirty seconds, or for five minutes? It may be true throughout a period of thirty seconds or five minutes that one takes this word token to have that meaning, but doing so is not a *perceptual* state and need not involve seeing the inscription throughout the period. One does perceptually recognize the word and grasp its meaning, but this is a momentary occurrence (or two of them), not a continuous state, even if the recognition or grasping comes only with difficulty. My point is not that the state of seeing a picture as a man is one of constantly discovering new fictional truths. Rather it is the constant *possibility* of making new discoveries that sustains the state.

Goodman emphasizes the open-endedness of examinations of pictures, and he connects it with his claim that pictures necessarily belong to "dense" symbol systems. ("A scheme is syntactically dense if it provides for infinitely many characters so ordered that between each two there is a third."[22] So there will always be further more precise assessments of a mark which would refine our judgment as to what character it belongs to.) Pictorial systems need not be dense. A system of mosaics, for instance, might fail to be dense without failing to be pictorial. But pictorial systems do tend to be dense *up to a point*, at least, a point which is often beyond the limits of discrimination

21. In many cases we can see the blobs before seeing the limit approaching. But the reverse is less likely.
22. *Languages of Art*, p. 136.

when pictures are examined in the expected manner. And this fact contributes to the open-endedness of pictorial investigations. The important point is that we can now see *why* pictorial systems are dense to the extent that they are. Density contributes to a significant analogy between visual investigations of picture worlds and visual investigations of the real world, and so to the ease with which the former are imagined to be the latter.

Another significant analogy between examining the world of a picture and examining, visually, the real world concerns what is easy to ascertain and what is difficult, and what mistakes the perceiver is susceptible to. In these respects also examinations of both of these kinds contrast sharply with readers' investigations of the worlds of verbal representations.

In estimating the height of a tree by looking at it, we are more likely to make small errors than large ones. It is easier to mistake an 85-foot-tall-tree for an 85.0001-foot tree than for one which is merely 35 feet tall. This holds for picture trees as well as for real ones: in estimating the height of trees in Hobbema's painting, we are more likely to make small mistakes than larger ones.

The reverse is often true for trees in stories. The numerals 3 and 8 are readily mistaken for each other. An inattentive reader might easily take an 85-foot-tall (fictional) tree to be merely 35 feet tall. This enormous mistake is much *more* likely than many smaller ones. The reader is not apt to suppose that the tree in the story is 85.0001 feet high rather than a mere 85 feet high, since "85" and "85.0001" are easily distinguishable.

It is relatively easy to confuse a *house* in a story with a *horse* or a *hearse*, a *cat* with a *cot*, a *madam* with a *madman, intellectuality* with *ineffectuality, taxis* with *taxes,* and so on. But when we examine either the real world by looking at it or picture worlds, houses are more easily mistaken for barns or woodsheds than for hearses or horses, cats are harder to distinguish from puppies than from cots, and so on.[23]

The mistakes perceivers are susceptible to correspond to similarities among things themselves. Things that are hard to discriminate perceptually are things that really are similar in some respect. An 85-foot tree resembles one which is 85.0001 feet tall more closely than it does a 35-foot tree. Houses are more like barns and woodsheds than

23. What I call mistakes about picture trees and story trees are, of course, mistakes about fictional truths. If it is easy to be mistaken about which of two propositions is true, it is often easy to be mistaken about which of them is fictional in a depiction, but mistakes about which of them is fictional in a story are much less likely.

horses or hearses. In fact, the degree of similarity explains the likelihood of confusion. It is *because* 85- and 85.0001-foot trees are similar that they are difficult to distinguish. So there is a substantial correlation between difficulty of discrimination, when we look at the real world, and similarities among things. In *this* sense we can be said to perceive things as they really are.

(Some will prefer to say that the correlation is between difficulty of discrimination and *what we think of* as resemblances; some claim that there is no such thing as similarity in things themselves, that similarity is *only* a matter of our ways of thinking or our conceptual schemes. We regard the things we do as being similar, sometimes, precisely because they are easily confused when examined in ways which otherwise count as perceptual. If similarity relative to our conceptual scheme is the only kind there is, facts about our discriminative capacities might be said to *create* similarities. We can still allow that similarities make things difficult to discriminate perceptually, however. What count as similarities for us, what respects of resemblance there are relative to our conceptual scheme, is determined in part by which discriminations are easy to make and which difficult, given our usual modes of perception. The fact that certain things are similar in these respects explains the difficulty of discriminating them.)[24]

Pictorial representations largely preserve this correlation. But descriptions scramble the real similarity relations (or what we think of as similarity relations). Houses are not much like horses or hearses. The difficulty of distinguishing a house from a horse in a story has nothing to do with similarities between the house and horses; it is due to similarities between the *words* used to describe them. So we think of the words as getting between us and what we are reading about, blocking our view of objects, in a way that pictorial representations do not. The words thus make it awkward to imagine ourselves seeing the objects when we read the words.

We now have the tools to understand a couple of possible representational systems mentioned by Richard Wollheim: "We could imagine a painting of a landscape in which, say, the colours were reversed so that every object—tree, river, rocks—was depicted in the complementary of its real colour: or we could imagine, could we not?, an even more radical reconstruction of the scene, in which it was first fragmented into various sections and these sections were then totally rearranged without respect for the look of the landscape, according to

24. See Walton, "Transparent Pictures," § 8.

a formula?" These paintings would not be depictive, he suggests, "since it is only by means of an inference, or as the result of a 'derivation', that we are able to go from the drawing to what it is said to depict. There is no longer any question of seeing the latter in the former. We have now not a picture that we look at, but a puzzle that we unravel."[25]

We can agree that if "reading" a representation is an inferential process of the kind described, if one must first ascertain its relevant features and then figure out, according to a formula, what fictional truths are generated, we do not see what is represented in the representation. Normally the viewer of Hobbema's millscape just looks and sees that fictionally there is a mill with a red roof near a grove of trees. If we could not do this more or less automatically, the canvas would not be a picture for us. The reason, I would add, is that the process of figuring out from characteristics of the two-dimensional pattern of paint on canvas, with the aid of a formula, that fictionally there is a red-roofed mill (for example) is hardly such that one can vividly imagine it to be an instance of observing an actual scene and noticing that there is a red-roofed mill. For noticing this does not involve any similar figuring; we just look and see.

What about Wollheim's color-reversed representation, and the systematically scrambled one? Is it *impossible* that they should be pictures? I suspect that with sufficient practice we could become so familiar with these systems and so adept at "reading" representations in them that we would not have to figure out what fictional truths are generated but could just look and see. If we did, Wollheim would apparently be willing to call the representations pictures. But I am skeptical. The ability to read representations automatically is clearly not sufficient for their being pictures; we read words automatically, after all.

Consider a Scrambled System whereby the parts of pictures in some normal system are rearranged according to the accompanying schema.

Normal

1	2	3
4	5	6

Scrambled

6	4	2
5	3	1

25. "On Drawing an Object," p. 25.

8.2a · Normal, witch right.

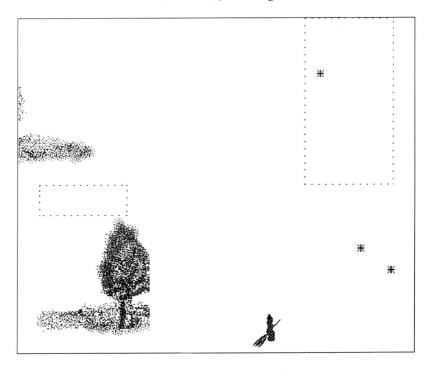

8.2b · Scrambled, witch right.

8.3a · Normal, witch left.

8.3b · Scrambled, witch left.

Figure 8.2b (without the rectangles) is the scrambled version of the normal picture, figure 8.2a. Understood in their own systems, they generate the same fictional truths: the "world of the picture" is the same in both cases. Each depicts a tree in the center of the scene and a witch on the far right and above it. Since the Scrambled System is foreign to us, we have to do some calculating to figure out what is going on in figure 8.2b. We understand 8.2a much more readily.

But suppose that after long experience we develop the ability to "read" pictures of both kinds automatically. There still will be important differences in the processes of investigating them. The scrambling drastically alters the ease or difficulty with which various fictional truths are ascertained, even for observers equally fluent in the two systems. A viewer practiced in reading scrambled pictures could presumably tell at a glance that the witch in 8.2b is not near the center of the scene above the tree but is far to one side or the other. (If she were in the center, her portrayal on the picture surface would be in one of the two rectangular areas, and it obviously is not.) But it is not so easy even for the practiced viewer to tell *which* side of the scene she is on, whether she is far to the left or far to the right, whether she is coming or going. In 8.2b she is on the right. In 8.3b she is on the left. These two pictures are not readily distinguishable.

Contrast the unscrambled versions of these pictures, figures 8.2a and 8.3a. In figure 8.3a the witch is approaching on the far left; figure 8.2a shows her far to the right on her way to other mischief. It is easy to tell which is which.

Examining the worlds of ordinary pictures like these is clearly more like looking at the real world than is examining the worlds of the scrambled ones, even for a viewer thoroughly fluent in the Scrambled System. When in real life would one notice quickly that something is *either* far to the right or far to the left and not be able to tell which without looking much more closely? The consequences for one's visual game of make-believe would be severe.

I do not suggest that the scrambled pictures are not pictures. Looking at them is in many other respects like looking at the world, and they do function as props in reasonably rich and vivid visual games of make-believe. Certainly each of their six segments qualifies as a picture. The differences between them and their unscrambled cousins are nevertheless substantial.

Note that the Scrambled System, no less than the unscrambled one, has every right to be regarded as "dense" in Goodman's sense (both syntactically and semantically).[26] Goodman's theory does not distin-

26. And it is just as "replete." See Goodman, *Languages of Art*, p. 230.

guish between them. The Scrambled System differs from the ordinary one, however, with respect to what Kent Bach calls "continuous correlation" and what Elliott Sober calls "perspicuity."[27] Roughly, the orderings of pictures correspond to the orderings of scenes of the kinds depicted in the case of the normal system but not in that of the scrambled one.

Wollheim's Scrambled System is not just an academic exercise. Artists of various stripes have employed what amount to scramblings in their work, most obviously the cubists,[28] although the principles on which their scramblings are based are typically very unsystematic and much more complex than those employed in our artificial example. Often viewers have to divine the system by which the pieces are arranged from the picture itself. Consider Paul Citroën's photograph *Metropolis* (1923) (figure 8.4). Flashbacks and flash-forwards in film have similar consequences. We see more clearly now how serious a mistake it is to regard cubism, for instance, as just a system *different* from others, one with different conventions which we must get used to. It is a system that affects substantially the nature of the visual games in which works function as props, quite apart from our familiarity with it. The difference I have described bears out the common characterization of cubism as a more intellectual, less visual pictorial style than earlier ones.[29]

8.3.   STYLES OF DEPICTION

Depictions differ from representations of other kinds by virtue of the games of make-believe appreciators are to play with them. We have just noted a difference of this sort among depictions themselves. There are many others. The significance of many features of pictorial styles lies in their effects on viewers' games. When the games played with certain depictions can be regarded as richer or more vivid perceptually than those played with certain others, we might speak of differences of "realism" (of one sort); thus the scramblings of cubism lessen its realism in one respect. Some important differences among games are not easily so regarded. Let us look at some examples.

27. Bach, "Part of What a Picture Is," and Sober, *Simplicity*.

28. "[Picasso] presents us here [in *Desmoiselles d'Avignon*] with the female form dismembered and reassembled in a way that allows us to see the back and front at the same time, a device that became a keystone of cubism" (Penrose, "In Praise of Illusion," pp. 248–249).

29. "[Cubism] is the art of painting new structures out of elements borrowed not from the reality of sight, but from the reality of insight" (Apollinaire, *Cubist Painters,* p. 17).

Sloppy Style and Idealized Shapes

Figure 8.5 is in what I will call a *Sloppy Style* of depiction. It would be uncharitable and boorish to insist that the casing of the computer in the picture is warped, that the right side fails to connect with the top, that half of the keyboard is missing. True, the lines of the sketch are

8.4 · Paul Citroën, *Metropolis*. © Paul Citroën / VAGA New York, 1989.

not straight and do not connect with one another as they would in a precise architectural drawing, and the keyboard is only partially portrayed. But this *is* Sloppy Style, after all, and lines in Sloppy Style are *expected* to be sloppy. Their sloppiness is not to be read into the fictional world but is to be accepted as inevitable in the style regardless of what is being portrayed. We can reasonably allow that fictionally the computer is a perfectly whole and healthy one, notwithstanding the sloppiness of the portrayal. Certainly Apple Computer, Inc., and its advertising agency expect the sketch to be so understood. (A principle of charity may be operative, or what the artist evidently meant to be fictional may be understood to affect what is fictional.)

How then does this sketch differ from a carefully precise and

8.5 · Manual cover, © Apple Computer, Inc. Used with permission. Apple Macintosh and the Macintosh logo are registered trademarks of Apple Computer, Inc.

8.6 · Paul Klee, *Mountains in Winter,* 11 × 14⅜ inches, watercolor and brush on cardboard (1925). Copyright © ARS N.Y. / Cosmopress, 1989. Museum of Fine Arts Berne, Hermann und Margrit Rupf-Stiftung © 1989, Copyright by Cosmopress, Genf.

detailed rendition of the same subject? Largely in the visual games of make-believe in which they figure. In both cases the viewer fictionally sees an unbroken, undamaged Macintosh computer. But nothing which the viewer of the Sloppy Style sketch might do is easily imagined to be looking carefully to see just how true the sides of the machine are. He will not, fictionally, examine the computer closely for damage.[30] Once we see that it is in Sloppy Style, we realize that further investigation of the lines of the drawing will not reveal fictional truths about details of the computer's construction; it is fictional more or less by default that its condition is normal. The person who looks at the more precise drawing, however, might very well fictionally engage in a close scrutiny of its construction. The more precise drawing thus admits of visual games which are richer in some respects than ones we will play with the Sloppy Style sketch.

(A more important difference between these examples, although one less central to our present concerns, is that the Sloppy Style sketch

30. It is not fictional that he cannot examine it closely for damage; probably it is fictional that he can. But it cannot be fictional that he does.

contains an intimation of human warmth and computer friendliness which a more precise drawing is likely to lack. This might be understood in terms of an alternative game to be played with the sketch in which fictionally it is drawn by a fallible and feeling and not overly fastidious human being—not by a machine. See § 7.6.)

Paul Klee's *Mountains in Winter* (figure 8.6) is of an opposite kind. Here the lines are straight but the mountains are not. We can reasonably take for granted that fictionally the mountains are rough and ragged, as befits all self-respecting mountains, but we will not fictionally look to see that they are, or fictionally examine the particular dimensions of the raggedness.

Similar observations can be made about the idealized shapes of cubist and other works. Is it fictional that a person has an angular head if the picture uses angular shapes to portray it? Not if the angularity is thought of as being simply a feature of the style, regardless of what is depicted. Picasso's *Portrait of Daniel-Henry Kahnweiler* (figure 8.7) does not portray Kahnweiler as exotically deformed. But our visual game of make-believe is severely limited in certain ways. There will be no such thing as fictionally gazing fondly at the gentle curve of his brow, or fictionally being slightly intimidated by his aggressive, prominent chin.

Light

Some pictures portray very explicitly the play of light on the surfaces of objects, rendering shadows and reflections overtly and in great detail. Vermeer's works do, and so do many photographs. Other pictures concentrate on the shapes, positions, colors, and textures of objects while ignoring how light is reflected from them. These include outline drawings and assorted ancient, "primitive," and twentieth-century works. Vermeer's *Girl Reading Letter by Open Window* (figure 8.8) will serve as an example of the first kind. The second is illustrated by Matisse's *Red Studio* (figure 8.9), in which the solid, homogeneously colored tablecloth and wall are portrayed by solid-colored, homogeneous stretches of canvas, ignoring shadows, differing angles of the incidence of light on different parts of the tablecloth, and so on.

What exactly does this difference amount to? Shall we say that the Vermeer contains "information" of certain kinds which the Matisse lacks? Perhaps. But the paintings differ less in this regard than might first appear. It would not be fair to say that whereas the Vermeer

8.7 · Pablo Picasso, *Portrait of Daniel-Henry Kahnweiler*, 100.6 × 72.8 cm, oil on canvas (1910). Copyright © ARS N.Y. / SPADEM, 1989. Courtesy of The Art Institute of Chicago. Gift of Mrs. Gilbert W. Chapman in memory of Charles B. Goodspeed, 1948.561. Copyright © 1989 The Art Institute of Chicago.

generates fictional truths about the play of light, the Matisse does not. It is clear that the main illumination in the Matisse comes from the large window on the left. (The window is open, and since the scene is a daytime one, we should expect it to be the main source of illumination.) So we can reasonably infer that (fictionally) the vase casts a shadow on the table in the direction away from the window, for example. This is implied by fictional truths about the window, and so on. The fact that Matisse did not use a darker patch of paint to portray the shadow, as Vermeer would have, may be construed as a characteristic of the style in which this picture is painted, not as indicating the absence of a shadow in the depicted scene.[31]

The Red Studio does, then, generate fictional truths about the play of light. It does not generate as detailed or specific ones as we find in *Girl Reading Letter,* to be sure; there is *more* information about light and shadow in the Vermeer than in the Matisse. But a more important difference between them concerns not what fictional truths are generated but the manner in which they are generated and the effect that that has on our visual games of make-believe.

Whereas in the Matisse fictional truths about shadows and reflections are implied by fictional truths about the location of the window, the position and shape of the vase, and so on, the Vermeer generates fictional truths about shadows and reflections more directly. But fictional truths about the position and shape of objects are in some cases generated more directly by the Matisse than by the Vermeer. Vermeer uses reflections and shadows to indicate the folds of the draperies and the texture of surfaces. The fact that fictionally the draperies fall in such and such a manner is implied by the fact that fictionally light is reflected from various parts of them in a certain way. In short, the relations of dependency among fictional truths run in opposite directions in the two cases. In the Matisse, fictional truths about the play of light depend on fictional truths about three-dimensional objects. In

---

31. There is room for doubt about this construal. But many ordinary line drawings are obviously to be interpreted in this way, and they can serve to illustrate my point. It is fictional, in many line drawings, that there are shadows and reflections, even if the drawing does not explicitly portray them.

I do not doubt the aesthetic importance of the absence of explicitly portrayed shadows and reflections in the Matisse; this feature of the painting's style contributes much to its expressive character. But neither the supposition that it is fictional that there are no shadows nor the supposition that it is not fictional that there are shadows is required to explain this contribution. It can be understood to derive from the truncation of spectators' games of make-believe, which I will describe shortly, rather than from what is or is not fictional in the work world.

8.8 · Jan Vermeer of Delft, *Girl Reading Letter by Open Window*, oil on canvas (c. 1658). Gemäldegalerie Alte Meister—Staatliche Kunstsamm-lungen, Dresden.

the Vermeer, fictional truths about three-dimensional objects depend, to a considerable extent, on fictional truths about the play of light.[32]

---

32. Which work is thought to correspond best to the way the world is may depend on one's metaphysical theory. A phenomenalist might pick the Vermeer, a materialist the Matisse. My present concern is with how pictures relate not to how the world is or is thought to be but to how we perceive it.

8.9 · Henri Matisse, *The Red Studio*, $71\frac{1}{4}$ inches × 7 feet $2\frac{1}{4}$ inches, oil on canvas (1911). Collection, The Museum of Modern Art, New York. Mrs. Simon Guggenheim Fund.

There is a corresponding difference in how viewers discover fictional truths of the two kinds. Fictional truths about the play of light enable the spectator of the Vermeer to ascertain fictional truths about the spatial configurations of objects. But the viewer of the Matisse must base such judgments on other things—most obviously on lines in the painting indicating the edges of objects. Our access to the world of the Vermeer corresponds better to the access perceivers have to the real world. In real life, reflections and shadows have a lot to do with our judgments of the spatial properties of three-dimensional objects.

It is easily understood that when we observe the Vermeer, fictionally we perceive the topography of the drapes by perceiving the patterns of light and shadow on them. But this is not what is crucial. One might reasonably allow that it is fictional in our game with the

Matisse as well that our perception of the attitudes of objects is dependent on our perception of light and shade. (This fictional truth derives from something like the Reality Principle, discussed in § 4.2.)

The difference that does obtain between the two pictures comes out most dramatically when the observer investigates the perceptual cues underlying his perception of fictional truths about three-dimensional objects. The viewer of *Girl Reading Letter* inevitably imagines himself to be probing the grounds of his judgments about objects of the kind represented. Fictionally he notices that certain reflections and shadows are important cues. But the viewer of *The Red Studio* who embarks on similar reflections is soon forced out of the game of make-believe. It may be fictional that shadows and reflections serve him as cues, but nothing he does is naturally imagined to be investigating and discovering these cues. Examining the *actual* cues underlying his awareness of fictional truths about three-dimensional objects is not, for these cues do not include fictional truths about light and shadow. The visual games one plays with the Matisse are thus attenuated in a way the visual games one plays with the Vermeer are not.

Often in real life we pay no attention to shadows and reflections; we concentrate on the spatial configurations of three-dimensional objects, not even noticing the cues on which our judgments of these matters are based. In contemplating the Vermeer, we may also fail to notice fictional truths about the play of light which serve as cues for our perception of fictional truths about three-dimensional objects. When this is so, is our experience no different from that of the viewer of Matisse's painting? In both cases we simply look and see that, fictionally, objects are arranged in certain ways, thereby fictionally looking at objects and seeing how they are arranged; the mechanics of the process by which we tell may seem not to be part of the experience. But I believe that a vague realization of the possibility of fictionally probing the cues underlying one's perceptions of three-dimensional objects is present in one's experience of the Vermeer and significantly colors it, even if one pays no attention to the portrayal of light and shadow. This realization—the realization of the potential richness of his visual game of make-believe—is an important part of what makes so vivid the viewer's imaginings of his viewings that they are observations of the real world.

Translations

Most depiction involves what we might call *translation* of one sort or another. Pictures portray three-dimensional arrays of objects on two-dimensional surfaces. Pencil sketches and most sculptures render multicolored scenes monochromatically. Movement is depicted in static media. Panoramic scenes are reduced to tiny canvases or stages. Statues expand retired heroes to larger-than-life size. When motion is used to portray motion, as in film and theater, time may be either contracted or expanded. Musical portrayals reduce natural sounds to diatonic ones.

Such translations inevitably result in some attenuation of appreciators' perceptual games. It is not fictional of viewers' observations of pencil sketches that they are observations of colors. (Fictional truths about colors may be generated, however, at least indirectly; that fictionally a thing is red may be implied by the fact that fictionally it is a stop sign. And it may be fictional that the viewer observes the colors.) It will not be fictional either that the viewer of Eugène Delacroix's *Oriental Lion Hunt* waits to see which lions and which hunters survive or that he does not. The use of both slow motion and fast motion in film obscures certain aspects of the events portrayed (while revealing others); each makes it hard to detect fictional truths which would be evident in normal motion. Details are lost in fast motion; things go by too quickly. In slow motion the details may obscure the overall pattern of movement. In both cases the actual speed at which, fictionally, the events transpire may be hard to judge. These inabilities to detect what is fictional translate, of course, into its not being fictional that we detect this or that truth.

The long-standing debate about whether to render everything in a painting, from frame to frame and from foreground to background, with equal clarity and distinctness can be understood in terms of the effects the artist's choice has on viewers' visual games.[33] Those who object to this practice claim that it is contrary to the way we actually see the world: only those things in the central focal area of our visual field and whose distance from us corresponds to the focus of our eyes are distinct; the periphery of our visual field and the background when we focus on the foreground, or the foreground when we focus on the background, are fuzzy.

A viewer of Andrea Mantegna's *Adoration of the Shepherds* (figure 8.10) might see that fictionally there is a series of S curves in the road in the far background and also that fictionally Mary, in the fore-

---

33. "After many practical experiments I found the closest truth to Nature IN PHOTOGRAPHY *(from the physiological point of view)* was to be obtained by throwing background of the picture out of focus to an extent which did not produce *destruction* of structure" (P. H. Emerson, 1893, quoted in Nancy Newhall, *P. H. Emerson,* p. 99). See also Gombrich, "Standards of Truth"; Gombrich's citation of Herman von Helmholtz; and Snyder, "Picturing Vision," pp. 502, 516.

8.10 · Andrea Mantegna, *The Adoration of the Shepherds*, $15\frac{3}{4} \times 21\frac{7}{8}$ inches, tempera on wood transferred from wood (1450–1460). The Metropolitan Museum of Art, Anonymous Gift, 1932.

ground, is wearing a blue cape, and he might note that fictionally Joseph on the far left is wearing sandals while one of the shepherds on the far right is barefoot—all without changing his focus or the direction of his gaze. To acquire the corresponding information about a real scene, observed from a corresponding point of view, would require changing focus and looking from side to side. What does this do to the observer's visual game? I doubt that we will want to say that fictionally he takes in all of this information without moving or refocusing his eyes. And if we did, there would be no good answer to the question of how fictionally he manages this visual feat. If we assume that fictionally his visual capacities are normal and ordinary, there will be no actual refocusing or redirecting of his gaze which fictionally constitutes such.

Probably, also, it will be relatively easy to make mistakes about whether something is in the foreground or the background in the picture. One might confuse a tuft of hair on one of the angels with an island in the distant river. Corresponding mistakes about the real world are unlikely because of the difference in the sharpness of objects at different distances from the observer. (Hogarth capitalizes on this point in *False Perspective*, figure 1.2.) This lessens the richness and/or vivacity of the observer's game.

Will a depiction in which the background (or alternatively the foreground) and the edges are indistinct be more realistic? (Antoine Watteau's *Embarcation for Cythera* has a narrow depth of field, as do photographs taken with sufficiently large lens apertures. Fuzzy edges are less common in painting and more difficult to achieve in photography.) Such depictions have their own limitations. An observer of an actual scene can change his focus and look in different directions. What is fuzzy in one's first look can be focused in one's second. But no mode of examining the selectively blurred picture easily counts as fictionally attending to what was first indistinct. The viewer can attend to any part of it, of course, but the blurred images remain blurred. A closer look at them reveals details of the paint on the canvas but little in the way of fictional truths about what is depicted. So looking closer is unlikely to make it fictional that one focuses on certain objects in the world, thereby seeing them more distinctly. Examining *The Embarcation* is more closely analogous to looking at a scene with a rather unnatural fixed stare, a single unchanging focus of attention, than to a more normal examination of a scene, in which one's eyes and attention rove around. Moreover, this fixed stare is forced on the viewer; it is not an option which he chooses. Charity may favor allowing, by default, that fictionally the spectator of the Watteau observes the scene in a normal manner; but there will be little to be said about the specifics, about what, fictionally, he looks at when and for how long.

The choice here—between homogeneous clarity à la Mantegna and selective fuzziness—is forced by the "translation" of a three-dimensional panoramic scene to a small two-dimensional surface. (*The Adoration* is only $15\frac{3}{4}$ inches by $21\frac{7}{8}$ inches.) One can to some extent have it both ways by using a large canvas or screen, thus utilizing the natural differences between the center and the periphery of our visual fields. At any one moment some features of the depiction are in focus and others are not, even if the portrayal is equally sharp throughout, and which ones are in focus changes as we move our eyes. So naturally it is fictional of our changes of attention vis à vis the depiction that they are changes of attention vis à vis the scene. And fictionally one can *choose* what to look at. (The artist or filmmaker can still effectively control the viewer's attention by a variety of devices, but only if the viewer submits to his control.)

Although translations of these various sorts mean a lessening of one variety of realism, they entail neither that the work is less realistic *tout court* than it would have been otherwise, whatever that might mean, nor that it is less interesting or beautiful or valuable. Indeed, the elegance with which such translations are achieved is an important part of the beauty of many representational works.

8.4. REALISM

Realism is a monster with many heads desperately in need of disentangling. We can now separate a few strands from the snarl.

Some kinds of realism consist in correspondences between work worlds and the actual world. The more "similar" the world of a work is to the real world, the more realistic it may be said to be. This standard is neither simple nor univocal. We might ask either how much of what is fictional in the work is also true, or how much of what is true is fictional. An accurate but sketchy line drawing of Boston Harbor may score high on the first criterion; a detailed and only partially doctored photograph may be the winner on the second. We might ask how *likely* or *unlikely* it is, in one or another sense, that what is fictional should be true, or that propositions of the *kinds* that are fictional should be true, how far from the realm of possibility the fictional world is. There will be decisions to be made about how much to weigh various particular points of similarity and difference.

Whatever correspondences are taken to constitute realism, elements of fantasy in a work—rings that make their wearers invisible, time-travel machines, transformations of people into animals, societies of six-inch-tall people—will probably reduce them. But even the most fantastic works are obviously capable of extraordinary "realism" of another sort. Tolkien's *Lord of the Rings* trilogy achieves it. It may seem that the dissimilarities of the world of *The Lord of the Rings* to the real one—many of them anyway—do not even count against its realism. It does not somehow manage to be realistic in spite of these differences, by virtue of similarities which outweigh the differences; rather it presents a very dissimilar, fantastic world in an enormously realistic manner. The fact that slimes of the sort Charles faces in the theater are unheard of in reality does nothing to lessen the film's "terrifying" realism. Science fiction films can be as realistic as documentaries. And the most accurate and detailed portrayal of real-world events can be remote, "unconvincing"—unrealistic. Not all realism is a matter of correspondence.

We have recently been working with a different notion of realism, one consisting in the richness and vivacity of appreciators' games of make-believe. Our concern now is with perceptual games. But we can speak more generally of the richness and vivacity of whatever games are played with representations of a given sort. Correspondences between work worlds and the real one can affect the richness and vivacity of appreciators' games, no doubt. But the character of the games depends substantially on the manner in which fictional truths are generated, not just which ones are generated. Again we see that important attributes of a work reside not in its fictional world but in the games appreciators play with it.

Besides assessing the richness and vivacity of games of make-believe, we can consider the ways in which *game* worlds do and do not correspond to reality. We can compare what is fictional about what and how appreciators perceive with how and what we perceive in real life. Game worlds can be as fantastic as work worlds ever are. Frequently they inherit fantasy from the associated work worlds. When I look at a picture of a fire-breathing dragon, it is fictional that I see a fire-breathing dragon. *That* is something I have never actually seen and do not expect to. But if there were such beasts it would not be surprising if they were visible. Given that fictionally there are such, given that they are included in the picture world and hence in my game world, it is not fantastic that fictionally I see them.

But game worlds can have fantastic elements of their own. Pictures sometimes show us perfectly ordinary things that we cannot see in real life, or not easily, or are unlikely to: hibernating bears, genes, DNA molecules, electrical currents, fetuses *in utero,* stars so distant or dark they can only be inferred from their effects. Some pictures portray things in a way that reveals aspects of them that are rarely or never visible: the position at a single moment of the four hooves of a galloping horse, individual drops of water in the photographically frozen spray of a waterfall, a view of a domestic scene from directly above, a view from between the jaws of an angry hippopotamus. So it is sometimes fictional in viewers' games that they see things which they cannot or do not see in real life. Their perceptual game worlds are fantastic, even if the work worlds are perfectly ordinary. Fictionally they see molecules, hibernating bears, hippopotamuses' tonsils. Fictionally they observe that all four hooves of a galloping horse are in the air simultaneously.

(A *photograph* may allow us *actually* to see what could not be seen otherwise—the position at a given moment of the galloping horse's four hooves, for instance. But it may also be *fictional* that we see this when we observe the photograph. The fact that we actually see it does not make our fictionally doing so any less fantastic. For whereas we actually see it with the aid of a photograph, it is fictional that we see it with the naked eye, and *that* remains impossible.)[34]

As with fantastic fictions generally, there is likely to be considerable indeterminacy in our game worlds, and silly questions can be cultivated. How, fictionally, do we manage to see viruses and electrons? Is our eyesight astoundingly acute? Are we (fictionally) looking through a microscope or a cloud chamber? (Probably not.) How did we get attached to the ceiling above the domestic scene? When there are no answers we have indeterminacy: it may be neither fictional that stupendously acute eyesight is responsible for our perceptual achievements nor fictional that it is not. Such indeterminacy makes for a certain attenuation of the perceptual game; there will be fewer visual actions which fictionally we perform. It is not fictional that we see with stupendously acute eyesight, nor that we see with ordinary eyesight. The game may have considerable richness and vivacity nonetheless.

If the fact that fictionally viewers of a picture see subatomic particles or the tonsils of an angry hippopotamus is counted against its "realism" on the grounds that the game world is in this respect fantastic, that it fails to correspond to the real one, this fact also counts, in a

---

34. I explain and defend these points in "Transparent Pictures."

different way, *for* "realism." For it is probably fictional that we learn about the electrons or hippopotamus tonsils, come to understand them in a special way, by seeing them. Fictionally we acquire information or achieve insight of sorts which microscopes actually enable us to achieve about the things they make visible. (When we have reason to think that the portrayal is accurate, we may actually achieve such insight from our experience with the picture.) Moreover, I would argue, it is fictional that we enjoy a kind of "perceptual contact" with the particles or the tonsils that does not reduce to the acquisition of information or knowledge. Fictionally we *actually see* them!—even if, fictionally, the view is too brief or blurry to yield significant knowledge. This too is a point for "realism," even if such perceptual contact with electrons or angry hippopotamus tonsils is out of the question in real life.[35]

These observations concerning depictive "realism" are enormously incomplete. I scarcely mentioned the most important aspect of "photographic" realism, which is the fact that to look at a photograph of something is literally, actually, to see the thing itself.[36] There are other important strands in the tangle of realism that I have not mentioned.

8.5.   CROSS-MODAL DEPICTION

> There issued from the distended and motionless jaws a voice—
> such as it would be madness in me to attempt describing . . . No
> similar sounds have ever jarred upon the ear of humanity . . .
> [The intonation] impressed me (I fear, indeed, that it will be
> impossible to make myself comprehended) as gelatinous or
> glutinous matters impress the sense of touch.
> Edgar Allan Poe, "Facts in the Case of M. Valdemar"

Fantasy has limits. We noted in Chapter 4 a tendency to construe work worlds so as to minimize dissimilarities from the real one (or from how we mutually believe the real one to be). Similar considerations affect game worlds. Cross-modal depiction, "translation" from one sense modality to another, would seem ordinarily to involve games with worlds too fantastic to be acceptable. Pictures—represen-

35. See Walton, "Transparent Pictures."

36. One's game of make-believe with a photograph is superimposed on the basic and peculiar photographic function of assisting our actual perception. The dialectic between what we actually see via photographs, when viewing films, for instance, and what fictionally we see is fascinating and important. See ibid.

tations that are depictive in some respects—can portray (generate fictional truths about) nonvisual phenomena, of course. The question is whether *this* portrayal is depiction. The indirect representation of the sound of a shot by means of the sudden rising of a flock of birds in *The Docks of New York* is clearly not depiction. Seeing the images of the rising birds is not, fictionally, perceiving the shot. What about the portrayal in cartoons of sounds or patterns of thermal radiation or smells by means of concentric arcs or wavy lines emanating from the source—a gong or a campfire or a garbage heap? It is probably not fictional that we *see* sounds or smells or heat when we see the picture, nor is our looking at the picture fictionally a looking at such nonvisual phenomena.

Genes and distant stars are different. Although they are not (normally) visible, especially not to the naked eye, we understand well enough what it would be like to see them, even what it would be like to see them with the naked eye, which probably is what fictionally we do. We have an impression of understanding what it would be like to see subatomic particles or electrical currents, I suppose, even if it involves misconceptions about what they are. But we haven't the foggiest idea what it would be like to see sounds or smells, nor do we easily imagine that we understand this.[37] So it is unlikely to be fictional that we see them.

Is it fictional that we *hear* sounds or *smell* smells or *feel* heat when we look at the picture? Possibly. But it is most unlikely that we are to imagine of our perception of the picture, of our *looking* at it, that *it* is an instance of hearing or smelling or feeling. (And if we did, would putting the picture in better light or squinting fictionally improve our hearing or smelling or feeling?) It might as well be fictional of one's eating a watermelon that it is an instance of climbing the mast of a pirate ship. So the cartoon probably does not depict the sounds or smells that it represents.

Why are weather maps, charts, and graphs so often not comfortably classed as pictures? Mainly because the information they contain is so often nonvisual, even nonperceptual. It would have to be fictional of our visually examining a weather map, for example, that it is a perceiving (seeing? feeling?) of temperatures and high-pressure systems. Inspecting a line graph would have to be, fictionally, perceiving the rate of growth of the national debt as a percentage of GNP over the last ten years, for instance. Even when a graph does provide

---

37. Unless physicists who identify sounds or smells with sound waves or effluents are right. Even so, we do not understand what it would be to see them as sounds or smells.

information about visual phenomena, it is unlikely to allow sufficiently rich or vivid visual games to qualify as a depiction. Consider a bar graph indicating the number of trees growing on various lots. (This is in part a consequence of the lack of *repleteness* Goodman takes to be decisive.[38] This lack is not decisive, but now we see how it is important.) Moreover, the fact that graphs, for instance, are not usually thought of as having the function of serving as props in visual games, used as they so frequently are for nonvisual information, makes it less likely that a particular one will be so understood even if it can be. There is a convention of sorts to the contrary.

Goodman accommodates cross-modal depiction without the slightest hesitation.[39] A scheme of visual symbols correlated with auditory or olfactory referents might well be dense, or as nearly so as depictions ever are, and no less replete. This argues against Goodman's account, for cross-modal depiction is surely awkward at best, and it is not very common. These facts need to be explained. (Cross-modal representation by *nondepictive* means is commonplace and perfectly natural.) Resemblance theorists appear to do better on this score. They can say that a requirement that depictions look like (or sound like or feel like) what they depict rules out pictures depicting nonvisual phenomena.[40]

Some "translations" other than crossings of perceptual modalities probably should be treated similarly. Temporal features are sometimes represented spatially; motion may be portrayed in a still picture by outlines of successive positions of the object in motion.[41] Insofar as we resist saying that the act of ascertaining the temporal order in which, fictionally, events occur (by noting the spatial relations among their images on the picture) is fictionally an act of observing their temporal order, we may conclude that in *this* respect the picture is not depictive.

8.6. MUSICAL DEPICTIONS

My examples have been limited, rather dangerously perhaps, to the visual arts. I defined depiction broadly, in terms of *perceptual* games

---

38. *Languages of Art*, pp. 228–230. One scheme is more "replete" than another if more of its features are "constitutive," fewer are "dismissed as contingent."

39. Ibid., p. 231.

40. Novitz does say this (*Pictures and Their Use*, p. 12).

41. Another example is the photo-finish photograph discussed in Snyder and Allen, "Photography, Vision, and Representation," pp. 157–159.

of make-believe, and noted that not all depictions are visual. But we must not assume that depiction in the nonvisual arts will be straight-forwardly analogous to depiction in the visual ones. What about musical depictions?

Representation appears to be much less common and much less important in music than it is in painting. In painting representation-ality is the norm; "nonobjective," "nonfigurative" painting requires justification and has had to fight for legitimacy.[42] The reverse seems to hold in music. Program music is often regarded as distinctly inferior to "pure" or "absolute" music. In their different ways, pro-gram music and nonfigurative painting are both oddities.

Representation in music is not limited to blatant program music, of course, although it is not easy to say how pervasive it is. There are representational elements, obvious and subtle ones, in much prepon-derantly absolute music, such as Beethoven's *Pastoral* Symphony. Music combined with words or pictures often makes a contribution to the generation of fictional truths even if it would not be representa-tional by itself. In film it may be fictional that a character suddenly realizes something at a particular moment because of a sudden bright-ening of the background music. There is the tone painting of baroque vocal music, where the instrumental parts reinforce or illustrate the meaning of the text. It may turn out that musical expressiveness is sometimes to be understood as a species of representation. And if one is determined to, one *can* find representationality in—or impose it on—almost any passage of music. But let us look first at uncontrover-sial cases.

When music is representational, is it *depictive*? Music and painting appear to be alike in being "perceptual" arts—the one visual and the other auditory—in contrast to literature. So we might expect music's mode of representation, like painting's, to be perceptual, depictive. The reason why painting qualifies as a visual art and the novel does not, I have suggested, is that paintings are props in visual games of make-believe and novels are not. If music is a perceptual art, won't musical works be props in perceptual games also, auditory ones, when they are props at all? The answer is, often not.

Some music does depict. In one passage of Beethoven's *Missa Sol-emnis* the listener fictionally hears nails being driven into the cross. One's hearing of trumpet passages in Bach's cantata *Der Himmel Lacht, die Erde Jubilieret,* is, fictionally, hearing laughter. Other

---

42. But much "nonfigurative" painting is representational in our sense. See § 1.8.

music depicts booming cannons, raging storms, alpine horn calls, galloping horses, flowing water, buzzing flies, sighing, weeping, church bells, steam locomotives, and of course chirping birds.

Representational music is depictive, typically, when it represents auditory phenomena. But as often as not—*more* often than not, I think—what it represents is not auditory. A suddenly rising scale represents David slinging the stone at Goliath in one of Johann Kuhnau's *Biblical Sonatas* for organ. Fourteenth-century Italian *caccias* use melodic imitation to portray the chase of the hunt. Not only is such cross-modal representation common in music (insofar as it is representational at all), but sometimes what is represented is not even visual or otherwise perceptual: patience, pain (by dissonance), obedience (by imitation), arrivals and returns, struggles, harmony in human relations. Think of Strauss's tone poems, Vivaldi's *Four Seasons,* the portraits of Elgar's *Enigma Variations,* perhaps Scott Joplin's *Wall Street Rag.* The musical representations that seem most childish, silly, unmusical appear to be those that represent, depict sounds.[43] More "abstract" representations—representations of arrivals, of conflict, of feelings—often seem more intimately integrated into the musical structure, and less offensive to musical purists. (Possibly they less obviously qualify as *representations,* however.)

Cross-modal representation in music, as in painting, is unlikely to be depiction, and certainly representation of nonperceptual things or events is not. It is not fictional of the listener that he hears or otherwise perceives someone's ascending into heaven, or at least it is not fictional of his hearing an ascending passage of music that it is such a perceiving. And certainly the listener does not fictionally perceive someone's patience or obedience or arrival at a destination. So depiction would seem to be far less important and far less central in music than in painting, even insofar as music is representational. The apparent affinity we noted between music and painting is partly illusory. Music is less perceptual, less an aural art than painting is a visual one.

But there is a way of understanding music that recaptures some of this apparent affinity, and that will encourage regarding music as depictive far more often than it is usually considered even representational. I have suggested elsewhere that, in the case of much "expressive" music, it may be fictional not that one sees or hears or otherwise perceives external things but that one experiences or is aware of

43. Haydn is reported to have apologized for the croaking frogs in *The Seasons,* "saying that this [French rubbish] had been forced on him by a friend." See Tovey, "Programme Music," p. 171.

(one's own) feelings or emotions or sensations or sentiments or moods.[44] The listener imagines experiencing excitement, passion, fervor, despair, conflict, feelings of exuberance, of striving, of determination, of well-being, of trepidation, of repose. Moreover, I suggest, it may be fictional of one's actual awareness of auditory sensations (not one's perception of sounds) that it is an awareness of such feelings. In place of fictional perception of external objects we have fictional introspection or self-awareness. If I am right, this is likely to be true even of such stalwarts of musical purity as Bach's *Art of the Fugue;* and to whatever extent introspection is analogous to the "external" senses, it will be reasonable to expand our understanding of "depiction" to include them.

(The spectator of a picture may also, fictionally, be aware of feelings. But it is not fictional of her experiencing of visual sensations that that is an experiencing of her feelings. It strikes me that auditory sensations are somehow more suitable for this role than visual ones are, perhaps because introspecting is in some way more like hearing than like seeing.)

There is another important difference between ("pure") music and painting. In the case of painting we recognize both worlds of works and worlds of appreciators' games of make-believe. A picture generates the fictional truths of the picture world, and it combines with the activities and experiences of the observer to generate the fictional truths of the world of his game. If in listening to music one engages in a game in which fictionally one experiences certain feelings or sensations, there is a game world. But it is not evident that we must recognize a work world as well. Are any fictional truths generated by the music alone, apart from anyone's listening to it?

When one observes a picture of a house it is fictional in one's game that one sees a house. Fictionally the house exists independently of one's seeing it, as houses are wont to do, and it is natural that the picture itself, which also exists apart from anyone's viewing it, should make it fictional that the house exists. This and other fictional truths generated by the picture alone constitute the content of the picture's world. But when, fictionally, a listener experiences feelings of well-being or pangs of pain, there may be no fictional truths for which the music alone is responsible. It need not be fictional that his feelings are feelings of or about any particular independently existing object or situation or event. Sometimes, perhaps, the fact that fictionally a feeling of a certain sort is felt implies that fictionally there is some-

---

44. Walton, "What Is Abstract About the Art of Music?"

thing or other that is its object. But it need not be fictional that the feeling is directed toward something whose fictional existence is established by the music itself. There may be no fictionality at all until we listen—none apart from listeners' games of make-believe. Game worlds are paramount in music in a way they are not in painting. The music still qualifies as representational in our sense: its function is to serve as a prop in listeners' games. But much music differs in this important respect from painting and other paradigmatically representational arts. (Recall that ad hoc props, which for different reasons may be considered to lack work worlds, might be denied representationality. See § 1.7.)

To the extent that these suggestions are right, we can explain the impression that the appreciation of music is a more personal, private experience than the appreciation of painting and literature. Listening to music is thus more like dreaming; one's imaginative activity is largely solitary. You and I will not, fictionally, notice or learn about something and later compare our attitudes, responses, reactions to it, when we attend a concert together, as we might if we looked at a painting together or read the same novel. We might explain to each other what fictionally we feel, when we listen to music (insofar as we can put it into words); this is like telling our dreams at breakfast. And it can be fictional that we compare notes on what we feel. But we cannot fictionally compare what we feel about such and such a mutually observed event or situation or person. We end up talking about the *music* (whether *it* is anguished or serene or bombastic, or how we respond to it) rather than participating verbally with other listeners in a game of make-believe using it as a prop.

Music also differs from painting in another way when it is depictive, a way having to do with the "points of view" from which things are depicted.

8.7.   POINTS OF VIEW (IN DEPICTIONS)

> Up ahead we glimpse Thomas driving through Hyde Park, camera moving in towards the car. This is how the car would appear to a vigilant but hidden eye, determined never to let it out of sight, keeping hot on its trail.
>
> Screenplay for Michelangelo Antonioni's *Blow-Up*

What is it for a depiction to depict things from a certain point of view? One sense is obvious. The point of view consists in the perspective from which, fictionally, we perceive when we examine the depiction. Fictionally we see Hobbema's red-roofed mill from a point a couple of hundred yards downstream on the left bank of the river. A depiction's point of view is a function of the propositions of this sort that are fictional in appreciators' (authorized) games. (We might include, also, propositions about the lighting and other circumstances in which fictionally we see what we see.)

Is depiction *necessarily* from a point of view in this sense? No. When one observes a freestanding sculpture, it is fictional that one sees from a certain angle and distance. But the depiction itself does not determine this fictional perspective; it depends on where the viewer happens to be standing in relation to the sculpture, and it changes as he moves. So the *work* has no particular point of view. We could say that it has none at all, or we might credit it with multiple ones, infinitely many of them.

Some pictures are said to have multiple points of view. If we focus on one part of Picasso's *Demoiselles d'Avignon* (figure 8.11), it will be fictional that we see a woman's face from the front; if we focus on another, it will be fictional that we see it in profile. The possibilities are limited, however; the picture does more to determine from what point of view it is fictional that we see than the freestanding sculpture does. But the viewer who merely focuses on parts of the painting, one after another, would be missing a lot; the look of the whole is important. For this reason it would be misleading to think of pictures like this as collages of separate depictions, each with its own specific point of view. (Also there will be no determinate boundaries between elements of the collage, and some elements will overlap; the depiction of an eye in *Les Demoiselles* is shared by the frontal and profile views.)

When one does see the whole, it will be fictional, arguably, that one sees the woman from the front and at the same time fictional that one sees her from the side, though not, surely, fictional that one sees her simultaneously from both angles. Alternatively we might hold that the different points of view cancel each other out, and that it is fictional neither that we see her frontally nor in profile—although it *is* fictional that we see her. (The choice may be of a kind familiar from Chapter 4: one between regarding the fictional truths about our point of view as unemphasized and taking them to be absent.) On this alternative the picture has multiple points of view only in the sense that were one part of it isolated from its surroundings it would depict the woman from the front, whereas another part, similarly isolated, would depict her from the side.

In any case the possibility of indeterminacy in our visual games

8.11 · Pablo Picasso, *Les Demoiselles d'Avignon,* 8 feet × 7 feet 8 inches, oil on canvas (1907). Copyright © ARS N.Y. / SPADEM, 1989. Collection, The Museum of Modern Art, New York. Acquired through the Lillie P. Bliss Bequest.

with respect to the point of view from which fictionally we see needs to be taken into account. There are obvious instances of indeterminacy of this sort. When we see a stick figure drawing with a circle for the head but no face or other features, there may be no answer to the question whether it is fictional that we are seeing a person from the front or from the back. But it is fictional that our view is an approximately horizontal one, that we are not seeing him or her from straight above or directly below, so the depiction is not entirely lacking in point of view. Often it is impossible to say at all precisely from what distance it is fictional that we see, although the angle of vision may be quite definite. I see no reason why appreciators' (authorized) games could not in principle be entirely indeterminate with respect to the angle and distance from which fictionally they see; depictions could conceivably be entirely lacking in point of view. It is not implausible that some complex cubist works should be construed approximately thus, and (as we will see shortly) it is likely that some musical depictions should be. (Similarly I do not see any reason to assume that all visualization must be from a point of view. It may be fictional in the world of one's imagination that one sees, without there being any point of view from which fictionally one sees.)[45]

The more subtle questions about particular cases are probably best left to art historians and critics. Having multiple points of view shades imperceptibly into having none. Perhaps experts will have opinions about Egyptian and other ancient depictions, about pre-Renaissance works, children's and "primitive" drawings. It does matter sometimes what we say. Subtleties of emphasis and differences in the ways appreciators respond to depictions of various sorts will be clarified and explained by what is or is not fictional about from where, and how in other respects, we see.

Musical depictions are especially weak in point of view. When sounds are depicted, very little is fictional, usually, with respect to the angle and distance from which fictionally we hear. No doubt this is because hearing, in real life, typically gives us less definite information about angle and distance than seeing does. When it is fictional of the listener that she hears a brook gurgling, is it fictional that she hears it from upstream or downstream, from the side or from above, from near or from afar?

The notion of point of view may not even apply to self-awareness. Are there different perspectives from which one may "observe" one's feelings or sensations? (How does "observing" them from different points of view differ from "observing" different feelings or sensations?) If in listening to music it is fictional that we are introspectively aware of our feelings or sensations, it may not even make sense to ask what, fictionally, our point of view is. We *can* say, however, that it is fictional that we are aware of certain feelings or sensations from a

45. Cf. Williams, "Imagination and the Self," p. 34.

first-person rather than a third-person perspective, that fictionally we observe them in ourselves rather than discover them in others.

But even this sort of point of view may be absent from some musical depictions—or musical representations anyway. Some passages of music are reasonably construed as representing struggles, arrivals, conflicts, achievements. Listeners are to imagine a struggle occurring, for example, although many details of the struggle—who is struggling about what and why, whether the struggle is a physical one or, for instance, a business or political competition or a struggle within someone's psyche—are left open. It may be unclear even whether the listener herself is a participant in the imagined struggle. Does she imagine *herself* struggling, or does she just imagine others doing so? I, for one, find it impossible to say, even when it seems to me reasonably clear that a passage does portray a struggle and that my experience involves imagining one. I imagine *someone* struggling, but I imagine neither myself struggling nor others doing so.[46] So a struggle (or an arrival, or a success) may be represented in music neither from a first- nor from a third-person point of view.

Is such representation depiction? Is the listener to imagine *perceiving* a struggle (allowing introspective self-awareness to count as one kind of perception)? The mode of perception may be indeterminate. It need not be fictional that it is, for example, by a combination of introspection, kinesthetic sensation, and vision that one perceives the struggle (one's own), nor that one merely sees and/or hears it occurring (a struggle among others). It might still be fictional that in some manner or other one perceives the struggle. One has a sense of its occurring *here and now,* which suggests that one's access to it is perceptual rather than, for instance, by hearsay. I find it not implausible, also, that one is to imagine one's auditory sensations to be sense impressions of a struggle, although one's imagining is indeterminate with respect to the modality of the sense impressions. So perhaps the struggle is depicted. If it is, we have an instance of depiction radically lacking in what might be called point of view.[47]

Some works depict things not just from a certain angle and distance but from the perspective of a certain person or kind of person. There are the many so-called subjective shots in film, which portray what a

---

46. Another possibility is imagining that I am struggling, but not in a first-person manner, or not from the inside. Even if I do not imagine whose struggle it is, mine or someone else's, I may imagine, from the inside, being aware of it.

47. See Walton, "What Is Abstract About the Art of Music?"

8.12 · Ingmar Bergman, *Hour of the Wolf*, still (1968). The dinner guests.
Museum of Modern Art (Film Stills Archive). William Allen & Mrs. Maria

character sees and how things look to him. The final shot of Fritz Lang's *You Only Live Once* shows Eddie's last visual experience before he dies. An earlier shot in the same film is apparently from the point of view of a frog.[48] Van Gogh's *Herbage aux Papillons* is from a butterfly's point of view. The dinner scene in Bergman's *Hour of the Wolf* (figure 8.12) portrays the diners, as seen by the severely disturbed artist Borg, as grotesquely positioned and threatening. Francesco Parmigianino's *Self-Portrait in a Convex Mirror* presents the artist's view of himself in the mirror.

In film the usual technique is to show first a character looking at something and then what he is looking at, the second shot being understood to portray how, fictionally, things look to the character. (What he notices, for instance, may be indicated by what is in focus.) The two shots are sometimes combined, in effect, in still pictures. In cartoons the portrayal of the perceiving character's view is enclosed in a balloon attached to the portrayal of the character. But balloons are not necessary. In Rousseau's *Dream* we see the dreamer and her dream image in the same frame. (It is assumed that her dream image does not include herself lying on the couch.) We might understand Munch's painting *The Scream* (figure 8.13) to portray how things look to the woman in the foreground. In *L'Herbage aux Papillons*, however, the perceiving butterfly is implied but not shown. The view presented in Parmigianino's *Self-Portrait* is partly of the perceiver himself, so he is portrayed along with it.

Does depicting things from Eddie's or a butterfly's point of view involve its being fictional in one's game that one *is* Eddie or a butterfly as he or it perceives those things? Does the viewer of the depiction imagine himself to be Eddie, or Parmigianino, or a frog, or a butterfly? I don't know.[49] The question is a close cousin of the question

---

48. See Wilson, *Narration in Light*, p. 31.
49. What is novel is the extreme care in rendering

> The velleities of the rounded reflecting surface
> (It is the first mirror portrait),
> So that you could be fooled for a moment
> Before you realize the reflection
> Isn't yours. You feel then like one of those
> Hoffmann characters who have been deprived
> Of a reflection, except that the whole of me
> Is seen to be supplanted by the strict
> Otherness of the painter in his
> Other room. We have surprised him
> At work, but no, he has surprised us
> As he works.

John Ashbery, "Self-Portrait in a Convex Mirror," p. 74.

whether in empathizing with a friend I imagine myself to *be* him or whether I merely imagine having experiences or feelings that I think he is having. (See §§ 1.4, 7.2.) Point-of-view shots might be construed in the latter manner. Rather than imagining oneself to be Eddie or a frog, the spectator might imagine having perceptual experiences of certain sorts, ones one takes it to be fictional that Eddie or a frog is experiencing. A rather different kind of case will illustrate this possibility.

8.13 · Edvard Munch, *The Scream,* 36 × 29 inches (1893). Nasjonalgalleriet, Oslo.

Akira Kurosawa's film *Rashomon* portrays things not as characters *see* them but as they *describe* them. The focus is on a confrontation between a samurai traveling with his wife in a forest and a bandit, recounted by the participants afterwards at an inquest. In each case the witness begins his testimony, and then we see the incident as he or she claims it to have occurred.[50] The accounts differ, so we see (as it were) several incompatible versions of the same event. In the bandit's version he killed the samurai; in the wife's, she did. Presumably at least one of them is lying; the testimony of one or both of them does not correspond to what he or she saw. So in viewing the sequence illustrating the testimony we do not "see through the character's eyes," as we do in watching *You Only Live Once*. Our view is not the character's. Thus there is little reason to suppose that fictionally the spectator is the character, or to expect him to imagine that he is. What the spectator does do, of course, is to learn how fictionally the character testified at the inquest.

Can we allow even that the spectator fictionally sees? If it is not fictional that the wife killed the samurai, as she claims, how can it be fictional that I see her doing so?

Let us distinguish the various sequences of the film from the film as a whole and from one another. We can think of the sequence illustrating each witness's testimony as having its own separate fictional world, and combining with the rest of the film to establish the world of the film. The viewer plays separate games of make-believe with the sequences, which are distinct from the game he plays with the whole. It is fictional in the sequence illustrating the wife's testimony that she *does* kill her husband, and it is fictional in my game with it that I see her do so. The sequence illustrating the bandit's testimony is a prop in a game in which it is fictional that I see *him* do the deed. But in the film as a whole no determinate proposition about who killed the samurai is fictional, and it is not fictional in my game with the whole that I see who did it. (This makes the whole somewhat less a depiction than it would otherwise have been, although its parts are fully depictive.)

But the whole depends on the parts. What happens in the world of a given sequence is, in the world of the whole, what the witness in question claims to have happened. (This is an instance of the implication of one fictional truth by others, but the implied and the implying fictional truths belong to different worlds.) And what, fictionally, I

50. The film's structure is actually more complicated than this, but the simplifications will make it easier to illustrate my point.

see, in my game with the sequence, is what, fictionally, I hear the witness testify to have occurred, in my game with the whole. This, of course, is what I mean in describing the sequence as an *illustration* of the testimony. It *shows* us what, according to his testimony, transpired.

This interpretation accords well with the experience of watching the film. The viewer is caught up in the drama of the individual sequences, forgetting, more or less, the framing courtroom proceedings, and imagining vividly the wife stabbing her husband (for example)—until a cut to the courtroom jolts him back to the world of the whole, whereupon he imagines only that the wife testified to having killed her husband. (One does not focus separately, to the same extent, on the spatial parts of a cubist painting, which is one reason for my reservations about thinking of it as a collage.)

Analogous construals of ordinary point-of-view shots such as those in *You Only Live Once* are possible, if less inevitable. We could think of the final shot of the film as a prop in a separate momentary game, illustrating how, in the world of the whole, Eddie sees. It is fictional in that game that one sees thus, and it is fictional in the whole and in one's game with the whole that Eddie does. We need not take it to be fictional in *any* world that the spectator is Eddie, nor must we suppose that he imagines himself to be Eddie.

Recall Rubens' *Toilette of Venus* (figure 4.2), which shows reflected in the mirror what Venus sees in it, not what would be seen from the spectator's point of view. The portrayal of the mirror can be regarded as a separate depiction illustrating what, fictionally, in the world of the whole, Venus sees in it.

L'Herbage aux Papillons is not easily divided into relevant spatial or temporal parts, but one could think of it as having a depictive aspect which makes it fictional that the viewer sees thus, and that this aspect is at a second stage understood to illustrate how fictionally things appear to another butterfly.

Whatever one prefers to say, in the various kinds of cases in which a depiction portrays things from a character's perceptual point of view, about whether the spectator imagines being identical to the perceiving character, what is important is that she share the character's perspective. She participates in a visual game of make-believe using part or all of the depiction as a prop, and it is fictional that she sees in a way in which, fictionally, the character does—whether through the character's eyes or her own; she imagines seeing thus.

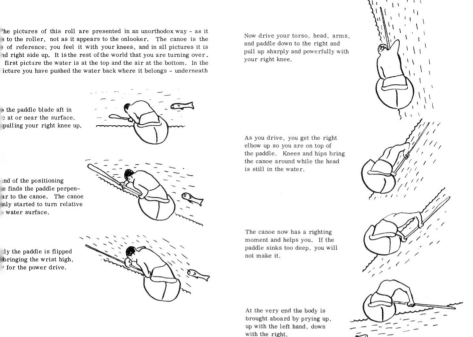

The pictures of this roll are presented in an unorthodox way – as it
is to the roller, not as it appears to the onlooker. The canoe is the
[...] of reference; you feel it with your knees, and in all pictures it is
[...]d right side up. It is the rest of the world that you are turning over.
[...] first picture the water is at the top and the air at the bottom. In the
[...]icture you have pushed the water back where it belongs – underneath

Now drive your torso, head, arms,
and paddle down to the right and
pull up sharply and powerfully with
your right knee.

[...] the paddle blade aft in
[...] at or near the surface.
[...]pulling your right knee up.

As you drive, you get the right
elbow up so you are on top of
the paddle. Knees and hips bring
the canoe around while the head
is still in the water.

[...]nd of the positioning
[...]e finds the paddle perpen-
[...]r to the canoe. The canoe
[...]ly started to turn relative
[...] water surface.

The canoe now has a righting
moment and helps you. If the
paddle sinks too deep, you will
not make it.

[...]ly the paddle is flipped
[...]bringing the wrist high,
[...] for the power drive.

At the very end the body is
brought aboard by prying up,
up with the left hand, down
with the right.

8.14 · Eskimo roll diagram, from Robert E. McNair, *Basic River Canoeing,*
3rd edition (American Camping Association, 1972). Copyright © American
Camping Association, Inc., Martinsville, Indiana. 1968. 1–800–428–2267.
Reproduced by permission.

Such participation is essential to our experience of depictions like
these, just as imagining feeling as one takes another to feel—if not
imagining being him and feeling thus—is essential to the experience
of empathy. Indeed, we might regard the spectator as "empathizing"
with the character's perceptual experience, and this "perceptual
empathy," for Borg, for example, may contribute to "empathy" with
his disturbed state of mind.

Figure 8.14 illustrates how to perform an Eskimo roll, how to right
an overturned slalom (closed) canoe. The sketches can be taken in
part as showing how, fictionally, the canoeist in the picture sees
(excluding, of course, the portrayal of his own back). The point in this
case is not especially to foster "empathy" for or understanding of the
pictured canoeist, however, but to give us a feeling for what it is like

to execute the maneuver so we can do it ourselves. What is important is that we imagine having a certain experience.[51] The fact that what, fictionally, we experience is what it is fictional that the paddler experiences is incidental, although a realization of this may contribute to our imagining having the experience.

The viewer's visual game of make-believe is crucial. It is crucial that I imagine *myself* rolling over; that fictionally the world and the horizon revolve relative to *me*, in *my* field of vision. That is what gives me a vivid sense of what it is like to do the roll. The effect would be entirely different and not nearly as instructive if the sketches were all right side up, with water below and sky above. What is fictional in the world of the *pictures* would surely be the same in that case. The difference would be in viewers' games of make-believe; fictionally one would have the visual experiences of a spectator watching someone else perform a roll rather than those of a roller.[52] This is dramatic confirmation of the necessity even in this simple example of recognizing the role of depictions as props in viewers' visual games of make-believe.

Those who think of pictures in terms of seeing-as or seeing-in might easily overlook this difference. It does not consist in what one sees them as or what one sees in them, but rather in the manner in which one sees—that to be explained in terms of one's visual game of make-believe.

8.8. CONCLUSION

Understanding depiction in terms of perceptual games of make-believe has proved fruitful in many ways—in explaining realism, points of view, and other aspects of depictive styles, as well as in differentiating depiction from description. It brings out what is peculiarly visual about pictorial representation. It supports the pre-theoretical impression that the contrast between depiction and description (between "showing" and "telling," to put it crudely) is a fundamental one and that whether a representation is depictive or not is a significant fact about it. The significance mirrors the importance

51. Our imagined experience is of course not just visual but kinesthetic and tactile also. Fictionally experiencing in these nonvisual ways is partly a result of fictionally seeing in a certain way.

52. "The Eskimo roll is a challenge to teacher and student alike . . . There is an understanding problem because the spectator sees the boater roll around; the boater sees and feels the world turning about him. The transition from observing to doing is very confusing" (McNair, *Basic River Canoeing*, p. 89).

perception has in our lives and the ways in which what we do and do not actually perceive matters.

This account of depiction assists us also in understanding its rivals. We observed how "density," "repleteness," and "continuous correlation" contribute to the richness and vivacity of our visual games (by enhancing the open-endedness of investigations of picture worlds, or by ensuring correspondences in what is easy or difficult to ascertain perceptually about fictional worlds and about the real one). The same can be said for various other attributes of representations or representational systems or our responses to them which have been declared by one theorist or another to be wholly or partially constitutive of depictiveness (or pictoriality). One writer locates pictoriality in the representation of "co-visible" properties—properties visible from a given point at a given time—and in the (alleged) fact that the features by means of which depictions represent color values (including brightness relations) serve also to represent shapes.[53] Another fixes on the fact that pictures engage the recognitional capacities we use in real-life perception, that our ability to interpret pictures depends on our ability to recognize things of the kinds they depict, and on "natural generativity"—roughly, our ability, once we have mastered a pictorial system sufficiently to interpret some pictures in it, to understand indefinitely many others without doing anything like learning new vocabulary.[54]

Each of these traits, when and to the extent that it is present, makes for analogies between looking at pictures and looking at things which encourage visual games of make-believe. If a representation portrays co-visible properties, the properties whose portrayal we see simultaneously in looking at it are ones we might perceive simultaneously while looking at the world. Thanks to the second feature, it is by seeing depictions of color and brightness values that we ascertain depictions of shapes, just as, in real life, we detect shapes visually by perceiving variations of color and brightness. Our perceptual capacities are engaged when we perceive reality (obviously!), as they are claimed to be when we interpret pictures. (This explains how the capacity to recognize an actual thing can be acquired by looking at pictures of it.) "Natural generativity" links up with our ability to perceive new things intelligibly without special training.[55]

53. Karelis, "The Las Meninas Literature."

54. Schier, *Deeper into Pictures*, pp. 43–56.

55. The reader can consult Schier's account of "natural generativity" to confirm this observation. My hasty remarks here are not meant to do justice to either his or Karelis' proposals.

We noted how the capacity of a representation to be understood without decoding, without inference, which Wollheim considers necessary for depiction (although it is not part of his definition), is conducive to visual games of make-believe. The fluency with a pictorial system Goodman declares to be the touchstone of realism is no doubt conducive to such games in just the same way.

Even resemblance comes into play—particular specifiable respects in which depictions (sometimes) look like what they depict. It is no accident that green paint is ordinarily used to portray green leaves (although the depicting and depicted shades of green may be rather different). If we want to represent leaves in such a manner that noticing the fact that fictionally they are green will be, fictionally, seeing their greenness, the obvious thing to do is to use green to represent their greenness.

The diversity of these purported marks of depiction, considered in their own terms, is disconcerting. The proposed definitions do not give the impression of being attempts to capture similar intuitions. And none of them has the intuitive plausibility that the appeal to ill-defined notions of *overall* similarity has. Density, continuous correlation, natural generativity, and so on, do tend to correlate with the things we ordinarily call pictures. But they are likely to strike one, even pretheoretically, as peripheral and symptomatic, as unsatisfyingly remote from the essence of depiction. Definitions in terms of them do not provide the insight we expect from a theory, however well they succeed in delimiting the extension of the class. One is left wondering, to various extents in the various instances, what is important about pictoriality so defined, whether the contrast between depiction and description is a fundamental one after all, whether what makes a depiction realistic has anything to do with what makes it a depiction in the first place, whether one's account of depiction will help to illuminate significant dimensions of pictorial styles, and in some cases what is especially visual about pictures and perceptual about depictions.

Now we see this motley crew united in a common purpose: the encouragement of rich and vivid perceptual games of make-believe. None of the mentioned features lies at the heart of pictoriality, but none is related only accidentally to it either. Their influence on perceptual games suggests how their presence or absence can be important and how they figure in variations of pictorial style. Our make-believe account of depiction provides a place for each of them and puts it there. To the various other advantages of which this account may boast we can add this: What seems on the surface a jumbled profusion of ad hoc proposals of uncertain motivation offering minimal insight begins to make sense in light of it.

The reader will notice that I have left no room for nonfictional depiction. Pictures are fiction by definition (*works* of fiction, when they are works). Of course they are used frequently for instruction, for conveying information, for keeping records, in addition to fulfilling their role in make-believe. But to possess that role, to have the job of serving as a prop in games of make-believe, whether or not visual ones, is to be fiction, in the sense explained in Chapter 2.

Words are different; they often instruct or inform without invoking make-believe. Some verbal texts are fiction and some are not. So *description* and *depiction*—the alliteration notwithstanding—are not parallel concepts. One is a species of fiction, the other cuts across that category. "Description" ("words," "verbal symbols") is to be defined in semantic and/or syntactic terms, I suppose; depiction is a pragmatic notion, a matter of the use to which things with semantic content are to be put.

There is good reason to recognize this pragmatic category and to give it a central place in our view of things. The use of pictures in visual games is in a certain way prior to their possession of semantic content. It is nearly always by using pictures in make-believe that we ascertain what "information" they contain, what propositions they pick out. It is when we find ourselves "seeing a picture as a deer" or "seeing a deer in it," imagining seeing a deer, that we recognize it to portray a deer, to specify and make fictional the proposition that a deer is bounding across a meadow or grazing by a stream. "Reading" pictures without engaging in make-believe, by merely noting the colors and shapes on the picture surface and invoking rules or principles, is difficult, to say the least, especially when the propositions to be read are specific and subtle (that a deer looks up with a slightly wary expression, that ripples break the glistening light on the surface of the water). This means that when pictures are used to communicate information, to instruct or inform or remind, it is by means of their role in make-believe that they serve this other purpose. We must use a picture in a visual game in order to understand what is being said by means of it.

This epistemological point is just a symptom of a more important substantive one. It is probably *by virtue* of the fact that a picture is easily or naturally used (by appropriately sensitive viewers) as a prop in games in which one fictionally sees a deer that it can be said to pick out the proposition that there is a deer. The relevant principles of generation may be such that what it can easily be "seen as" has a lot to do with what it is a picture of, what it makes fictional. Its semantic content, the propositions it picks out, are simply the ones it makes fictional. Using a picture in make-believe is not just a *convenient* means of extracting its "information" but the fundamental or primary one. What one decides in this way is likely to be definitive. The semantic content of words, by contrast, is accessible more directly and is independent of uses they might have in make-believe.

9

Verbal Representations

Words are well suited for use in make-believe. They come with built-in semantic and syntactic properties whereby they can be combined in innumerable ways to indicate a wide range of propositions. Although their original or primary purpose may be to serve in ordinary communication as vehicles of assertion or query or request, or as a medium of thought, they can readily be employed to prescribe imaginings. One can use words specifying a given proposition to ask others to imagine it. If a collection of words, a verbal or written text, is itself thought of as issuing such prescriptions, it is a prop; and if it is its function to be a prop, it is a representation in our sense. Some literary works might be thought of in just this way, as simply mandating the imagining of the propositions their sentences specify. But most of them play a more complex role in make-believe.

9.1. VERBAL DEPICTION

I mentioned in the previous chapter that words do not serve well in *perceptual* games of make-believe, that they do not readily function as depictions. This needs clarification. Words can easily depict words. The words "General Delivery" on David Gilmore Blythe's painting *The Post Office* depict an inscription of those words over a post office window. Observing the words on the canvas is, fictionally, seeing that inscription. Words uttered by actors are depictive. In hearing the words pronounced on stage by Sir Laurence Olivier, the playgoer fictionally hears Hamlet speaking. In these cases the utterances or marks are *reflexive* depictions; they depict themselves. "Concrete" poems, whose words are arranged on the page so as to form a picture of a tree or a house or whatever, are depictions but not usually reflexive ones.

The semantic properties of words are not essential to these depictive roles. Words thought of as meaningless sounds or shapes might depict the same; the meanings of the words in a concrete poem do not contribute to its depiction of a tree or house. But semantic attributes do almost invariably come into play. Fictionally the words on the wall of the post office *mean* "general delivery"; the meanings of the words Olivier utters are, fictionally, what Hamlet's words mean.

Few novels are as richly depictive as the words on *The Post Office* and Olivier's utterances, but many are props in at least sketchy perceptual games. Reading *Gulliver's Travels* is, fictionally, reading a ship's logbook. The representation of epistles by epistolary novels such as Samuel Richardson's *Pamela,* of an autobiography by *Tristram Shandy,* and of journals, diaries, and notes by other literary works approaches depiction. But the games in which these works serve are only minimally perceptual; reading is about the only perceptual action that, fictionally, one performs. If one examines the printed text of *Gulliver's Travels,* it will not be fictional that one examines the handwriting of the logbook or observes the formation of the letters beyond recognizing what letters they are. The typographical eccentricities and the blank and black pages of *Tristram* add a little more perceptuality to the reader's game with it. If a copy of an epistolary novel contains a cursive signature, that will be a full-fledged signature-picture. But when *written* texts represent *spoken* words (not written quotations of what was spoken previously), depiction drops out almost entirely. We have seen how unlikely cross-modal depiction is. In some such cases it will be fictional of the reader that he hears the words spoken; it may even be fictional that the speaker addresses him. But it will not be fictional of the reader's actual perceiving of the text, his reading it, that that is a hearing of the speaking of the words.

Gulliver's Travels is primarily about Gulliver and his various adventures (not to mention the real-world butts of the satire), not the logbook. The representation of meaningful words is a device for representing things of the sorts the words describe. But *this* representing is not depicting at all. It is not fictional that, as we read the novel, we see Gulliver or watch his adventures. Here is the truth in our observation that words are ill suited for perceptual games. Insofar as the semantic characteristics of literary works determine what they represent, specifying the propositions they make fictional, their representing is most unlikely to be depiction. What words find it hard to depict is what they describe (unless they happen to describe words).

The fact that games involving words are sometimes perceptual in important ways and sometimes hardly perceptual at all illustrates the immense variety of their uses in make-believe. Verbal representations are not united by anything beyond the fact that they employ words. But one kind of verbal representation, *narration,* is especially central, and I suspect that it is the historical ancestor of many others. This is not the place to launch a full-fledged examination of "narratology." But we can note several crucial junctures at which our general picture of representation can make contributions.

9.2. NARRATION

> You don't know about me without you have read a book by the name of *The Adventures of Tom Sawyer;* but that ain't no matter. That book was made by Mr. Mark Twain, and he told the truth, mainly. There was things which he stretched, but mainly he told the truth. That is nothing. I never seen anybody but lied one time or another.
>
> Mark Twain, *Huckleberry Finn*

When words represent words, it is only to be expected that they should represent them not only as being meaningful but also as being used in ordinary ways. It is often fictional of the words (the word types if not the tokens) composing verbal representations that some-one reports events or expresses attitudes by means of them, or sets them down in writing to a friend or in contributing to a diary, or that in uttering them he argues or pleads or raves or muses. Representations composed of words which, fictionally, a character speaks or writes are *narrated* representations, and the character who fictionally speaks or writes them is the *narrator.*[1]

When fictionally a narrator quotes another character directly (and accurately), it is fictional of the words (word types) of the text that the quoted as well as the quoting character uses (or used) them. I expect that we will want to avoid counting the quoted character a narrator. In any case, the difference between the quoted character's relation to the text and that of the quoting character is significant: it is likely to

---

1. A work whose words are merely such that, fictionally, there is someone or other who utters or writes them does not thereby have a narrator. To speak informally, the words must, fictionally, be those of a *particular* character. Readers are to imagine not just that the words are uttered or written by someone; they are to imagine someone's uttering or writing them, or someone's having done so.

be fictional in our games that we read or hear the speech of the latter but not the speech of the former.

Narrators are commonly distinguished from (real-life) authors. What is meant when critics or theorists insist on this distinction is usually that properties of the narrator are not to be attributed to the author. If it is fictional that the narrator disapproves of certain kinds of activities, for instance, we must not assume that the author actually does. The point is well taken, but this is a confused way of making it. The real-life author can be his work's narrator; it can be fictional of *him* that he speaks or writes the words of the text.[2] Yet it remains illegitimate to infer simply from the fact that the narrator (= the author) fictionally possesses such-and-such characteristics, that he actually possesses them. (Even if the author is not the narrator, the two may "share" indefinitely many properties; the narrator may be a mouthpiece through which the author speaks.)

There need be no such thing as *the* narrator of a narrated work. Different narrators can replace one another in quick succession. In most plays (written or performed) there is a new narrator for every several lines of text; each of the speaking characters is the narrator, in our sense, of the lines attributed to it. Novels which, in representing conversation, omit the "he said"s (and perhaps some which do not as well) can be understood similarly:

—Hello . . .
—It's Fanny!
—Hello? Who is this?
—It's me, Fanny! Is Mrs. Nené around?[3]

This passage has two alternating narrators. The words of the text are not, fictionally, spoken by someone in quoting the two conversants, but it is fictional that the conversants speak them. Some take narrators to be *unifying* features of the works containing them. Narrators can serve this purpose, but obviously they do not always do so.

If it is fictional of the words of a narration that someone speaks or writes them, it is likely to be fictional in readers' games that they hear him speaking or read what he has written: fictionally we hear the narrator recounting adventures, or fictionally we read his letters or

2. Witold Gombrowicz is probably the narrator of his *Pornografia:* "And now suddenly there appeared before me the possibility of a warm idyll in a spring I thought irrevocably ended . . . I wanted nothing more. I had had enough of this agony. I, a Polish writer, I, Gombrowicz, chased after this will-o'-the-wisp as a fish chases its bait" (p. 41).

3. Puig, *Heartbreak Tango,* p. 131.

logbook or diary or autobiography. Sometimes it is fictional that the narrator addresses us (see § 6.5); sometimes it is fictional that we overhear him talking to someone else or to himself or read what he wrote for other eyes. Often it is indeterminate how fictionally we manage to see or hear his words, and to ask may be to ask a silly question. We might treat cases in which fictionally the narrator addresses someone other than the (real-life) reader or listener like point-of-view shots in film. (See § 8.7.) When I read the passage of Manuel Puig's *Heartbreak Tango* portraying the letter of May 12, 1947, from Nélida Fernández de Massa to Mrs. Etchepare (p. 10), I might be understood to be engaging temporarily in a game with this passage in which fictionally I am the one addressed. I leave open the question whether this involves my imagining being Mrs. Etchapare. In any case, the manner in which fictionally I am addressed will be the manner in which it is fictional in the work as a whole and in my game with *it* that Mrs. Etchapare is addressed. I learn how fictionally she is addressed by noting how fictionally (in my game with the passage) I am addressed. Construals like this may be undermotivated when I can plausibly be understood as fictionally overhearing or "overreading" discourse addressed to another—when, for example, it is fictional that I might have discovered the narrator's old correspondence in an attic (even if it is not fictional that I did discover it there). They are more tempting when it is fictional that the recipient of the letter destroyed it immediately, or that the narrator conversed with his narratee in private. In any case, insofar as the reader or listener "empathizes" with the character addressed, I presume that she imagines either being him or at least being addressed in the way in which fictionally the character is addressed.

Narrators are often said to *mediate* our access to the "events of the story"; those events are presented to us *indirectly* through them. This is frequently true, but in several different ways which need to be kept distinct: (a) Fictional truths about Gulliver's adventures are implied by fictional truths about what he wrote in his logbook; they are generated indirectly. (b) Readers ascertain the former fictional truths on the basis of the latter ones. And (c) it is fictional that the reader learns of Gulliver's adventures by reading the logbook.

We do not ordinarily find quite the same indirection in depiction. Fictional truths about objects depicted may be generated indirectly, it is true, implied by fictional truths about how things appear. (Perhaps they always are.) We may ascertain the former fictional truths on the basis of the latter (even if we do not specifically note the latter). And it may be fictional that we judge what is the case from what appears to be the case. But the route to these implied fictional truths does not in general go through another (fictional) consciousness, like that of a narrator. It is fictional truths in our game worlds about how things appear to *us* that imply fictional truths about how they are. And fictionally we see things for ourselves, even if we must judge how they are from how they appear. *Hour of the Wolf* and *Rashomon* are exceptions: how fictionally things are (in the world of the whole) depends (in part) on how fictionally they appear to Borg, or how fictionally they are described by the various witnesses. (It is not so clear that fictionally we judge how things are from how they appear to Borg, or from how they are described by the witnesses.) Even so, it is fictional in our game *with the particular scene or sequence* that we see things for ourselves. And how fictionally in the scene or sequence they are depends on how fictionally they appear to us.

In narrated representations what are called *omniscience* and *effacement* of the narrator can soften this effect and provide an "immediacy" of access to the events of the story approaching that normal for depiction. (They do not, of course, make readers' games *perceptual*.) But we will soon see that narrators do not always mediate at all, in all or even any of the ways I have described.

Narrators come in all shapes and sizes. The variety is evident from even a casual survey of familiar literary works and what critics say about them. But some of the conceptual tools commonly used in describing narrators are rather crude and have encouraged the misconstrual or neglect of important features of certain narrative arrangements. I have in mind especially discussions of the "trustworthiness" or "reliability" of narrators, of their relation to the story they tell or the incidents they relate, and of their relation to the reader. What is needed, in many instances, is more sensitivity to the distinction between what is fictional and what is true, and more attention to which fictional worlds various fictional truths belong to.

9.3. TWO KINDS OF RELIABILITY

Some narrators are said to be more "trustworthy" or "reliable" than others. In saying this one may have in mind either of two very different points. One is a matter of what propositions about narrators are fictional.[4] Sometimes it is fictional that the narrator is highly reliable,

---

4. A reminder: There are no propositions about purely fictional characters, and hence none that are fictional. I am in this respect engaging in pretense myself, in a manner I will explain in Chapter 10.

that he is intelligent, perceptive, honest, knowledgeable. Sometimes it is fictional that he is ignorant or confused or deceptive or self-deceived or prejudiced or neurotic. It is (perhaps) fictional in Thomas Mann's "Death in Venice" that the narrator is a "wise and rational psychologist."[5] It is fictional in Nabokov's *Pale Fire* that Charles Kinbote deceives himself about John Shade's interest in him.

Fictional truths about narrators are often implied largely or entirely by fictional truths about their verbal behavior. *Pale Fire* consists solely of what is fictionally Kinbote's edition of a poem by John Shade, with a foreword, commentary, and index (whose longest entry by far is "Charles Kinbote," under which one subheading is "his modesty"). We judge on the basis of what Kinbote says and how he says it, especially in the interminable commentary, that fictionally he has deceived himself. Another narrator destroys his credibility, as follows:

> For there are many things which I have forgotten, many things which cannot be told, many things which are not tellable, many things of unspeakable nature!

> Therefore I reconstruct
>   I invent (a little)
>   I distort
>   I simulate
>   I dissimulate
>   I suggest
>   I exaggerate.[6]

The inferences we draw from fictional truths about narrators' verbal behavior often mirror inferences we would be likely to make in real life. (The Reality and/or Mutual Belief principles of implication are prominently involved.) How reliable, fictionally, the narrator is frequently approximates the extent to which his manner of speaking would enhance the credibility of a real-life reporter. But in real life we usually have a wider range of information on which to base our judgments. When the entirety of a work is to be attributed to a single narrator, what he says or writes is *all* we have to go on. We cannot run background checks on his character or verify independently what he tells us. (It may be fictional that we can, but it cannot be fictional that we do.)

---

5. Cohn, *Transparent Minds*, p. 26.
6. Federman, *Take It or Leave It*, p. 87.

Fictional truths about narrators' reliability frequently affect what other fictional truths are implied. If it is fictional that the narrator is honest, intelligent, and knowledgeable, that and the fact that fictionally he asserts such and such are likely to imply that fictionally such and such is the case. If fictionally he is confused, ignorant, or a liar, these implications may not go through. We may even decide that fictionally such and such is not the case, perhaps partly *because* it is fictional that he says that it is. Ford Maddox Ford's *Good Soldier* and other standard examples of works with "unreliable" narrators illustrate this point. So narrators who are "reliable," in the sense that it is fictional that they are, are often "reliable" in a second sense as well: What fictionally they say is a reliable indication that fictionally it is true.

But these two kinds of "reliability" do not always go together. Sometimes there is a (perhaps "conventional") principle of implication directing us to accept as fictional whatever (or almost whatever) it is fictional that the narrator claims to be the case, without considering fictional truths about his character. This, it seems to me, is approximately how most works with so-called omniscient narrators are best understood. The label is misleading, for it is not usually fictional that the narrator is omniscient—nor that he is perfectly honest or godlike or telepathic or clairvoyant or disincarnated or supernatural.[7] It may even be fictional that he is *not* omniscient. There may be specific intimations of his fallibility,[8] or it may simply be assumed that fictionally he is an ordinary mortal with a normal complement of failings, vices, shortcomings, limitations (as it is so often assumed that fictionally characters have blood in their veins). Alternatively, it may be indeterminate how knowledgeable, fictionally, he is. Yet it may be understood that whatever he is portrayed as saying is true, that if fictionally he says that *p*, the fictionality of *p* itself is automatically implied, regardless of what is or is not fictional about his knowledgeability and honesty. It will be fictional that he *knows* that *p*, I suppose, and (in our games) that we take his word for it, if it is

7. Not in the work world or in authorized games of make-believe. But perhaps in easily envisionable *unofficial* games. See § 10.4.

8. "He was an old man, beyond a doubt, with wrinkles and crow's-feet round eyes and mouth" suggests that, fictionally, not everything is beyond doubt for the narrator of "Death in Venice." Specific uncertainties are implied later: "Could they not see that he was old, that he had no right to wear the clothes they wore or pretend to be one of them? But they were used to him, it seemed; they suffered him among them, they paid back his jokes in kind and the playful pokes in the ribs he gave them. How could they?" (Mann, "Death in Venice," p. 17).

fictional that he says that *p*. But questions such as "How did he find that out?" "Why should we believe him?" "How can he know so-and-so's secret thoughts—better even than she does herself?" are silly. They are not to be asked and, if they are asked, are not to be answered by "Because (fictionally) he is omniscient."[9]

The advantages of this arrangement are obvious. It enables the author cleanly and crisply to establish fictional truths about the characters and events described—including fictional truths about their innermost thoughts and feelings—and to provide readers sure access to them. He need only put into the mouth of his "omniscient" narrator words expressing what he wants made fictional. The uncertainties of sorting out the testimony of a fallible and human reporter, of judging his character solely, in some cases, on the basis of his testimony, and deciding what to accept and what not to, are bypassed. Yet fictionally the narrator *is* human and fallible, or at least it is not fictional that he is not. The "realism" of the story is not disturbed by the presence of a character with exotically supernatural powers. True, the mere fact that fictionally the narrator knows and tells what he does—what in many cases a real-life human reporter could not know—may be "unrealistic." But this divergence from the real world can be localized and more or less ignored. If it is fictional that the narrator is fallibly human, we may (fictionally) empathize with him, or respond to him in various ways as we do to other human characters. But to the extent that his fictionally knowing and telling what he does is taken to imply that fictionally he possesses supernatural powers, empathy and understanding are less easy to come by. It is hard to relate to exotically supernatural beings.

The fantastic elements in the fictional world are significant, however, even if they are localized. Arrangements whereby what fictionally the narrator says is automatically fictional itself, whether by virtue of a "convention" to that effect or because it is fictional that the narrator is omniscient (and omnitruthful), are purchased at a price in "realism" in one or more of the senses mentioned in § 8.4. There will be failures of correspondence, through indeterminacy, between the fictional world and the real one or adjacent possible ones, even where there is no *conflict* (as there is when it is fictional that someone speaks with authority about matters that, in the real world, no one could

9. A typical example of the fuzziness of these two notions of "trustworthiness" is Wayne Booth's definition of "omniscience": "Complete privilege [to know what could not be learned by strictly natural means or limited to realistic vision and inference] is what we usually call omniscience" (*Rhetoric of Fiction*, p. 160).

know). There will be indeterminacy concerning the extent of the narrator's knowledge beyond what he explicitly says, if it is not fictional that he is omniscient, as well as concerning how fictionally he acquired it and why his word should be trusted. Indeterminacies in the work world, here as elsewhere, have the effect of stunting our games of make-believe. It is unlikely to be fictional of the reader that he speculates about how the narrator learned what he knows or whether his word should be accepted and why, that initially he is skeptical of the narrator's claims but chooses finally, for one reason or another, to accept them, and so on. If it is not fictional that the narrator is omniscient, there will probably be no answer to the question of why, fictionally, we believe him. If it is fictional that we believe him because he is omniscient (and truthful), it will not be fictional that we have such-and-such reasons for thinking him so.

But these sacrifices in realism, involving both discrepancies between the fictional world and the real one and stuntings of our games of make-believe, purchase realism of another sort. They facilitate the generation of a rich array of fictional truths about the characters and events the narrator describes, and this results in games rich with respect to what fictionally we know about those characters and events, if not with respect to how we know it. Fictionally we have a lot to think about. In sorting through what is fictional, tracing implications in various directions, it is fictional that we reflect on, speculate about, and consider in any of many ways the events described by the narrator.

The trade-off is much like the one we discussed in connection with pictures depicting things not ordinarily or ever visible in real life: genes, DNA molecules, the tonsils of an angry hippopotamus. (See § 8.4.) That fictionally we see genes or DNA molecules is a fantastic element in the worlds of our games, a sharp departure from what is true or likely in the real world. And it is largely indeterminate how fictionally we manage to see these things. Our game worlds are thus attenuated. But we *do* fictionally see them. A rich collection of detailed fictional truths about their physical properties is generated, and when we learn these fictional truths, it is fictional that we (somehow or other) acquire unusually intimate knowledge of them. Likewise, a novel with an "omniscient" and perfectly "reliable" narrator—whether it is fictional that he is so, or whether implications about what is fictional go through as though it is—can easily generate fictional truths about the most intimate attributes of the characters the narrator describes. It is fictional in the reader's game that she knows about these attributes, however fantastic the fictional truths about her acquisition of this knowledge are, and however little is fictional about the source of her information. This intimate knowledge of the described characters, which fictionally the reader possesses, may encourage "empathy" with them, if not with the narrator.[10]

We have noted again and again similar sacrifices for similar benefits. We tolerate Emily Dickinson's verbosity (as it were), English in the mouths of Frenchmen, the optical irregularities of *Toilette of Venus,* transparent fourth walls (in theater and film), observers at the Creation, and strangers' eyes in the dressing rooms of shy maidens, all for the sake of facilitating the generation of detailed fictional truths about characters or events and giving us access to them. (See §§ 4.5, 6.6.)

Why recognize a narrator at all when it is automatic that what fictionally he says is itself fictional? Why not just say that, by convention, whatever the sentences of the work express is fictional, without supposing it fictional that anyone speaks or writes them? In that case it will not be fictional even that we learn of the events of the story by being told, but this may seem an artificial intrusion in a "realistic" work anyway, when what is told are intimate secrets of the heart. Why not let it be *entirely* indeterminate how fictionally we learn? I will consider this option in § 9.5.

9.4. NONVERBAL NARRATION

Sometimes it is fictional only that the words of a text (or some of them) are *thought* by a character, not that he speaks or writes them; some passages, or even entire works, are best construed as "internal monologues." Manuel Puig uses two unconventional devices for making it fictional of (some of) his words that a character merely thinks them. Here is one: Fanny's prevailing thoughts while with Pancho in the dark: the mistress can't see me, I won't tell my friend about it, I didn't dance with those fellows from the bank, I didn't dance with the students ma'am, I didn't dance with the kind you told me never to dance with.[11] Puig's other device is to use italics for words that, fictionally, the characters think but do not utter:

—May I? *she turns my stomach*

10. "The most real, the 'roundest' characters of fiction are those we know most intimately, precisely in ways we could never know people in real life" (Cohn, *Transparent Minds,* p. 5).

11. *Heartbreak Tango,* p. 86.

—Yes, please come in. I was waiting for you. *here's shorty all dressed up*

—You know how to keep plants, don't you? *but the house is nothing*

—It's the only thing I would regret leaving, if I leave Vallejos . . . *so stop staring at the broken floor tiles! dressed to kill, expensive wool coat, expensive felt hat*[12]

Sometimes it is not fictional of the words of the text even that a character thinks them, but just that he would think them if he were reflective or articulate enough or had an opportunity to do so. At the beginning of *Sunset Boulevard* we hear the voice of a character while observing his body face down in a swimming pool. The words are hardly ones it could be fictional that he is thinking, let alone uttering. Perhaps it is fictional that he would use them if he could speak from the dead, or something of the sort. It is probably fictional, sometimes, that a text expresses a character's fantasies or dreams or desires, but in words he would never be likely to use.

It does not much matter whether we restrict the notion of narration to cases in which it is fictional that the words of a work are such that a character utters or writes them, or count any character to whom the words are fictionally to be "attributed" in one way or another a narrator. But we must recognize not only the imprecision of the latter definition but also significant differences among instances it can be taken to cover. If it is fictional that the narrator only thinks the words of the text, the reader is dealt out of the game in important respects. It will not be fictional that he reads or hears the narrator's words, although presumably it will be fictional that he knows (somehow or other) that the narrator thinks them. The game thus loses even the minimal perceptuality that games with works containing speaking or writing narrators often have.

There is an alternative way of understanding many works, however, which diminishes this difference. We might allow that one part or aspect of a work considered alone establishes a world in which fictionally the character does speak or write, although it is fictional in the world of the work *as a whole* only that he thinks them (if even that). The voice-over narration in *Sunset Boulevard* thus illustrates what, in the world of the whole, Gillis would say if he could speak from the dead; it illustrates this by making it fictional in a secondary world that he does speak thus. The viewer does play a game, then, in

12. Ibid., pp. 164–165.

which it is fictional that he hears Gillis speak, a game in which the voice-over narration considered alone is a prop, and which is distinct from the game he plays with the film as a whole. This alternative parallels our way of understanding *Rashomon*. (See § 8.7.)

9.5. ABSENT AND EFFACED NARRATORS

It doesn't pay to get overly exercised about the question of whether all literary works have narrators or just how many do. But it will be useful to consider what can be said on this issue.

Narrators are certainly not inevitable in representations composed of words. It is entirely possible to understand a verbal text as simply making the propositions its words express fictional without making it fictional that those words are spoken or written by anyone or in any way to be attributed to anyone. (We might think of the choice as that between understanding a text to be preceded implicitly by "Let's imagine that" or "Let's imagine someone saying [writing, thinking] that.") We have noted how very "thin" the narrators of some works are, if there are such, how little can be said about them. This may argue against recognizing them. There are also the awkward cases in which narrators apparently could not have learned of the events they describe or cannot report them—because they are events of an unknowable sort or because no one was present when they occurred or because the narrator was dead then or when he supposedly reports their occurrence. We noted that, in cases of "omniscience," consideration of what sort of person the narrator is may be irrelevant; what fictionally he says is automatically fictional itself, regardless. None of this *forces* us to deny the presence of narrators. There are familiar ways of treating similar puzzles: We can accept indeterminacies and refuse to pursue silly questions; we can declare a narrator to be "effaced"—meaning that fictional truths about him are deemphasized and probably that there are few of them (*not* that it is fictional that he is effaced). But one may wonder what point there is, in many instances, in insisting that there are narrators.

Various considerations have been adduced in favor of recognizing narrators in all or nearly all literary works. I will sketch two, formulating them in terms of our theory, and also a third which may not be familiar. First, we are so used to declarative sentences being employed to report events and describe people and situations that, when we experience a literary work, we almost inevitably imagine someone's using or having used its sentences thus. And it is scarcely a

366 MODES AND MANNERS

strain to regard these nearly unavoidable imaginings to be prescribed. (The point need not be that such uses of words are in any sense fundamental or basic or essential; their mere pervasiveness may explain our propensity to engage in these imaginings.)

The words of many or most literary works contain hints of feelings or attitudes or inclinations or impressions concerning the events of the story that are best attributed to a narrator, even if in most respects he remains far in the background, and even if his attitudes and so on are irrelevant to deciding whether (fictionally) what he says is true (as they are in many cases of "omniscience"). It may be fictional that he describes the events with irony or pleasure or assurance or relief, in a tone of contempt or compassion or scorn or sympathy or resignation or despair, hesitantly or eagerly. These attitudes may be expressed explicitly, by means of adverbs such as "fortunately," "strangely," "sadly," "apparently," for instance, but they may also come out in more subtle ways.

Must we attribute these attitudes to a narrator? Might they not belong to the actual author of the literary work instead? No, in many cases. The author does not (actually) have attitudes toward the characters and situations of the story (not, anyway, when they are *merely* fictional and he knows that they are).[13] Wolterstorff claims that the author may have "implied with his words, or *presented* himself as implying," that he has the attitudes in question. To present himself thus, Wolterstorff says, is to "pretend," to "fictionalize about himself," to "put on a persona."[14] But what this means, surely, is that it may be fictional that the author regards the characters and situations in certain ways and expresses this in the words of the text. This makes the author a narrator.

A third reason for recognizing narrators in some instances, even when they are very inexplicit, is this: Sometimes in "real life" it is important to us that certain things be said or certain attitudes expressed, even if everyone involved fully realizes the truth of what is said or shares the attitudes expressed. We derive a certain satisfaction from the saying or expressing itself. (This is an important function of funerals and other rituals and ceremonies.) So one would expect it to be important, sometimes, that it be fictional that things be said and that it be fictional in our games that we hear them said, quite apart

13. The author may actually have attitudes concerning *fictional truths* about the characters and situations, and express them in the words of the text, but this is quite a different matter, as we shall see, and it fails to explain many textual features that need explaining.
14. *Works and Worlds*, p. 178.

from our learning that they are fictional and/or our fictionally learning or knowing that they are true. It is not enough to suppose merely that the words of the text make it fictional that the propositions expressed are true or the attitudes appropriate.

What should we conclude? I prefer to be relatively liberal in recognizing narrators, to speak of their effacement, usually, rather than their absence.[15] There are literary works such that little or nothing would be lost by taking them to be narratorless. But recognizing narrators in a wide range of cases, while allowing that some may have scarcely any significance for criticism or appreciation, encourages sensitivity to the subtlest hints of narratorial intrusions and facilitates recognizing infinitely fine variations in the degrees (and kinds) of prominence narrators in different works have, without presuming an artificially sharp break between narrated and unnarrated works.

Having said this, however, we must note special cases in which it is a particular strain to recognize narrators.[16] The following words are not easily thought of as those of a person describing a country fair:

> *Country fair, Sunday, April 26, 1937, in the Spanish Meadow: Its Course and Denouement*
>
>> Opening time: 6:30 P.M.
>> Price of tickets: one peso for the gentlemen, twenty cents for the ladies.
>> First dance performed by the musical band called Los Armónicos: tango "Don Juan."
>> Lady most admired in the course of the evening: Raquel Rodríguez.
>> Prevailing perfume: that which emanated from the leaves of the eucalyptus trees surrounding the Spanish Meadow . . .
>> Gentleman who attended the fair with the intention of breaking into Fanny's existence: Francisco Catalino Páez, also known as Pancho . . .
>> Barometric circumstances which facilitated the fulfillment of Pancho's intentions: the pleasantly cool temperature, 61 degrees Fahrenheit, and the new moon.
>> Chance circumstance which facilitated said intentions: the approach of a ferocious-looking stray dog who frightened Fanny and gave rise to an unmistakable show of courage on the part of Pancho, which awakened in Fanny a warm sense of security.[17]

15. This is approximately Chatman's recommendation in *Story and Discourse*.
16. Narrating reporters anyway. See § 9.6.
17. Puig, *Heartbreak Tango*, pp. 83–85.

Narrators—perfectly unobjectionable ones—do sometimes speak in ways real people do not—in iambic pentameter, for instance. But a passage in iambic pentameter is likely to be a recognizable transformation or adaptation of what might be said in real life, and a transformation of a conventional sort; we can think of it as an ordinary utterance dressed up to fit a particular literary genre.[18] The passage just quoted is harder to think of in this way.

What is important is not deciding where to draw the line between literary works with (effaced) narrators and ones lacking them or whether to draw such a line at all. But we need to be sensitive to the subtleties to be found in various works. We need to have at our fingertips conceptual tools adequate to whatever writers of fiction might throw our way.

I have considered only *reporting* narrators so far. It may sometimes be reasonable or mandatory that we recognize a *storytelling* narrator, even when we need not or should not recognize a reporting one—even, perhaps, in cases like that of the passage just quoted.

9.6. STORYTELLING NARRATORS

When a narrator fictionally speaks or writes the words constituting the text of a literary work, we need to ask what, fictionally, he does with them. Frequently it is fictional that he reports actual events or describes real people or situations. But it can be fictional that a narrator uses the words of the text to tell a story or write a novel or spin a yarn. There are *reporting* narrators and there are *storytelling* narrators. In some cases it is fictional that the narrator speaks or writes nonfictionally, but in others it is fictional that he creates a fiction. Some narrators, fictionally, speak of actual things and events, or purport to; others make things up.[19]

The difference between reporting and storytelling narrators is critical in considering how narrators are related to the "action" of a story, to the characters and situations and events of which they speak. The first question to ask is whether the act of narrating and the narrated events belong to the same fictional world. They do when it is fictional that the events are actual ones which the narrator recounts. That Robinson Crusoe was shipwrecked and lived as he did on his

18. One might regard similarly the sentences of literary works which Banfield, in *Unspeakable Sentences,* claims cannot be attributed to narrators.

19. That these several distinctions do not coincide is clear from Chapter 3. It is possible for a narrator to be both a reporting and a storytelling one.

island, and that he tells of these adventures, are both fictional in the world of *Robinson Crusoe* (and in readers' game worlds as well). In this and like cases we can ask a battery of familiar questions about the narrator's relation to the happenings he describes, within the world they share: Is it fictional that he participated in them or merely observed them? Did he, fictionally, play a central role in them or a bit part? Is it fictional that he witnessed them with his own eyes or learned of them by hearsay or in some other way? (Or is it indeterminate how fictionally he came to know about them?) Is it fictional that he gives a blow-by-blow account of them as they occur or soon after, or that he dredges them up from his memory? Is it fictional that he reports them honestly and accurately, or that he twists them to suit his own purposes?

A reporting narrator may be remote from the events he describes, either in the sense that fictionally he had nothing to do with them or in the sense that there simply are no significant fictional truths regarding what connections he might have had with them (or even how he knows about them); the work may be indeterminate in this regard. In the latter case, especially, there may be an informal sense in which the events take place in a different "world" from that in which the narrator reports them. But so long as it is fictional that he is reporting happenings that actually occurred, whatever else is or is not fictional, he and those happenings belong to the same fictional world (in our sense).

If, however, it is fictional that the narrator, in speaking or writing the words of the text, is spinning a yarn or telling a tale or authoring a novel, and fictional that he made up the events of which he speaks, his narrating and those events belong to different worlds. The world of the work contains only the telling; the events occur in a world within the work world. It is fictional in the work world that he creates a fiction in which it is (merely) fictional that those events transpire. Questions about how, fictionally, the narrator learned of them or whether and how he participated in them will not even arise, since it is fictional that they did not actually occur.[20] The questions to be asked are not ones about his relation to the events (within a fictional world), but rather the very different questions about how, fictionally, he is related to *fictional truths* about them.

In § 3.6 I discussed works that represent themselves as representations. It is fictional that the words of *Vanity Fair* constitute a repre-

20. But it might be fictional in the work world that it is fictional in the world of his story that he participated in them, or observed them.

sentation in which it is fictional that Becky Sharp marries Rawdon Crawley. It is also fictional that the writer of those words told a tale in which fictionally Becky marries Crawley; *Vanity Fair* has a storytelling narrator. Works which (at times, anyway) explicitly portray their narrators as producing works of fiction are not uncommon (*Tom Jones*, Barth's "Life Story"). But many in which this is not at all explicit can, with some plausibility, be understood similarly.

What are called *implied authors*, and those *apparent artists*, as I have named them,[21] that occur in literary works, can often be understood as storytelling narrators. In reading a story or a novel we may have an impression of what sort of person wrote it, or of the author's objectives in writing it, or of the manner in which it was written. It might seem to be the work of someone with racist attitudes, or someone who is insensitive or frightened or neurotic. It may seem to have been written in an attempt to be funny or to advance the cause of socialism. Or quickly, or laboriously, or carelessly. This impression may be an indication of what sort of person actually wrote the novel or told the story or how or why he did so. But often we are interested in the impression for its own sake and cultivate it, regardless of whether it corresponds to reality. The fact that a story *seems* to have been meant to be funny may be an important fact about it quite apart from how it actually was meant. Its seeming so may create an atmosphere of delicious anticipation. Or it might spoil the humor by making it too predictable or by raising listeners' expectations; sometimes it is best to tell a funny story with a straight face, in a way that makes it seem meant not to be funny (even if the listeners know better). A literary work in a bold or compulsive or carefree style, or a passionate or pretentious or sentimental or flamboyant one, is one that gives the impression of having been written boldly or compulsively or in a carefree manner or by a passionate or pretentious or sentimental or flamboyant person, whether or not it actually was. And the style itself is of interest to us. Sick jokes appear to be the product of sick minds.

When we are interested in the impression a text gives of how or why or by what sort of person it was written, apart from how reliable or unreliable that impression is, it is likely that we *imagine* someone of that sort writing it thus. If it is part of the function of the work to prescribe such imaginings, if it is fictional that its author was a person of that sort and composed it in that manner or for those reasons, the

---

21. Walton, "Points of View" and "Style." In these essays I say much more about the nature and importance of apparent artists than I do here, although I do not explain them in terms of make-believe.

fictional author is the (or a) narrator of the work—a *storytelling* narrator, if it is fictional that in writing it he created a work of fiction.

When it is fictional that the narrator of a work of fiction produces a work of fiction, it is usually fictional of the actual work, the story *we* read, that *it* is the fiction the narrator has produced.[22] After all, the words of the actual story are such that fictionally it is in writing or uttering *them* that the narrator tells his story. Not only is it fictional that the narrator of *Vanity Fair* writes a novel; it is fictional that he writes *Vanity Fair*.

If the actual story, containing the words it contains, is fictionally the story the narrator tells, we should expect the fictional truths it is fictional that it generates to be ones it actually generates. It is not *just* fictional that *Vanity Fair,* a novel composed by the narrator, makes it fictional that Becky Sharp marries Rawdon Crawley; *Vanity Fair* actually does make it fictional that she marries him.

This was our observation in § 7.6. Readers regard *Vanity Fair* in two ways, as establishing two distinct (first-order) work worlds: one in which it is fictional that the narrator tells a story in which it is fictional that various events, including Becky's marriage, transpire, and one in which it is fictional that those events actually transpire. The reader shifts between two games of make-believe corresponding to the two work worlds, sometimes concentrating on the narrator, the fictional storyteller and his telling of the story, sometimes on the content of the story (although he may be aware of both simultaneously). The same can be said of less explicit examples. It may be fictional in a story that it is a *story* about love and plunder written hastily by an ambitious but none too talented aspiring author. And it may be fictional in the story, but in a distinct work world, that characters engage in assorted acts of love and plunder. The reader may concentrate alternately on how fictionally the story came about, on the impression it gives of its author and his motives and manner, and on the acts of love and plunder.

The storytelling narrator and the events of which he speaks still do not share a world, but they are now seen to belong to worlds on the same level, work worlds, though different ones. This opens up certain questions concerning relations between fictional truths about the narrating and fictional truths about the narrated events (as opposed to

22. This is not inevitable. It might be fictional, in an actual short story, S, that its words are the opening words of an epic novel written by author N. N is the narrator of S; it is S-fictional that its words are his. And it is S-fictional that in producing them he is creating a fiction. But it may not be S-fictional that S itself is the epic he creates.

questions about how fictionally the narrator and his narrating are related to the events, or how fictionally the former are related to fictional truths about the latter). We can ask, for instance, how the text of the story manages to generate both groups of fictional truths at once, how the author's decisions to establish certain fictional truths about the storyteller's character and motives affect what is made fictional, in the other work world, about (for instance) actions of love and plunder.

It is obvious that a single literary work or a single passage can have both a storytelling narrator and a reporting narrator. A story in which it is fictional that R reports incidents of love and plunder may be such that fictionally it is a story told by S. It is fictional, of the words of the work, that R speaks or writes them in recounting incidents involving love and plunder. It is also fictional of those words, in a different work world, that S tells a story by means of them, a story in which R recounts incidents of love and plunder. The potential for fascinating entanglements and interpretive confusion is evident.

Keeping in mind the various relations that may hold between narrators and the "action" of a story, and especially the difference between storytelling narrators and reporting ones, will help us sort out the ways in which narrators do and do not mediate between the (actual) reader and the "action," and what might be meant in speaking of the "point of view" from which the "action" is portrayed.

9.7.   MEDIATION

Storytelling narrators do not mediate readers' access to the events of which they speak in the ways reporting narrators typically do.

We noted in § 9.2 several different ways in which reporting narrators may mediate. Let us sketch them a little more explicitly. Fictional truths about the "action" of a story often depend on fictional truths about what a reporting narrator says. It is because it is fictional that Gulliver wrote what he did in his logbook that it is fictional that he visited Lilliput. The fact that, fictionally, a narrator tells of performing heroic deeds and speaks emphatically, persistently, defensively about how honorably he behaved might imply that it is fictional that he did *not* behave honorably or heroically. What is fictional about what actually happened depends on what, fictionally, the narrator says and how he says it, whether or not it is fictional that things happened as he said they did. Perhaps the fact that fictionally the narrator speaks or writes the words of the text is a *primary* fictional truth, one that depends on no others. It may even be the only one; all of the other fictional truths the work generates may flow from it.

Insofar as fictional truths about the "action" of the story depend on fictional truths about the narrator's verbal behavior, the reader will infer the former from the latter. We note, first, what fictionally the narrator says and how he says it, and judge from this what, fictionally, actually occurred. In making these inferences we must pay attention to what is fictional about the narrator's character, personality, and circumstances, just as we need to take into account the character and circumstances of real people in order to decide when to believe them. Whether we judge it fictional that things happened as the narrator says they did or that they did not depends to a significant extent on our judgments about how perceptive or intelligent or honest it is fictional that he is, on whether, fictionally, he is prejudiced or confused or has an interest in concealing the truth; it depends (in many cases) on whatever bears on the narrator's "reliability" in the first of our two senses. We rely on the narrator for our information about the rest of the fictional world—on his eyes and mind as well as his words—even when we disbelieve what he says.

Not only do we actually access what is fictional about the events of the story through fictional truths about the narrator; it is fictional in our games that our access to the events is through him. It is fictional that we learn about them from his reports and whatever they reveal about his character, personality, and circumstances. It may be fictional that the reader judges from the defensive manner in which the narrator insists that he behaved honorably that he actually behaved otherwise.

Thus do reporting narrators sometimes mediate our access to the events of the story, in the several senses mentioned earlier. But only sometimes. We have seen that "omniscient" narrators—when this means that whatever, fictionally, the narrator says is automatically fictional itself—are partial exceptions. Perhaps no narrated representations fit very exactly the simple picture I have just outlined. But it is clear that some approximation of it applies to many of them. Reporting narrators do frequently fill something like the mediating roles I have described.

Storytelling narrators, however, do not. A story about a boy raised an orphan who embarks on a quest for fame and fortune, let's say, might give the impression of having been written by someone who is perceptive, or stupid, or wise, or neurotic, or self-serving, or brutally honest. We may decide that we are to imagine this, that it is fictional (in one work world) that the story is the creation of a storyteller of such and such a sort and was written with certain intentions. But this is unlikely to affect what propositions the story makes fictional (in the other work world) concerning the orphan and his search. Even if the story appears to be a tale told by an idiot—even if it is fictionally the creation of a raving lunatic and a liar whose judgment, whose *reports*, we would never trust—this need not make us doubt that, fictionally, the orphan's search was successful, if the story says it was. The story itself is there before us; we can read it and decide for ourselves what fate the protagonist came to. If we decide that he found his fortune, then we have, simply, a story about an orphan who succeeded, a story which, fictionally, was composed by a lunatic and a liar. The story, together with the fictional world in which the protagonist's search was successful, is fictionally the creation of a lunatic and a liar.

Indeed, fictional truths about the storytelling narrator are likely to depend on fictional truths about the orphan, rather than vice versa. It is probably because of the manner in which, fictionally, the protagonist goes about searching for fame and fortune or what happens to him along the way that the story gives the impression of having been composed by a lunatic; the fact that fictionally the protagonist is crazy himself might play a part. No sane author would write a story like that, we might think, and we may decide that fictionally the storyteller was insane (perhaps that the actual storyteller was insane as well). A sick joke, one that is fictionally the product of a diseased mind, is sick because of its content, because of what fictionally its characters say and do. We don't usually decide first that the joke is a sick one and then draw conclusions from that about its plot and characters.

Not only do we not determine what is fictional about the orphan boy's quest from what is fictional about the storyteller; it is certainly not fictional in our games that we ascertain how the orphan conducted his search and how successful he was on the basis of what kind of person told the tale, his motives in telling it, and so on. In this sense also storytelling narrators fail to mediate as reporting narrators frequently do. (This difference is a natural consequence of differences between real-life reporters and real-life storytellers. In judging whether to believe a reporter's report we must consider the source, but we need not, in general, attend especially to a storyteller in order to ascertain the content of his story. See Chapter 2.)

Two qualifications are in order. First, I do not claim that storytelling narrators *cannot* mediate. In special cases probably they do, in at least two of the ways I have discussed. A Sloppy Style drawing like figure 8.5 is arguably such that, fictionally, it was created sloppily or by a sloppy person. This may be part of what makes it fictional (in a different work world) that the computer is whole and healthy, and we may infer the latter fictional truth (partly) from the former. It is certainly not fictional in our games, however, that among our reasons for judging the computer to be whole is the fact that the the artist was sloppy. No doubt there are literary analogues of this example, literary works whose content depends on a principle of charity triggered by what is fictional of the storyteller.

The second qualification is this: The storytelling narrator may mediate our access to the events of which he speaks in a way different from those we have considered. There are two different work worlds, one in which it is fictional that the storytelling narrator tells his story and one in which it is fictional that the protagonist seeks fame and fortune. But it is fictional in the first of these worlds that it is *fictional* that the orphan boy searches for fame and fortune; his quest occurs both in a work world and also in a world within a (different) work world. The storytelling narrator does, in a way, mediate our access to the latter occurrence. It is fictional in our games that we learn fictional truths about the quest by reading the story responsible for them, the storyteller's story. But this need not involve attention to fictional truths about the narrator's personality or circumstances. We need not even realize that fictionally the story was written by someone, nor need it be fictional that we realize this, in order for it to be fictional that it is from reading what the storyteller wrote that we learn what is fictional about the quest.

9.8. POINTS OF VIEW IN NARRATED REPRESENTATIONS

A literary work's "perspective" or "point of view," in one sense anyway, is often identified with that of the reporting narrator, with whatever is fictional about his position with respect to the events of which he speaks, his spatial and temporal relations to them, what he does and does not know about them, and the sources of his knowledge, his attitudes toward them. And the work may be said to portray the events from his perspective, since he mediates readers' access to them. Storytelling narrators also have perspectives or points of view—that is, it is fictional that they do—although the work does not in the same way present the events of the story from their perspective. It presents the events and *also* the storytelling narrator's perspective, but not the former via the latter.

Moreover, the storytelling narrator's views are not views *of the events of the story* in the sense that the reporting narrator's are. The world in which fictionally the orphan's search for fame and fortune actually occurs is not the one in which fictionally the storytelling narrator resides. There is no world in which it might be fictional that he is aware of its actual occurrence and views it in one way or another; there is no world in which he learns of the orphan, by one means or another, and applauds or admires or despises or pities him—although it may be fictional, in the storyteller's world, that he plays a game in which it is *fictional* that he knows about the orphan and thinks well or ill of him. It may also be fictional that the story-teller actually has attitudes concerning the *story* and the *fictional truths* it generates about the orphan. He may (fictionally) take the fact that fictionally the orphan behaves as he does to imply that fictionally he acts wisely or foolishly or honorably or childishly. It may be fictional that the storyteller thinks the fictional truths about the orphan are such as to make for a funny story, or an exciting or boring or instructive one, or a best-seller. The storytelling narrator views the orphan and his world *from the outside,* whereas a reporting narrator, one who fictionally reports what actually took place, sees it *from within.*

Literary works often contain or present points of view other than those of narrators, of course, whether reporting or storytelling ones. And sometimes characters and events are portrayed from other points of view. Gérard Genette urges us to observe a distinction between *voice* and *mood,* between "the question *who is the character whose point of view orients the narrative perspective?* and the very different question *who is the narrator?*—or, more simply, the question *who sees?* and the question *who speaks?*"[23] I would insist only on not supposing that there must be such a thing as *the* "character whose point of view orients the narrative perspective," a single one (even in a single passage of the work), and on recognizing at least the nominal presence of the reporting narrator's (the speaker's) perspective, in many cases, even when the dominant point of view is that of another character.

When a reporting narrator straightforwardly describes how another character views things, the perspectives of both have roles to

23. *Narrative Discourse,* p. 186. See also Chatman, *Story and Discourse,* pp. 151–158.

play. The work presents the narrator's view of the character's view of events. (It may be clear that, fictionally, the narrator considers the character's view to be distorted or inappropriate.) Sometimes it is fictional that the narrator indicates or portrays a character's view in one or another less straightforward manner.

Critics have been especially interested in works in which the narrator (speaker) seems somehow to take on or adopt the perspective of another character, in which, as some have vaguely described it, the two perspectives tend to merge or fuse.[24] In many such cases it is fictional that the narrator shows what he takes the character's view of things to be by pretending to express that view himself. When (fictionally) the narrator explicitly quotes the character, directly or indirectly, he may be pretending to speak as he thinks the character does or might. (See § 6.3.) But sometimes such mimicry is less obvious.

One familiar technique for presenting the perspective of a character other than the narrator is to use what Wayne Booth has called a "third-person centre of consciousness."[25] Rather than (fictionally) describing the character's views or perspective or attitudes concerning certain events or saying explicitly what she does and does not know, by quoting her or otherwise, the narrator simply (fictionally) describes the events, restricting what he reports about them to what the character knows or notices or thinks important, and reporting them in a manner expressive of the attitudes the character takes of them. Strether is the "third-person centre of consciousness" in Henry James's novel *The Ambassadors*.[26]

> Strether's first question, when he reached the hotel, was about his friend; yet on his learning that Waymarsh was apparently not to arrive till evening he was not wholly disconcerted. A telegram from him bespeaking a room "only if not noisy," with the answer paid, was produced for the inquirer at the office, so that the understanding that they should meet at Chester rather than at Liverpool remained to that extent sound. The same secret principle, however, that had prompted Strether not absolutely to desire Waymarsh's presence at the dock, that had led him thus to postpone for a few hours his enjoyment of it, now operated to make him feel that he could still wait without disappointment.[27]

24. Pascal, *Dual Voice*, p. 26.
25. Booth, "Distance and Point-of-View," p. 94.
26. Booth calls the character whose perspective is thus presented the narrator, but I find this confusing, as does Genette. Strether is not himself, fictionally, the speaker of the words of the text, the narrator in our sense.
27. *The Ambassadors*, opening sentences.

The narrator unabashedly describes Strether's state of mind, which Strether presumably knows well, but reports only the evidence available to Strether concerning Waymarsh's intended arrival—the telegram—and speculates on its import ("apparently").

How do we know that what fictionally the narrator reports is limited to what fictionally the character knows? Often this is obvious simply because the facts which (fictionally) the narrator reports are ones we would expect the character to know, ones we assume that he knows. But once the pattern is set, once the precedent of restricting what fictionally the narrator reports to what fictionally the character knows or notices is established, the fact that the narrator does or does not mention something may itself be understood to make it fictional that the character does or does not know or notice it. Propositions about epistemological aspects of the character's point of view are thus made fictional without being expressed explicitly.

We can understand it to be fictional, in many such cases, that the narrator deliberately limits what he reports to what the character knows as a way of indicating or emphasizing what knowledge the character does and does not possess. We frequently do this in ordinary life. When I recount a friend's brush with the law, I may avoid saying whether or not he ended up spending the night in jail while describing how the brush began in order to dramatize the fact that *he* did not know then where he would spend the night. It can easily be fictional that a narrator portrays a character's state of knowledge or ignorance in this ordinary manner.

It has been suggested that this literary technique somehow gives the reader a sense of what a certain perspective is like, a feeling for how things seem from a certain standpoint, and encourages empathy with the character whose perspective it is. It is fictional in the reader's game that his own view of things is in important respects like the character's. Fictionally he knows and notices just what the character does, since that is what, fictionally, the narrator reports (even though the way in which fictionally the reader learns what she knows—from the narrator's reports—is different from the ways in which the character does). Also, the order in which fictionally the reader learns of things from what the narrator says is likely to approximate the order in which the character discovers them. So what, fictionally, the two are and are not surprised to learn will tend to coincide.

There is an analogy to be drawn between this novelistic technique and point-of-view shots in film. What fictionally viewers of the dinner sequence in *Hour of the Wolf* see and what they notice, what is portrayed on the screen and what is in focus, is understood to be what fictionally Johan Borg sees and notices. In this respect (and others also) the view which, fictionally, viewers have of the dinner is like Borg's.

The words in which (fictionally) the narrator of *The Ambassadors* describes things are an approximation of ones which (fictionally) Strether might use in expressing his knowledge of them. But this is not true of the narrator's references to Strether in the third person, nor of many of his uses of the past tense. Strether would express his knowledge of his reaction to the delay (if he is self-conscious about it) by saying, "*I am* not wholly disconcerted," not "He was not wholly disconcerted." The best depictive analogy may be point-of-view shots showing what the character whose view is presented sees together with shots of the seeing character, or still pictures that show both a seeing character and the scene as he sees it: Rousseau's *Dream*, the Eskimo roll diagrams (figure 8.13), perhaps Munch's *Scream* (figure 8.13).

There is nothing in any of these depictions, however, corresponding to the reporting narrator in *The Ambassadors*. What fictionally we hear *from the narrator* is what fictionally Strether thinks or knows. But it is what fictionally we see for ourselves that fictionally Borg sees.

My suggestion is that, fictionally, the narrator speaks as though he himself were, in many respects, in the epistemological position he attributes to the character, reporting what he takes the character to know and remaining silent about what he takes the character not to know. In some cases we might understand it to be fictional that the narrator *pretends* to be in that epistemological position, as a way of indicating that the character is, the pretense consisting in participation in a game of make-believe. The following passage from *The Trial*, portraying Josef K's thoughts just before his execution, encourages an understanding of this kind:

> His glance fell on the top storey of the house adjoining the quarry. With a flicker as of a light going up, the casements of a window there suddenly flew open, a human figure, faint and insubstantial at that distance and that height, leaned abruptly far forward and stretched both arms still farther. Who was it? A friend? A good man? Someone who sympathized? Someone who wanted to help? Was it one person only? Or was it mankind? Was help at hand? Were there arguments in his favour that one had overlooked? Of course there must be. Logic is doubtless unshakable, but it cannot

withstand a man who wants to go on living. Where was the High
Court, to which he had never penetrated?[28]

We can take the following to be fictional in the world of *The Trial:* In
asking, "Who was it? A friend? . . . ," the narrator pretends to wonder who the person leaning out the window was, whether a friend, a
good man, and so on. The narrator plays a game in which it is
fictional that he wonders thus. His purpose in engaging in this pretense is to show what questions went through K's mind while await-
ing execution. (In this case the narrator indicates K's occurrent
thoughts, not just what he knew—and didn't know.) The narrator is
not mimicking K's exact *words,* the words he takes K to have thought
to himself. K presumably thought, "Who *is* it? . . . *Are* there arguments in *my* favor. . . ?" But the *facts* the narrator pretends to
express uncertainty about while recounting K's execution—the identity of the person leaning out the window and so on—are ones he
portrays K as having wondered about at the time.

(It may be fictional in the work world that the narrator knows who
the person in the window is while pretending not to; more likely, I
think, it is fictional neither that he knows nor that he does not know.)

Sometimes it is fictional that the narrator pretends to express other
aspects of a character's point of view—her attitudes, for instance—as
a way of showing how the character does view things. Ann Banfield
points out that the sentiments expressed by the exclamations in this
passage: "What a lark! What a plunge! For so it had always seemed to
her when . . . she had burst open the French windows and plunged at
Bourton"[29] must be attributed to Mrs. Dalloway (the character
referred to by "her") and not to a narrator. But we can think of a
(reporting) narrator as (fictionally) *pretending* to express these sentiments, thereby indicating how Mrs. Dalloway felt.

Concerning this passage from George Eliot's *Daniel Deronda:*
"Gwendolen's dominant regret was that after all she had only nine
louis to add to the four in her purse; these Jew dealers were so
unscrupulous in taking advantage of Christians unfortunate at play!"
one critic has commented: "It will be observed that the second,
exclamatory sentence, though grammatically identical with the first,
cannot like the first be an authorial statement—since it asserts an
opinion the novel sets out to show is a prejudice—but must express a

28. Kafka, *The Trial,* quoted in Cohn, *Transparent Minds,* pp. 122–123.
29. Opening passage of Virginia Woolf, *Mrs. Dalloway,* quoted and discussed in Banfield, *Unspeakable Sentences,* p. 66.

view held by the character, Gwendolen."[30] My suggestion is that (fictionally) the reporting narrator pretends to express this anti-Semitic attitude in order to show what Gwendolen actually thinks. (The similarity to my proposal in § 6.3 about how to understand irony will be obvious.)

I am tempted even to regard the narrator of the following passage from Joyce's *Portrait of the Artist as a Young Man* (fictionally) as pretending to confess Stephen Dedalus' guilt, to express *his* penitent feelings, to avow *his* intention of telling all, to declare *his* determination not to be deterred by the fact that everyone will know. (I take it that no one but Stephen himself could actually perform most of these actions.)

> The slide was shot to suddenly. The penitent came out. He was next. He stood up in terror and walked blindly into the box.
>
> At last it had come. He knelt in the silent gloom and raised his eyes to the white crucifix suspended above him. God could see that he was sorry. He would tell all his sins. His confession would be long, long. Everybody in the chapel would know then what a sinner he had been. Let them know. It was true. But God had promised to forgive him if he was sorry. He was sorry. He clasped his hands.[31]

This pretense, if such it be, is of course thoroughly betrayed; it is perfectly clear that (fictionally) the narrator is not actually doing what he pretends to do. But the betrayal does not cancel the pretending, and the betrayal need not be undesirable if the objective of the pretending is not to fool people but rather to indicate what Stephen confessed and expressed and avowed to himself.

If this is too much to swallow, one might allow at least that (fictionally) the narrator is pretending to perform certain actions which he could actually perform: exclaiming about how long the confession will be, expressing the expectation that everybody will know, noting and remarking on the gravity of the sins.

I do not insist that we take the narrator in any of these cases (fictionally) to be pretending to speak or think or act in the manner in which he portrays the character as speaking or thinking or acting. But the fact that such interpretations are open to us is itself significant. A more cautious alternative would be to take it to be fictional that the narrator suggests the possibility of such pretense without actually

---

30. Pascal, *Dual Voice*, p. vii.
31. Quoted in Cohn, *Transparent Minds*, p. 102.

engaging in it, or pretends to pretend. In most cases we can easily imagine a vocal reading of the text which would make recognizing that (fictionally) the narrator actually engages in the pretense in question nearly unavoidable: a reading of "these Jew dealers were so unscrupulous in taking advantage of Christians unfortunate at play!" in a tone dripping with contempt, a rendition of "He was sorry" in a manner that would be expressive of deep remorse and contrition were the sentence in the first person.

Needless to say, the foregoing falls far short of a comprehensive or systematic account of mediation and points of view in literary representations. But we have observed several significant ways in which the make-believe theory can contribute clarity and insight to these much-discussed issues. Perhaps they will suggest others as well.

PART FOUR

Semantics and Ontology

Doing without Fictitious Entities

We all know that there is no King Lear, that Shake-speare's play is mere fiction. We learned at our mothers' knees that "Peter and the Wolf" is "just a story" and that Peter and the Wolf never were. But if we are asked whether there are such *characters* as Lear and Peter, the answer first on our lips is that indeed there are. In one breath we endorse the truism that there are no dragons, unicorns, and fairies and never have been any. In the next we find ourselves allowing that *of course* there are, *in fiction,* dragons, unicorns, fairies, and all the rest. Such are the conflicting intuitions of which the problem of the ontological status of fictional entities is born.

These conflicts have provoked philosophers to a variety of unseemly contortions. Some have introduced a distinction between being and existence, or between what there is and what exists or is actual: Lear and Grendel do not *exist,* it is said, yet they *are.*[1] (The artificiality of this move is evident from the fact that pretheoretically it seems just as acceptable to deny that there "are" any such things as Lear and Grendel as it is to deny that they "exist," and just as acceptable to affirm that they "exist" as to affirm that there "are" such.) Sometimes it is claimed that Lear and Grendel do exist but are not real, or that they enjoy fictional but not actual existence or exist in a fictional realm but not in actuality. These various devices look like voodoo metaphysics. It is hard to escape the impression that they are tricks designed to camouflage a contradiction, tricks whereby ontological respectability is offered to King Lear and his cohorts with one hand only to be taken back with the other.

An equally unappealing alternative is to deny fictions[2] any sort of existence or being, while insisting that nevertheless we can and do

1. For example in Meinong, "Theory of Objects."
2. In Part Four I will mean by "fictions" and "fictional entities" things that are *merely* fictional. These uses contrast with those of earlier chapters, in which "fictions" or "fictional

refer to them and talk about them.[3] This mandates a simple rejection of the ordinary claim that *there is* such a character as Lear. More important, it saddles us with an awkward puzzle about how to construe reference. Causal theories of reference will be unavailable, since nonentities cannot be causes; indeed reference will turn out not to be a relation at all. This tactic amounts to another misbegotten attempt to have it both ways, to smuggle in the existence of fictions amidst denials of their existence.

The urge to stand with feet on both sides of the fence arises from the fact that each side has its problems; from each the grass seems greener on the other. Those who accept fictional entities and those who reject them both have a lot of explaining to do. Nonbelievers must account for the many apparent references to fictions in ordinary discourse. If there is no King Lear and we know it, what are we saying when we say that King Lear had three daughters or that he is a character in Shakespeare's play? Believers must confront the fact that, in many contexts, we easily and naturally deny that there is a Lear and that there are such things as dragons and unicorns. They must also say what *sorts* of things these are, if there are such, what properties they have.

Believers have found themselves forced into awkward positions on this score also, construing characters and other fictions as exotica of one sort or another.[4] Some take them to be "incomplete" objects, exempt from the law of the excluded middle. (Lady Macbeth possesses neither the property of having more than two children nor that of not having more than two.) Terence Parsons allows that Sherlock Holmes might have had the property of having talked with Gladstone without Gladstone having had the property of having talked with Sherlock Holmes.[5] Partly to escape uncomfortable consequences like these, other believers deny characters such ordinary properties as that of being a person and that of having three daughters, allowing them

---

entities" may be actual as well as fictional, and also with the use of "fictions" to mean *works* of fiction.

3. Margolis, *Art and Philosophy*, pp. 252–263.

4. The several views cited here about the nature of fictions and variations on them (many of which are more sophisticated than my brief comments would suggest) are to be found in Castañeda, "Fiction and Reality"; Fine, "Problem of Non-Existence"; Howell, "Fictional Objects" and "Review of Parsons"; Lamarque, "Fiction and Reality"; Meinong, "Theory of Objects"; Parsons, *Non-Existent Objects*; Routley, *Exploring Meinong's Jungle*; Van Inwagen, "Creatures of Fiction"; Wolterstorff, *Works and Worlds*; Woods, *Logic of Fiction*.

5. *Non-Existent Objects*, pp. 59–60.

only properties like that of having had personhood attributed to them in a story, or that of being such that fictionally (or "in-a-story") they are human, or that of being in some way partially constituted by personhood. Some take fictional objects to be abstract entities (types or kinds or collections of properties), and some take them to exist necessarily and eternally. On some accounts different works cannot be about the same character unless exactly the same properties are attributed to it in each; and if exactly the same properties are attributed to two characters in a single work, it is said that they are not two but one,[6] or none.[7]

All of these various conceptions of fictional objects collide with our usual ways of speaking. We describe fictions as we would ordinary concrete particulars. We speak of Lear and Lady Macbeth as though they are subject to the law of the excluded middle just as Louis XIV is. Lear is a man who had three daughters, we say, without hinting that he is *really* an abstraction who is above such mundane attributes. We speak as though Lear came to be on a certain occasion. (But on what occasion? When he was born, or when Shakespeare wrote the play?) We say that the Hamlet in *Hamlet* and the Hamlet in Stoppard's *Rosencrantz and Guildenstern Are Dead* are one and the same, although the properties ascribed to him in each are not entirely the same. And on reading *The Tale of the Flopsy Bunnies*[8] we easily allow that there are six distinct bunnies, since the story says there are, even though it does not tell us how they differ from one another. If we have a naive, pretheoretical commitment to fictional people and things, it would seem to be a commitment to people and things that are in most respects perfectly ordinary. Theories built to accommodate what is supposed to be a pretheoretical ontological commitment, especially the more sophisticated ones, find themselves having to reinterpret radically the entities in question.

So far nothing has been settled. No matter what theory we end up with, some ordinary and obviously true observations will have to be construed in a way that is not entirely literal and straightforward. Something funny is going on in fiction, however we look at it.

Theorists on both sides have attempted, with varying degrees of success, to paraphrase the statements they cannot take at face value or to indicate in some other way how they are to be construed. But this is

6. Wolterstorff, *Works and Worlds*, p. 146. See Fine, "Problem of Non-Existence," and Walton, "Review of Wolterstorff," pp. 187–189.

7. Parsons, *Non-Existent Objects*, pp. 190–194.

8. Beatrix Potter, *The Tale of the Flopsy Bunnies*.

not enough. Any theory worth its salt will endeavor also to explain *why* we express ourselves in the ways we do. If in saying "King Lear has three daughters" one is not referring to a certain King Lear, or if one is not attributing to what is referred to the property of having three daughters, we need to know not only what it is that is being said but also why we say it in the potentially misleading way we do. Why do we speak as if we were attributing the property of having three daughters to something we pick out with the name "King Lear" if that is not what we are doing? If to say that there is no Grendel or that there are no dragons is to say something about what *sort* of things Grendel or dragons are, to say that they are *fictional* or *nonexistent* entities rather than actual ones, we need an explanation of why we put it this way. Why should we disguise what are really observations about the *nature* of certain objects as denials that there are such? Moreover, we need a reasonably *systematic* way of understanding the various kinds of things concerning fiction which are said, not a piecemeal, ad hoc arrangement for each individual anomaly.[9] We want a systematic and comprehensive way of conceiving the whole business of fiction.

Our vision must extend beyond the metaphysical and semantic issues before us now to the aesthetic ones we explored in previous chapters. Even before embarking on that exploration we found reason to suppose that the two groups of issues are intimately intertwined, in particular that the experience of being "caught up in a story" is closely linked with our conflicting intuitions about the status of fictional entities. The notion of make-believe, which served us well in the treatment of aesthetic questions and was central to our understanding of that experience, will be the key to the semantic and metaphysical questions also.

Many discussions of the status of fictitious entities, by realists especially, proceed without so much as mentioning make-believe or pretense or imagining or anything of the sort. This is surprising, for it seems obvious that, whatever the fate of the specifics of my theory, *some* such notion must have a prominent place in any adequate account of the institution of fiction. No doubt make-believe or pretense could be tacked on to nearly any theory, as an afterthought. But the result is bound to be unsatisfyingly disjointed. *After* recognizing fictional entities and specifying what sorts of things they are and how they enter into our discourse, one might add that people engage in

9. Howell has emphasized this ("Fictional Objects," p. 153).

certain imaginings or pretense (that we pretend or imagine of fictional entities that they are actual, or that they have existence as well as being, or that they are particulars rather than properties or kinds). But this is too late. Make-believe or some close relative seems so fundamental to the institution that one would expect it to have a lot

10.1 · Patrick Maynard, "You Don't Exist!" Copyright © Patrick Maynard, 1990.

to do with the question of what and whether fictions are. Better to bring it on board at the start.

It is my contention, briefly, that when realists claim with a straight face that people refer to and talk about fictional entities and that our theory must postulate them in order to make sense of what people say, they are overlooking or underemphasizing the element of make-believe that lies at the heart of the institution. They mistake the *pretense* of referring to fictions, combined with a serious interest in this pretense, for genuine ontological commitment. We are so deeply immersed in make-believe that it infects even theorizing itself. Our job is to extricate ourselves enough to be able to see how pervasive it is.

One more preliminary: My resistance to fictional objects is not part of a suspicion of abstract entities in general. It does not derive from broad empiricist or nominalist tendencies that would apply equally to properties, numbers, propositions, and meanings. Any general prejudice in favor of concrete kickable objects and any good reasons for banishing abstractions will of course affect fictional entities, insofar as they are thought of as abstractions. But such reasons are not mine. Indeed I have shamelessly helped myself to properties and propositions in the preceding chapters, and I will use them now in explaining away fictional entities. There are important intuitive grounds for being wary of fictional entities that are not readily applicable to abstractions generally. Among the data with which realist accounts of fiction must contend is the fact that in many ordinary nontheoretical contexts people naturally make what appear to be claims that fictions do not exist, that there are no such things. There are no similarly ordinary denials of the existence of properties and numbers. We rarely have occasion to point out that there is no such thing as redness or that the number seventeen does not exist in anything like the nontheoretical spirit in which we do sometimes observe that there is no King Lear or that there are no dragons. It is only after acquiring philosophical axes to grind that some seek to banish numbers and properties from the universe. That Peter Rabbit is not an inhabitant of the universe seems a truism of common sense (even though there are pretheoretical intuitions tending in the opposite direction as well).

10.2.   SPEAKING WITHIN AND ABOUT FICTIONAL WORLDS

> Even at its best, its most deadly serious, criticism, like art, is partly a game.
>
> John Gardner, *On Moral Fiction*

Virtually all discussions of the ontological status of fictional entities, whether realist or irrealist, start with the observation that people
commonly make assertions that appear to be about fictional entities,
and that these assertions are in many cases assertions of truths. To
begin this way is to begin on the wrong foot. The problem is not that
this observation is incorrect. We *do* say things like "Tom Sawyer
attended his own funeral" and "Don Quixote is a character invented
by Cervantes" assertively, and frequently what we assert thereby is
true. The mistake lies in taking this as our starting point. There is
another way in which utterances of such sentences can and do function, one that is more fundamental (even if less common) and that
points the way to an understanding of the problematic assertive uses.
The more fundamental utterances are acts of pretense, acts of participation in games of make-believe.

Recall Stephen, who pronounced, "That is a ship," in an assertive
tone of voice while pointing to an appropriate spot on Van der
Velde's *Shore at Scheveningen* (See § 6.3). We encountered difficulties
in attempting to understand him to be describing the world of the
painting. "That is a ship," in its context, seemed not to express a
proposition that Stephen could plausibly be claiming to be fictional in
the picture world, for we could not find an appropriate referent for
the demonstrative "that." These difficulties pushed us toward the idea
that Stephen was merely pretending to refer to something by means of
the demonstrative and to say of it that it is a ship. The time has come
to develop this suggestion and to try it out on other kinds of cases. If
there is no Gulliver and there are no Lilliputians, there are no propositions about them. So there would seem to be no such thing as the
proposition that Gulliver was captured by the Lilliputians.[10] To say
"Gulliver was captured by the Lilliputians" cannot, then, be to
attribute fictionality to this proposition, to say that fictionally Gulliver was captured by the Lilliputians. Could it be that the speaker is
engaging in pretense?

I speak of *pretense* here, but gingerly. This is no more than a
shorthand way of describing acts of verbal participation in games of
make-believe. To pretend to rob a bank is actually to do something
that makes it fictional in one's game that one robs a bank, and fictional of what one actually does that it is an instance of robbing a

---

10. We might allow that this sentence (in its context) does, in a way, express a proposition, but not a proposition about Gulliver and the Lilliputians, and not one to which the
speaker could be attributing fictionality. The proposition it expresses is simply the one
which, I will claim, we are likely to assert by means of it. It is not because the sentence
expresses the proposition it does that a speaker can or does assert what he asserts by means
of it.

bank. Let us add that the pretender imagines accordingly—he imagines what he does to be a robbing of a bank. "Pretense" so understood has nothing to do with deception, of course. Also, to pretend to do something in this sense is entirely compatible with actually doing it. The child playing cops and robbers who yells "Stop, Thief!" makes it fictional that he shouts those words, and it is fictional of his actual shouting of them that it is an instance of doing so. He pretends to shout "Stop, Thief!" by actually shouting it, although he *only* pretends to apprehend a robber.

I noted in § 6.3 how pervasive verbal participation is in children's games of make-believe and expressed the expectation that appreciators frequently participate verbally in the games they play with representations, that when one says things like "That is a ship," "There are several ships offshore," "Gulliver was captured by the Lilliputians," and "Ivan was furious with Smerdyakov," it may be fictional that one is recounting events or reporting on states of affairs. Understanding such remarks in this way locates the speaker *within* a fictional world (the world of his game) and has him contributing to it. This contrasts with the usual assumption that the speaker is making a genuine assertion about a fictional world (a work world) from a perspective outside of it, that he is saying something about what fictional truths it contains. The pretense construal has the appreciator pretending to describe the real world rather than actually describing a fictional one.

How much of our discourse concerning representational works of art is to be understood as pretense, as verbal participation in games of make-believe? In some cases the pretense interpretation applies with no strain at all. Tears come to the eyes of a reader of *Anna Karenina* as he learns of Anna's suicide, and he mumbles to himself, "Oh no! Poor Anna; she didn't deserve that fate." Fictionally he mourns Anna's death and laments the circumstances that led to it. When Charles, watching the horror movie, leans toward his companion and exclaims, "Yikes! Watch out! Here comes the slime!" he is pretending to declare that a slime is coming; fictionally he does so. If he were just describing a fictional world, he could have made this explicit; he could have said instead, "A slime is coming, in the world of the movie." But this variant lacks the original's air of desperation; Charles's exclamatory tone is absurdly out of place when the fictional status of the danger is made explicit. (Compare an actor playing Horatio in *Hamlet,* who exclaims, when the ghost appears, "Look, my lord, it comes, in the fictional world of the play!" or suppose Gregory shouts, "Watch out! There's a bear in the thicket, in the

world of the game!") Charles is engaging in pretense. He makes it
fictional of himself that he proclaims the imminent arrival of a slime
in a spirit of desperation appropriate to the occasion. "Yikes!" and
"Watch out!" do not even appear to be descriptions, and thus not
descriptions of the fictional world. But they are easily understood.
Charles is pretending to express amazement or terror and pretending
to issue a (serious) warning. Fictionally he is doing these things.

Many utterances about works of fiction involve no similarly obvious pretense, however. There is sober, detached criticism, distant
observation, cold academic analysis, abstract theorizing. In discussing
"anachronies" in literary works, Gérard Genette, referring to a novel
by Santeuil, observes that "Jean, after several years, again finds the
hotel where Marie Kossichef, whom he once loved, lives, and com-
pares the impressions he has today with those that he once thought he
would be experiencing today,"[11] and proceeds to contrast the order
of the parts of the text with the order of the events they portray in the
story world. It hardly seems that Genette has interrupted his serious
theorizing to play a game, to pretend. And he does seem really to have
pointed out features of the world of the novel. Demonstratives like
Stephen's occur in the most sober criticism. The driest academic lecturer might indicate a particular spot on Hieronymus Bosch's *Hay-
wagon* with a pointer, saying "That is a pig," and proceed to discourse on its iconographic import. One recounts the plot of a movie
or a novel to a friend who must decide whether to see or buy it. In the
course of explaining why a work fascinated or upset or bored us, or
why we think it good or bad, we describe what the characters were
like and what they did. Make-believe seems remote in cases such as
these. Isn't one actually describing a fictional world rather than pretending to describe the real world?

One suggestion would be to distinguish *appreciation* from *criticism,* and to treat separately the remarks people make in the course
of engaging in these different activities. The appreciator is caught up
in the spirit of the work and plays along with it, participating in a
game in which the work is a prop. (I ignore for the moment the
nonparticipatory appreciation discussed in § 7.6.) The critic, by contrast, considers the work and the games to be played with it from
without, from an onlooker's point of view, describing matter-of-
factly what fictional truths it generates.

The situation is not this simple, of course, even if we assume that

11. *Narrative Discourse,* pp. 37–38.

appreciation is mainly a matter of pretending and criticism is mainly observing and describing. Appreciation and criticism, participation and observation, are not very separate. One can hardly do either without doing the other, and nearly simultaneously. In order to appreciate a work one must notice what it makes fictional; one must be sensitive to the fictional world. To this extent the appreciator must be a critic. The critic usually cannot get very far in describing the world of a work unless she allows herself to be caught up in the spirit of pretense to some extent, as appreciators are. Insofar as the Reality or Mutual Belief principles of implication are applicable, extrapolation involves deciding what would be the case if certain other things were, or what would be the case given the truth of relevant background beliefs shared in the artist's community. It helps greatly to put oneself in the shoes of one who knows or believes the premises and the background, to imagine being in that situation, and to observe what else one then finds oneself imagining. This is what the critic does when she engages in a game of make-believe, when she is also an appreciator. Appreciation (participatory appreciation) and criticism are intimately intertwined, and so are the activities of pretending to describe the real world and actually describing a fictional one.

Indeed we often do both at once. Pretending to talk about the real world is frequently a way of actually talking about a fictional one. In other contexts also it is not uncommon for one to pretend to say one thing by way of actually saying something else. A diner jokingly remarks that he could eat a rhinoceros, in order to indicate, seriously, that he is hungry. Smith declares in a sarcastic tone of voice, "Jones is a superhero," thereby implying or suggesting or asserting that Jones thinks thus of himself. A critic-appreciator pretending to claim (seriously) that there is a country inhabited by six-inch-tall people may be pointing out that it is fictional in *Gulliver's Travels* that this is so. Verbal participation may thus be much more prevalent than one might have thought. Even when it is perfectly obvious that a speaker is making serious claims about a fictional world, we need not deny that he is engaging in pretense, that he is participating verbally in a game of make-believe.[12]

Sometimes the dual nature of an utterance is transparent. A teacher of literature remarks on Willy Loman's sad plight with an air of gravity and an expression of deep concern ("Poor Willy," he begins), in the course of discussing the allegorical or symbolic significance of

12. Evans emphasizes the exploitation of make-believe for purposes of serious assertion (*Varieties of Reference*, pp. 363–364).

his troubles. It may be evident both that he is pretending to describe a real human tragedy in a properly sympathetic manner, and also that in doing this he is making sober observations about the world of the play.

One aspect of a dual performance may be emphasized over the other. The pretense is what matters in some cases. The speaker may delight in playing along with the fiction but may scarcely care about informing others about the fictional world. If he is also describing the fictional world, this may be a mere by-product of his pretending. In sober criticism, however, pretense, if there is any, may be no more than a convenient vehicle for describing the fictional world.

How do we decide whether there is pretense at all, especially when the emphasis is on the (genuine) assertion? What determines whether a genuine assertion is being made in cases with the opposite emphasis? The answers depend on how we are to understand asserting and pretending (participation). I have no account of assertion to offer. Sometimes, no doubt, it will be best to say that in pretending, the speaker does something weaker than asserting—that he merely implies or suggests or gives it to be understood that the fictional world is of a certain sort. Where exactly the line is to be drawn need not concern us.

What about pretending? Although some may be willing to allow that critics engage at least in pro forma games of make-believe even in the driest academic settings, many will prefer to speak of pretense and participation only in more obvious cases, like that of the professor who blatantly acts the part of a sympathetic observer as he discusses Willy Loman. This difference, too, is inherently fuzzy, and we can happily leave it that way. It is worth noting, however, that even on a narrow construction, even if we do not regard the sober critic as pretending, weakly, to recount real-world events, pretense may be lurking in the background. The critic may be *pretending* to pretend to recount real events—it may be fictional that he is participating verbally in a game—or he may be deliberately going through the motions of so pretending. (See § 7.6.) Performing either of *these* actions would naturally substitute for actually pretending to recount real events as a way of describing the fictional world of the work; the hearer can be expected to get the point in either case. Alternatively, a speaker's utterances may be props in a game for others to play, and he may intend them as such, even if he does not participate in it himself. In saying "Tom Sawyer attended his own funeral," a person may not imagine himself to be claiming that a certain Tom Sawyer attended his own funeral or consider himself subject to a prescription to so imagine, but there may be a charge to his listeners to do so. Make-believe thus comes into the picture, although the speaker is not in our sense pretending to assert that someone attended his own funeral.

Insofar as statements appearing to be about fictional entities are uttered in pretense, they introduce no metaphysical mysteries. When Sally says "Tom Sawyer attended his own funeral" in pretense, it is *fictional* in her game that there is someone whom she calls Tom Sawyer and who she claims attended his own funeral. We need not suppose that there really is any such person. We need not suppose even that there is someone, or some character, about whom Sally *pretends* to speak, nor that there is a proposition she pretends to assert. Her utterance is fully intelligible as an act of participation if we take it to be *merely* fictional, not true, that her words express a proposition, that they express a proposition about someone whom she calls Tom Sawyer, and that she asserts such a proposition to be true.

If this were the whole story, we could dispense with fictitious entities forthwith, dismissing apparent references to them as mere pretense. But it isn't. The fact remains that in saying things like "Tom Sawyer attended his own funeral," we are sometimes making genuine assertions, whether or not we are at the same time engaging in pretense. Our task is to explain what is being asserted in these cases. (The question is not what the sentences themselves mean or what propositions *they* express. My position is that the sentences have no meanings beyond their ordinary literal ones, and I prefer to regard those appearing to denote purely fictional entities as not expressing propositions at all.)

The key to understanding assertive uses of sentences appearing to make reference to fictional entities is to take as primary their use in pretense. What is asserted by means of them is to be understood in terms of their role in make-believe.

10.3. ORDINARY STATEMENTS

Statements appearing to make reference to fictitious entities are of several kinds. The simplest and most basic ones—let us call them *ordinary* statements concerning fiction—are ones like these:

(1) Tom Sawyer attended his own funeral.
(2) The murderer hid the body under the floorboards. (said in connection with Edgar Allan Poe's "Telltale Heart")

(3) That is a unicorn. (said while pointing toward one of the Unicorn Tapestries)

These are such that phrases like "in *The Adventures of Tom Sawyer*," "in the story," and "in the world of the picture" can comfortably be attached to them with a result that seems equivalent to the original. This will do as a rough test for ordinariness.

Construing (1), for example, as short for

(1a) In the world of *The Adventures of Tom Sawyer*, Tom Sawyer attended his own funeral

does not solve our problem, of course. This longer statement retains the apparent reference to Tom Sawyer; it appears to describe him as being such that in the world of Mark Twain's novel he attended his own funeral.

Not all ordinary statements contain apparent references to merely fictional entities. Some are about real things rather than fictitious ones. Some do not even have the form of statements about particulars:

(4) Caesar was warned about the Ides of March. (said in connection with Shakespeare's play)

(5) Giant mosquitoes raised in the North Woods were used to drill wells in Arizona. (said in connection with the Paul Bunyan stories)

Our problem is with fictional entities, but we should seek a general account of ordinary statements applicable to those that do not appear to refer to such as well as those that do.

Ordinary statements are linked to what I have called *authorized* games of make-believe—games of the sort it is the function of representations to serve in. There is nothing to stop us from using a work however we like, of course. One might devise a game in which marks like those on the pages of *Remembrance of Things Past* are fictionally footprints of tiny Martians. We could choose to count the splotches of red paint on Brueghel's *Wedding Dance* as, fictionally, blood spilled at the scene of a heinous crime. But these are not the standard or accepted uses of these works or the uses for which they were designed; it is not their function to serve in games like these. Such games are not authorized for them.

Whether or not a game is authorized is a matter of what principles of make-believe are operative in it. It is the "rules" of a game that are or are not authorized, not the "moves" players make. It may be inadvisable, even improper to behave in front of the Mona Lisa so as to make it fictional that one studiously avoids looking La Gioconda in the eye. But the game is still an authorized one if the principles whereby this and other fictional truths are generated are the accepted ones for works of this sort. A reader of *Tom Sawyer* may be participating in an authorized game when she says "Tom never played hooky," even though it is fictional, if the game is authorized, that Tom did on occasion play hooky.

Ordinary statements are ones that are understood to be such that they might naturally be uttered in pretense in the course of *authorized* games of make-believe. It is this actual or envisioned pretense—acts of verbal participation in authorized games—that holds the key to understanding assertive uses of such statements.

It is uncontroversial that some ordinary statements are *acceptable* or *appropriate* and others are not. To say "Tom Sawyer attended his own funeral" is justified in a way that saying "Tom Sawyer never played hooky" is not.[13] This acceptability and unacceptability easily pass as truth and falsity, thus encouraging construing the utterances as genuine assertions. But we must not make this move too quickly, for reasons that are now evident. Actions of almost any kind, acts of pretense included, can be appropriate or inappropriate for any of a variety of reasons. Appreciators are expected to play games of kinds authorized for the works they appreciate and, when they participate verbally, to make it fictional of themselves in such games that they speak truths rather than falsehoods. In pretending to assert that there are giant well-drilling mosquitoes in Arizona, Robert makes it fictional of himself in a game authorized for the Paul Bunyan stories that he speaks truly; his act of pretense is in *this* way appropriate. Sally's pretending to refer to someone by means of the name Tom Sawyer and to say of him that he attended his own funeral is appropriate for the same reason. For Robert to pretend to claim that Arizona is devoid of well-drilling mosquitoes, or for Sally to pretend to say of someone she refers to as Tom Sawyer that he traveled by spaceship to Neptune would be inappropriate, unacceptable, for then it would be fictional of the speaker, if the game is an authorized one, that he or she asserts a falsehood. There is no need to assume that in engaging in acts of pretense like these one is genuinely asserting something that is true or false in order to explain the acceptability or unacceptability of the utterances.

But the fact that acts of pretense can themselves be appropriate or

13. Woods (*Logic of Fiction*) speaks of "bet sensitivity." If you bet on Tom's having attended his own funeral, you win; if you bet on his having never played hooky, you lose.

inappropriate creates an obvious opportunity for making assertions by means of them. One can indicate to others what behavior is appropriate in a given situation simply by behaving in the appropriate way. A native of an exotic culture might inform his alien guests that the snake livers are to be eaten with the parrot's nest sauce by going ahead and doing so. If it is awkward or improper to discuss Harold's winning of a prize before it is officially announced, one way of indicating that the announcement has been made, that the subject of Harold's good fortune is now a properly discussable one, would be to begin discussing it. Doing something is sometimes a way of claiming that it is proper or acceptable to do it.

So in pretending to assert that there are giant well-drilling mosquitoes in Arizona, Robert may be saying that it is appropriate or acceptable in the circumstances to so pretend. Sally, likewise, may be construed as calling attention to the fact that it is appropriate to engage in the pretense she engages in when she says, "Tom Sawyer attended his own funeral." The appropriateness or acceptability in question is of a particular kind, that of fictionally speaking the truth in a game of make-believe authorized for the work in question. So Robert and Sally can be regarded as claiming that to pretend as they do is to make it fictional of oneself, in a game authorized by the Paul Bunyan stories or *Tom Sawyer*, that one speaks truly.

I will be more explicit later about what they are asserting, how to paraphrase their claims. But deciding on a paraphrase is not strictly necessary. All we need for our purposes are truth conditions for such assertions, a specification of the circumstances in which the speaker will be (genuinely) asserting something true. If no such entity as Tom Sawyer is required for the truth of whatever it is that Sally asserts, her apparently referring use of "Tom Sawyer" provides no reason to believe in such a thing.

What makes Sally's assertion true, I suggest, is simply the fact that it is fictional in her (authorized) game that she speaks truly. In general, when a participant in a game of make-believe authorized by a given representation fictionally asserts something by uttering an ordinary statement and in doing so makes a genuine assertion, what she genuinely asserts is true if and only if it is fictional in the game that she speaks truly.[14] Our discussion of how to paraphrase such assertions will lend support to this principle. But for now the reader may want

14. This is close to the truth condition Gareth Evans proposes for statements concerning fiction (*Varieties of Reference*, chap. 10). He does not say how to paraphrase them. Evans' attempt to account for apparent references to fictional entities in terms of make-believe is, as far as it goes, much like mine in spirit and in some of its details.

to satisfy himself that no clear counterexamples come easily to mind.

Fictional entities are obviously not needed for this truth condition to be satisfied. Whether it is satisfied or not in a given case depends on the nature of the work in question and on what principles of generation are in force in games authorized for it. It is fictional in Sally's authorized game that she speaks truly—hence what Sally actually asserts is true—because the principles of generation for games authorized for *Tom Sawyer* are such that, given the words of the text, to speak as Sally does is fictionally to speak truly. No such thing as Tom Sawyer comes into the picture at all.

What is it that Sally genuinely asserts? How are claims like hers to be paraphrased? Is she asserting simply that the truth condition, as stated, is satisfied in her case, that it is fictional in a game authorized for *Tom Sawyer* that she speaks truly? No, she is not speaking about herself. Nor is she speaking about her action or the words she uses. (She may be *implying* or *suggesting* something about herself, however.) What she asserts could be asserted by someone else using different words. Diyan makes the same claim when she says (in Indonesian), "*Tom Sawyer menghadiri upacara pengkebumian dirinya.*" Diyan's assertion is certainly not about Sally or Sally's action or the words Sally used. So neither is Sally's.

Sally's claim is that the novel *Tom Sawyer* is such that to behave in a certain way, to engage in an act of pretense of a certain kind while participating in a game authorized for it, is fictionally to speak the truth. Sally and Diyan both pretend in the manner in question. They indicate the relevant kind of pretense by exemplifying it.[15] Let's name this kind of pretense K. Sally's (and Diyan's) assertion can then be paraphrased as follows:

(1b) *The Adventures of Tom Sawyer* is such that one who engages in pretense of kind K in a game authorized for it makes it fictional of himself in that game that he speaks truly.

Paraphrases of this form work for ordinary statements generally. In saying (5) ("Giant mosquitoes raised in the North Woods were used to drill wells in Arizona") Robert asserts that

(5a) The Paul Bunyan stories are such that one who engages in pretense of kind K^* in a game authorized for them makes it fictional of himself in that game that he speaks truly,

15. I will shortly consider a speaker, Sam, who asserts what Sally and Diyan do without engaging in pretense.

where K^* is a kind of pretense exemplified by Robert's utterance of (5).

What are the kinds of pretense K and K^*? When there is no apparent reference to fictitious entities, as in Robert's case, there is a purely descriptive way of specifying the relevant kind of pretense. Robert pretends to assert the proposition that giant mosquitoes raised in the North Woods were used to drill wells in Arizona; fictionally he does so. This is what counts as engaging in pretense of kind K^*. Robert's claim, then, is that

> (5b) The Paul Bunyan stories are such that one who fictionally asserts that giant mosquitoes raised in the North Woods were used to drill wells in Arizona, in a game authorized for these stories, makes it fictional of himself in that game that he speaks truly.

It is easy to see how this can be said by someone else using different words. Roberto might utter, "Mosquitos gigantes criados en los Bosques del Norte fueron utilizados para perforar pozos en Arizona," thereby pretending to assert that giant mosquitoes from the North Woods were used to drill wells in Arizona, and actually asserting that to so pretend in a game authorized for the Paul Bunyan stories is fictionally to speak truly.

The last formulation suggests a simpler one which, although not strictly equivalent, is near enough for many purposes. What is it about the Paul Bunyan stories by virtue of which one who fictionally asserts that giant mosquitoes raised in the North Woods were used to drill wells in Arizona, in an authorized game, fictionally speaks truly? The fact that it is fictional in those stories that giant mosquitoes raised in the North Woods were used to drill wells in Arizona.[16] So Robert's assertion might be glossed as, simply,

> (5c) It is fictional in the Paul Bunyan stories that giant mosquitoes raised in the North Woods were used to drill wells in Arizona.[17]

This gives the same result as the familiar suggestion that in saying (5) Robert has merely omitted, left implicit, some such phrase as "it is fictional in the Paul Bunyan stories that," or "it is true in the stories that." But it is misleading to think of (5) as derived from (5c)

16. Since this is fictional in the stories, it is fictional in any game authorized for them. So when it is fictional in an authorized game that one claims this to be so, it is fictional in it that what one claims is true.

17. See § 10.5.

by abbreviation. The shorter statement is better regarded as the primary one.

There is no corresponding simple paraphrase or gloss of Sally's "Tom Sawyer attended his own funeral," for reasons already mentioned. The longer paraphrase, (5b), of Robert's remark has the advantage over the shorter one of displaying the affinity between Robert's statement and other ordinary statements such as Sally's.

Sally's assertion ("Tom Sawyer attended his own funeral") is about a kind of pretense that I dubbed kind K. I know of no informative individuating description that can be given of this kind of pretense. To pretend in this way is not to pretend to assert the proposition that Tom Sawyer attended his own funeral, if there is no such proposition. It is to pretend to make an assertion, more specifically, to pretend to assert de re of someone that he attended his own funeral. But not all acts of pretense of *this* sort are of kind K. We need not insist that an individuating description be provided, however. The reference of "K" can be fixed by pointing to examples, such as the pretense Sally herself displays, although the meaning of "K" is not tied to any particular instances.[18]

Sally specifies K by indicating, displaying, a single instance of it, her own act of pretense. This would not suffice without some understanding about what kind of a kind K is, for there are many different kinds to which Sally's act of pretense belongs. One can specify a shade of color by pointing to a single instance, but only if it is understood that the kind indicated is a shade of color, one whose instances are exactly alike in color. Sally can succeed in indicating K by displaying the one instance only if there is an understanding about how to decide whether another act of pretense belongs to the kind indicated. This does not mean that we must be able to extract a crucial (nonrelational) property from the sample which we can check for in its absence. But we must know what relation an act of pretense must bear to the sample to be of the same relevant kind. What relation does Diyan's act of pretense bear to Sally's by virtue of which both belong to the same kind of the right kind?

Robert and Roberto will point the way. Let us for a moment think of them as participating in a single extended game of make-believe in which the Paul Bunyan stories are props. It is fictional in this game that both of them make the same claim, assert the same proposition. This is the crucial relation between their acts of pretense. It happens

18. I am relying on Kripke's account of natural kind terms in *Naming and Necessity*.

also that there really is a proposition—the proposition that giant mosquitoes raised in the North Woods were used to drill wells in Arizona—which fictionally both assert. But this is not essential. There is no proposition which fictionally both Sally and Diyan assert. Nonetheless it is fictional, in an extended game understood to include both of their actions, that there is a single proposition which both assert. Fictionally both attribute the property of having attended one's own funeral to someone; and fictionally there is a single person to whom both attribute this property. It happens that fictionally they use the same name, "Tom Sawyer," to refer to the person to whom they attribute this property. But this is not necessary either. Instead of "Tom Sawyer attended his own funeral" Sally might say, "Huckleberry Finn's best friend attended his own funeral." It still is fictional that what she asserts is what she would assert in saying "Tom Sawyer attended his own funeral." One might even make up a new name. Diyan might announce, "Let's call Tom Sawyer Su Quitopo, and then assert, "Su Quitopo attended his own funeral" (or "Su Quitopo menghadiri upacara pengkebumian diriunya"). In either case it will be fictional that what she asserts is what Sally asserts in saying "Tom Sawyer attended his own funeral"; the pretense is still of kind K. And what is actually asserted remains the same—that *The Adventures of Tom Sawyer* is such that to so pretend in an authorized game is fictionally to speak truly.[19]

Is it legitimate to think of Sally and Diyan as participating in a single extended game of make-believe? I have usually regarded different appreciators as playing their own separate games. But it is not obvious that they must be so regarded, even if each is unaware of the other's participation. (They could be thought of in both ways at once; we might regard Sally as playing a game of her own, which also is part of a larger game in which Diyan also participates.) In any case, we can regard this inclusive game as an *unofficial* but very natural one, like ones I will discuss in the following section.[20]

19. If space is relative, if nothing is in motion or at rest simpliciter but only relative to something else, one might specify a class of things as those that are at rest relative to a given object, e.g., Saturn, by indicating one member of the class (e.g., Saturn) and the relation other things must bear to it to be members. It is in this way that kind K is to be specified.

The affinity to Davidson's account of indirect discourse will be obvious: "When I say that Galileo said that the earth moves, I represent Galileo and myself as same-sayers" ("On Saying That").

20. An alternative account of what makes Sally's and Diyan's pretense of the same kind might be in terms of the actual circumstances by virtue of which it is fictional that they assert the same proposition—perhaps the fact that if Sally and Diyan were making genuine assertions, they would be asserting the same proposition.

I understand Sally and Diyan, as well as Robert and Roberto, to be engaging in pretense as they make genuine assertions. But one need not engage in pretense in order to assert what they assert. One must specify the relevant kind of pretense, but this can be done without exemplifying it. Sam says what Sally does, "Tom Sawyer attended his own funeral," but not in a spirit of pretense. Like Sally, he is (genuinely) asserting that *The Adventures of Tom Sawyer* is such that to engage in pretense of kind *K* is, in authorized games, fictionally to speak the truth. But he refers to *K* not by displaying an example of it but by going through the motions of pretending in that manner, by using words which if used pretendingly would most likely be used in that kind of pretense.

What is the fate of fictional entities after all this? There is a sense in which we do not have a ready paraphrase of Sally's assertion that eliminates her apparent reference to Tom Sawyer, another way of saying the same thing in ordinary English. The paraphrase I suggested does not contain a reference to Tom Sawyer. But it requires the introduction of a technical term, "*K*," which was explained, whose reference was fixed, by pointing to the use of a sentence containing the name "Tom Sawyer," to an instance of the kind *K*. Should we conclude that a commitment to fictional entities is deeply embedded in our language and conceptual scheme, even if there aren't really any? No. For it is the use of names like "Tom Sawyer" *in pretense* that enables us to fix the reference of "*K*." To pretend to refer to someone with the name "Tom Sawyer" is not in any interesting sense to be committed to there being a referent of that name. What we should conclude is that it is our pretendings to assert, our games of make-believe, that are central to our conceptual scheme. It is that, not an ontological commitment to fictional entities, that plays an important role in our structuring of the world.

Some readers will be distressed by the complexity of my paraphrases of what appear to be simple, everyday utterances. They need not worry. If what Sally means by (1), made explicit, is as complicated as (1b), this is a good reason to have the simpler way of saying it. One would expect the language to devise a manageable equivalent of (1b) just because (1b) is so awkwardly complex. But how can Sally be meaning all *that* when she utters (1)? Certainly she does not have anything like (1b) specifically in mind, nor does she have the resources to formulate it. In one sense she does *not* mean all that. She thinks in terms of statements like (1), not ones like (1b). So for her, what she says *is* relatively simple.

(Simplicity and complexity, we might add, are in the syntax of one's language or the language of one's thought.) Nevertheless, (1b) indicates, in an explicit form needed for theoretical purposes, the state of affairs Sally claims to obtain when she asserts (1).

One concern about complex paraphrases of seemingly simple utterances may be this: A candidate paraphrase might be constructed by stitching together in an ad hoc fashion multiple clauses designed to avoid an assortment of counterexamples. The result is likely to be an unperspicuous jumble which leaves it unclear why what is said is worth saying, why, if the paraphrase captures what is said by means of the paraphrased utterance, people should be interested in it. (The presumption is that what we have simple ways of saying are things we sometimes find it important to say.) My paraphrases do not have this problem. The facts people express by means of statements like (1), if my account is right, are facts one would expect them to find important. Given that the (authorized) games appreciators play with works of art are important, people are bound to be interested in what sorts of pretendings-to-assert are, fictionally in these games, assertions of truths, in when participants are and when they are not, fictionally, speaking truly.

In proposing a paraphrase one should also be prepared to explain how it happens that what is said came to be expressed in the particular way people express it. Why do we use one abbreviated or simplified or indirect way of saying it rather than some other one? My account of ordinary statements has a convincing story to tell on this score also. It is common, as we noted, to express the idea that a certain kind of behavior is appropriate simply by engaging in it. To say things like "Tom attended his own funeral" assertively is just another instance of this common pattern.

Of the various kinds of statements containing apparent references to fictitious entities, it is not the ordinary ones that create the most pressure to recognize such entities. Others are more ornery. But even the orneriest seem to me to be recognizable variants of the ordinary pattern. I will investigate two main kinds of variation, one in the following section and the other in § 11.1.

10.4.   UNOFFICIAL GAMES

Ah, happy, happy boughs! that cannot shed
Your leaves, nor ever bid the Spring adieu;

> And, happy melodist, unwearied,
>   For ever piping songs for ever new;
> More happy love! more happy, happy love!
>   For ever warm and still to be enjoyed,
>   For ever panting, and for ever young;
>   John Keats, "Ode on a Grecian Urn"

> Michelangelo dissolves the end wall of the Sistine Chapel so that
> we can exit the church through heaven and hell, moving out of
> the Renaissance toward Caravaggio's world, a world of sensuality
> and spatial incongruity beyond even Michelangelo's imagination.
>   Frank Stella, *Working Space*

Games authorized for works of fiction—games in which it is the function of works to serve as props—are not the only ones people play with them. Often we devise our own, or modify authorized ones, altering the principles whereby works contribute to the generation of fictional truths. We play special games for special purposes. Sometimes in doing so we follow unorthodox traditions of one sort or another. Sometimes we improvise on the spot. Many unauthorized games are fragmentary, our participation in them constituting a momentary turn in the course of a conversation. Sometimes—even more so than in the case of authorized games—we do not so much participate in them as merely allude to them. Nevertheless much of what we say concerning representations must be understood in terms of such games. In order to avoid the implication that they are somehow illicit, I will speak of *unofficial* games of make-believe rather than unauthorized ones.

One can of course stipulate arbitrary principles of make-believe, thereby establishing a new kind of game. But many unofficial games are perfectly natural and are readily understood without stipulation. A game in which to caress a sculpture of a person is fictionally to caress a person is unauthorized for most traditional sculptures. It is not the function of most eighteenth-century portraits to serve as props in games in which throwing darts at them is fictionally to throw darts at the person portrayed. But these games could hardly be more easily grasped. To insist on pursuing silly questions is frequently to transform an authorized game into an unofficial one, as when one demands to know why the diners in Leonardo's *Last Supper* all sit on one side of the table (see § 4.5).

Many nonordinary statements made in pretense can be construed as contributions to unofficial games. Even if the speaker is not actually engaging in pretense, such statements, in the contexts in which they are made, often suggest or imply unofficial games of certain sorts, ones in which a person speaking similarly in a similar context might well be participating. To say, concerning a performance of Gilbert and Sullivan's *H.M.S. Pinafore,* whose action takes place on the ship's quarterdeck,

(6) The orchestra is in the water,

is to suggest a game in which the orchestra pit is, fictionally, the ocean off the bow of the ship.

(7) A vandal attacked Mary with a hammer,

in a context in which reference to the attack on Michelangelo's *Pietà* can be expected, suggests a game in which attacking a sculpture is fictionally to attack what the sculpture portrays.

(8) Little Orphan Annie has been eight years old for over forty
     years now

fits easily into a slightly unorthodox but fully intelligible game in which the fact that the cartoon strip has lasted for forty years plays a crucial role in making it fictional that there is a wide-eyed girl named Annie who has been eight for that long. To say of an actress playing Desdemona

(9) She died nine times in the last two weeks

is readily understood to involve a slightly perverse game of a not dissimilar kind.

Comparisons between characters in different works can be thought of as contributions to unofficial games which combine in natural ways games authorized for the various works.

(10) Robinson Crusoe was more resourceful than Gulliver

suggests a game in which Defoe's *Robinson Crusoe* and Swift's *Gulliver's Travels* are both props, and in which each functions much as it does in games authorized for it. To speak informally, Crusoe and Gulliver are both characters in the world of the combination game, and each brings to it the degree of resourcefulness he exhibits in his home world.

Identifying a character of one work with a character of another, as when one says concerning Homer's *Odyssey* and Tennyson's poem *Ulysses*

(11) Ulysses is Odysseus,

may be to play a game similarly combining these two works.[21]

What happens if there is a conflict between two works that are props in a single unofficial game? In the *Odyssey*, Odysseus (= Ulysses) returns home. In the *Inferno* he does not.[22] This conflict need not be confronted in the fragmentary unofficial game in which, speaking of the *Odyssey* and the *Inferno*, one remarks, "Odysseus is Ulysses." Probably it is clear that, in saying this, fictionally one speaks truly, but there is no need to dwell on other aspects of the unofficial game in which these two works are props. If we do insist on pursuing the game further, there are several alternatives. We might take it to be fictional that a person speaks truly if he says, "Odysseus (= Ulysses) both did and did not return home," or alternatively, if he says, "Odysseus (= Ulysses) returned home, but is falsely portrayed in the *Inferno* as not doing so." (The latter way of understanding the game makes the *Inferno* a reflexive prop, one that generates fictional truths about itself.) One may well dismiss the matter on the grounds that the questions are silly.

How are assertive uses of statements like (6)–(11) to be understood? If the speaker is making a serious assertion, in addition to implying and possibly participating in a game of make-believe of a certain sort, what is he asserting, and under what conditions is his assertion true?

The answers parallel those we gave for assertive uses of ordinary statements, except that in place of authorized games we must substitute the implied unofficial games. Suppose that the speaker is engaging in pretense, participating verbally in a game of the implied sort as well as genuinely asserting something. Then he is asserting something true if and only if it is fictional in that game that he speaks truly. If he is not engaging in pretense, what he asserts is true if and only if it would be fictional in a game of the implied sort that he speaks truly were he playing one. What is he asserting? That the situation is such that to pretend in the way exemplified or indicated is fictionally to speak truly, in a game of the implied sort.

This account can be taken to subsume the one we gave for ordinary

21. If it is fictional in this case that one speaks truly, this is so because of a certain causal connection between the two works, a causal connection of whatever kind it is that occurs between a biography of X and a commentary on it written by someone who knows of X only from the biography, by virtue of which the name "X" in the commentary refers to whomever it refers to in the biography.

22. I borrow this example from Howell, "Fictional Objects," p. 171.

statements. We need only take ordinary statements in their contexts to imply games authorized for the works under discussion. This gives us a unified treatment of assertive uses of both ordinary statements and the nonordinary ones discussed so far.

But there is a difference in how the implied games are to be specified in the two kinds of cases. Implied unofficial games are to be specified as games in which such-and-such principles of generation are operative. Games implied by ordinary statements are to be specified as ones that are authorized by the work in question, whatever their principles of generation. What Doreen asserts in saying "There is a unicorn in a corral," on viewing one of the Unicorn Tapestries, is true just in case the tapestry is such that, in whatever games are authorized for it, if it is fictional that a person claims there is a unicorn in a corral, it is fictional that truth is spoken. Doreen's assertion is one that would be true if the colors of the tapestry were different from what they actually are, but, because of a compensating difference in the games of make-believe authorized for the work, it still is fictional in authorized games that there is a unicorn in a corral.[23] What Doreen (actually) asserts would not be true if the tapestry were embedded in a cultural context in which games authorized for it have different principles of generation such that it is not fictional in authorized games that a unicorn is in a corral. By contrast, the claim one makes in saying (6), for instance, or (10) is true if and only if, in any game with such-and-such principles of generation, to pretend in a given manner is fictionally to speak truly.

A wide range of statements concerning fiction can be understood in terms of implied unofficial games of make-believe in the manner I have described. Here is an assortment of additional examples:

(12) Oscar Wilde killed off Dorian Gray by putting a knife through his heart.
(13) Most children like E.T. better than Mickey Mouse.
(14) Sherlock Holmes is more famous than any other detective.
(15) Vanquished by reality, by Spain, Don Quixote died in his native village in the year 1614. He was survived but a short time by Miguel de Cervantes.[24]

How do we decide what sort of unofficial game is implied in a given case? How do we know whether to look for an implied unofficial

23. It is arguable that the stories could not have contained different words and still be the stories they are. Nevertheless we can ask what would be the case if they did.
24. Borges, "Parable of Cervantes and the *Quixote*," p. 242.

game at all, rather than taking a given statement to be ordinary? There is no easy recipe. It is by virtue of a complicated and shifting array of contextual features and prior precedents that one construal of a given statement is more reasonable than another. The prospects for systematizing the principles involved are no better than the prospects for systematizing the principles of generation for work worlds or the "rules" for understanding metaphors.

There is, I suppose, an initial presumption that statements concerning fiction are to be regarded as ordinary in the absence of good reasons to construe them otherwise (and a similar presumption in favor of interpreting utterances literally rather than metaphorically). Beyond that, a principle of charity is operative. Understanding an utterance in a way that would make it an absurd or blatantly false or trivial or stupid thing to say is to be avoided if an alternative is available. Speakers are to be saved from assininity, when possible. It is blatantly obvious that to say (10) ("Robinson Crusoe was more resourceful than Gulliver") would not be fictionally to speak the truth in games authorized either for *Robinson Crusoe* or for *Gulliver's Travels*. (Perhaps it would be fictional that the speaker does not even speak sensibly.) It is blatantly obvious that if the utterance were construed as an ordinary statement, what the speaker genuinely asserts would not be true. So we look for a salient unofficial game and a more reasonable nonordinary construal. In this case we take an unofficial game in which *Robinson Crusoe* and *Gulliver's Travels* are both props to be implied. It is at least arguable that to say "Robinson Crusoe was more resourceful than Gulliver" in such a game would be, fictionally, to speak truly, and hence that a genuine assertion made by saying this would be true. The principle of charity is no guarantee of truth, of course. "A vandal attacked Mary with a wrench" may well imply the same game that "A vandal attacked Mary with a hammer" does, but to say the former is fictionally, in that game, to speak falsely.

What besides charity is involved? Precedents are important; there are certain more or less standard patterns of implication, even when the implied games are not authorized ones. The practice of combining unrelated works in a single unofficial game is well entrenched. Unofficial games in which to author a fiction about people and things of certain kinds is fictionally to create such, as when one says

(16) Jane Austen created Emma Woodhouse,

are commonplace, as are games in which to make it fictional that something has certain properties is fictionally to give something those properties.

Other implications take more novel routes. Consider

(17) The guests at the Last Supper are gradually fading away,

said during a conversation about Leonardo's fading *Last Supper,* as well as (9) and Stella's comment about the Sistine Chapel. The difference between relatively standard ways in which unofficial games are implied and novel ones bears comparison with that between moribund and fresh metaphors.

The unofficial games I have mentioned so far, though not authorized by works of fiction, are inspired by them and are easily thought of as modifications of authorized games. But unofficial games need not have anything to do with authorized ones and can arise with no works of fiction in sight. An anthropologist discussing the tenets of an alien religion might play along with its practitioners, speaking as they would. "This is the ceremony that brings rain," he might say, or "Vishnu needs to be appeased." These remarks may in effect be observations about what the natives think. But in speaking thus the anthropologist may be participating in a game, or hinting at one, in which what the natives believe is thereby fictional, one in which it is fictional that he speaks truly just in case his utterance is in accord with their beliefs. Games based in this way on what others believe rather than on works of fiction, or on what appears or is purported to be the case, or what one takes to be illusion or superstition, games in which the participant "plays along with," colludes or connives with, beliefs he does not accept, will be important shortly.[25]

10.5. VARIATIONS

The way of treating statements concerning fiction that I have proposed is not meant to be taken rigidly. A certain looseness infects their interpretation, especially when unofficial games of make-believe are involved (even if it is clear what unofficial games are implied).

A similar looseness is to be found in simpler cases. The action of

25. Evans emphasizes that make-believe can grow out of "shared illusions . . . or mistaken testimony, not originally the product of any artistic or imaginative process" (*Varieties of Reference,* p. 353).

discussing Harold's prize may serve to get across to an audience several different pieces of information (in addition to whatever is said explicitly). The speaker may, by discussing the award, succeed in informing her listeners that it is proper or appropriate to discuss it; she may inform them also of a salient circumstance that is responsible for this propriety, of the fact that the award has been officially announced, for example. Probably it is by means of indicating the former that the speaker convinces her audience of the latter. It is because listeners are made aware of the propriety of discussing Harold's good fortune that they take the condition for this propriety to be satisfied.

A speaker does not necessarily assert whatever she manages to induce her audience to believe. What is being asserted in this case will depend on details of the example, on features of the context and/or the speaker's state of mind which we need not try to specify, as well as on one's favored account of assertion. It may be plausible to regard the speaker as asserting that it is proper to discuss the award, while implying or suggesting that the official announcement has been made. Or she may be best regarded as asserting the latter and merely implying or suggesting the former. Or she may be asserting both, or neither. Or there may be no clear answer as to exactly what assertion she is making.

Statements concerning fiction may present similar choices. I suggested that in making such a statement one asserts that to pretend in a certain manner in games of an implied sort is fictionally to speak truly; one asserts that it is in this way appropriate to so pretend. But it may be more reasonable in some cases to take the speaker to be asserting the presence of a certain circumstance responsible for the propriety. To say (6) ("The orchestra is in the water") may be simply a slightly colorful way of claiming that the orchestra is in the pit where it belongs. For this is what makes it fictional in games of the implied sort, of a person who pretends in the relevant manner, that he speaks truly. On this interpretation the speaker's assertion is not about pretense or games of make-believe. Nevertheless pretense comes into play. The speaker may be engaging in pretense as a means of asserting what he does; it may be fictional (in an unofficial game) that he is claiming that the orchestra is in the water. Probably he is calling attention to pretense of that kind even if he is not engaging in it, and implying or suggesting, if not asserting, that to pretend thus in a game of a certain sort is fictionally to speak truly. It is by implying or suggesting this that he expects to inform his audience of the presence of the orchestra in the pit. The suitability of the words "The orchestra is in the water" for asserting that the orchestra is in the pit depends on their conjuring up this pretense.

Let us look at a different example:

(18) Napoleon was more pompous than Caesar

(understood not as a historical observation but as a claim concerning Shakespeare's play and Tolstoy's novel, one that might be expressed as "Shakespeare's Julius Caesar was more pompous than Tolstoy's Napoleon"). A paraphrase of the kind I suggested earlier would go like this:

(18a) *Julius Caesar* and *War and Peace* are such that to pretend to assert that Napoleon is more pompous than Caesar, in a game of such and such a sort, is fictionally to speak truly,

where games of the relevant sort are certain unofficial ones in which the two works serve together as props. But the speaker may seem merely to be drawing a comparison between the worlds of the two works, not saying anything about any unofficial games of make-believe. We may find plausible some such paraphrase as this:

(18b) There is a degree of pompousness such that it is fictional in *War and Peace* that Napoleon is pompous to that degree, and it is fictional in *Julius Caesar* that Caesar is not.[26]

These two proposed paraphrases are not equivalent, but they are closely related. The truth of (18a) depends on the truth of (18b). Unofficial games of the kind mentioned in (18a) are ones whose fictional truths depend in certain ways on what is fictional in the worlds of the two works. Propositions about the degree of Caesar's or Napoleon's pomposity, which are fictional in *Julius Caesar* or *War and Peace,* are fictional also in the unofficial combination games. If these propositions are as described in (18b), it is fictional in these games that Napoleon is more pompous than Caesar, and a participant who fictionally asserts that he is fictionally speaks truly.

So we can expect some looseness between the two interpretations. Saying (18) may serve to get across to an audience either or both of the facts expressed by (18a) and (18b). Depending on the circumstances (and one's account of assertion) it may be reasonable to regard the speaker as asserting either of them (or both, or neither).

26. See Howell, "Fictional Objects," p. 154; Parsons, *Non-Existent Objects,* pp. 169–170; and Parsons' reference to Prior.

Probably the fact expressed by (18b) is more important than that expressed by (18a). People are likely to be more interested in what is fictional in work worlds (and hence in authorized games) than in what is fictional in a more or less ad hoc unofficial game. So perhaps (18) is more likely to be used to make the claim paraphrased by (18b) than that paraphrased by (18a). But the means by which one makes the former claim, in using this sentence, is that of indicating, implying the fact about the unofficial game that (18a) expresses.

The reader may want to try out similar alternative paraphrases of other statements. To assert

(11) Ulysses is Odysseus,
(12) Oscar Wilde killed off Dorian Gray by putting a knife through his heart,
(14) Sherlock Holmes is more famous than any other detective,
(19) The chess players have been studying the board intently for over a century without making a move (said with reference to Daumier's *Chess Players*)

may amount to asserting, respectively, that

(11a) Tennyson's *Ulysses* bears such and such a genetic relation to Homer's *Odyssey*,
(12a) Oscar Wilde wrote *The Picture of Dorian Gray* in such a way that to pretend in a certain manner [the manner in which a reader normally would pretend in saying "Dorian Gray died of a knife through the heart"] in a game authorized for *The Picture of Dorian Gray* is fictionally to speak truly,
(14a) There is a degree of fame such that no real detective is famous to that degree, and to pretend in a certain manner [in the manner in which one who says "Sherlock Holmes is famous to that degree" normally would be pretending] in a game authorized for the Sherlock Holmes stories is fictionally to speak truly,
(19a) Daumier's *Chess Players,* which portrays chess players intently studying the board, has existed for over a century.

Considered by themselves, these paraphrases appear to be a diverse lot. To rest with them alone would be to treat the paraphrased statements in an ad hoc, piecemeal fashion. But each of the paraphrases specifies a salient circumstance by virtue of which one who utters the sentence in question in pretense would fictionally be speaking truly, in an implied unofficial game. This explains how we get to the various different paraphrases in each case, how it happens that uttering the words in question serves as a way of asserting what the paraphrases express. This common background role of unofficial games gives us the "smooth and uniform" handling of these and similar statements Howell rightly insists on. Indeed we have gone one better. We have uncovered a systematic connection between statements like these and ordinary ones, ones that concern authorized rather than unofficial games.

In § 10.3 we noted an alternative way of paraphrasing some ordinary statements. Rather than taking (5) ("Giant mosquitoes raised in the North Woods were used to drill wells in Arizona") to be the claim that fictionally to assert that giant mosquitoes from the North Woods were used to drill wells in Arizona, in a game authorized for the Paul Bunyan stories, is fictionally to speak truly, we might construe it simply as the claim that it is fictional in those stories that such mosquitoes were so used. This alternative fits the by now familiar pattern. The second paraphrase expresses the fact that makes the first one true.

Some implausible paraphrases fit this pattern also. The arrangement of colors and shapes in Breughel's *Wedding Dance* is responsible for the fact that it is fictional in games authorized for it that one speaks truly when fictionally one asserts that peasants are making merry. Why shouldn't one say "Peasants are making merry" as a way of describing this arrangement? It is not inconceivable that one should do so, of course. But a statement detailing the relevant colored splotches would hardly seem to capture what is said in normal cases. Part of the explanation for the failure of this paraphrase is that ordinarily we are not much interested in the relevant combination of colors and shapes for its own sake, but are very interested in, and so are likely to talk about, what is fictional in the world of the painting and in the worlds of games authorized for it. We may not even notice the precise characteristics of color and line that make it fictional that peasants are making merry.[27]

In other cases circumstances responsible for the fact that pretending in the manner in question is fictionally to speak truly may be of far

---

27. A viewer may be interested in the painting as an abstract design, apart from what fictional truths it generates. But it is unlikely that he will be interested in the particular combination of colors and shapes that makes it fictional that peasants are making merry. Moreover, to indicate these features by saying "Peasants are making merry" is certain to call attention to their representational function rather than to the features themselves.

more interest than the fact that this is fictional. These are the cases in which it is plausible that what the speaker asserts is simply that those circumstances obtain. It is important to note that even when make-believe is involved crucially in determining what it is that a person says, the content of what he says may involve no mention of pretense or make-believe or anything of the sort.

There is room for further tinkering with the interpretation of statements concerning fiction, especially those involving unofficial games.[28] But I expect that most if not all reasonable candidates for paraphrases will be connected in one way or another with the idea that to pretend in a certain manner in a game of a certain sort is fictionally to speak truly. None of the paraphrases I have suggested threatens to force fictional entities on us. Neither, I believe, do any plausible variations in sight.

10.6.   LOGICAL FORM

Paraphrases must preserve the logical form of the statements they paraphrase and the entailment relations obtaining among them. Peter Van Inwagen has expressed skepticism about whether paraphrases like those I propose for statements concerning fiction satisfy this requirement.[29]

> (20) There is a fictional character who, for every novel, either appears in that novel or is a model for a character who does

appears to have a certain complex quantificational structure, he points out, one that validates the inference from (20) to

> (21) If no character appears in every novel, then some character is modeled on another character.

But none of the paraphrases of (20) and (21) I recommend has these logical forms. On our primary model, both will be paraphrased by something of this form:

> To engage in pretense of kind K is fictionally to speak truly in a game of such and such a sort

28. Here is an alternative way of construing "Ulysses is Odysseus." It may be understood that, because of the genetic relation between the two works, one is to keep in mind certain aspects of Homer's *Odyssey* and its authorized games while reading Tennyson's poem. The point of uttering this sentence might be to get this fact across, and *this* may be what is being asserted.

29. "Pretence and Paraphrase," a response to an early sketch of my theory. See also Van Inwagen, "Creatures of Fiction," pp. 304–305.

(the relevant kind of pretense being different in the two cases). An alternative is to regard (20) and (21) as attesting to circumstances which, if present, would make it fictional of one who pretends in the relevant manner that he speaks truly (circumstances concerning the corpus of extant novels). Obviously we cannot expect any such paraphrases to mirror the quantificational structures exhibited by (20) and (21). Paraphrases of neither kind show (20) to entail (21) by virtue of logical form.

Not only can we live with this result; we will thrive on it. Recall, first, that what our paraphrases seek to capture is what speakers say in uttering the sentences cited, not what the sentences themselves mean or what propositions *they* express, if any. What speakers say simply does not have the logical forms indicated by the sentences they use. To assume otherwise would be question begging. But we do need to explain why people use sentences displaying logical forms different from those of what they assert in uttering them. And it certainly *seems* as though what is said by means of (21) follows deductively from what is said by means of (20); it is not easy to envisage accepting (20) while dissenting from (21). If the quantificational structures of what is said do not guarantee this entailment, what does? If the entailment does not hold, why does it seem to? Explanations are easily provided, but first let us say a little more about what speakers might assert by means of (20) and (21).

Utterances of (20) and (21) can be understood to involve unofficial games of a rather ordinary sort, ones with some approximation of the following features: (a) All novels are props in them and most of what is fictional in any novel is fictional in them; the unofficial games combine the games authorized for each individual novel in a way familiar from § 10.4. (b) It is fictional in these combination games that the universe is divided into realms corresponding to the various novels.[30] To say that "a character appears in a certain novel" is, fictionally, to locate a person in a certain realm. (c) To write a novel of a certain sort is to make it fictional of oneself, in games of the implied sort, that one creates people ("characters") and endows them with certain properties. (Compare "Jane Austen created Emma Wood-house.") (d) When, as we say, an author "models a character on some preexisting character," it is fictional that he creates someone to be like some other person, that he makes someone in the image of someone else. (In speaking of "characters" rather than "people" the speaker

---

30. This is not an uncommon feature of unofficial games that combine other games, although there may be little to be said about what fictionally these realms are or what it is fictionally for things to belong to the same or different ones. (See § 11.1.)

betrays his pretense, but this does not affect the content of the assertion. See § 11.1.)

It is fictional in unofficial games of the kind implied, no doubt, that (20) and (21)—the sentences themselves—express propositions that have the logical structures they appear to have, ones by virtue of which (20) entails (21). And it is fictional of Ellen, if she utters (20) assertively while participating in such a game, that what she asserts entails, by virtue of logical form alone, what would be asserted by (21). This partly explains the impression that what Ellen actually asserts by means of (20) thus entails what would be asserted by (21).

What does Ellen genuinely assert by means of (20)? In the simplest and primary case (unlikely though it may be) she is participating in an unofficial game of the sort described and asserting that to pretend as she does is fictionally to speak truly. Her pretense is a kind of pretending to assert something of the form displayed by that sentence; it is fictional that she asserts a proposition of that form. So naturally she uses that sentence, even though what she actually asserts about this kind of pretense has a very different form.

If Ellen speaks of this kind of pretense without engaging in it, she still refers to it. If, rather than speaking about it she is pointing out the presence of circumstances by virtue of which to so pretend is fictionally to speak truly, it is by indicating the kind of pretense that she calls attention to the circumstances she claims to obtain. In either case the sentence she uses, (20), displaying the logical form it does, suits her purpose, since to pretend in the manner she refers to or indicates is fictionally to assert something of that form.

But it is *only* fictional, not true, that (20) has a quantificational structure such as to entail (21). And it is at most fictional, not true, that what is asserted by means of (20) entails by virtue of logical form alone what is asserted by (21). Nevertheless, one may be speaking truly in asserting

(22) Statement (20) entails (21) by virtue of logical form alone.

Assertions of (22) can themselves be understood as we understand other statements concerning fiction. The speaker, in the primary case, indicates a kind of pretense—the pretense of asserting that (20) entails (21) by virtue of logical form alone—and claims that to so pretend in an unofficial game of an implied sort (the kind implied by (20) and (21)) is fictionally to speak truly. *This* claim is true, even though (20) does not entail (21) by virtue of logical form alone; (22) taken literally is false. The moral of the story, again, is that we must take care to distinguish between fictionality and truth, between what is the case and what is merely pretended to be the case.

The likelihood of confusion is enhanced by the fact that what is asserted by (20) probably *does* entail what is asserted by (21), though not by virtue of logical form alone. The principles constituting the implied games of make-believe are likely to be such that it cannot be fictional that to assert (20) is to speak truly unless it is fictional that to assert (21) is to speak truly. The unofficial games would have to be rather exotic logical fantasies for this not to be so. And the principles are likely to be such that the circumstances required to make it fictional that one speaks truly in asserting (20) are ones that make it fictional that one speaks truly in asserting (21). No wonder it is difficult to conceive of (20) being true and (21) false.

11
Existence

11.1. BETRAYAL AND DISAVOWAL

When people pretend, they sometimes betray their pretense; they indicate more or less explicitly that they are just pretending. Ordinary statements concerning fiction and the nonordinary ones considered so far will be misunderstood if their pretense goes unrecognized. So betrayal may be called for. To assert

(22) A whaler with an ivory leg pursued a great white whale

is to speak as though one is seriously asserting that such an event took place. We must judge from the context that the speaker is only pretending to do so (or alluding to such pretense). When there is danger of confusion, one can betray the pretense. One may say, for instance,

(23) In Melville's novel *Moby Dick* a whaler with an ivory leg pursued a great white whale.

The betrayal calls attention to the pretense (actual or implied) and makes it clear that that is what is being talked about. (It probably does not in this case alter what it is that is being genuinely asserted. The speaker asserts that to pretend in the manner indicated—to pretend to assert that a whaler with an ivory leg pursued a great white whale—in a game authorized for *Moby Dick* is fictionally to speak truly.)

Betrayal is an important job of phrases like "in the story" and "in the world of the picture." But it can be effected by a variety of other means as well. Pretense can be betrayed by speaking explicitly of "(fictional) characters," as in

(24) Mrs. Moore, a character in E. M. Forster's *Passage to India,* had a nervous breakdown.

Statements concerning unofficial games of make-believe can have their pretense betrayed, as can ordinary ones. One may say,

(25) The orchestra is in the water, as it were,

in place of (6) ("The orchestra is in the water"), or

(26) The Robinson Crusoe in Defoe's novel was more resourceful than Swift's Gulliver,

rather than (10) ("Robinson Crusoe was more resourceful than Gulliver").

Does the speaker engage in the pretense he betrays? Is betrayed pretense still pretense? Certainly it can be. But it doesn't matter if it is not, since one may allude to a kind of pretense and talk about it without exemplifying it. The speaker of (23) may not actually be engaging in the pretense which he betrays. The betrayal indicates that he is not really claiming that a whaler with an ivory leg pursued a great white whale, that he is *at most* pretending to do so, and that in any case it is this kind of pretense that he is talking about.

Sometimes we go beyond betrayal to *disavow* what is pretended, declaring in effect that if one were really to assert in the pretended manner, one would not be asserting a truth. A person who says,

(27) It is *only* in Kafka's *Metamorphosis* that someone was transformed into an insect,

not only makes it clear that he is not claiming that someone was transformed into an insect. He also declares that to claim this would not be to assert a truth, that nobody ever was really transformed into an insect.

We observed that the betrayal in (23) does not affect the content of the assertion; it serves to clarify that "a whaler with an ivory leg pursued a great white whale" is to be taken as an (ordinary) statement concerning fiction. But the disavowal in (27) is part (at least) of what the speaker asserts. He does not assert merely what would be asserted by the ordinary statement "Someone was transformed into an insect." He indicates a certain kind of pretense in order to disavow what is pretended, not just to claim that to pretend thus in games of a certain sort would be fictionally to speak truly.

Betrayal and disavowal have obvious affinities with the practice discussed in § 7.6 of designing representations so as to discourage participation, employing devices that call special attention to the medium or to the fact that a story is just a story or a picture just a picture. In both instances pretense, participation—be it actual or envisaged, betrayed or disavowed or discouraged—is nonetheless central.

The kinds of pretense we have considered so far are kinds of pretending-to-assert; to engage in pretense of these kinds is, fictionally, to perform an act of assertion. Some of them involve pretendings-to-refer, as when, fictionally, one refers to a certain Tom Sawyer and asserts of him that he attended his own funeral. But sometimes we exemplify or indicate a kind of pretending-to-refer independently of any pretending-to-assert, and go on to comment on it. We do this when we say,

> (28) Gregor Samsa is a (purely fictional) character in *The Metamorphosis.*

In using the name "Gregor Samsa" the speaker pretends to refer to something or alludes to a kind of pretending-to-refer. He then betrays this pretense, making it clear that it is only fictional that he is referring to something. (He also disavows part of what he pretends, as we shall see.)

In this case the speaker acknowledges that to pretend in the indicated manner in a game authorized for *The Metamorphosis* would be fictionally to refer to something. One need not specify the work, however. To say

> (29) Gregor Samsa is a (purely fictional) character

is to acknowledge, while betraying the pretense, only that *there is* a work in whose authorized games so pretending is fictionally to refer successfully. One can avoid acknowledging even this, as in

> (30) Gregor Samsa does not exist.

To betray pretense is to step outside of it and comment on it. In the examples I have discussed, betrayal is effected by means of a phrase appended to words that are or might be uttered in pretense. The appended phrase is not itself uttered in pretense, it seems, nor does it contribute to specifying a kind of pretense. It serves merely to comment on the kind of pretense specified by the words to which it is attached.

But there is a way of regarding many such appendages as being themselves part of a pretense—a pretense different from the one they betray. The form that many betrayals (and disavowals) take is revealing. Statement (29) has the grammatical structure of an ordinary singular statement whereby the speaker attributes a property to the referent of the subject expression. It is not this, of course. Nor does my account of it have the speaker *pretending* to say of something to which he refers as Gregor Samsa that it is a fictional character. Statement (29) would seem to concern games authorized for *The Metamorphosis,* but it is not to be treated as an ordinary statement like "Gregor Samsa was transformed into an insect." For to assert (29), as I am understanding it, is to assert something true; but it is not fictional in a game authorized for *The Metamorphosis,* of one who says this in pretense, that one expresses a truth. (To speak informally, within the novel and within games authorized for it, Gregor is not merely a fictional character but a real person.)

But there may be an unofficial game in which one who says (29) fictionally speaks the truth, a game in which it is fictional that there are two kinds of people: "real" people and "fictional characters." The speaker can be regarded as participating in this unofficial game, as fictionally referring to something by means of the name "Gregor Samsa" and attributing to the referent a property he specifies by the predicate "is a fictional character." (It does not matter that there is no such property as that of being a fictional character. The speaker is pretending that these words pick out a property; it is fictional in the unofficial game that they do.) By engaging in one pretense the speaker betrays another. In fictionally speaking the truth, in the unofficial game, he indicates that he is only pretending, in an authorized game, to refer by means of the proper name (or alluding to such pretense).

It is not surprising that there should be unofficial games of the kind described. Once we pretend to refer to something with the name "Gregor Samsa," the temptation to go on and pretend to attribute properties to what we are referring to will be, for creatures as given to make-believe as humans are, all but irresistible. Sometimes we must indicate that the pretending-to-refer is just pretense, so we betray it. We could, and sometimes do, entirely abandon the pretense, unmask it from without, as when we say, "There is no such thing (or person) as Gregor Samsa," or " 'Gregor Samsa' does not denote anything." But we may prefer to retain something of the form if not the spirit of pretense even as we betray it. The betrayal is effected by means of a further pretense. We pretend to attribute a property to something referred to as "Gregor Samsa" by attaching the predicate "is a fictional character" to the name, thereby making it clear that we are only pretending to refer to something. (One way to let on that one is just joking without simply saying so, seriously, and spoiling the fun, is to push the joke further, to the point of blatant absurdity. One thus makes it obvious that the joke is a joke without having to abandon it.)

Other devices of betrayal can also be thought of as contributions to unofficial games superimposed on authorized ones. Perhaps it is fictional in an unofficial game that "existence is a predicate," or rather that the predicate "exists" expresses a genuine property, one that some but not all things possess, and that "does not exist" expresses its complement. So it might be fictional that one who utters (30) truly attributes a property to someone he refers to as "Gregor Samsa"; one may make this fictional while betraying the pretense of using the name to refer to someone. It may be fictional in an unofficial game that the universe consists of several realms, the "real world" and various "fictional worlds," each with its own inhabitants. To say

(31) In the world of Kafka's *Metamorphosis* a boy was transformed into an insect

may be fictionally to assert, truly, that the transformation of a boy into an insect occurred in a certain part or realm of the universe. (Woody Allen invoked an unofficial game of the latter sort when he expressed a preference for existing in comics rather than in real life.)

It will be noticed that what is fictional in unofficial games like those I have just described, what we pretend to be the case—that there are things that have a property expressed by the predicate "is a merely fictional character," for instance, and that "exists" expresses a property some things lack—is just what some theorists of a realist persuasion claim actually to be the case. Their mistake is one of excessive literal-mindedness, one of mistaking pretense for what is pretended.

11.2.   CLAIMS OF EXISTENCE AND NONEXISTENCE

We recently came close to a way of understanding negative existential statements like (28), (29), and

(30) Gregor Samsa does not exist.

To assert any of these, I suggested, is to indicate and to betray a kind of pretending-to-refer (possibly by engaging in or alluding to a further pretense).[1]

Here is a worry: We want our account of (30) to fit in with a way of treating singular existence claims generally. But many such claims involve no obvious pretense or make-believe, especially ones that

1. It is possible to understand (30) as a claim about what exists "within the story" rather than what "really" exists. So understood it is false and "Gregor exists" is true, both being ordinary statements and neither involving betrayal. I am trying to explicate claims about what "really" exists.

have nothing to do with novels or other works of fiction. People affirm or deny the existence of Vulcan, the Fountain of Youth, Homer, the Loch Ness monster, and the mole in the State Department as well as Gregor Samsa, Gulliver, and Robinson Crusoe. Stephen Schiffer remarked that Gareth Evans' treatment of negative existentials in terms of make-believe seems not to apply to examples such as

(32) Qaddafi does not exist and never has existed: there is no such person. (said "in a possible world just like ours but for the truth of that utterance")

For "the truth conditions of the imagined utterance would surely make no reference to any pretense or make believe engaged in by the speaker and his audience."[2]

We must not be rushed into a blanket dismissal of attempts to explain existence claims in terms of make-believe. Such an account need not presume that the speaker or his audience actually engages in pretense or make-believe, as we know; he may call their attention to a kind of pretense without instantiating it. And the utterance might imply games of a sort no one has ever played or ever will, yet which the audience understands clearly. We remember, also, that unofficial games need not be linked to any recognized work of fiction. Nevertheless, existence claims do not involve make-believe as directly or essentially as do assertions like those discussed in Chapter 10. This goes for affirmations and denials of the existence of Gregor Samsa, Gulliver, and Robinson Crusoe as well as Vulcan, Homer, and the mole in the State Department.

In uttering (30) one betrays a kind of pretense, as we observed. But the betrayal does not constitute the content of the speaker's assertion. His assertion is rather a *disavowal*, and disavowals (those we are considering anyway) are comments not on pretendings but on what is or might be pretended. In using the name "Gregor Samsa" the speaker indicates not only a kind of pretending-to-refer but also a kind of pretending-to-*attempt*-to-refer. What he disavows is the attempt to refer, or attempts to refer of the pretended kind. His claim is that to attempt to refer in this manner would not be to succeed in referring to anything.[3] Pretense comes in only as a way of picking out

2. Schiffer, "Review of Gareth Evans," p. 42.

3. It follows from this that one who pretends to refer (successfully), in the indicated manner, would be *merely* pretending. So he betrays the pretending-to-refer as well as the pretending-to-attempt-to-refer. The awkwardness here derives from the fact that "referring," unlike "asserting," implies success. To refer is to succeed in picking something out; to assert is not always to succeed in saying something true.

the kind of attempted referring he wishes to disavow; he specifies it by pretending to make such an attempt or by indicating this kind of pretense.

There are other ways of picking out kinds of attempted referring. One might do so without conjuring up any pretense, by actually making an attempt of the relevant kind; or one might use words that are or are likely to be used in such an attempt. In asserting (32) or

(33) Vulcan does not exist,

one pronounces a name, "Vulcan" or "Qaddafi," that has actually been used in attempts to refer, and proceeds to disavow attempts of that kind. The speaker does not himself attempt to refer, at least not seriously—since he goes on to pronounce such attempts failures, to disavow them. But the audience knows what sort of attempt he is disavowing if it is familiar with uses of the name by those who believe in Vulcan or Qaddafi. There is no need for the speaker to pretend to attempt to refer, fictionally to do so, or to allude to such pretense, in order to indicate the kind of attempted reference he then disavows. In asserting (30) one does pretend to refer by means of "Gregor Samsa" or indicates such pretense, but this is not essential to the content of one's assertion; what one asserts is simply that to attempt to refer in a certain manner is to fail.

Displaying or indicating a possible or actual act of attempted reference can succeed in picking out a kind to which it belongs only if it is understood what relation other attempts must have to a sample in order to be of the same kind. (See § 10.3.) Make-believe may come into the picture here. Attempts to refer by means of "la Fuente de la Edad," by Ponce de León and by others who believed the same reports of a spring with magical powers, are of the kind one disavows when one says, "The Fountain of Youth does not exist." So are some serious uses of translations of this phrase into other languages, of other names that might have been used in place of it, and of pronouns and definite descriptions appropriately linked to these. What makes these attempts attempts of the same kind is the fact that it is fictional in an implied unofficial game that they are successful references to the same thing. This game is of course one in which what Ponce de León believed is fictional, and in which it is fictional that there is (or was) a single water hole with magical powers that was referred to in all of these instances.

"Gregor Samsa" may never actually have been used in a serious referring attempt of the kind one disavows in saying (30), but we know what would count as making such an attempt. A person who took *The Metamorphosis* to be a serious report and who recounts what he thinks he learned from it would do so. Other (incredibly) naive readers of Kafka's text and people who learn of Gregor from them will be such that, in an obvious game of make-believe, it is fictional that there is a single person named "Gregor Samsa" to whom they all refer. (*This* game may be an authorized one, apart perhaps from the fact that different readers participate in it.)

The details of these games will depend largely on what one takes actually to be required for two (successful) acts of referring to be referrings to the same thing. I believe that historical connections between the instances are crucial. If there happens to be an actual person named "Gregor Samsa" about whom Kafka was entirely igno-rant, to speak about *him* will not be, fictionally, to refer to what a naive reader of *The Metamorphosis* is referring to, and *these* attempts to refer will not be of the relevant kind. I will not try to be more specific than this.

There are alternative ways of explaining what holds a kind of attempted referring together, ones in which make-believe has a less essential role. One is in terms of the circumstances (including histor-ical connections among the instances) responsible for its being fic-tional in games of the relevant sort that a single thing is referred to. Or one might suggest simply that two attempts to refer are of the same kind just in case *if* they are or were successful, the referents are or would be the same. (This last alternative will not do as it stands.)

What about positive (singular) existence claims? They are *avowals* of kinds of attempted reference. To assert

(34) Homer exists

is to claim that to attempt to refer in a certain manner—the manner in which people ordinarily attempt to refer when they use the name "Homer"—is to succeed in referring to something. The speaker's use of "Homer" may itself be an attempt of this kind, and a successful one. This is not incompatible with his pretending to make such an attempt, playing a game in which fictionally he does so, or his allud-ing to such pretense. But he need not do either in order to say what he is saying. He need only specify, in one way or another, the relevant kind of attempted reference and avow it—declare it successful. One who takes the Paul Bunyan stories to be linked (in a certain way) to an actual historical figure might assert "Paul Bunyan exists," perhaps indicating thereby a kind of pretending-to-refer, but asserting simply that to attempt to refer in a certain manner is to succeed.

Existence claims "about fictional entities" thus accord with existence claims generally and differ sharply from much of our other discourse concerning fiction. Much of this discourse consists of assertions that to pretend in a certain manner in a game of a certain sort is fictionally to speak truly. Affirmations and denials of existence are not similarly about pretense or make-believe, even when it is the existence of "fictional entities" that is affirmed or denied.

But this is not the whole story. Many existence claims have more to do with make-believe than this last conclusion indicates, and can be construed as analogous in important ways to other statements concerning fiction. Recall that betrayal of pretense can, in many cases, be thought of as effected by means of a further pretense. The same goes for disavowal, since devices of betrayal often double as devices of disavowal. When one asserts (29) or (30), it may be fictional that one uses "Gregor Samsa" referringly and attributes a property to the referent by means of the predicate "is a (purely fictional) character" or "does not exist." It is by thus pretending to assert that the speaker betrays the pretended reference and, we now know, disavows attempted referrings of the pretended kind. So the statement implies unofficial games in which it is fictional that there are two kinds of people—"actual" ones and "(merely fictional) characters"—or that some people "exist" and others do not.

Other instances of betrayal and/or disavowal are not hard to construe as implying games in which it is fictional that there are "mythical" beasts as well as "real" ones; or that some exploits and adventures and enormous fish that got away are "hoaxes" or are "imaginary" whereas others are "genuine"; or that oases can be either "illusory" or "real"; or that among the many trucks in the universe some are "toys," and bears come in "stuffed" as well as "flesh-and-blood" varieties. (We engage in games like these when we say things like, "Tubby is a very sweet bear and a dear friend; it's too bad he isn't real"; "Lacings, straps, and other devices to keep a [life] jacket from riding up range from effective to nonexistent";[4] and "Mythical beasts are not very dangerous.")

The quotes are there to remind us that there are no such properties as being mythical or illusory or imaginary or fake or real or genuine,

4. *Consumer Reports* (July 1988), 435.

not even ones which it is fictional that anything possesses. (Also, being stuffed or a toy is not a property that bears or trucks might possess.) It is only fictional that predicates like "fake," "mythical," "illusory," "real," and "actual" express properties. When we participate in the appropriate games, we pretend to attribute properties by means of them, but there are no properties that we thus pretend to attribute to anything.[5]

Unofficial games of the sort described may be implied by existence statements having no connection with works of fiction. We can think of "Vulcan," for instance, as, fictionally, naming a planet which lacks the property expressed by "exists," a property Pluto enjoys.

Statements like "There is no Vulcan" and "There is no Robinson Crusoe," whose grammatical form is not straightforwardly that of singular predications, are less easily construed as involving a secondary pretense than is (33). The speaker indicates and disavows a kind of referring, possibly by indicating or even engaging in a kind of pretending-to-refer. But he probably does not do so by indicating a pretense of attributing a property to something referred to.

Thinking of existence claims as involving a secondary pretense of the kind described enables us to subsume them under our account of predicative statements concerning fiction. On our primary model, the speaker of (30) or (33) indicates a kind of pretending-to-assert (more specifically a kind of pretending-to-attribute-a-property-to-something) and claims that to pretend thus in an (unofficial) game of the implied sort is to speak truly. We can expect existence statements to be true and false in the same instances whether they are understood this way or in the way I proposed previously. For surely the implied games are such that it is fictional that one speaks truly when one says "X exists," just in case referring attempts of the kind one indicates in uttering "X" would be successful. And it is fictional that one speaks truly in saying "X doesn't exist," just in case referring attempts of that kind would be unsuccessful.[6]

The primary model puts pretense and make-believe back in the content of what is asserted by means of existence statements; affirmations or denials of the existence even of Vulcan and Qaddafi will be assertions about kinds of pretense and (unofficial) games of make-

5. I do not agree with Evans that "exists" is sometimes used "to signify a first-level concept, true of everything" (*Varieties of Reference*, p. 345). It may be fictional that it is used thus, however.

6. In the case of positive existence claims, one actually makes such an attempt. So we can say that it is fictional that one speaks truly in uttering "X exists," just in case one actually succeeds in referring by means of "X."

believe. Our familiar variant on the primary model is available, however. It may be best to construe singular existence statements as attesting to the presence of a circumstance responsible for the fact that to pretend-to-assert in the indicated manner is fictionally to speak truly, not as claiming that this is fictional. (We noticed in § 10.5 that statements involving unofficial games are especially likely to fit such a construal.) The relevant circumstance in the case of existence statements is the fact that to attempt to refer in the indicated manner is to succeed, or to fail, in referring to something. We thus return to our original account of existence claims. But now we understand how sentences like (30) and (33) come to be used to say what they do. We have discovered an unexpected continuity between existence claims like them and the predicative statements they resemble so closely— both predicative statements genuinely attributing properties to (actual) things and ones appearing to attribute ordinary properties to fictitious things. We have also achieved a unified account of existence statements, ones having nothing to do with works of fiction as well as ones concerning "fictitious entities," and we have done this without taking the former to be claims about pretense or make-believe.

The notion of make-believe is of course essential in achieving these results, even if it has no place in the content of existence claims.

Works Cited

Aldis, Owen. *Play Fighting.* New York: Academic Press, 1975.

Allen, Woody. Quoted in *Newsweek* (June 1976): 46.

Antonioni, Michelangelo. *Blow-Up: A Film by Michelangelo Antonioni.* New York: Simon and Schuster, 1971.

Apollinaire, Guillaume. *The Cubist Painters: Aesthetic Meditations.* Translated by Lionel Abel. New York: G. Wittenborn, Schultz, 1949.

Apuleius. *The Golden Ass.* Translated by Jack Lindsay. Bloomington: Indiana University Press, 1960.

Aristotle. *Poetics.* Translated by Gerald F. Else. Ann Arbor: Ann Arbor Paperbacks, University of Michigan Press, 1970.

Arnheim, Rudolf. "The Robin and the Saint." In *Toward a Psychology of Art.* Berkeley: University of California Press, 1966.

———— *Film as Art.* Berkeley: University of California Press, 1966.

Ashbery, John. "Self-Portrait in a Convex Mirror." In *Self-Portrait in a Convex Mirror.* New York: Viking, 1975.

Bach, Kent. "Part of What a Picture Is." *British Journal of Aesthetics* 10 (1970): 119–137.

Banfield, Ann. "Narrative Style and the Grammar of Direct and Indirect Speech." *Foundations of Language* 10 (1973): 1–39.

———— *Unspeakable Sentences: Narration and Representation in the Language of Fiction.* Boston: Routledge and Kegan Paul, 1982.

Barth, John. "Frame Tale." In *Lost in the Funhouse.* New York: Bantam Books, 1969.

———— "Life Story." In *Lost in the Funhouse.* New York: Bantam Books, 1969.

Baum, L. Frank. *The Road to Oz.* New York: Ballantine Books, 1972.

Baxandall, Michael. *Painting and Experience in Fifteenth-Century Italy.* London: Oxford University Press, 1972.

Bazin, André. *What Is Cinema?* Edited and translated by Hugh Gray. Berkeley: University of California Press, 1971.

Beardsley, Monroe. *Aesthetics: Problems in the Philosophy of Criticism.* 2d ed. New York: Harcourt Brace Jovanovich, 1980.

———— "Fiction as Representation." *Synthese* 46 (1981): 291–313.

———— *The Possibility of Criticism.* Detroit: Wayne State University Press, 1970.

Bennett, John G. "Depiction and Convention." *The Monist* 58 (April 1974): 255–268.

Berkeley, George. *Three Dialogues between Hylas and Philonous.* In *Berke-*

ley's Philosophical Writings. Edited by David Armstrong. New York: Collier, 1965.

Bernstein, Leonard. CBS Interview (November 24, 1979).

Bettelheim, Bruno. *The Uses of Enchantment: The Meaning and Importance of Fairy Tales.* New York: Knopf, 1977.

Booth, Wayne. "Distance and Point-of-View: An Essay in Classification." In *The Theory of the Novel.* Edited by Phillip Stevick. New York: Free Press, 1967.

———— *The Rhetoric of Fiction.* Chicago: University of Chicago Press, 1961.

Borges, Jorge Luis. "Everything and Nothing." In *Labyrinths: Selected Stories and Other Writings.* Edited by Donald A. Yates and James E. Irby. New York: New Directions, 1964.

———— "Parable of Cervantes and the *Quixote*." In *Labyrinths: Selected Stories and Other Writings.* Edited by Donald A. Yates and James E. Irby. New York: New Directions, 1964.

———— "Tlön, Uqbar, Orbis Tertius." In *Labyrinths: Selected Stories and Other Writings.* Edited by Donald A. Yates and James E. Irby. New York: New Directions, 1964.

Braudy, Leo. *The World in a Frame.* Garden City, N.Y.: Anchor, 1976.

Calvino, Italo. *If on a Winter's Night a Traveler.* Translated by William Weaver. New York: Harcourt Brace Jovanovich, 1981.

Casey, Edward S. *Imagining: A Phenomenological Study.* Bloomington: Indiana University Press, 1976.

Castañeda, Hector-Neri. "Fiction and Reality: Their Fundamental Connections: An Essay on the Ontology of Total Experience." *Poetics* 8 (1979): 31–62.

Charlton, William. "Feeling for the Fictitious." *British Journal of Aesthetics* (1984): 206–216.

Chatman, Seymour. *Story and Discourse: Narrative Structure in Fiction and Film.* Ithaca: Cornell University Press, 1978.

Chisholm, Roderick. *The First Person: An Essay on Reference and Intentionality.* Minneapolis: University of Minnesota Press, 1981.

Clark, Herbert H., and Richard J. Gerrig. "On the Pretense Theory of Irony." *Journal of Experimental Psychology: General* 113 (1984): 121–126.

Clark, Ralph W. "Fictional Entities: Talking about Them and Having Feelings about Them." *Philosophical Studies* 38 (1980): 341–349.

Cohn, Dorrit. *Transparent Minds: Narrative Modes for Presenting Consciousness in Fiction.* Princeton: Princeton University Press, 1978.

Coleridge, Samuel. *Selected Poetry and Prose.* Edited by Elizabeth Schneider. New York: Holt, Rinehart, and Winston, 1951.

Conrad, Joseph. *The Secret Agent.* Garden City, N.Y.: Doubleday, 1953.

Cortázar, Julio. "Blow-Up." In *Blow-Up and Other Stories.* Translated by Paul Blackburn. New York: Macmillan (Collier), 1968.

———— "Continuity of Parks." In *Blow-Up and Other Stories*. New York: Macmillan (Collier), 1968.

Currie, Gregory. "Fictional Truth." *Philosophical Studies* 50 (1986): 195–212.

———— "What is Fiction?" *The Journal of Aesthetics and Art Criticism* 63, no. 4 (Summer 1985): 385–392.

Danto, Arthur C. *The Transfiguration of the Commonplace*. Cambridge, Mass.: Harvard University Press, 1981.

Darwin, Charles. *The Expression of Emotions in Man and Animals*. Chicago: University of Chicago Press, 1965.

Davidson, Donald. "On Saying That." *Inquiries into Truth and Interpretation*. Oxford: Clarendon Press, 1984.

Donnellan, Keith. "Reference and Definite Descriptions." *Philosophical Review* 75 (July 1966): 281–304.

———— "Speaking of Nothing." *Philosophical Review* 83 (1974): 3–31.

Dostoyevsky, Fyodor. "Notes from the Underground." In *Notes from the Underground, White Nights, The Dream of a Ridiculous Man, and Selections from The House of the Dead*. Translated by Andrew R. MacAndrew. New York: New American Library, 1980.

Doyle, Sir Arthur Conan. "The Adventures of the Empty House." In *The Complete Sherlock Holmes*. Garden City, N.Y.: Doubleday, 1930.

Eaton, Marcia. "Liars, Ranters, and Dramatic Speakers." In *Art and Philosophy*. Edited by William Kennick. 2d ed. New York: St. Martin's, 1979.

Evans, Gareth. *The Varieties of Reference*. Edited by John McDowell. Oxford: Oxford University Press, 1982.

Farrell, Daniel M. "Recent Work on the Emotions." *Analyse und Kritik* 10 (1988): 71–102.

Federman, Raymond. *Take It or Leave It*. Excerpt in *Statements: New Fiction from the Fiction Collective*. Assembled by Jonathan Baumbach. New York: George Braziller, 1975.

Fielding, Henry. *Tom Jones*. Harmondsworth, Middlesex, England: Penguin, 1966.

Fine, Kit. "The Problem of Non-Existence: I. Internalism." *Topoi* 1 (1982): 97–140.

Fish, Stanley. "How to Do Things with Austin and Searle." In *Is There a Text in This Class? The Authority of Interpretive Communities*. Cambridge, Mass.: Harvard University Press, 1980.

Fried, Michael. *Absorption and Theatricality: Painting and Beholder in the Age of Diderot*. Berkeley: University of California Press, 1980.

———— *Realism, Writing, Disfiguration: On Thomas Eakins and Stephen Crane*. Chicago: University of Chicago Press, 1987.

Gale, Richard. "The Fictive Use of Language." *Philosophy* 46 (1971): 324–339.

Gardner, John. *On Moral Fiction*. New York: Basic Books, 1977.

Genette, Gérard. *Narrative Discourse: An Essay in Method.* Translated by Jane E. Lewin. Ithaca, N.Y.: Cornell University Press, 1983.

Gombrich, Ernst. *Art and Illusion.* 2d ed. New York: Pantheon Books, 1961.

———— "Meditations on a Hobby Horse, or the Roots of Artistic Form." In *Meditations on a Hobby Horse and Other Essays on the Theory of Art.* London: Phaidon, 1965.

———— "Standards of Truth: The Arrested Image and the Moving Eye." *Critical Inquiry* 7, no. 2 (Winter 1980): 237–273.

Gombrowicz, Witold. *Pornografia.* Translated by Alastair Hamilton. New York: Grove Press, 1966.

Goodman, Nelson. "Fiction for Five Fingers." *Philosophy and Literature* (October 1982): 162–164.

———— *Languages of Art.* Indianapolis: Bobbs-Merrill, 1968.

———— *Ways of World-Making.* Indianapolis: Hackett, 1978.

Greenspan, Patricia. "Emotions as Evaluations." *Pacific Philosophical Quarterly* 62 (1981): 158–169.

Grice, Paul. "Meaning." *Philosophical Review* 66 (1957): 377–388.

Halliwell, Leslie. *The Filmgoer's Companion.* New York: Avon, 1974.

Hazlitt, William. *The Characters of Shakespeare's Plays.* London: C. H. Reynell, 1817.

Hermerén, Göran. *Representation and Meaning in the Visual Arts.* Lund: Lärsomedelsförlagen (Scandinavian University Books), 1969.

Howell, Robert. "Fictional Objects: How They Are and How They Aren't." *Poetics* 8 (1979): 129–177.

———— "Review of Parsons, *Nonexistent Objects.*" *Journal of Philosophy* 80, no. 3 (1983): 163–173.

Hume, David. *An Enquiry Concerning Human Understanding.* Edited by Antony Flew. La Salle, Ill.: Open Court, 1988.

———— "Of the Standard of Taste." In *Of the Standard of Taste and Other Essays.* Edited by John W. Lenz. Indianapolis: Bobbs-Merrill, 1965.

———— "Of Tragedy." In *Of the Standard of Taste and Other Essays.* Edited by John W. Lenz. Indianapolis: Bobbs-Merrill, 1965.

Hyslop, Alec. "Emotions and Fictional Characters." *Australasian Journal of Philosophy* 64, no. 3 (September 1986): 289–297.

James, Henry. *The Ambassadors.* New York: Harper and Brothers, 1902–3.

Kael, Pauline. *I Lost It at the Movies.* Boston: Atlantic–Little, Brown, 1965.

———— *Kiss Kiss Bang Bang.* Boston: Little, Brown, 1965.

Kafka, Franz. "The Burrow." Translated by Willa and Edwin Muir. In *Franz Kafka: The Complete Stories.* Edited by Nahum N. Glatzer. New York: Schocken Books, 1971.

———— "The Metamorphosis." Translated by Willa and Edwin Muir. In *Franz Kafka: The Complete Stories.* Edited by Nahum N. Glatzer. New York: Schocken Books, 1971.

Karelis, Charles. "The Las Meninas Literature—and Its Lesson." In *Creation and Interpretation.* Edited by Raphael Stern. New York: Haven Publications, 1985.

Keats, John. "Ode on a Grecian Urn." In *The Mentor Book of Major British Poets.* Edited by Oscar Williams. New York: The New American Library, 1963.

Kraut, Robert. "Feelings in Context." *Journal of Philosophy* 83, no. 11 (November 1986): 642–652.

Kripke, Saul. *Naming and Necessity.* Cambridge, Mass.: Harvard University Press, 1973.

——— *Wittgenstein on Rules and Private Language: An Elementary Exposition.* Cambridge, Mass.: Harvard University Press, 1982.

Laing, R. D. *Knots.* New York: Random House, 1972.

Lamarque, Peter. "Fiction and Reality." In *Philosophy and Fiction: Essays in Literary Aesthetics.* Aberdeen: Aberdeen University Press, 1983.

——— "How Can We Fear and Pity Fictions?" *British Journal of Aesthetics* 21, no. 4 (Autumn 1981): 291–304.

Lem, Stanislaw. *A Perfect Vacuum: Perfect Reviews of Nonexistent Books.* Translated by Michael Kandel. New York: Harcourt Brace Jovanovich, 1971.

Leonardo da Vinci. *Treatise on Painting.* Edited by A. P. McMahon. Princeton: Princeton University Press, 1956.

Levinson, Jerrold. "What a Musical Work Is." *Journal of Philosophy* 77, no. 1 (January 1980): 5–28.

Lewis, David. "Attitudes De Dicto and De Se." In *Philosophical Papers. Vol. 1.* New York: Oxford University Press, 1983.

——— *Convention.* Cambridge, Mass.: Harvard University Press, 1969.

——— *Counterfactuals.* Oxford: Blackwell, 1973.

——— "Truth in Fiction." In *Philosophical Papers. Vol. 1.* New York: Oxford University Press, 1983.

Locke, John. *An Essay Concerning Human Understanding.* New York: Dover, 1959.

MacDonald, Margaret. "The Language of Fiction." In *Art and Philosophy.* Edited by W. E. Kennick. 2d ed. New York: St. Martin's, 1979.

Mailer, Norman. *The Executioner's Song.* Boston: Little, Brown, 1979.

Mann, Thomas. "Death in Venice." *Death in Venice and Seven Other Stories.* Translated by H. T. Lowe-Porter. New York: Random House, 1936.

Mannison, Don. "On Being Moved by Fiction." *Philosophy* 60, no. 231 (January 1985): 71–87.

Margolis, Joseph. *Art and Philosophy.* Brighton: Harvester, 1980.

Márquez, Gabriel García. "The Incredible and Sad Tale of Innocent Erendira and Her Heartless Grandmother." In *Innocent Erendira and Other Stories.* Translated by Gregory Rabassa. New York: Harper and Row, 1978.

Martin, Pete. "Pete Martin Calls on Hitchcock." In *Film Makers on Film Making*. Edited by Harry Geduld. Bloomington: Indiana University Press, 1971.

McNair, Robert E. *Basic River Canoeing*. 3d ed. Martinsville, Ind.: American Camping Association, Bradford Woods, 1972.

McPhee, John. *The Pine Barrens*. New York: Farrar, Straus, and Giroux, 1967.

Meinong, Alexius. "The Theory of Objects." Translated by Isaac Levi, D. B. Terrell, and Roderick M. Chisholm. In *Realism and the Background of Phenomenology*. Edited by Roderick M. Chisholm. New York: Free Press, 1960.

Melville, Herman. *Moby Dick*. New York: Random House, 1930.

Meyer, Leonard. *Emotion and Meaning in Music*. Chicago: University of Chicago Press, 1956.

——— "On Rehearing Music." In *Music, the Arts, and Ideas*. Chicago: University of Chicago Press, 1967.

Morreall, John. "Enjoying Negative Emotions in Fiction." *Philosophy and Literature* 9, no. 1 (April 1985): 95–103.

Mothersill, Mary. *Beauty Restored*. Oxford: Oxford University Press, 1984.

Nabokov, Vladimir. *Pnin*. New York: Doubleday, 1957.

Newfield, Jack. "Journalism: Old, New, and Corporate." *The Reporter as Artist: A Look at the New Journalism Controversy*. Edited by Ronald Weber. New York: Hastings House, 1974.

Newhall, Nancy. *P. H. Emerson: The Fight for Photography as a Fine Art*. New York: Aperture, 1975.

Novitz, David. "Fiction, Imagination, and Emotion." *Journal of Aesthetics and Art Criticism* 38, no. 3 (Spring 1980): 279–288.

——— *Knowledge, Fiction, and Imagination*. Philadelphia: Temple University Press, 1987.

——— *Pictures and Their Use in Communication*. The Hague: Martinus Nijhoff, 1977.

O'Brien, Flann. *At Swim-Two-Birds*. London: MacGibbon and Kee, 1966.

Ohmann, Richard. "Speech Acts and the Definition of Literature." *Philosophy and Rhetoric* 4 (1971): 1–19.

Opie, I., and P. Opie. *Children's Games in Street and Playground*. Oxford: Oxford University Press, 1969.

Panofsky, Erwin. "Die Perspektive als 'Symbolische Form.'" In *Aufsätze zu Grundfragen der Kunstwissenschaft*. Berlin: 1964.

——— "Style and Medium in the Motion Pictures." In *Film Theory and Criticism: Introductory Readings*. Edited by Gerald Mast and Marshall Cohen. 2d ed. New York: Oxford University Press, 1979.

Parsons, Terence. *Nonexistent Objects*. New Haven: Yale University Press, 1980.

——— "Review of John Woods, *The Logic of Fiction: A Philosophical Sounding of Deviant Logic.*" *Synthese* 39 (1978): 155–164.

Pascal, Roy. *The Dual Voice.* Totowa, N.J.: Rowan and Littlefield, 1977.

Pavel, Thomas G. *Fictional Worlds.* Cambridge, Mass.: Harvard University Press, 1986.

Peacocke, Christopher. "Depiction." *The Philosophical Review* (July 1987): 383–410.

——— "Imagination, Experience, and Possibility: A Berkeleian View Defended." In *Essays on Berkeley: A Tercentennial Celebration.* Edited by John Foster and Howard Robinson. Oxford: Clarendon Press, 1985.

——— *Sense and Content.* Oxford: Oxford University Press, 1983.

Peirce, Charles Sanders. *The Collected Papers of Charles Sanders Peirce.* Vols. 1–6. Edited by Charles Hartshorne and Paul Weiss. Cambridge, Mass.: Harvard University Press. 1931–1935.

Penrose, Roland. "In Praise of Illusion." In *Illusion in Nature and Art.* Edited by R. L. Gregory and E. H. Gombrich. London: Duckworth, 1973.

Plantinga, Alvin. *The Nature of Necessity.* Oxford: Oxford University Press, 1974.

Podro, Michael. *The Critical Historians of Art.* New Haven: Yale University Press, 1982.

Poe, Edgar Allan. "Facts in the Case of M. Valdemar." In *The Portable Poe.* Edited by Philip Van Doren Stern. New York: Viking, 1945.

Potter, Beatrix. *The Tale of the Flopsy Bunnies.* New York: Frederick Warne and Co., 1909.

Pratt, Mary Louise. *Toward a Speech Act Theory of Literary Discourse.* Bloomington: Indiana University Press, 1977.

Price, H. H. *Belief.* London: George Allen and Unwin, 1969.

Puig, Manuel. *Heartbreak Tango.* Translated by Suzanne Jill Levine. New York: Vintage, 1981.

Robbe-Grillet, Alain. "Jealousy." In *Two Novels by Robbe-Grillet (Jealousy and In the Labyrinth).* Translated by Richard Howard. New York: Grove Press, 1965.

Roberts, Robert C. "What an Emotion Is: A Sketch." *The Philosophical Review* 97, no. 2 (April 1988): 183–209.

Rorty, Richard. "Is There a Problem about Fictional Discourse?" In *Consequences of Pragmatism (Essays: 1972–1980).* Minneapolis: University of Minnesota Press, 1982.

——— "The World Well Lost." *Journal of Philosophy* 69, no. 19 (1972): 3–18.

Rose, Barbara. *American Art since 1900: A Critical History.* London: Thames and Hudson, 1967.

Routley, Richard. *Exploring Meinong's Jungle and Beyond: An Investigation of Noneism and the Theory of Items.* Canberra: Research School of Social Sciences, Australian National University, 1980.

Rubin, Kenneth H., Greta G. Fein, and Brian Vandenberg. "Play." In *Socialization, Personality, and Social Development*. Edited by E. Mavis Hetherington. Vol. 4 of *Handbook of Child Psychology*. 4th ed. Edited by Paul H. Mussen. New York: John Wiley and Sons, 1983.

Ryan, Marie-Laure. "Fiction, Non-Factuals, and the Principle of Minimal Departure." *Poetics* 8 (1980): 403–422.

Savile, Anthony. *The Test of Time: An Essay in Philosophical Aesthetics*. Oxford: Oxford University Press, 1982.

Schier, Flint. *Deeper into Pictures*. Cambridge: Cambridge University Press, 1986.

Schiffer, Stephen. *Meaning*. Oxford: Oxford University Press, 1972.

———— "Review of Gareth Evans, *The Varieties of Reference*." *Journal of Philosophy* 85, no. 1 (January 1988): 33–42.

Scholes, Robert. *Structural Fabulation*. Notre Dame, Ind.: University of Notre Dame Press, 1975.

Scruton, Roger. *Art and Imagination*. London: Methuen, 1974.

Searle, John. "The Logical Status of Fictional Discourse." *New Literary History* 6 (1975): 319–332.

———— *Speech Acts: An Essay in the Philosophy of Language*. Cambridge: Cambridge University Press, 1969.

Shakespeare, William. *A Midsummer Night's Dream*. In *William Shakespeare: The Complete Works*. Edited by Charles Jasper Sisson. New York: Harper and Brothers, n.d. (Preface dated 1953.)

———— *Othello*. In *William Shakespeare: The Complete Works*. Edited by Charles Jasper Sisson. New York: Harper and Brothers, n.d. (Preface dated 1953.)

Sheikh, Anees A., and John Shaffer, eds. *The Potential of Fantasy and the Imagination*. New York: Brandon House, 1979.

Sidney, Sir Phillip. *An Apology for Poetry, or The Defense of Poesy*. Edited by Geoffrey M. A. Shepherd. London: Thomas Nelson and Sons, Ltd., 1965.

Silverstein, Shel. "Slithergadee." In *Uncle Shelby's Zoo: Don't Bump the Glump*. New York: Simon and Schuster, 1964.

Singer, Jerome L. *The Child's World of Make-Believe: Experimental Studies of Imaginative Play*. New York: Academic Press, 1973.

Skulsky, H. "On Being Moved by Fiction." *Journal of Aesthetics and Art Criticism* 39 (1980): 5–14.

Smith, Barbara Herrnstein. *On the Margins of Discourse: The Relation of Literature to Language*. Chicago: University of Chicago Press, 1978.

Snyder, Joel. "Picturing Vision." *Critical Inquiry* 6 (Spring 1980): 499–526.

Snyder, Joel, and Neil Walsh Allen. "Photography, Vision, and Representation." *Critical Inquiry* 2, no. 1 (Autumn 1975): 143–169.

Sober, Elliott. *Simplicity*. Oxford: Oxford University Press, 1975.

Stalnaker, Robert. "A Theory of Conditionals." In *Studies in Logical Theory*. Edited by Nicholas Rescher. Oxford: Blackwell, 1968.

Steinberg, Leo. "The Eye Is Part of the Mind." *Partisan Review* 22, no. 2 (1953): 194–212.

Stella, Frank. *Working Space: The Charles Eliot Norton Lectures, 1983–84*. Cambridge, Mass.: Harvard University Press, 1986.

Strawson, Peter. "Imagination and Perception." In *Experience and Theory*. Edited by Lawrence Foster and J. W. Swanson. N.p.: University of Massachusetts Press, 1970.

Thackeray, William Makepeace. *Vanity Fair: A Novel without a Hero*. New York: Modern Library, 1950.

Thurber, James. "The Macbeth Murder Mystery." In *The Thurber Carnival*. New York: Dell, 1962.

Tolkien, J. R. R. "On Fairy-Stories." In *The Monsters and the Critics, and Other Essays*. Edited by Christopher Tolkien. Boston: Houghton Mifflin, 1984.

Tovey, Donald Francis. "Programme Music." In *The Forms of Music*. Cleveland: World Publishing Company, 1956.

Toynbee, A. J. Quoted in *Webster's Third New International Dictionary*. Springfield, Mass.: G. and C. Merriam, 1971.

Twain, Mark (Samuel L. Clemens). *The Adventures of Huckleberry Finn (Tom Sawyer's Comrade)*. New York: Modern Library, 1985.

——— *The Adventures of Tom Sawyer*. Harmondsworth, Middlesex, England: Penguin, 1986.

Urmson, J. O. "Fiction." *American Philosophical Quarterly* 13, no. 2 (April 1976): 153–157.

Van Inwagen, Peter. "Creatures of Fiction." *American Philosophical Quarterly* 14 (1977): 299–308.

——— "Pretence and Paraphrase." In *The Reasons of Art: Artworks and the Formations of Philosophy / L'art a ses raisons: Les oeuvres d'art: Défis à la philosophie*. Edited by Peter J. McCormick. Ottawa: University of Ottawa Press, 1985.

Voltaire. *Candide*. In *Candide and Other Romances*. Translated by Richard Aldington. London: Abbey Library, n.d.

Walton, Kendall L. "Categories of Art." In *Art and Philosophy*. Edited by William Kennick. 2d and 3d eds. New York: St. Martin's, 1979.

——— "Linguistic Relativity." In *Conceptual Change*. Edited by Glenn Pearce and Patrick Maynard. Dordrecht, Holland: Reidel, 1973.

——— "Points of View in Narrative and Depictive Representation." *Noûs* 10 (1976): 49–61.

——— "Review of Nicholas Wolterstorff, *Works and Worlds of Art*." *Journal of Philosophy* 80 (1983): 179–193.

——— "Style and the Products and Processes of Art." In *The Concept of*

Style. Edited by Berel Lang. 2d ed. Ithaca, N.Y.: Cornell University Press, 1987.

———. "Transparent Pictures." *Critical Inquiry* 11 (1984): 246–277.

———. "What Is Abstract About the Art of Music?" *The Journal of Aesthetics and Art Criticism* 46, no. 3 (Spring 1988): 351–364.

Weber, Ronald. *The Literature of Fact: Literary Nonfiction in American Writing*. Athens, Ohio: Ohio University Press, 1980.

———. "Some Sort of Artistic Excitement." In *The Reporter as Artist: A Look at the New Journalism Controversy*. Edited by Ronald Weber. New York: Hastings House, 1974.

Williams, Bernard. "Imagination and the Self." In *Problems of the Self: Philosophical Papers, 1956–72*. Cambridge: Cambridge University Press, 1973.

Wilshire, Bruce. *Role Playing and Identity*. Bloomington: Indiana University Press, 1982.

Wilson, George M. *Narration in Light: Studies in Cinematic Point of View*. Baltimore: Johns Hopkins University Press, 1986.

Wittgenstein, Ludwig. *The Blue and Brown Books*. Oxford: Basil Blackwell, 1958.

———. *Philosophical Investigations*. Translated by G. E. M. Anscombe. 3d ed. New York: Macmillan, 1958.

Wodehouse, P. G. *How Right You Are, Jeeves*. New York: Harper and Row, 1985.

Wollheim, Richard. *Art and Its Objects*. 2d ed. Cambridge: Cambridge University Press, 1980.

———. "Imagination and Identification." In *On Art and the Mind*. Cambridge, Mass.: Harvard University Press, 1974.

———. "On Drawing an Object." In *On Art and the Mind*. Cambridge, Mass.: Harvard University Press, 1974.

———. *Painting as an Art*. Princeton: Princeton University Press, 1987.

———. *The Thread of Life*. Cambridge, Mass.: Harvard University Press, 1984.

Wolterstorff, Nicholas. *Works and Worlds of Art*. New York: Oxford University Press, 1980.

Woods, John. *The Logic of Fiction: A Philosophical Sounding of Deviant Logic*. The Hague: Mouton, 1974.

Index

Docks of New York, The (Joseph von Sternberg), 332
Donnellan, Keith, 124n
Dostoevski, Feodor, Notes from the Underground, 233
Doyle, Conan, "The Adventure of the Empty House," 263
Dreams, 16, 35, 43–51, 61, 68, 176–177, 182, 271, 272, 284, 337
Duchamp, Marcel, Nude Descending a Staircase, 171

Eaton, Marcia, 84n, 85n
"Effet de la Ligue," 113
Eisenstein, Elizabeth, 96n
Eliot, George, Daniel Deronda, 380
Emerson, P. H., 325
Emotions, 195–204, 241–259; and belief, 197–204, 244–245, 251–252; and half belief, 197–198; and inclinations to act, 198–199, 201–202, 203–204, 245–246; akin to belief-desire complexes, 202, 245; other than fear, 249–255; links between actual and fictional emotions, 252–253; negative, 255–258. See also Fear; Quasi emotions
Empathy, 237, 255, 272, 344, 347, 357, 361, 363
Entailment relations, among statements concerning fiction, 416
Epistolary novels, 231, 238, 354, 357
Escher, M. C., 64, 176, 237
Eskimo roll diagram, 347–348, 379
Evans, Gareth, 394n, 399n, 411n, 425, 429n
Evolutionary explanations, 245n, 272
Excluded middle, law of the, 386, 387. See also Indeterminate (incomplete) fictional worlds
Existence: and being, 385; is it a "predicate"?, 424, 428–429
Existence claims, 424–430; negative, 422, 424–427, 428, 429; ones unrelated to works of fiction, 424–428, 429; positive, 427–428; assimilated to predicative statements concerning fiction, 428–430; not about pretense, 428, 430
Expression, 1–2, 129, 173, 174, 334, 335–336

Fairy tales, 94n, 98, 146, 269, 283
Fantastic fictions, 163, 329, 331, 361, 362–363
Fear: fearing fictions, 195–204; fear of flying, 198–199. See also Emotions; Quasi emotions.
Federman, Raymond, Take It or Leave It, 359
Fiction and nonfiction, 1, 3, 70–105, 121; and pretended illocutionary actions, 81–83, 84–85; and represented illocutionary actions, 83–85. See also Depiction, fictional and nonfictional pictures
Fiction versus reality, 73, 77, 99. See also Truth and reality
Fictional spaces, 62–63
Fictional truths: defined, 35; what they are, distinguished from how they are generated, 139–140; emphasized and de-emphasized, 140, 148–150, 173, 174, 182, 239, 338. See also Accessibility of fictional truths and fictional worlds; Fictionality (of propositions)
Fictional worlds, 35–36, 41, 57–67, 69, 205–206; of appreciators' games, 58–61, 215–216, 273, 297, 329–331, 336–337; of works, 58–61, 62, 215–216, 273, 297, 336–337; what they are, 63–67; and classes of propositions, 64–67; and possible worlds, 64–66; as indicated classes of propositions, 66–67; worlds within worlds, 120–121, 283–285, 369, 370; isolation from the real world, 191–196, 205, 241; multiple work worlds, 285–287, 371–372, 374, 375. See also Accessibility of fictional truths and fictional worlds; Impossible fictional worlds; Indeterminate (incomplete) fictional worlds
Fictionality (of propositions), 35–51, 67, 69, 139, 218–219; in a world, 35–36, 58–61; and imagining, 36–38, 39–41, 43–49; defined, 39–40; and truth, 41–42, 101, 194, 205–208, 249; and other intentional properties, 204–208
Fictionality operators, omission of, 206–207, 221–224
Fiction-making, 77–89

Nonordinary statements concerning fiction, 406–411; paraphrases of, 408, 411–419; truth conditions of, 408; construed as not about pretense, 412–415, 416, 419

Novitz, David, 123n, 203n, 297n, 333n

Objectivity (of fictional truths and fictional worlds), 42, 67

Objects of imaginings, 25–35, 38–39, 69, 106, 116, 247, 294; as focuses of interest, 25–26, 34–35, 211

Objects of representation, 106–137, 212; their inessentiality to representationality, 122–130; objects of depiction, 297

O'Brien, Flann, *At Swim-Two-Birds,* 176, 208n

Ohmann, Richard, 77n, 78n, 84

Open-endedness of visual investigations, 307–309

Opera, 165, 177, 182

Opie, I., and P. Opie, 11n, 12n

Order of ascertaining fictional truths, 305–306

Ordinary statements concerning fiction, 396–405, 408, 423; truth conditions of, 399, 400; paraphrases of, 400, 404–405; alternative interpretations of, 401–410, 415; as elliptical, 401–402, 415; ones not made in pretense, 404. *See also* Statements concerning fiction

Ornamental representation, 239n, 280, 282–289; defined, 281–282; value of, 287–289; ornamental depiction, 296–297

Panofsky, Erwin, 163, 165, 298n

Paraphrases: complexity of, 404–405. *See also* Nonordinary statements concerning fiction; Ordinary statements concerning fiction

Parmigianino, *Self-Portrait in a Convex Mirror,* 343

Parsons, Terrence, 78n, 147n, 386, 387n, 413n

Participation in games of make-believe, 190, 208, 209–239, 364–365, 395, 406; using the Reality Principle and

the Mutual Belief Principle, 158–160, 166–167; defined, 209–210, 212; differences between children's and appreciators' games, 213, 224–226, 227, 228, 240–241; verbal, 220–224, 242, 337, 392, 394–396, 398; restrictions on, 224–229, 233–234, 235–236, 253–254; psychological, 228, 240–289; epistemological aspects of, 259–271; value of, 271–274, 287–289; inhibited, 274–282, 283, 284, 288, 421; imagined, 284. *See also* Appreciation, as participation; Games of make-believe, attenuated

Pascal, Roy, 377n, 380–381

Pavel, Thomas G., 7n

Peacocke, Christopher, 28, 237n, 296n

Peirce, Charles, 298

Peking Opera, 165

Penrose, Roland, 169, 173n, 314n

Perceptual contact, 331

Philosophical examples, 90, 281

Photography, 88, 327, 330, 331

Picasso, Pablo, 276; *Women Running on the Beach,* 169; *Bull's Head,* 276–277; *Les Desmoiselles d'Avignon,* 315n, 338; *Portrait of Daniel-Henry Kahnweiler,* 319

Pictures. *See* Depiction

Plantinga, Alvin, 19n, 78n, 131n

Podro, Michael, 298n

Poe, Edgar Allan, "The Tell-Tale Heart," 107

Points of view, 292

Points of view (in depictions), 337–348; multiple, 338, 340; absent, 340–341; first- and third-person, 341. *See also* Film, point-of-view shots

Points of view (in narrated representations), 375–382

Pollock, Jackson, 1, 56

Portraits, 234–235

Possible worlds, 57. *See also* Fictional worlds, and possible worlds

Potemkin (Sergei Eisenstein), 145, 147

Potter, Beatrix, *The Tale of the Flopsy Bunnies,* 387

Pratt, Mary Louise, 78n